RULES OF CONTRACT LAW

Selections from the Uniform Commercial Code,
the CISG, the Restatement (Second) of Contracts,
and the UNIDROIT Principles,
with Material on Contract Drafting
and Sample Examination Questions
2012–2013

RULES OF CONTRACT LAW

Selections from the Uniform Commercial Code, the CISG, the Restatement (Second) of Contracts, and the UNIDROIT Principles, with Material on Contract Drafting and Sample Examination Questions

2012–2013 Statutory Supplement

Charles L. Knapp
Joseph W. Cotchett Distinguished Professor of Law
University of California, Hastings College of the Law
Max E. Greenberg Professor Emeritus of Contract Law
New York University School of Law

Nathan M. Crystal
Distinguished Research Scholar
Charleston School of Law
Distinguished Professor Emeritus
University of South Carolina School of Law

Harry G. Prince
Professor of Law
University of California, Hastings College of the Law

Wolters Kluwer
Law & Business

Published by Wolters Kluwer Law & Business in New York.

Wolters Kluwer Law & Business serves customers worldwide with CCH, Aspen Publishers, and Kluwer Law International products. (www.wolterskluwerlb.com)

To contact Customer Service, e-mail customer.service@wolterskluwer.com, call 1-800-234-1660, fax 1-800-901-9075, or mail correspondence to:

Wolters Kluwer Law & Business
Attn: Order Department
PO Box 990
Frederick, MD 21705

Printed in the United States of America.

1 2 3 4 5 6 7 8 9 0

ISBN 978-1-4548-1856-4

ISSN 1556-0058

About Wolters Kluwer Law & Business

Wolters Kluwer Law & Business is a leading global provider of intelligent information and digital solutions for legal and business professionals in key specialty areas, and respected educational resources for professors and law students. Wolters Kluwer Law & Business connects legal and business professionals as well as those in the education market with timely, specialized authoritative content and information-enabled solutions to support success through productivity, accuracy and mobility.

Serving customers worldwide, Wolters Kluwer Law & Business products include those under the Aspen Publishers, CCH, Kluwer Law International, Loislaw, Best Case, ftwilliam.com and MediRegs family of products.

CCH products have been a trusted resource since 1913, and are highly regarded resources for legal, securities, antitrust and trade regulation, government contracting, banking, pension, payroll, employment and labor, and healthcare reimbursement and compliance professionals.

Aspen Publishers products provide essential information to attorneys, business professionals and law students. Written by preeminent authorities, the product line offers analytical and practical information in a range of specialty practice areas from securities law and intellectual property to mergers and acquisitions and pension/benefits. Aspen's trusted legal education resources provide professors and students with high-quality, up-to-date and effective resources for successful instruction and study in all areas of the law.

Kluwer Law International products provide the global business community with reliable international legal information in English. Legal practitioners, corporate counsel and business executives around the world rely on Kluwer Law journals, looseleafs, books, and electronic products for comprehensive information in many areas of international legal practice.

Loislaw is a comprehensive online legal research product providing legal content to law firm practitioners of various specializations. Loislaw provides attorneys with the ability to quickly and efficiently find the necessary legal information they need, when and where they need it, by facilitating access to primary law as well as state-specific law, records, forms and treatises.

Best Case Solutions is the leading bankruptcy software product to the bankruptcy industry. It provides software and workflow tools to flawlessly streamline petition preparation and the electronic filing process, while timely incorporating ever-changing court requirements.

ftwilliam.com offers employee benefits professionals the highest quality plan documents (retirement, welfare and non-qualified) and government forms (5500/PBGC, 1099 and IRS) software at highly competitive prices.

MediRegs products provide integrated health care compliance content and software solutions for professionals in healthcare, higher education and life sciences, including professionals in accounting, law and consulting.

Wolters Kluwer Law & Business, a division of Wolters Kluwer, is headquartered in New York. Wolters Kluwer is a market-leading global information services company focused on professionals.

Contents

RULES OF CONTRACT LAW

Selections from the Uniform Commercial Code,
the CISG, the Restatement (Second) of Contracts,
and the UNIDROIT Principles,
with Material on Contract Drafting
and Sample Examination Questions
2012–2013

Uniform Commercial Code (2011 Official Text)

EDITORS' NOTE[1]

History of the UCC

As the United States developed a national market economy during the nineteenth century, the number of business transactions across state lines increased dramatically. Many of these transactions were cumbersome, however, because of differences among the states on commercial subjects, such as negotiable instruments, sales, and warehousing. Recognizing these problems, a number of business lawyers suggested the need for greater uniformity among the states in commercial law.

In 1889 the legislature of New York, the leading commercial state at that time, passed a statute providing for the appointment of commissioners who were authorized to solicit the appointment of commissioners from other states for the purpose of preparing uniform state laws. In 1892 the first meeting of the National Conference of Commissioners on Uniform State Laws (NCCUSL) was held in connection with the annual meeting of the American Bar Association.[2] At first the Commissioners concentrated on technical questions, such as standardized forms for acknowledgment of instruments, but they soon ventured into more substantive areas. By the early part of the twentieth century, the Commissioners had prepared uniform acts on a number of commercial subjects: negotiable instruments, sales, warehouse receipts, bills of lading, and trust receipts, to name just a few.

Adopted in many states, the uniform acts did foster the cause of uniformity to some extent. A number of factors, however, limited the success of the National Conference. Professor and later Judge Robert Braucher summarized the problems as follows:

---

1. Matters covered in this Note are explored more fully in the following works: R. Braucher & Robert R. Riegert, Introduction to Commercial Transactions 19-31 (1977) and Nathan M. Crystal, Codification and the Rise of the Restatement Movement, 54 Wash. L. Rev. 239 (1979).
2. NCCUSL is now also referred to as the Uniform Law Commission or ULC.

[The history of the uniform acts] provides an illustration of four major difficulties which have afflicted uniform legislation: (1) difficulty in obtaining original enactment, (2) a tendency toward deviation from the official text at the time of the original adoption, (3) nonuniform judicial interpretation, and (4) difficulty in promulgating and obtaining enactment of uniform amendments.

Robert Braucher & Robert Riegert, Introduction to Commercial Transactions 21-22 (1977).

By 1940 it was apparent that many of the uniform acts adopted early in the century required revision. At the fiftieth annual meeting of the National Conference of Commissioners, William A. Schnader, the president of the Conference, called for the creation of a uniform commercial code. The Conference quickly adopted his suggestion, subject to obtaining funding. In 1944 the Conference combined forces with the American Law Institute (ALI) to sponsor the project, with Professor Karl Llewellyn of Columbia Law School as Chief Reporter.

After a lengthy process, involving circulation of drafts among advisors, business groups, and others, the National Conference and the ALI issued an official text of the proposed Code in 1951. Pennsylvania became the first state to adopt the Code, in 1953. The project received a major setback in 1956, however, when the New York Law Revision Commission, after a three-year study, advised the New York Legislature that the Code "is not satisfactory in its present form." The New York Law Revision Commission's study was published in a six-volume set and remains an important source of information about the Code.

The New York study caused the ALI and the National Conference to reexamine the Code. In 1958 the sponsoring organizations issued a revised Official Text. New York adopted this new version of the Code in 1962, and other states quickly followed suit. By 1968 the Code was in force in all jurisdictions except Louisiana, where only certain articles have been enacted. In 1961 the ALI and the National Conference created a Permanent Editorial Board for the Uniform Commercial Code to monitor developments in commercial law and propose revisions of the Code.

Nature and Scope of the UCC

Although titled a commercial code, the name is somewhat of a misnomer because the Code fails to cover a number of important commercial subjects. For instance, transactions involving real estate, insurance, and personal services are generally outside the scope of the Code. In addition, even for transactions subject to the Code, many aspects are regulated by other bodies of law. For example, Article 8 of the Code deals with title and transfer of investment securities, such as corporate stock. Most of the law regulating transactions in securities, however, lies outside the Code. Moreover, common law principles continue to govern transactions to which the Code is applicable unless specifically displaced by Code provisions. UCC §1-103(b).

Rather than a comprehensive code of commercial law, the UCC instead is a loosely related collection of revised versions of the most significant uniform acts adopted earlier in the twentieth century by the National Conference of Commissioners. Article 1 covers a number of general matters; it includes a section containing definitions that apply throughout the Code. UCC §1-201. Article 2, which is the principal part of the Code addressed in most contracts courses, deals with transactions involving the sale of goods. Article 2A deals with various aspects of leases of personal property, including formation of lease contracts, performance, and default. For several years the ALI and National Conference worked on a proposed Article 2B, dealing with computer information transactions. After much controversy over the provisions, the ALI and the National Conference decided that such rules should not be proposed as part of the UCC. Instead, the project was transformed into a separate Uniform Computer Information Transactions Act (UCITA). The Act was adopted by the National Conference (or ULC) in 1999, but not by the ALI. A more detailed discussion of UCITA is included in the Materials on Electronic Contracts later in this Supplement.

"Commercial paper"—checks, notes, and drafts—is the focus of Article 3; the processing of such instruments through the banking system is the subject of Article 4; fund transfers are the topic of Article 4A. Article 5 deals with the rights and liabilities of parties to "letters of credit." Article 6 establishes rules for "bulk sales," transactions in which the owner of a certain type of business sells substantially all of the assets of that business. (On recommendation of the ULC, a substantial majority of states have now repealed Article 6.) Article 7 governs "documents of title," such as bills of lading issued by carriers of goods or warehouse receipts issued by companies that are involved in the storage of goods. Article 8 regulates the ownership and transfer of investment securities. Finally, Article 9 provides for the creation and protection of security interests in most types of personal property, tangible and intangible.

Unlike the Restatements, which have only persuasive weight, the UCC is a statute and has the force of law. It is important to remember, however, that in each state the "law" is not the official text of the Code promulgated by the ALI and the ULC, but that state's own enacted version of the Official Code. Most states have made non-uniform changes in certain provisions of the Official Text. See U.C.C. Rep. Serv., State U.C.C. Variations.

Each section of the complete Official Text of the Code is accompanied by an Official Comment, which includes references to prior law, discussion of the purposes of the section, and definitional cross-references. What weight should be given to the discussion in the official comments? Since the state legislatures have not enacted the comments, they do not have the force of law. Nonetheless, court opinions frequently have given the comments substantial weight. See Joseph M. Perillo, Calamari and Perillo on Contracts 16 (6th ed. 2009). Examples of courts utilizing the Official Comments are readily available. See, e.g., Carlund Corp. v. Crown Center Redevelopment, 849 S.W.2d 647, 650 (Mo. Ct. App. 1993); B & W Glass, Inc. v. Weather Shield Mfg., Inc., 829 P.2d 809, 816 (Wyo. 1992) (comments treated as persuasive authority).

Revisions to Articles 1 and 2

This part of the Supplement includes the text of many sections from Articles 1 and 2 of the Code, along with a few provisions from Articles 3 and 9. Official Comments for some significant sections are included as well. A major revision of Article 1 was completed in 2001 and a less substantial revision of Article 2 was completed in 2003. Revised Article 1 had been adopted in 42 states as of May 1, 2012, and that version is also the official text as promulgated by the ALI and ULC. (The status of adoptions is reported at the ULC website [www.uniformlaws.org].) Thus, this supplement includes only the most recent version of Article 1. Notably, revised Article 1, as adopted in most states, will result in few, if any, substantive changes to the law. Specific changes to Article 1 are discussed below and a guide is also offered to help identify where comparable sections of pre-revision Article 1 are now located in revised Article 1. The relocation guide may be helpful because many reported opinions that you may read at this point will still contain citations to pre-revision Article 1 section numbers.

From the beginning the amendments to Article 2 appeared destined to have trouble gaining acceptance by the states and that proved correct. The drafting process for the Article 2 amendments began in 1988 and was not completed until 2003, some fifteen years later. The length of the drafting process accurately reflects that the various proposals ran into substantial opposition. For a discussion of those difficulties, see Richard E. Speidel, Introduction to Symposium on Proposed Revised Article 2, 54 SMU L. Rev. 787 (2001). Opposition was based on a number of factors, including a dispute about the degree to which revised Article 2 would contain protection for consumers, the potential application of Article 2 to computer software or information transactions, and a general sense among commercial sellers and buyers that pre-revision Article 2 was not in need of major change. Id. at 791-93. As of fall 2010, not a single state had adopted the revisions to Article 2 or had enacting legislation pending. Consequently, the ULC voted to withdraw the proposed amendments to Article 2 in January 2011 and the ALI membership concurred by vote in May 2011.[3] Thus, this supplement does not contain any of the proposed revisions to Article 2. While it is possible that courts may find some persuasive authority in the proposed amendments to Article 2, that potential value is very limited.

Notable Changes to Article 1

As noted above, the revisions to Article 1 contain very few significant changes in substance, if any at all; a number of sections have been relocated and given stylistic or technical updates. Initially, the most significant proposed change involved the choice of law provisions in §1-301. The first proposed version of §1-301 would have allowed parties to a nonconsumer transaction to choose applicable law from a state having no relationship to the transaction and that approach caused substantial controversy. See William J. Woodward, Jr., Contractual Choice of Law: Legislative Choice in an Era of Party Autonomy, 54 SMU L. Rev. 697 (2001). Indeed, the opposition was overwhelming and none of the states adopting revised Article 1 included the initial version of §1-301. Consequently, the ULC and the ALI decided in 2007 to revert back to the pre-revision choice of law rules that had been embodied in §1-105. See Keith A. Rowley, The Often Imitated, But Not Yet Duplicated, Revised Uniform Commercial Code Article 1, [internet publication available at http://www.law.unlv.edu/faculty/rowley/RA1.081511.pdf] (visited May 12, 2012). Thus, the uniform version of revised §1-301 on choice of law is now substantively identical to former §1-105.

---

3. A memorandum entitled, Recommendation of the Permanent Editorial Board for the Uniform Commercial Code to Withdraw the 2003 Amendments to UCC Articles 2 and 2A from the Official Text of the Uniform Commercial Code, and reporting the earlier vote of the ULC (or NCCUSL) to drop the proposal, was distributed to ALI membership in advance of the May 16-18, 2011 ALI Annual Meeting. (See 88th ALI Annual Meeting Drafts and Motions at http://2011am.ali.org/drafts-motions.cfm.) The report of the ALI membership vote to withdraw is found in the Annual Meeting Updates (http://2011am.ali.org/updates.cfm).

Another notable change in revised Article 1 involves the duty of good faith. Previously, the UCC offered two definitions of "good faith"; §1-201(19) provided a general definition applicable throughout the UCC that "good faith" meant simply "honesty in fact", while Article 2 included an additional definition of "good faith" in §2-103(1)(b), stating that "good faith" for merchants meant both "honesty in fact" and "the observance of reasonable commercial standards of fair dealing in the trade." Revised Article 1 now includes a unitary definition of "good faith" in §1-201(b)(20) that would apply throughout the UCC (except for Article 5) requiring both honesty in fact and the more objective standard of observance of reasonable commercial standards. This unitary definition in revised Article 1 would ostensibly be applicable to all parties, merchants and nonmerchants, but its effect on the obligations of nonmerchants remains unclear. See Robyn L. Meadows, Russell A. Hakes, Stephen L. Sepinuck, The Uniform Commercial Code Survey: Introduction, 59 Bus. Law. 1553 (2004); Keith A. Rowley, One for All, But None for (All of) One: Part 2 of 2, 12 Nev. Law. 28 (Aug. 2004). Not surprisingly, the states have been divided on whether to adopt the new unitary definition of good faith or to retain the bifurcated definition of "good faith" from the previous version of Article 1.[4] Ultimately, the duty of good faith for merchants and nonmerchants may very well be the same regardless of the definition adopted in a particular state.

Correlation Guide for Article 1

Topic	Location in Pre-revision Article 1	Location in Current Article 1
Code to be liberally construed to promote uniformity	§1-102(1), (2)	§1-103(a)
Code may be varied by agreement except if mandatory	§1-102(3), (4)	§1-302
Code supplemented by principles of law and equity	§1-103	§1-103(b)
Choice of law provisions	§1-105	§1-301
Remedies administered to achieve compensation	§1-106	§1-305
Ability to waive claim after breach	§1-107	§1-306
General definitions	§1-201	§1-201(b)
Duty of good faith in every contract performance and enforcement	§1-203	§1-304
What is reasonable time	§1-204	§1-205
Define usage of trade, course of dealings, course of performance	§1-205 (and §2-208)	§1-303

4. Compare Alabama (Code of Ala. §7-1-201 (2004)) and Hawaii (Haw. Rev. Stat §490:1-201(2004)) (maintaining the pre-revision definition of "good faith" as requiring only honesty in fact), with Texas (Tex. Bus. & Com. Code Ann. §1.201(b)(20)(2004)) and Delaware (6 Del. Code §1-201 (2005)) (adopting the revised version of "good faith" definition requiring honesty in fact and observance of commercially reasonable standards).

Topic	Location in Pre-revision Article 1	Location in Current Article 1
Option to accelerate payment at will	§1-208	§1-309
Definitions of notice and knowledge	§1-201(25)-(27)	§1-202
Lease distinguished from sale with security interest	§1-201(37)	§1-203

ARTICLE 1.   GENERAL PROVISIONS

Part 1.   General Provisions

ARTICLE 2.   SALES

Part 1.   Short Title, General Construction and
Subject Matter

ARTICLE 3. NEGOTIABLE INSTRUMENTS

Part 1. General Provisions and Definitions

ARTICLE 1.   GENERAL PROVISIONS

Part 1.   General Provisions

§1-102.   Scope of Article

This article applies to a transaction to the extent that it is governed by another article of [the Uniform Commercial Code].

§1-103.   Construction of [Uniform Commercial Code] to Promote Its Purposes and Policies; Applicability of Supplemental Principles of Law

(a) [The Uniform Commercial Code] must be liberally construed and applied to promote its underlying purposes and policies, which are:

(1) to simplify, clarify, and modernize the law governing commercial transactions;

(2) to permit the continued expansion of commercial practices through custom, usage, and agreement of the parties; and

(3) to make uniform the law among the various jurisdictions.

(b) Unless displaced by the particular provisions of [the Uniform Commercial Code], the principles of law and equity, including the law merchant and the law relative to capacity to contract, principal and agent, estoppel, fraud, misrepresentation, duress, coercion, mistake, bankruptcy, and other validating or invalidating cause supplement its provisions.

§1-108. Relation to Electronic Signatures in Global and National Commerce Act

This article modifies, limits, and supersedes the federal Electronic Signatures in Global and National Commerce Act, 15 U.S.C. Section 7001 et seq., except that nothing in this article modifies, limits, or supersedes Section 7001(c) of that Act or authorizes electronic delivery of any of the notices described in Section 7003(b) of that Act.

Part 2. General Definitions and Principles of Interpretation

§1-201. General Definitions

(a) Unless the context otherwise requires, words or phrases defined in this section, or in the additional definitions contained in other articles of [the Uniform Commercial Code] that apply to particular articles or parts thereof, have the meanings stated.

(b) Subject to definitions contained in other articles of [the Uniform Commercial Code] that apply to particular articles or parts thereof:

(1) "Action", in the sense of a judicial proceeding, includes recoupment, counterclaim, set-off, suit in equity, and any other proceeding in which rights are determined.

(2) "Aggrieved party" means a party entitled to pursue a remedy.

(3) "Agreement", as distinguished from "contract", means the bargain of the parties in fact, as found in their language or inferred from other circumstances, including course of performance, course of dealing, or usage of trade as provided in Section 1-303.

(4) "Bank" means a person engaged in the business of banking and includes a savings bank, savings and loan association, credit union, and trust company.

(5) "Bearer" means a person in possession of a negotiable instrument, document of title, or certificated security that is payable to bearer or indorsed in blank.

(6) "Bill of lading" means a document evidencing the receipt of goods for shipment issued by a person engaged in the business of transporting or forwarding goods.

(7) "Branch" includes a separately incorporated foreign branch of a bank.

(8) "Burden of establishing" a fact means the burden of persuading the trier of fact that the existence of the fact is more probable than its nonexistence.

(9) "Buyer in ordinary course of business" means a person that buys goods in good faith, without knowledge that the sale violates the rights of another person in the goods, and in the ordinary course from a person, other than a pawnbroker, in the business of selling goods of that kind. A person buys goods in the ordinary course if the sale to the person comports with the usual or customary practices in the kind of business in which the seller is engaged or with the seller's own usual or customary practices. A person that sells oil, gas, or other minerals at the wellhead or minehead is a person in the business of selling goods of that kind. A buyer in ordinary course of business may buy for cash, by exchange of other property, or on secured or unsecured credit, and

may acquire goods or documents of title under a preexisting contract for sale. Only a buyer that takes possession of the goods or has a right to recover the goods from the seller under Article 2 may be a buyer in ordinary course of business. "Buyer in ordinary course of business" does not include a person that acquires goods in a transfer in bulk or as security for or in total or partial satisfaction of a money debt.

(10) "Conspicuous", with reference to a term, means so written, displayed, or presented that a reasonable person against which it is to operate ought to have noticed it. Whether a term is "conspicuous" or not is a decision for the court. Conspicuous terms include the following:

(A) a heading in capitals equal to or greater in size than the surrounding text, or in contrasting type, font, or color to the surrounding text of the same or lesser size; and

(B) language in the body of a record or display in larger type than the surrounding text, or in contrasting type, font, or color to the surrounding text of the same size, or set off from surrounding text of the same size by symbols or other marks that call attention to the language.

(11) "Consumer" means an individual who enters into a transaction primarily for personal, family, or household purposes.

(12) "Contract", as distinguished from "agreement", means the total legal obligation that results from the parties' agreement as determined by [the Uniform Commercial Code] as supplemented by any other applicable laws.

(13) "Creditor" includes a general creditor, a secured creditor, a lien creditor, and any representative of creditors, including an assignee for the benefit of creditors, a trustee in bankruptcy, a receiver in equity, and an executor or administrator of an insolvent debtor's or assignor's estate.

(14) "Defendant" includes a person in the position of defendant in a counterclaim, cross-claim, or third-party claim.

(15) "Delivery", with respect to an instrument, document of title, or chattel paper, means voluntary transfer of possession.

(16) "Document of title" includes bill of lading, dock warrant, dock receipt, warehouse receipt or order for the delivery of goods, and also any other document which in the regular course of business or financing is treated as adequately evidencing that the person in possession of it is entitled to receive, hold, and dispose of the document and the goods it covers. To be a document of title, a document must purport to be issued by or addressed to a bailee and purport to cover goods in the bailee's possession which are either identified or are fungible portions of an identified mass.

(17) "Fault" means a default, breach, or wrongful act or omission.

(18) "Fungible goods" means:

(A) goods of which any unit, by nature or usage of trade, is the equivalent of any other like unit; or

(B) goods that by agreement are treated as equivalent.

(19) "Genuine" means free of forgery or counterfeiting.

(20) "Good faith," except as otherwise provided in Article 5, means honesty in fact and the observance of reasonable commercial standards of fair dealing.

(21) "Holder" means:

(A) the person in possession of a negotiable instrument that is payable either to bearer or to an identified person that is the person in possession; or

(B) the person in possession of a document of title if the goods are deliverable either to bearer or to the order of the person in possession.

(22) "Insolvency proceeding" includes an assignment for the benefit of creditors or other proceeding intended to liquidate or rehabilitate the estate of the person involved.

(23) "Insolvent" means:

(A) having generally ceased to pay debts in the ordinary course of business other than as a result of bona fide dispute;

(B) being unable to pay debts as they become due; or

(C) being insolvent within the meaning of federal bankruptcy law.

(24) "Money" means a medium of exchange currently authorized or adopted by a domestic or foreign government. The term includes a monetary unit of account established by an intergovernmental organization or by agreement between two or more countries.

(25) "Organization" means a person other than an individual.

(26) "Party", as distinguished from "third party", means a person that has engaged in a transaction or made an agreement subject to [the Uniform Commercial Code].

(27) "Person" means an individual, corporation, business trust, estate, trust, partnership, limited liability company, association, joint venture, government, governmental subdivision, agency, or instrumentality, public corporation, or any other legal or commercial entity.

(28) "Present value" means the amount as of a date certain of one or more sums payable in the future, discounted to the date certain by use of either an interest rate specified by the parties if that rate is not manifestly unreasonable at the time the transaction is entered into or, if an interest rate is not so specified, a commercially reasonable rate that takes into account the facts and circumstances at the time the transaction is entered into.

(29) "Purchase" means taking by sale, lease, discount, negotiation, mortgage, pledge, lien, security interest, issue or reissue, gift, or any other voluntary transaction creating an interest in property.

(30) "Purchaser" means a person that takes by purchase.

(31) "Record" means information that is inscribed on a tangible medium or that is stored in an electronic or other medium and is retrievable in perceivable form.

(32) "Remedy" means any remedial right to which an aggrieved party is entitled with or without resort to a tribunal.

(33) "Representative" means a person empowered to act for another, including an agent, an officer of a corporation or association, and a trustee, executor, or administrator of an estate.

(34) "Right" includes remedy.

(35) "Security interest" means an interest in personal property or fixtures which secures payment or performance of an obligation. "Security interest" includes any interest of a consignor and a buyer of accounts, chattel paper, a payment intangible, or a promissory note in a transaction that is subject to Article 9. "Security interest" does not include the special property interest of a buyer of goods on identification of those goods to a contract for sale under Section 2-401, but a buyer may also acquire a "security interest" by complying with Article 9. Except as otherwise provided in Section 2-505, the right of a

seller or lessor of goods under Article 2 or 2A to retain or acquire possession of the goods is not a "security interest", but a seller or lessor may also acquire a "security interest" by complying with Article 9. The retention or reservation of title by a seller of goods notwithstanding shipment or delivery to the buyer under Section 2-401 is limited in effect to a reservation of a "security interest." Whether a transaction in the form of a lease creates a "security interest" is determined pursuant to Section 1-203.

(36) "Send" in connection with a writing, record, or notice means:

(A) to deposit in the mail or deliver for transmission by any other usual means of communication with postage or cost of transmission provided for and properly addressed and, in the case of an instrument, to an address specified thereon or otherwise agreed, or if there be none to any address reasonable under the circumstances; or

(B) in any other way to cause to be received any record or notice within the time it would have arrived if properly sent.

(37) "Signed" includes using any symbol executed or adopted with present intention to adopt or accept a writing.

(38) "State" means a State of the United States, the District of Columbia, Puerto Rico, the United States Virgin Islands, or any territory or insular possession subject to the jurisdiction of the United States.

(39) "Surety" includes a guarantor or other secondary obligor.

(40) "Term" means a portion of an agreement that relates to a particular matter.

(41) "Unauthorized signature" means a signature made without actual, implied, or apparent authority. The term includes a forgery.

(42) "Warehouse receipt" means a receipt issued by a person engaged in the business of storing goods for hire.

(43) "Writing" includes printing, typewriting, or any other intentional reduction to tangible form. "Written" has a corresponding meaning.

§1-202. Notice; Knowledge

(a) Subject to subsection (f), a person has "notice" of a fact if the person:

(1) has actual knowledge of it;

(2) has received a notice or notification of it; or

(3) from all the facts and circumstances known to the person at the time in question, has reason to know that it exists.

(b) "Knowledge" means actual knowledge. "Knows" has a corresponding meaning.

(c) "Discover", "learn", or words of similar import refer to knowledge rather than to reason to know.

(d) A person "notifies" or "gives" a notice or notification to another person by taking such steps as may be reasonably required to inform the other person in ordinary course, whether or not the other person actually comes to know of it.

(e) Subject to subsection (f), a person "receives" a notice or notification when:

(1) it comes to that person's attention; or

(2) it is duly delivered in a form reasonable under the circumstances at the place of business through which the contract was made or at another location held out by that person as the place for receipt of such communications.

(f) Notice, knowledge, or a notice or notification received by an organization is effective for a particular transaction from the time it is brought to the attention of the individual conducting that transaction and, in any event, from the time it would have been brought to the individual's attention if the organization had exercised due diligence. An organization exercises due diligence if it maintains reasonable routines for communicating significant information to the person conducting the transaction and there is reasonable compliance with the routines. Due diligence does not require an individual acting for the organization to communicate information unless the communication is part of the individual's regular duties or the individual has reason to know of the transaction and that the transaction would be materially affected by the information.

§1-203. Lease Distinguished from Security Interest

(a) Whether a transaction in the form of a lease creates a lease or security interest is determined by the facts of each case.

(b) A transaction in the form of a lease creates a security interest if the consideration that the lessee is to pay the lessor for the right to possession and use of the goods is an obligation for the term of the lease and is not subject to termination by the lessee, and:

(1) the original term of the lease is equal to or greater than the remaining economic life of the goods;

(2) the lessee is bound to renew the lease for the remaining economic life of the goods or is bound to become the owner of the goods;

(3) the lessee has an option to renew the lease for the remaining economic life of the goods for no additional consideration or for nominal additional consideration upon compliance with the lease agreement; or

(4) the lessee has an option to become the owner of the goods for no additional consideration or for nominal additional consideration upon compliance with the lease agreement.

(c) A transaction in the form of a lease does not create a security interest merely because:

(1) the present value of the consideration the lessee is obligated to pay the lessor for the right to possession and use of the goods is substantially equal to or is greater than the fair market value of the goods at the time the lease is entered into;

(2) the lessee assumes risk of loss of the goods;

(3) the lessee agrees to pay, with respect to the goods, taxes, insurance, filing, recording, or registration fees, or service or maintenance costs;

(4) the lessee has an option to renew the lease or to become the owner of the goods;

(5) the lessee has an option to renew the lease for a fixed rent that is equal to or greater than the reasonably predictable fair market rent for the use of the goods for the term of the renewal at the time the option is to be performed; or

(6) the lessee has an option to become the owner of the goods for a fixed price that is equal to or greater than the reasonably predictable fair market value of the goods at the time the option is to be performed.

(d) Additional consideration is nominal if it is less than the lessee's reasonably predictable cost of performing under the lease agreement if the option is not exercised. Additional consideration is not nominal if:

(1) when the option to renew the lease is granted to the lessee, the rent is stated to be the fair market rent for the use of the goods for the term of the renewal determined at the time the option is to be performed; or

(2) when the option to become the owner of the goods is granted to the lessee, the price is stated to be the fair market value of the goods determined at the time the option is to be performed.

(e) The "remaining economic life of the goods" and "reasonably predictable" fair market rent, fair market value, or cost of performing under the lease agreement must be determined with reference to the facts and circumstances at the time the transaction is entered into.

§1-204. Value

Except as otherwise provided in Articles 3, 4, [and] 5, [and 6], a person gives value for rights if the person acquires them:

(1) in return for a binding commitment to extend credit or for the extension of immediately available credit, whether or not drawn upon and whether or not a charge-back is provided for in the event of difficulties in collection;

(2) as security for, or in total or partial satisfaction of, a preexisting claim;

(3) by accepting delivery under a preexisting contract for purchase; or

(4) in return for any consideration sufficient to support a simple contract.

§1-205. Reasonable Time; Seasonableness.

(a) Whether a time for taking an action required by [the Uniform Commercial Code] is reasonable depends on the nature, purpose, and circumstances of the action.

(b) An action is taken seasonably if it is taken at or within the time agreed or, if no time is agreed, at or within a reasonable time.

§1-206. Presumptions

Whenever [the Uniform Commercial Code] creates a "presumption" with respect to a fact, or provides that a fact is "presumed," the trier of fact must find the existence of the fact unless and until evidence is introduced that supports a finding of its nonexistence.

Part 3.   Territorial Applicability and General Rules

§1-301. Territorial Applicability; Parties' Power to Choose Applicable Law

(a) Except as otherwise provided in this section, when a transaction bears a reasonable relation to this state and also to another state or nation the parties may agree that the law either of this state or of such other state or nation shall govern their rights and duties.

(b) In the absence of an agreement effective under subsection (a), and except as provided in subsection (c), [the Uniform Commercial Code] applies to transactions bearing an appropriate relation to this state.

(c) If one of the following provisions of [the Uniform Commercial Code] specifies the applicable law, that provision governs and a contrary agreement is effective only to the extent permitted by the law so specified:

(1) Section 2-402;

(2) Sections 2A-105 and 2A-106;

(3) Section 4-102;

(4) Section 4A-507;

(5) Section 5-116;

[(6) Section 6-103;]

(7) Section 8-110;

(8) Sections 9-301 through 9-307.

Amended in 2008.

Official Comment

Source: Former Section 1-105.

Changes from former law: This section is substantively identical to former Section 1-105. Changes in language are stylistic only.

1. Subsection (a) states affirmatively the right of the parties to a multi-state transaction or a transaction involving foreign trade to choose their own law. That right is subject to the firm rules stated in the sections listed in subsection (c), and is limited to jurisdictions to which the transaction bears a "reasonable relation." In general, the test of "reasonable relation" is similar to that laid down by the Supreme Court in Seeman v. Philadelphia Warehouse Co., 274 U.S. 403, 47 S. Ct. 626, 71 L. Ed. 1123 (1927). Ordinarily the law chosen must be that of a jurisdiction where a significant enough portion of the making or performance of the contract is to occur or occurs. But an agreement as to choice of law may sometimes take effect as a shorthand expression of the intent of the parties as to matters governed by their agreement, even though the transaction has no significant contact with the jurisdiction chosen.

2. Where there is no agreement as to the governing law, the Act is applicable to any transaction having an "appropriate" relation to any state which enacts it. Of course, the Act applies to any transaction which takes place in its entirety in a state which has enacted the Act. But the mere fact that suit is brought in a state does not make it appropriate to apply the substantive law of that state. Cases where a relation to the enacting state is not "appropriate" include, for example, those where the parties have clearly contracted on the basis of some other law, as where the law of the place of contracting and the law of the place of contemplated performance are the same and are contrary to the law under the Code.

3. Where a transaction has significant contacts with a state which has enacted the Act and also with other jurisdictions, the question what relation is "appropriate" is left to judicial decision. In deciding that question, the court is not strictly bound by precedents established in other contexts. Thus a conflict-of-laws decision refusing to apply a purely local statute or rule of law to a particular multi-state transaction may not be valid precedent for refusal to apply

the Code in an analogous situation. Application of the Code in such circumstances may be justified by its comprehensiveness, by the policy of uniformity, and by the fact that it is in large part a reformulation and restatement of the law merchant and of the understanding of a business community which transcends state and even national boundaries. Compare Global Commerce Corp. v. Clark-Babbitt Industries, Inc., 239 F.2d 716, 719 (2d Cir. 1956). In particular, where a transaction is governed in large part by the Code, application of another law to some detail of performance because of an accident of geography may violate the commercial understanding of the parties.

4. Subsection (c) spells out essential limitations on the parties' right to choose the applicable law. Especially in Article 9 parties taking a security interest or asked to extend credit which may be subject to a security interest must have sure ways to find out whether and where to file and where to look for possible existing filings.

5. Sections 9-301 through 9-307 should be consulted as to the rules for perfection of security interests and agricultural liens and the effect of perfection and nonperfection and priority.

6. This section is subject to Section 1-102, which states the scope of Article 1. As that section indicates, the rules of Article 1, including this section, apply to a transaction to the extent that transaction is governed by one of the other Articles of the Uniform Commercial Code.

§1-302. Variation by Agreement

(a) Except as otherwise provided in subsection (b) or elsewhere in [the Uniform Commercial Code], the effect of provisions of [the Uniform Commercial Code] may be varied by agreement.

(b) The obligations of good faith, diligence, reasonableness, and care prescribed by [the Uniform Commercial Code] may not be disclaimed by agreement. The parties, by agreement, may determine the standards by which the performance of those obligations is to be measured if those standards are not manifestly unreasonable. Whenever [the Uniform Commercial Code] requires an action to be taken within a reasonable time, a time that is not manifestly unreasonable may be fixed by agreement.

(c) The presence in certain provisions of [the Uniform Commercial Code] of the phrase "unless otherwise agreed", or words of similar import, does not imply that the effect of other provisions may not be varied by agreement under this section.

§1-303. Course of Performance, Course of Dealing, and Usage of Trade

(a) A "course of performance" is a sequence of conduct between the parties to a particular transaction that exists if:

(1) the agreement of the parties with respect to the transaction involves repeated occasions for performance by a party; and

(2) the other party, with knowledge of the nature of the performance and opportunity for objection to it, accepts the performance or acquiesces in it without objection.

(b) A "course of dealing" is a sequence of conduct concerning previous trans-actions between the parties to a particular transaction that is fairly to be regarded as establishing a common basis of understanding for interpreting their expressions and other conduct.

(c) A "usage of trade" is any practice or method of dealing having such regularity of observance in a place, vocation, or trade as to justify an expectation that it will be observed with respect to the transaction in question. The existence and scope of such a usage must be proved as facts. If it is established that such a usage is embodied in a trade code or similar record, the interpretation of the record is a question of law.

(d) A course of performance or course of dealing between the parties or usage of trade in the vocation or trade in which they are engaged or of which they are or should be aware is relevant in ascertaining the meaning of the parties' agreement, may give particular meaning to specific terms of the agreement, and may supplement or qualify the terms of the agreement. A usage of trade applicable in the place in which part of the performance under the agreement is to occur may be so utilized as to that part of the performance.

(e) Except as otherwise provided in subsection (f), the express terms of an agreement and any applicable course of performance, course of dealing, or usage of trade must be construed whenever reasonable as consistent with each other. If such a construction is unreasonable:

(1) express terms prevail over course of performance, course of dealing, and usage of trade;

(2) course of performance prevails over course of dealing and usage of trade; and

(3) course of dealing prevails over usage of trade.

(f) Subject to Section 2-209, a course of performance is relevant to show a waiver or modification of any term inconsistent with the course of performance.

(g) Evidence of a relevant usage of trade offered by one party is not admissible unless that party has given the other party notice that the court finds sufficient to prevent unfair surprise to the other party.

Official Comments

Source: Former Sections 1-205, 2-208, and Section 2A-207.

Changes from former law: This section integrates the "course of perfor-mance" concept from Articles 2 and 2A into the principles of former Section 1-205, which deals with course of dealing and usage of trade. In so doing, the section slightly modifies the articulation of the course of performance rules to fit more comfortably with the approach and structure of former Section 1- 205. There are also slight modifications to be more consistent with the definition of "agreement" in former Section 1-201(3). . . .

§1-304. Obligation of Good Faith

Every contract or duty within [the Uniform Commercial Code] imposes an obli-gation of good faith in its performance and enforcement.

Official Comments

Source: Former Section 1-203.

Changes from former law: Except for changing the form of reference to the Uniform Commercial Code, this section is identical to former Section 1-203.

1. This section sets forth a basic principle running throughout the Uniform Commercial Code. The principle is that in commercial transactions good faith is required in the performance and enforcement of all agreements or duties. While this duty is explicitly stated in some provisions of the Uniform Commercial Code, the applicability of the duty is broader than merely these situations and applies generally, as stated in this section, to the performance or enforcement of every contract or duty within this Act. It is further implemented by Section 1-303 on course of dealing, course of performance, and usage of trade. This section does not support an independent cause of action for failure to perform or enforce in good faith. Rather, this section means that a failure to perform or enforce, in good faith, a specific duty or obligation under the contract, constitutes a breach of that contract or makes unavailable, under the particular circumstances, are medial right or power. This distinction makes it clear that the doctrine of good faith merely directs a court towards interpreting contracts within the commercial context in which they are created, performed, and enforced, and does not create a separate duty of fairness and reasonableness which can be independently breached.

2. "Performance and enforcement" of contracts and duties within the Uniform Commercial Code include the exercise of rights created by the Uniform Commercial Code.

§1-305.   Remedies to Be Liberally Administered

(a) The remedies provided by [the Uniform Commercial Code] must be liberally administered to the end that the aggrieved party may be put in as good a position as if the other party had fully performed but neither consequential or special damages nor penal damages may be had except as specifically provided in [the Uniform Commercial Code] or by other rule of law.

(b) Any right or obligation declared by [the Uniform Commercial Code] is enforceable by action unless the provision declaring it specifies a different and limited effect.

§1-306.   Waiver or Renunciation of Claim or Right After Breach

A claim or right arising out of an alleged breach may be discharged in whole or in part without consideration by agreement of the aggrieved party in an authenticated record.

§1-308.   Performance or Acceptance Under Reservation of Rights

(a) A party that with explicit reservation of rights performs or promises performance or assents to performance in a manner demanded or offered by the other party does not thereby prejudice the rights reserved. Such words as "without prejudice," "under protest," or the like are sufficient.

(b) Subsection (a) does not apply to an accord and satisfaction.

§1-309.   Option to Accelerate at Will

A term providing that one party or that party's successor in interest may accelerate payment or performance or require collateral or additional collateral "at will" or when the party "deems itself insecure," or words of similar import, means that the party has power to do so only if that party in good faith believes that the prospect of payment or performance is impaired. The burden of establishing lack of good faith is on the party against which the power has been exercised.

ARTICLE 2.   SALES

Part 1.   Short Title, General Construction and Subject Matter

§2-102.   Scope; Certain Security and Other Transactions Excluded from This Article

Unless the context otherwise requires, this Article applies to transactions in goods; it does not apply to any transaction which although in the form of an unconditional contract to sell or present sale is intended to operate only as a security transaction nor does this Article impair or repeal any statute regulating sales to consumers, farmers or other specified classes of buyers.

§2-103.   Definitions and Index of Definitions

(1) In this Article unless the context otherwise requires
(a) "Buyer" means a person who buys or contracts to buy goods.
(b) "Good faith" in the case of a merchant means honesty in fact and the observance of reasonable commercial standards of fair dealing in the trade.
(c) "Receipt" of goods means taking physical possession of them.
(d) "Seller" means a person who sells or contracts to sell goods.
(2) Other definitions applying to this Article or to specified Parts thereof, and the sections in which they appear are:
"Acceptance." Section 2-606.
"Banker's credit." Section 2-325.
"Between merchants." Section 2-104.
"Cancellation." Section 2-106(4).
"Commercial unit." Section 2-105.
"Confirmed credit." Section 2-325.
"Conforming to contract." Section 2-106.

"Contract for sale." Section 2-106.
"Cover." Section 2-712.
"Entrusting." Section 2-403.
"Financing agency." Section 2-104.
"Future goods." Section 2-105.
"Goods." Section 2-105.
"Identification." Section 2-501.
"Installment contract." Section 2-612.
"Letter of Credit." Section 2-325.
"Lot." Section 2-105.
"Merchant." Section 2-104.
"Overseas." Section 2-323.
"Person in position of seller." Section 2-707.
"Present sale." Section 2-106.
"Sale." Section 2-106.
"Sale on approval." Section 2-326.
"Sale or return." Section 2-326.
"Termination." Section 2-106.
(3) The following definitions in other Articles apply to this Article:
"Check." Section 3-104.
"Consignee." Section 7-102.
"Consignor." Section 7-102.
"Consumer goods." Section 9-102.
"Dishonor." Section 3-502.
"Draft." Section 3-104.
[As amended in 1999 to conform to Revised Article 9 (2000) of the Code.]
(4) In addition Article 1 contains general definitions and principles of construction and interpretation applicable throughout this Article.

§2-104. Definitions: "Merchant"; "Between Merchants"; "Financing Agency"

(1) "Merchant" means a person who deals in goods of the kind or otherwise by his occupation holds himself out as having knowledge or skill peculiar to the practices or goods involved in the transaction or to whom such knowledge or skill may be attributed by his employment of an agent or broker or other intermediary who by his occupation holds himself out as having such knowledge or skill.

(2) "Financing agency" means a bank, finance company or other person who in the ordinary course of business makes advances against goods or documents of title or who by arrangement with either the seller or the buyer intervenes in ordinary course to make or collect payment due or claimed under the contract for sale, as by purchasing or paying the seller's draft or making advances against it or by merely taking it for collection whether or not documents of title accompany the draft. "Financing agency" includes also a bank or other person who similarly intervenes between persons who are in the position of seller and buyer in respect to the goods (Section 2-707).

(3) "Between merchants" means in any transaction with respect to which both parties are chargeable with the knowledge or skill of merchants.

Official Comment

Prior Uniform Statutory Provision: None. But see Sections 15(2), (5), 16(c), 45(2) and 71, Uniform Sales Act, and Sections 35 and 37, Uniform Bills of Lading Act for examples of the policy expressly provided for in this Article.

Purposes:

1. This Article assumes that transactions between professionals in a given field require special and clear rules which may not apply to a casual or inexperienced seller or buyer. It thus adopts a policy of expressly stating rules applicable "between merchants" and "as against a merchant" wherever they are needed instead of making them depend upon the circumstances of each case as in the statutes cited above. This section lays the foundation of this policy by defining those who are to be regarded as professionals or "merchants" and by stating when a transaction is deemed to be "between merchants."

2. The term "merchant" as defined here roots in the "law merchant" concept of a professional in business. The professional status under the definition may be based upon specialized knowledge as to the goods, specialized knowledge as to business practices, or specialized knowledge as to both and which kind of specialized knowledge may be sufficient to establish the merchant status is indicated by the nature of the provisions.

The special provisions as to merchants appear only in this Article and they are of three kinds. Sections 2-201(2), 2-205, 2-207 and 2-209 dealing with the statute of frauds, firm offers, confirmatory memoranda and modification rest on normal business practices which are or ought to be typical of and familiar to any person in business. For purposes of these sections almost every person in business would, therefore, be deemed to be a "merchant" under the language "who ... by his occupation holds himself out as having knowledge or skill peculiar to the practices ... involved in the transaction ..." since the practices involved in the transaction are non-specialized business practices such as answering mail. In this type of provision, banks or even universities, for example, well may be "merchants." But even these sections only apply to a merchant in his mercantile capacity; a lawyer or bank president buying fishing tackle for his own use is not a merchant.

On the other hand, in Section 2-314 on the warranty of merchantability, such warranty is implied only "if the seller is a merchant with respect to goods of that kind." Obviously this qualification restricts the implied warranty to a much smaller group than everyone who is engaged in business and requires a professional status as to particular kinds of goods. The exception in Section 2-402(2) for retention of possession by a merchant-seller falls in the same class; as does Section 2-403(2) on entrusting of possession to a merchant "who deals in goods of that kind."

A third group of sections includes 2-103(1)(b), which provides that in the case of a merchant "good faith" includes observance of reasonable commercial standards of fair dealing in the trade; 2-327(1)(c), 2-603 and 2-605, dealing with responsibilities of merchant buyers to follow seller's instructions, etc.; 2-509 on risk of loss, and 2-609 on adequate assurance of performance. This group of sections applies to persons who are merchants under either the "practices" or the "goods" aspect of the definition of merchant.

3. The "or to whom such knowledge or skill may be attributed by his employment of an agent or broker . . ." clause of the definition of merchant means that even persons such as universities, for example, can come within the definition of merchant if they have regular purchasing departments or business personnel who are familiar with business practices and who are equipped to take any action required.

Cross References:

Point 1: See Sections 1-102 and 1-203.

Point 2: See Sections 2-314, 2-315 and 2-320 to 2-325, of this Article, and Article 9.

Definitional Cross References:

"Bank." Section 1-201.

"Buyer." Section 2-103.

"Contract for sale." Section 2-106.

"Document of title." Section 1-201.

"Draft." Section 3-104.

"Goods." Section 2-105.

"Person." Section 1-201.

"Purchase." Section 1-201.

"Seller." Section 2-103.

§2-105. Definitions: Transferability; "Goods"; "Future" Goods; "Lot"; "Commercial Unit"

(1) "Goods" means all things (including specially manufactured goods) which are movable at the time of identification to the contract for sale other than the money in which the price is to be paid, investment securities (Article 8) and things in action. "Goods" also includes the unborn young of animals and growing crops and other identified things attached to realty as described in the section on goods to be severed from realty (Section 2-107).

(2) Goods must be both existing and identified before any interest in them can pass. Goods which are not both existing and identified are "future" goods. A purported present sale of future goods or of any interest therein operates as a contract to sell.

(3) There may be a sale of a part interest in existing identified goods.

(4) An undivided share in an identified bulk of fungible goods is sufficiently identified to be sold although the quantity of the bulk is not determined. Any agreed proportion of such a bulk or any quantity thereof agreed upon by number, weight or other measure may to the extent of the seller's interest in the bulk be sold to the buyer who then becomes an owner in common.

(5) "Lot" means a parcel or a single article which is the subject matter of a separate sale or delivery, whether or not it is sufficient to perform the contract.

(6) "Commercial unit" means such a unit of goods as by commercial usage is a single whole for purposes of sale and division of which materially impairs its character or value on the market or in use. A commercial unit may be a single article (as a machine) or a set of articles (as a suite of furniture or an assortment of sizes) or a quantity (as a bale, gross, or carload) or any other unit treated in use or in the relevant market as a single whole.

§2-106. Definitions: "Contract"; "Agreement"; "Contract for Sale"; "Sale"; "Present Sale"; "Conforming" to Contract; "Termination"; "Cancellation"

(1) In this Article unless the context otherwise requires "contract" and "agreement" are limited to those relating to the present or future sale of goods. "Contract for sale" includes both a present sale of goods and a contract to sell goods at a future time. A "sale" consists in the passing of title from the seller to the buyer for a price (Section 2-401). A "present sale" means a sale which is accomplished by the making of the contract.

(2) Goods or conduct including any part of a performance are "conforming" or conform to the contract when they are in accordance with the obligations under the contract.

(3) "Termination" occurs when either party pursuant to a power created by agreement or law puts an end to the contract otherwise than for its breach. On "termination" all obligations which are still executory on both sides are discharged but any right based on prior breach or performance survives.

(4) "Cancellation" occurs when either party puts an end to the contract for breach by the other and its effect is the same as that of "termination" except that the cancelling party also retains any remedy for breach of the whole contract or any unperformed balance.

Part 2. Form, Formation and Readjustment of Contract

§2-201. Formal Requirements; Statute of Frauds

(1) Except as otherwise provided in this section a contract for the sale of goods for the price of $500 or more is not enforceable by way of action or defense unless there is some writing sufficient to indicate that a contract for sale has been made between the parties and signed by the party against whom enforcement is sought or by his authorized agent or broker. A writing is not insufficient because it omits or incorrectly states a term agreed upon but the contract is not enforceable under this paragraph beyond the quantity of goods shown in such writing.

(2) Between merchants if within a reasonable time a writing in confirmation of the contract and sufficient against the sender is received and the party receiving it has reason to know its contents, it satisfies the requirements of subsection (1) against such party unless written notice of objection to its contents is given within 10 days after it is received.

(3) A contract which does not satisfy the requirements of subsection (1) but which is valid in other respects is enforceable

(a) if the goods are to be specially manufactured for the buyer and are not suitable for sale to others in the ordinary course of the seller's business and the seller, before notice of repudiation is received and under circumstances which reasonably indicate that the goods are for the buyer, has made either a substantial beginning of their manufacture or commitments for their procurement; or

(b) if the party against whom enforcement is sought admits in his pleading, testimony or otherwise in court that a contract for sale was made, but the contract is not enforceable under this provision beyond the quantity of goods admitted; or

(c) with respect to goods for which payment has been made and accepted or which have been received and accepted (Sec. 2-606).

Official Comment

Prior Uniform Statutory Provision: Section 4, Uniform Sales Act (which was based on Section 17 of the Statute of 29 Charles II).

Changes: Completely rephrased; restricted to sale of goods. See also Sections 1-206, 8-319 and 9-203.

Purposes of Changes: The changed phraseology of this section is intended to make it clear that:

1. The required writing need not contain all the material terms of the contract and such material terms as are stated need not be precisely stated. All that is required is that the writing afford a basis for believing that the offered oral evidence rests on a real transaction. It may be written in lead pencil on a scratch pad. It need not indicate which party is the buyer and which the seller. The only term which must appear is the quantity term which need not be accurately stated but recovery is limited to the amount stated. The price, time and place of payment or delivery, the general quality of the goods, or any particular warranties may all be omitted.

Special emphasis must be placed on the permissibility of omitting the price term in view of the insistence of some courts on the express inclusion of this term even where the parties have contracted on the basis of a published price list. In many valid contracts for sale the parties do not mention the price in express terms, the buyer being bound to pay and the seller to accept a reasonable price which the trier of the fact may well be trusted to determine. Again, frequently the price is not mentioned since the parties have based their agreement on a price list or catalogue known to both of them and this list serves as an efficient safeguard against perjury. Finally, "market" prices and valuations that are current in the vicinity constitute a similar check. Thus if the price is not stated in the memorandum it can normally be supplied without danger of fraud. Of course if the "price" consists of goods rather than money the quantity of goods must be stated.

Only three definite and invariable requirements as to the memorandum are made by this subsection. First, it must evidence a contract for the sale of goods; second, it must be "signed," a word which includes any authentication which identifies the party to be charged; and third, it must specify a quantity.

2. "Partial performance" as a substitute for the required memorandum can validate the contract only for the goods which have been accepted or for which payment has been made and accepted.

Receipt and acceptance either of goods or of the price constitutes an unambiguous overt admission by both parties that a contract actually exists. If the court can make a just apportionment, therefore, the agreed price of any goods actually delivered can be recovered without a writing or, if the price has been paid, the seller can be forced to deliver an apportionable part of the goods. The overt actions of the parties make admissible evidence of the other terms of the contract necessary to a just apportionment. This is true even though the actions of the parties are not in themselves inconsistent with a different transaction such as a consignment for resale or a mere loan of money.

Part performance by the buyer requires the delivery of something by him that is accepted by the seller as such performance. Thus, part payment may be made by money or check, accepted by the seller. If the agreed price consists of goods or services, then they must also have been delivered and accepted.

3. Between merchants, failure to answer a written confirmation of a contract within ten days of receipt is tantamount to a writing under subsection (2) and is sufficient against both parties under subsection (1). The only effect, however, is to take away from the party who fails to answer the defense of the Statute of Frauds; the burden of persuading the trier of fact that a contract was in fact made orally prior to the written confirmation is unaffected. Compare the effect of a failure to reply under Section 2-207.

4. Failure to satisfy the requirements of this section does not render the contract void for all purposes, but merely prevents it from being judicially enforced in favor of a party to the contract. For example, a buyer who takes possession of goods as provided in an oral contract which the seller has not meanwhile repudiated, is not a trespasser. Nor would the Statute of Frauds provisions of this section be a defense to a third person who wrongfully induces a party to refuse to perform an oral contract, even though the injured party cannot maintain an action for damages against the party so refusing to perform.

5. The requirement of "signing" is discussed in the comment to Section 1-201.

6. It is not necessary that the writing be delivered to anybody. It need not be signed or authenticated by both parties but it is, of course, not sufficient against one who has not signed it. Prior to a dispute no one can determine which party's signing of the memorandum may be necessary but from the time of contracting each party should be aware that to him it is signing by the other which is important.

7. If the making of a contract is admitted in court, either in a written pleading, by stipulation or by oral statement before the court, no additional writing is necessary for protection against fraud. Under this section it is no longer possible to admit the contract in court and still treat the Statute as a defense. However, the contract is not thus conclusively established. The admission so made by a party is itself evidential against him of the truth of the facts so admitted and of nothing more; as against the other party, it is not evidential at all.

Cross References:

See Sections 1-201, 2-202, 2-207, 2-209 and 2-304.

Definitional Cross References:

"Action." Section 1-201.
"Between merchants." Section 2-104.
"Buyer." Section 2-103.
"Contract." Section 1-201.
"Contract for sale." Section 2-106.

"Goods." Section 2-105.
"Notice." Section 1-201.
"Party." Section 1-201.
"Reasonable time." Section 1-204.
"Sale." Section 2-106.
"Seller." Section 2-103.

§2-202. Final Written Expression: Parol or Extrinsic Evidence

Terms with respect to which the confirmatory memoranda of the parties agree or which are otherwise set forth in a writing intended by the parties as a final expression of their agreement with respect to such terms as are included therein may not be contradicted by evidence of any prior agreement or of a contemporaneous oral agreement but may be explained or supplemented

(a) by course of dealing or usage of trade (Section 1-205) or by course of performance (Section 2-208); and

(b) by evidence of consistent additional terms unless the court finds the writing to have been intended also as a complete and exclusive statement of the terms of the agreement.

Official Comment

Prior Uniform Statutory Provision: None.

Purposes:
1. This section definitely rejects:

(a) Any assumption that because a writing has been worked out which is final on some matters, it is to be taken as including all the matters agreed upon;

(b) The premise that the language used has the meaning attributable to such language by rules of construction existing in the law rather than the meaning which arises out of the commercial context in which it was used; and

(c) The requirement that a condition precedent to the admissibility of the type of evidence specified in paragraph (a) is an original determination by the court that the language used is ambiguous.

2. Paragraph (a) makes admissible evidence of course of dealing, usage of trade and course of performance to explain or supplement the terms of any writing stating the agreement of the parties in order that the true understanding of the parties as to the agreement may be reached. Such writings are to be read on the assumption that the course of prior dealings between the parties and the usages of trade were taken for granted when the document was phrased. Unless carefully negated they have become an element of the meaning of the words used. Similarly, the course of actual performance by the parties is considered the best indication of what they intended the writing to mean.

3. Under paragraph (b) consistent additional terms, not reduced to writing, may be proved unless the court finds that the writing was intended by both

parties as a complete and exclusive statement of all the terms. If the additional terms are such that, if agreed upon, they would certainly have been included in the document in the view of the court, then evidence of their alleged making must be kept from the trier of fact.

Cross References:
Point 3: Sections 1-205, 2-207, 2-302 and 2-316.

Definitional Cross References:
"Agreed" and "agreement." Section 1-201.
"Course of dealing." Section 1-205.
"Parties." Section 1-201.
"Term." Section 1-201.
"Usage of trade." Section 1-205.
"Written" and "writing." Section 1-201.

§2-203. Seals Inoperative

The affixing of a seal to a writing evidencing a contract for sale or an offer to buy or sell goods does not constitute the writing a sealed instrument and the law with respect to sealed instruments does not apply to such a contract or offer.

§2-204. Formation in General

(1) A contract for sale of goods may be made in any manner sufficient to show agreement, including conduct by both parties which recognizes the existence of such a contract.

(2) An agreement sufficient to constitute a contract for sale may be found even though the moment of its making is undetermined.

(3) Even though one or more terms are left open a contract for sale does not fail for indefiniteness if the parties have intended to make a contract and there is a reasonably certain basis for giving an appropriate remedy.

Official Comment

Prior Uniform Statutory Provisions: Sections 1 and 3, Uniform Sales Act.

Changes: Completely rewritten by this and other sections of this Article.

Purposes of Changes:
Subsection (1) continues without change the basic policy of recognizing any manner of expression of agreement, oral, written or otherwise. The legal effect of such an agreement is, of course, qualified by other provisions of this Article.

Under subsection (1) appropriate conduct by the parties may be sufficient to establish an agreement. Subsection (2) is directed primarily to the situation where the interchanged correspondence does not disclose the exact point at which the deal was closed, but the actions of the parties indicate that a binding obligation has been undertaken.

Subsection (3) states the principle as to "open terms" underlying later sections of the Article. If the parties intend to enter into a binding agreement, this subsection recognizes that agreement as valid in law, despite missing terms, if there is any reasonably certain basis for granting a remedy. The test is not certainty as to what the parties were to do nor as to the exact amount of damages due the plaintiff. Nor is the fact that one or more terms are left to be agreed upon enough of itself to defeat an otherwise adequate agreement. Rather, commercial standards on the point of "indefiniteness" are intended to be applied, this Act making provision elsewhere for missing terms needed for performance, open price, remedies and the like.

The more terms the parties leave open, the less likely it is that they have intended to conclude a binding agreement, but their actions may be frequently conclusive on the matter despite the omissions.

Cross References:
Subsection (1): Sections 1-103, 2-201 and 2-302.
Subsection (2): Sections 2-205 through 2-209.
Subsection (3): See Part 3.

Definitional Cross References:
"Agreement." Section 1-201.
"Contract." Section 1-201.
"Contract for sale." Section 2-106.
"Goods." Section 2-105.
"Party." Section 1-201.
"Remedy." Section 1-201.
"Term." Section 1-201.

§2-205. Firm Offers

An offer by a merchant to buy or sell goods in a signed writing which by its terms gives assurance that it will be held open is not revocable, for lack of consideration, during the time stated or if no time is stated for a reasonable time, but in no event may such period of irrevocability exceed three months; but any such term of assurance on a form supplied by the offeree must be separately signed by the offeror.

Official Comment

Prior Uniform Statutory Provision: Sections 1 and 3, Uniform Sales Act.

Changes: Completely rewritten by this and other sections of this Article.

Purposes of Changes:
1. This section is intended to modify the former rule which required that "firm offers" be sustained by consideration in order to bind, and to require instead that they must merely be characterized as such and expressed in signed writings.

2. The primary purpose of this section is to give effect to the deliberate intention of a merchant to make a current firm offer binding. The deliberation

is shown in the case of an individualized document by the merchant's signature to the offer, and in the case of an offer included on a form supplied by the other party to the transaction by the separate signing of the particular clause which contains the offer. "Signed" here also includes authentication but the reasonableness of the authentication herein allowed must be determined in the light of the purpose of the section. The circumstances surrounding the signing may justify something less than a formal signature or initialing but typically the kind of authentication involved here would consist of a minimum of initialing of the clause involved. A handwritten memorandum on the writer's letterhead purporting in its terms to "confirm" a firm offer already made would be enough to satisfy this section, although not subscribed, since under the circumstances it could not be considered a memorandum of mere negotiation and it would adequately show its own authenticity. Similarly, an authorized telegram will suffice, and this is true even though the original draft contained only a typewritten signature. However, despite settled courses of dealing or usages of the trade whereby firm offers are made by oral communication and relied upon without more evidence, such offers remain revocable under this Article since authentication by a writing is the essence of this section.

3. This section is intended to apply to current "firm" offers and not to long term options, and an outside time limit of three months during which such offers remain irrevocable has been set. The three month period during which firm offers remain irrevocable under this section need not be stated by days or by date. If the offer states that it is "guaranteed" or "firm" until the happening of a contingency which will occur within the three month period, it will remain irrevocable until that event. A promise made for a longer period will operate under this section to bind the offeror only for the first three months of the period but may of course be renewed. If supported by consideration it may continue for as long as the parties specify. This section deals only with the offer which is not supported by consideration.

4. Protection is afforded against the inadvertent signing of a firm offer when contained in a form prepared by the offeree by requiring that such a clause be separately authenticated. If the offer clause is called to the offeror's attention and he separately authenticates it, he will be bound; Section 2-302 may operate, however, to prevent an unconscionable result which otherwise would flow from other terms appearing in the form.

5. Safeguards are provided to offer relief in the case of material mistake by virtue of the requirement of good faith and the general law of mistake.

Cross References:
   Point 1: Section 1-102.
   Point 2: Section 1-102.
   Point 3: Section 2-201.
   Point 5: Section 2-302.

Definitional Cross References:
   "Goods." Section 2-105.
   "Merchant." Section 2-104.
   "Signed." Section 1-201.
   "Writing." Section 1-201.

§2-206. Offer and Acceptance in Formation of Contract

(1) Unless otherwise unambiguously indicated by the language or circumstances

(a) an offer to make a contract shall be construed as inviting acceptance in any manner and by any medium reasonable in the circumstances;

(b) an order or other offer to buy goods for prompt or current shipment shall be construed as inviting acceptance either by a prompt promise to ship or by the prompt or current shipment of conforming or non-conforming goods, but such a shipment of non-conforming goods does not constitute an acceptance if the seller seasonably notifies the buyer that the shipment is offered only as an accommodation to the buyer.

(2) Where the beginning of a requested performance is a reasonable mode of acceptance an offeror who is not notified of acceptance within a reasonable time may treat the offer as having lapsed before acceptance.

§2-207. Additional Terms in Acceptance or Confirmation

Can subvert mirror image rule

(1) A definite and seasonable expression of acceptance or a written confirmation which is sent within a reasonable time operates as an acceptance even though it states terms additional to or different from those offered or agreed upon, unless acceptance is expressly made conditional on assent to the additional or different terms. *last clause creates limited acceptance if you include specific language.*

(2) The additional terms are to be construed as proposals for addition to the contract. Between merchants such terms become part of the contract *automatically* unless:

(a) the offer expressly limits acceptance to the terms of the offer;

(b) they materially alter it; or

(c) notification of objection to them has already been given or is given within a reasonable time after notice of them is received.

(3) Conduct by both parties which recognizes the existence of a contract is sufficient to establish a contract for sale although the writings of the parties do not otherwise establish a contract. In such case the terms of the particular contract consist of those terms on which the writings of the parties agree, together with any supplementary terms incorporated under any other provisions of this Act.

Official Comment

Prior Uniform Statutory Provision: Sections 1 and 3, Uniform Sales Act.

Changes: Completely rewritten by this and other sections of this Article.

Purposes of Changes:

1. This section is intended to deal with two typical situations. The one is the written confirmation, where an agreement has been reached either orally or by informal correspondence between the parties and is followed by one or both of the parties sending formal memoranda embodying the terms so far as agreed upon and adding terms not discussed. The other situation is offer and acceptance, in which a wire or letter expressed and intended as an acceptance or

the closing of an agreement adds further minor suggestions or proposals such as "ship by Tuesday," "rush," "ship draft against bill of lading inspection allowed," or the like. A frequent example of the second situation is the exchange of printed purchase order and acceptance (sometimes called "acknowledgment") forms. Because the forms are oriented to the thinking of the respective drafting parties, the terms contained in them often do not correspond. Often the seller's form contains terms different from or additional to those set forth in the buyer's form. Nevertheless, the parties proceed with the transaction.

2. Under this Article a proposed deal which in commercial understanding has in fact been closed is recognized as a contract. Therefore, any additional matter contained in the confirmation or in the acceptance falls within subsection (2) and must be regarded as a proposal for an added term unless the acceptance is made conditional on the acceptance of the additional or different terms.

3. Whether or not additional or different terms will become part of the agreement depends upon the provisions of subsection (2). If they are such as materially to alter the original bargain, they will not be included unless expressly agreed to by the other party. If, however, they are terms which would not so change the bargain they will be incorporated unless notice of objection to them has already been given or is given within a reasonable time.

4. Examples of typical clauses which would normally "materially alter" the contract and so result in surprise or hardship if incorporated without express awareness by the other party are: a clause negating such standard warranties as that of merchantability or fitness for a particular purpose in circumstances in which either warranty normally attaches; a clause requiring a guaranty of 90% or 100% deliveries in a case such as a contract by cannery, where the usage of the trade allows greater quantity leeways; a clause reserving to the seller the power to cancel upon the buyer's failure to meet any invoice when due; a clause requiring that complaints be made in a time materially shorter than customary or reasonable.

5. Examples of clauses which involve no element of unreasonable surprise and which therefore are to be incorporated in the contract unless notice of objection is seasonably given are: a clause setting forth and perhaps enlarging slightly upon the seller's exemption due to supervening causes beyond his control, similar to those covered by the provision of this Article on merchant's excuse by failure of presupposed conditions or a clause fixing in advance any reasonable formula of proration under such circumstances; a clause fixing a reasonable time for complaints within customary limits, or in the case of a purchase for sub-sale, providing for inspection by the sub-purchaser; a clause providing for interest on overdue invoices or fixing the seller's standard credit terms where they are within the range of trade practice and do not limit any credit bargained for; a clause limiting the right of rejection for defects which fall within the customary trade tolerances for acceptance "with adjustment" or otherwise limiting remedy in a reasonable manner (see Sections 2-718 and 2-719).

6. If no answer is received within a reasonable time after additional terms are proposed, it is both fair and commercially sound to assume that their inclusion has been assented to. Where clauses on confirming forms sent by both parties conflict each party must be assumed to object to a clause of the other conflicting

with one on the confirmation sent by himself. As a result the requirement that there be notice of objection which is found in subsection (2) is satisfied and the conflicting terms do not become a part of the contract. The contract then consists of the terms originally expressly agreed to, terms on which the confirmations agree, and terms supplied by this Act, including subsection (2). The written confirmation is also subject to Section 2-201. Under that section a failure to respond permits enforcement of a prior oral agreement; under this section a failure to respond permits additional terms to become part of the agreement.

7. In many cases, as where goods are shipped, accepted and paid for before any dispute arises, there is no question whether a contract has been made. In such cases, where the writings of the parties do not establish a contract, it is not necessary to determine which act or document constituted the offer and which the acceptance. See Section 2-204. The only question is what terms are included in the contract, and subsection (3) furnishes the governing rule.

Cross References:

See generally Section 2-302.

Point 5: Sections 2-513, 2-602, 2-607, 2-609, 2-612, 2-614, 2-615, 2-616, 2-718 and 2-719.

Point 6: Sections 1-102 and 2-104.

Definitional Cross References:

"Between merchants." Section 2-104.

"Contract." Section 1-201.

"Notification." Section 1-201.

"Reasonable time." Section 1-204.

"Seasonably." Section 1-204.

"Send." Section 1-201.

"Term." Section 1-201.

"Written." Section 1-201.

§2-208. Course of Performance or Practical Construction

(1) Where the contract for sale involves repeated occasions for performance by either party with knowledge of the nature of the performance and opportunity for objection to it by the other, any course of performance accepted or acquiesced in without objection shall be relevant to determine the meaning of the agreement.

(2) The express terms of the agreement and any such course of performance, as well as any course of dealing and usage of trade, shall be construed whenever reasonable as consistent with each other; but when such construction is unreasonable, express terms shall control course of performance and course of performance shall control both course of dealing and usage of trade (Section 1-205).

(3) Subject to the provisions of the next section on modification and waiver, such course of performance shall be relevant to show a waiver or modification of any term inconsistent with such course of performance.

[**Note:** *This Section should be deleted if the jurisdiction has adopted revised Article 1.*]

Official Comment

Prior Uniform Statutory Provision: No such general provision but concept of this section recognized by terms such as "course of dealing," "the circumstances of the case," "the conduct of the parties," etc., in Uniform Sales Act.

Purposes:

1. The parties themselves know best what they have meant by their words of agreement and their action under that agreement is the best indication of what that meaning was. This section thus rounds out the set of factors which determines the meaning of the "agreement" and therefore also of the "unless otherwise agreed" qualification to various provisions of this Article.

2. Under this section a course of performance is always relevant to determine the meaning of the agreement. Express mention of course of performance elsewhere in this Article carries no contrary implication when there is a failure to refer to it in other sections.

3. Where it is difficult to determine whether a particular act merely sheds light on the meaning of the agreement or represents a waiver of a term of the agreement, the preference is in favor of "waiver" whenever such construction, plus the application of the provisions on the reinstatement of rights waived (see Section 2-209), is needed to preserve the flexible character of commercial contracts and to prevent surprise or other hardship.

4. A single occasion of conduct does not fall within the language of this section but other sections such as the ones on silence after acceptance and failure to specify particular defects can affect the parties' rights on a single occasion (see Sections 2-605 and 2-607).

Cross References:

Point 1: Section 1-201.

Point 2: Section 2-202.

Point 3: Sections 2-209, 2-601 and 2-607.

Point 4: Sections 2-605 and 2-607.

§2-209.   Modification, Rescission and Waiver

(1) An agreement modifying a contract within this Article needs no consideration to be binding.

(2) A signed agreement which excludes modification or rescission except by a signed writing cannot be otherwise modified or rescinded, but except as between merchants such a requirement on a form supplied by the merchant must be separately signed by the other party.

(3) The requirements of the statute of frauds section of this Article (Section 2-201) must be satisfied if the contract as modified is within its provisions.

(4) Although an attempt at modification or rescission does not satisfy the requirements of subsection (2) or (3) it can operate as a waiver.

(5) A party who has made a waiver affecting an executory portion of the contract may retract the waiver by reasonable notification received by the other party that strict performance will be required of any term waived, unless the retraction would be unjust in view of a material change of position in reliance on the waiver.

Official Comment

Prior Uniform Statutory Provision: Subsection (1)—Compare Section 1, Uniform Written Obligations Act; Subsections (2) to (5)—none.

Purposes of Changes and New Matter:

1. This section seeks to protect and make effective all necessary and desirable modifications of sales contracts without regard to the technicalities which at present hamper such adjustments.

2. Subsection (1) provides that an agreement modifying a sales contract needs no consideration to be binding.

However, modifications made thereunder must meet the test of good faith imposed by this Act. The effective use of bad faith to escape performance on the original contract terms is barred, and the extortion of a "modification" without legitimate commercial reason is ineffective as a violation of the duty of good faith. Nor can a mere technical consideration support a modification made in bad faith.

The test of "good faith" between merchants or as against merchants includes "observance of reasonable commercial standards of fair dealing in the trade" (Section 2-103), and may in some situations require an objectively demonstrable reason for seeking a modification. But such matters as a market shift which makes performance come to involve a loss may provide such a reason even though there is no such unforeseen difficulty as would make out a legal excuse from performance under Sections 2-615 and 2-616.

3. Subsections (2) and (3) are intended to protect against false allegations of oral modifications. "Modification or rescission" includes abandonment or other change by mutual consent, contrary to the decision in Green v. Doniger, 300 N.Y. 238, 90 N.E.2d 56 (1949); it does not include unilateral "termination" or "cancellation" as defined in Section 2-106.

The Statute of Frauds provisions of this Article are expressly applied to modifications by subsection (3). Under those provisions the "delivery and acceptance" test is limited to the goods which have been accepted, that is, to the past. "Modification" for the future cannot therefore be conjured up by oral testimony if the price involved is $500.00 or more since such modification must be shown at least by an authenticated memo. And since a memo is limited in its effect to the quantity of goods set forth in it there is safeguard against oral evidence.

Subsection (2) permits the parties in effect to make their own Statute of Frauds as regards any future modification of the contract by giving effect to a clause in a signed agreement which expressly requires any modification to be by signed writing. But note that if a consumer is to be held to such a clause on a form supplied by a merchant it must be separately signed.

4. Subsection (4) is intended, despite the provisions of subsections (2) and (3), to prevent contractual provisions excluding modification except by a signed writing from limiting in other respects the legal effect of the parties' actual later conduct. The effect of such conduct as a waiver is further regulated in subsection (5).

Cross References:

Point 1: Section 1-203.

Point 2: Sections 1-201, 1-203, 2-615 and 2-616.
Point 3: Sections 2-106, 2-201 and 2-202.
Point 4: Sections 2-202 and 2-208.

Definitional Cross References:
"Agreement." Section 1-201.
"Between merchants." Section 2-104.
"Contract." Section 1-201.
"Notification." Section 1-201.
"Signed." Section 1-201.
"Term." Section 1-201.
"Writing." Section 1-201.

§2-210. Delegation of Performance; Assignment of Rights

(1) A party may perform his duty through a delegate unless otherwise agreed or unless the other party has a substantial interest in having his original promisor perform or control the acts required by the contract. No delegation of performance relieves the party delegating of any duty to perform or any liability for breach.

(2) Except as otherwise provided in Section 9-406, unless otherwise agreed, all rights of either seller or buyer can be assigned except where the assignment would materially change the duty of the other party, or increase materially the burden or risk imposed on him by his contract, or impair materially his chance of obtaining return performance. A right to damages for breach of the whole contract or a right arising out of the assignor's due performance of his entire obligation can be assigned despite agreement otherwise.

(3) The creation, attachment, perfection, or enforcement of a security interest in the seller's interest under a contract is not a transfer that materially changes the duty of or increases materially the burden or risk imposed on the buyer or impairs materially the buyer's chance of obtaining return performance within the purview of subsection (2) unless, and then only to the extent that, enforcement actually results in a delegation of material performance of the seller. Even in that event, the creation, attachment, perfection, and enforcement of the security interest remain effective, but (i) the seller is liable to the buyer for damages caused by the delegation to the extent that the damages could not reasonably be prevented by the buyer, and (ii) a court having jurisdiction may grant other appropriate relief, including cancellation of the contract for sale or an injunction against enforcement of the security interest or consummation of the enforcement.

(4) Unless the circumstances indicate the contrary a prohibition of assignment of "the contract" is to be construed as barring only the delegation to the assignee of the assignor's performance.

(5) An assignment of "the contract" or of "all my rights under the contract" or an assignment in similar general terms is an assignment of rights and unless the language or the circumstances (as in an assignment for security) indicate the contrary, it is delegation of performance of the duties of the assignor and its acceptance by the assignee constitutes a promise by him to perform those duties.

This promise is enforceable by either the assignor or the other party to the original contract.

(6) The other party may treat any assignment which delegates performance as creating reasonable grounds for insecurity and may without prejudice to his rights against the assignor demand assurances from the assignee (Section 2-609).

[As amended in 1999 to conform to Revised Article 9 (2000) of the Code.]

Official Comment

Prior Uniform Statutory Provision: None.

Purposes:
1. Generally, this section recognizes both delegation of performance and assignability as normal and permissible incidents of a contract for the sale of goods.

2. Delegation of performance, either in conjunction with an assignment or otherwise, is provided for by subsection (1) where no substantial reason can be shown as to why the delegated performance will not be as satisfactory as personal performance.

3. Under subsection (2) rights which are no longer executory such as a right to damages for breach may be assigned although the agreement prohibits assignment. In such cases no question of delegation of any performance is involved. Subsection (2) is subject to Section 9-406, which makes rights to payment for goods sold ("accounts"), whether or not earned, freely alienable notwithstanding a contrary agreement or rule of law.

4. The nature of the contract or the circumstances of the case, however, may bar assignment of the contract even where delegation of performance is not involved. This Article and this section are intended to clarify this problem, particularly in cases dealing with output requirement and exclusive dealing contracts. In the first place the section on requirements and exclusive dealing removes from the construction of the original contract most of the "personal discretion" element by substituting the reasonably objective standard of good faith operation of the plant or business to be supplied. Secondly, the section on insecurity and assurances, which is specifically referred to in subsection (6) of this section, frees the other party from the doubts and uncertainty which may afflict him under an assignment of the character in question by permitting him to demand adequate assurance of due performance without which he may suspend his own performance. Subsection (6) is not in any way intended to limit the effect of the section on insecurity and assurances and the word "performance" includes the giving of orders under a requirements contract. Of course, in any case where a material personal discretion is sought to be transferred, effective assignment is barred by subsection (2).

5. Subsection (5) lays down a general rule of construction distinguishing between a normal commercial assignment, which substitutes the assignee for the assignor both as to rights and duties, and a financing assignment in which only the assignor's rights are transferred.

This Article takes no position on the possibility of extending some recognition or power to the original parties to work out normal commercial readjustments of the contract in the case of financing assignments even after the original obligor has been notified of the assignment. This question is dealt with in the Article on Secured Transactions (Article 9).

6. Subsection (6) recognizes that the non-assigning original party has a stake in the reliability of the person with whom he has closed the original contract, and is, therefore, entitled to due assurance that any delegated performance will be properly forthcoming.

7. This section is not intended as a complete statement of the law of delegation and assignment but is limited to clarifying a few points doubtful under the case law. Particularly, neither this section nor this Article touches directly on such questions as the need or effect of notice of the assignment, the rights of successive assignees, or any question of the form of an assignment, either as between the parties or as against any third parties. Some of these questions are dealt with in Article 9.

Cross References:
> Point 3: Articles 5 and 9.
> Point 4: Sections 2-306 and 2-609.
> Point 5: Article 9, Sections 9-317 and 9-318.
> Point 7: Article 9.

Definitional Cross References:
> "Agreement." Section 1-201.
> "Buyer." Section 2-103.
> "Contract." Section 1-201.
> "Party." Section 1-201.
> "Rights." Section 1-201.
> "Seller." Section 2-103.
> "Term." Section 1-201.

Part 3.   General Obligation and Construction of Contract

§2-301.   General Obligations of Parties

The obligation of the seller is to transfer and deliver and that of the buyer is to accept and pay in accordance with the contract.

§2-302.   Unconscionable Contract or Clause

(1) If the court as a matter of law finds the contract or any clause of the contract to have been unconscionable at the time it was made the court may refuse to enforce the contract, or it may enforce the remainder of the contract without the unconscionable clause, or it may so limit the application of any unconscionable clause as to avoid any unconscionable result.

(2) When it is claimed or appears to the court that the contract or any clause thereof may be unconscionable the parties shall be afforded a reasonable opportunity to present evidence as to its commercial setting, purpose and effect to aid the court in making the determination.

Official Comment

Prior Uniform Statutory Provision: None.

Purposes:

1. This section is intended to make it possible for the courts to police explicitly against the contracts or clauses which they find to be unconscionable. In the past such policing has been accomplished by adverse construction of language, by manipulation of the rules of offer and acceptance or by determinations that the clause is contrary to public policy or to the dominant purpose of the contract. This section is intended to allow the court to pass directly on the unconscionability of the contract or particular clause therein and to make a conclusion of law as to its unconscionability. The basic test is whether, in the light of the general commercial background and the commercial needs of the particular trade or case, the clauses involved are so one-sided as to be unconscionable under the circumstances existing at the time of the making of the contract. Subsection (2) makes it clear that it is proper for the court to hear evidence upon these questions. The principle is one of the prevention of oppression and unfair surprise (Cf. Campbell Soup Co. v. Wentz, 172 F.2d 80, 3d Cir. 1948) and not of disturbance of allocation of risks because of superior bargaining power. The underlying basis of this section is illustrated by the results in cases such as the following:

Kansas City Wholesale Grocery Co. v. Weber Packing Corporation, 93 Utah 414, 73 P.2d 1272 (1937), where a clause limiting time for complaints was held inapplicable to latent defects in a shipment of catsup which could be discovered only by microscopic analysis; Hardy v. General Motors Acceptance Corporation, 38 Ga. App. 463, 144 S.E. 327 (1928), holding that a disclaimer of warranty clause applied only to express warranties, thus letting in a fair implied warranty; Andrews Bros. v. Singer & Co. (1934 CA) 1 K.B. 17, holding that where a car with substantial mileage was delivered instead of a "new" car, a disclaimer of warranties, including those "implied," left unaffected an "express obligation" on the description, even though the Sale of Goods Act called such an implied warranty; New Prague Flouring Mill Co. v. G.A. Spears, 194 Iowa 417, 189 N.W. 815 (1922), holding that a clause permitting the seller, upon the buyer's failure to supply shipping instructions, to cancel, ship, or allow delivery date to be indefinitely postponed 30 days at a time by the inaction, does not indefinitely postpone the date of measuring damages for the buyer's breach, to the seller's advantage; and Kansas Flour Mills Co. v. Dirks, 100 Kan. 376, 164 P. 273 (1917), where under a similar clause in a rising market the court permitted the buyer to measure his damages for non-delivery at the end of only one 30 day postponement; Green v. Arcos, Ltd. (1931 CA) 47 T.L.R. 336, where a blanket clause prohibiting rejection of shipments by the buyer was restricted to apply to shipments where discrepancies represented merely mercantile variations; Meyer v. Packard Cleveland Motor Co., 106 Ohio St. 328, 140 N.E. 118 (1922), in which the court held that a "waiver" of all agreements not specified did not preclude implied warranty of fitness of a rebuilt dump truck for ordinary use as a dump truck; Austin Co. v. J. H. Tillman Co., 104 Or. 541, 209 P. 131 (1922), where a clause limiting the buyer's remedy to return was held to be applicable only if the seller had delivered a machine needed for a construction job which reasonably met the contract description; Bekkevold v. Potts, 173 Minn. 87, 216 N.W. 790, 59 A.L.R. 1164 (1927), refusing to allow warranty of fitness for purpose imposed by law to be negated by clause excluding all warranties "made" by the seller; Robert A. Munroe & Co. v. Meyer (1930) 2 K.B. 312, holding that the warranty of description overrides a clause reading "with all faults and defects" where adulterated meat not up to the contract description was delivered.

2. Under this section the court, in its discretion, may refuse to enforce the contract as a whole if it is permeated by the unconscionability, or it may strike any single clause or group of clauses which are so tainted or which are contrary to the essential purpose of the agreement, or it may simply limit unconscionable clauses so as to avoid unconscionable results.

3. The present section is addressed to the court, and the decision is to be made by it. The commercial evidence referred to in subsection (2) is for the court's consideration, not the jury's. Only the agreement which results from the court's action on these matters is to be submitted to the general triers of the facts.

Definitional Cross Reference:
"Contract." Section 1-201.

§2-305. Open Price Term

(1) The parties if they so intend can conclude a contract for sale even though the price is not settled. In such a case the price is a reasonable price at the time for delivery if
　　(a) nothing is said as to price; or
　　(b) the price is left to be agreed by the parties and they fail to agree; or
　　(c) the price is to be fixed in terms of some agreed market or other standard as set or recorded by a third person or agency and it is not so set or recorded.
(2) A price to be fixed by the seller or by the buyer means a price for him to fix in good faith.
(3) When a price left to be fixed otherwise than by agreement of the parties fails to be fixed through fault of one party the other may at his option treat the contract as cancelled or himself fix a reasonable price.
(4) Where, however, the parties intend not to be bound unless the price be fixed or agreed and it is not fixed or agreed there is no contract. In such a case the buyer must return any goods already received or if unable so to do must pay their reasonable value at the time of delivery and the seller must return any portion of the price paid on account.

Official Comment

Prior Uniform Statutory Provision: Sections 9 and 10, Uniform Sales Act.

Changes: Completely rewritten.

Purposes of Changes:

1. This section applies when the price term is left open on the making of an agreement which is nevertheless intended by the parties to be a binding agreement. This Article rejects in these instances the formula that "an agreement to agree is unenforceable" if the case falls within subsection (1) of this section, and rejects also defecting such agreements on the ground of "indefiniteness." Instead this Article recognizes the dominant intention of the parties to have the deal continue to be binding upon both. As to future performance, since this Article recognizes remedies such as cover (Section 2-712), resale (Section 2-706) and specific performance (Section 2-716) which go beyond any mere arithmetic as between contract price and market price, there is usually a "reasonably certain basis for granting an appropriate remedy for breach" so that the contract need not fail for indefiniteness.

2. Under some circumstances the postponement of agreement on price will mean that no deal has really been concluded, and this is made express in the preamble of subsection (1) ("The parties *if they so intend*") and in subsection (4). Whether or not this is so is, in most cases, a question to be determined by the trier of fact.

3. Subsection (2), dealing with the situation where the price is to be fixed by one party rejects the uncommercial idea that an agreement that the seller may fix the price means that he may fix any price he may wish by the express qualification that the price so fixed must be fixed in good faith. Good faith includes observance of reasonable commercial standards of fair dealing in the trade if the party is a merchant (Section 2-103). But in the normal case a "posted price" or a future seller's or buyer's "given price," "price in effect," "market price," or the like satisfies the good faith requirement.

4. The section recognizes that there may be cases in which a particular person's judgment is not chosen merely as a barometer or index of a fair price but is an essential condition to the parties' intent to make any contract at all. For example, the case where a known and trusted expert is to "value" a particular painting for which there is no market standard differs sharply from the situation where a named expert is to determine the grade of cotton, and the difference would support a finding that in the one the parties did not intend to make a binding agreement if that expert were unavailable whereas in the other they did so intend. Other circumstances would of course affect the validity of such a finding.

5. Under subsection (3), wrongful interference by one party with any agreed machinery for price fixing in the contract may be treated by the other party as a repudiation justifying cancellation, or merely as a failure to take cooperative action thus shifting to the aggrieved party the reasonable leeway in fixing the price.

6. Throughout the entire section, the purpose is to give effect to the agreement which has been made. That effect, however, is always conditioned by the requirement of good faith action which is made an inherent part of all contracts within this Act (Section 1-203).

Cross References:

Point 1: Sections 2-204(3) 2-706, 2-712 and 2-716.
Point 3: Section 2-103.
Point 5: Sections 2-311 and 2-610.
Point 6: Section 1-203.

Definitional Cross References:
"Agreement." Section 1-201.
"Burden of establishing." Section 1-201.
"Buyer." Section 2-103.
"Cancellation." Section 2-106.
"Contract." Section 1-201.
"Contract for sale." Section 2-106.
"Fault." Section 1-201.
"Goods." Section 2-105.
"Party." Section 1-201.
"Receipt of goods." Section 2-103.
"Seller." Section 2-103.
"Term." Section 1-201.

§2-306.   Output, Requirements and Exclusive Dealings

(1) A term which measures the quantity by the output of the seller or the requirements of the buyer means such actual output or requirements as may occur in good faith, except that no quantity unreasonably disproportionate to any stated estimate or in the absence of a stated estimate to any normal or otherwise comparable prior output or requirements may be tendered or demanded.

(2) A lawful agreement by either the seller or the buyer for exclusive dealing in the kind of goods concerned imposes unless otherwise agreed an obligation by the seller to use best efforts to supply the goods and by the buyer to use best efforts to promote their sale.

Official Comment

Prior Uniform Statutory Provision: None.

Purposes:

1. Subsection (1) of this section, in regard to output and requirements, applies to this specific problem the general approach of this Act which requires the reading of commercial background and intent into the language of any agreement and demands good faith in the performance of that agreement. It applies to such contracts of nonproducing establishments such as dealers or distributors as well as to manufacturing concerns.

2. Under this Article, a contract for output or requirements is not too indefinite since it is held to mean the actual good faith output or requirements of the particular party. Nor does such a contract lack mutuality of obligation since, under this section, the party who will determine quantity is required to operate his plant or conduct his business in good faith and according to commercial standards of fair dealing in the trade so that his output or requirements will approximate a reasonably foreseeable figure. Reasonable elasticity in the requirements is expressly envisaged by this section and good faith variations from prior requirements are permitted even when the variation may be such as to result in discontinuance. A shut-down by

a requirements buyer for lack of orders might be permissible when a shutdown merely to curtail losses would not. The essential test is whether the party is acting in good faith. Similarly, a sudden expansion of the plant by which requirements are to be measured would not be included within the scope of the contract as made but normal expansion undertaken in good faith would be within the scope of this section. One of the factors in an expansion situation would be whether the market price had risen greatly in a case in which the requirements contract contained a fixed price. Reasonable variation of an extreme sort is exemplified in Southwest Natural Gas Co. v. Oklahoma Portland Cement Co., 102 F.2d 630 (C.C.A. 10, 1939). This Article takes no position as to whether a requirements contract is a provable claim in bankruptcy.

3. If an estimate of output or requirements is included in the agreement, no quantity unreasonably disproportionate to it may be tendered or demanded. Any minimum or maximum set by the agreement shows a clear limit on the intended elasticity. In similar fashion, the agreed estimate is to be regarded as a center around which the parties intend the variation to occur.

4. When an enterprise is sold, the question may arise whether the buyer is bound by an existing output or requirements contract. That question is outside the scope of this Article, and is to be determined on other principles of law. Assuming that the contract continues, the output or requirements in the hands of the new owner continue to be measured by the actual good faith output or requirements under the normal operation of the enterprise prior to sale. The sale itself is not grounds for sudden expansion or decrease.

5. Subsection (2), on exclusive dealing, makes explicit the commercial rule embodied in this Act under which the parties to such contracts are held to have impliedly, even when not expressly, bound themselves to use reasonable diligence as well as good faith in their performance of the contract. Under such contracts the exclusive agent is required, although no express commitment has been made, to use reasonable effort and due diligence in the expansion of the market or the promotion of the product, as the case may be. The principal is expected under such a contract to refrain from supplying any other dealer or agent within the exclusive territory. An exclusive dealing agreement brings into play all of the good faith aspects of the output and requirement problems of subsection (1). It also raises questions of insecurity and right to adequate assurance under this Article.

Cross References:
Point 4: Section 2-210.
Point 5: Sections 1-203 and 2-609.

Definitional Cross References:
"Agreement." Section 1-201.
"Buyer." Section 2-103.
"Contract for sale." Section 2-106.
"Good faith." Section 1-201.
"Goods." Section 2-105.
"Party." Section 1-201.
"Term." Section 1-203.
"Seller." Section 2-101.

§2-307. Delivery in Single Lot or Several Lots

Unless otherwise agreed all goods called for by a contract for sale must be tendered in a single delivery and payment is due only on such tender but where the circumstances give either party the right to make or demand delivery in lots the price if it can be apportioned may be demanded for each lot.

§2-308. Absence of Specified Place for Delivery

Unless otherwise agreed
    (a) the place for delivery of goods is the seller's place of business or if he has none his residence; but
    (b) in a contract for sale of identified goods which to the knowledge of the parties at the time of contracting are in some other place, that place is the place for their delivery; and
    (c) documents of title may be delivered through customary banking channels.

§2-309. Absence of Specific Time Provisions; Notice of Termination

(1) The time for shipment or delivery or any other action under a contract if not provided in this Article or agreed upon shall be a reasonable time.

(2) Where the contract provides for successive performances but is indefinite in duration it is valid for a reasonable time but unless otherwise agreed may be terminated at any time by either party.

(3) Termination of a contract by one party except on the happening of an agreed event requires that reasonable notification be received by the other party and an agreement dispensing with notification is invalid if its operation would be unconscionable.

Official Comment

Prior Uniform Statutory Provision: Subsection (1)—see Sections 43(2), 45(2), 47(1) and 48, Uniform Sales Act, for policy continued under this Article; Section (2)—none; Subsection (3)—none.

Changes: Completely different in scope.

Purposes of Changes and New Matter:
    1. Subsection (I) requires that all actions taken under a sales contract must be taken within a reasonable time where no time has been agreed upon. The reasonable time under this provision turns on the criteria as to "reasonable time" and on good faith and commercial standards set forth in Sections 1-203, 1-204 and 2-103. It thus depends upon what constitutes acceptable commercial conduct in view of the nature, purpose and circumstances of the action to be taken. A greement as to a definite time, however, may be found in a term

implied from the contractual circumstances, usage of trade or course of dealing or performance as well as in an express term. Such cases fall outside of this subsection since in them the time for action is "agreed" by usage.

2. The time for payment, where not agreed upon, is related to the time for delivery; the particular problems which arise in connection with determining the appropriate time of payment and the time for any inspection before payment which is both allowed by law and demanded by the buyer are covered in Section 2-513.

3. The facts in regard to shipment and delivery differ so widely as to make detailed provision for them in the text of this Article impracticable. The applicable principles, however, make it clear that surprise is to be avoided, good faith judgment is to be protected, and notice or negotiation to reduce the uncertainty to certainty is to be favored.

4. When the time for delivery is left open, unreasonably early offers of or demands for delivery are intended to be read under this Article as expressions of desire or intention, requesting the assent or acquiescence of the other party, not as final positions which may amount without more to breach or to create breach by the other side. See Sections 2-207 and 2-609.

5. The obligation of good faith under this Act requires reasonable notification before a contract may be treated as breached because a reasonable time for delivery or demand has expired. This operates both in the case of a contract originally indefinite as to time and of one subsequently made indefinite by waiver.

When both parties let an originally reasonable time go by in silence, the course of conduct under the contract may be viewed as enlarging the reasonable time for tender or demand of performance. The contract may be terminated by abandonment.

6. Parties to a contract are not required in giving reasonable notification to fix, at peril of breach, a time which is in fact reasonable in the unforeseeable judgment of a later trier of fact. Effective communication of a proposed time limit calls for a response, so that failure to reply will make out acquiescence. Where objection is made, however, or if the demand is merely for information as to when goods will be delivered or will be ordered out, demand for assurances on the ground of insecurity may be made under this Article pending further negotiations. Only when a party insists on undue delay or on rejection of the other party's reasonable proposal is there a question of flat breach under the present section.

7. Subsection (2) applies a commercially reasonable view to resolve the conflict which has arisen in the cases as to contracts of indefinite duration. The "reasonable time" of duration appropriate to a given arrangement is limited by the circumstances. When the arrangement has been carried on by the parties over the years, the "reasonable time" can continue indefinitely and the contract will not terminate until notice.

8. Subsection (3) recognizes that the application of principles of good faith and sound commercial practice normally call for such notification of the termination of a going contract relationship as will give the other party reasonable time to seek a substitute arrangement. An agreement dispensing with notification or limiting the time for the seeking of a substitute arrangement is, of course, valid under this subsection unless the results of putting it into operation would be the creation of an unconscionable state of affairs.

9. Justifiable cancellation for breach is a remedy for breach and is not the kind of termination covered by the present subsection.

10. The requirement of notification is dispensed with where the contract provides for termination on the happening of an "agreed event." "Event" is a term chosen here to contrast with "option" or the like.

Cross References:
Point 1: Sections 1-203, 1-204 and 2-103.
Point 2: Sections 2-320, 2-321, 2-504, and 2-511 through 2-514.
Point 5: Section 1-203.
Point 6: Section 2-609.
Point 7: Section 2-204.
Point 9: Sections 2-106, 2-318, 2-610 and 2-703.

Definitional Cross References:
"Agreement." Section 1-201.
"Contract." Section 1-201.
"Notification." Section 1-201.
"Party." Section 1-201.
"Reasonable time." Section 1-204.
"Termination." Section 2-106.

§2-311. Options and Cooperation Respecting Performance

(1) An agreement for sale which is otherwise sufficiently definite (subsection (3) of Section 2-204) to be a contract is not made invalid by the fact that it leaves particulars of performance to be specified by one of the parties. Any such specification must be made in good faith and within limits set by commercial reasonableness.

(2) Unless otherwise agreed specifications relating to assortment of the goods are at the buyer's option and except as otherwise provided in subsections (1)(c) and (3) of Section 2-319 specifications or arrangements relating to shipment are at the seller's option.

(3) Where such specification would materially affect the other party's performance but is not seasonably made or where one party's cooperation is necessary to the agreed performance of the other but is not seasonably forthcoming, the other party in addition to all other remedies

(a) is excused for any resulting delay in his own performance; and

(b) may also either proceed to perform in any reasonable manner or after the time for a material part of his own performance treat the failure to specify or to cooperate as a breach by failure to deliver or accept the goods.

§2-312. Warranty of Title and Against Infringement; Buyer's Obligation Against Infringement

(1) Subject to subsection (2) there is in a contract for sale a warranty by the seller that

(a) the title conveyed shall be good, and its transfer rightful; and

(b) the goods shall be delivered free from any security interest or other lien or encumbrance of which the buyer at the time of contracting has no knowledge.

(2) A warranty under subsection (1) will be excluded or modified only by specific language or by circumstances which give the buyer reason to know that the person selling does not claim title in himself or that he is purporting to sell only such right or title as he or a third person may have.

(3) Unless otherwise agreed a seller who is a merchant regularly dealing in goods of the kind warrants that the goods shall be delivered free of the rightful claim of any third person by way of infringement or the like but a buyer who furnishes specifications to the seller must hold the seller harmless against any such claim which arises out of compliance with the specifications.

§2-313. Express Warranties by Affirmation, Promise, Description, Sample

(1) Express warranties by the seller are created as follows:

(a) Any affirmation of fact or promise made by the seller to the buyer which relates to the goods and becomes part of the basis of the bargain creates an express warranty that the goods shall conform to the affirmation or promise.

(b) Any description of the goods which is made part of the basis of the bargain creates an express warranty that the goods shall conform to the description.

(c) Any sample or model which is made part of the basis of the bargain creates an express warranty that the whole of the goods shall conform to the sample or model.

(2) It is not necessary to the creation of an express warranty that the seller use formal words such as "warrant" or "guarantee" or that he have a specific intention to make a warranty, but an affirmation merely of the value of the goods or a statement purporting to be merely the seller's opinion or commendation of the goods does not create a warranty.

Official Comment

Prior Uniform Statutory Provision: Sections 12, 14 and 16, Uniform Sales Act.

Changes: Rewritten.

Purposes of Changes: To consolidate and systematize basic principles with the result that:

1. "Express" warranties rest on "dickered" aspects of the individual bargain, and go so clearly to the essence of that bargain that words of disclaimer in a form are repugnant to the basic dickered terms. "Implied" warranties rest so clearly on a common factual situation or set of conditions that no particular language or action is necessary to evidence them and they will arise in such a situation unless unmistakably negated.

This section reverts to the older case law insofar as the warranties of description and sample are designated "express" rather than "implied."

2. Although this section is limited in its scope and direct purpose to warranties made by the seller to the buyer as part of a contract for sale, the warranty sections of this Article are not designed in any way to disturb those lines of case law growth which have recognized that warranties need not be confined either to sales contracts or to the direct parties to such a contract. They may arise in other appropriate circumstances such as in the case of bailments for hire, whether such bailment is itself the main contract or is merely a supplying of containers under a contract for the sale of their contents. The provisions of Section 2-318 on third party beneficiaries expressly recognize this case law development within one particular area. Beyond that, the matter is left to the case law with the intention that the policies of this Act may offer useful guidance in dealing with further cases as they arise.

3. The present section deals with affirmations of fact by the seller, descriptions of the goods or exhibitions of samples, exactly as any other part of a negotiation which ends in a contract is dealt with. No specific intention to make a warranty is necessary if any of these factors is made part of the basis of the bargain. In actual practice affirmations of fact made by the seller about the goods during a bargain are regarded as part of the description of those goods; hence no particular reliance on such statements need be shown in order to weave them into the fabric of the agreement. Rather, any fact which is to take such affirmations, once made, out of the agreement requires clear affirmative proof. The issue normally is one of fact.

4. In view of the principle that the whole purpose of the law of warranty is to determine what it is that the seller has in essence agreed to sell, the policy is adopted of those cases which refuse except in unusual circumstances to recognize a material deletion of the seller's obligation. Thus, a contract is normally a contract for a sale of something describable and described. A clause generally disclaiming "all warranties, express or implied" cannot reduce the seller's obligation with respect to such description and therefore cannot be given literal effect under Section 2-316.

This is not intended to mean that the parties, if they consciously desire, cannot make their own bargain as they wish. But in determining what they have agreed upon good faith is a factor and consideration should be given to the fact that the probability is small that a real price is intended to be exchanged for a pseudo-obligation.

5. Paragraph (1)(b) makes specific some of the principles set forth above when a description of the goods is given by the seller.

A description need not be by words. Technical specifications, blueprints and the like can afford more exact description than mere language and if made part of the basis of the bargain goods must conform with them. Past deliveries may set the description of quality, either expressly or impliedly by course of dealing. Of course, all descriptions by merchants must be read against the applicable trade usages with the general rules as to merchantability resolving any doubts.

6. The basic situation as to statements affecting the true essence of the bargain is no different when a sample or model is involved in the transaction. This section includes both a "sample" actually drawn from the bulk of goods which is the subject matter of the sale, and a "model" which is offered for

inspection when the subject matter is not at hand and which has not been drawn from the bulk of the goods.

Although the underlying principles are unchanged, the facts are often ambiguous when something is shown as illustrative, rather than as a straight sample. In general, the presumption is that any sample or model just as any affirmation of fact is intended to become a basis of the bargain. But there is no escape from the question of fact. When the seller exhibits a sample purporting to be drawn from an existing bulk, good faith of course requires that the sample be fairly drawn. But in mercantile experience the mere exhibition of a "sample" does not of itself show whether it is merely intended to "suggest" or to "be" the character of the subject-matter of the contract. The question is whether the seller has so acted with reference to the sample as to make him responsible that the whole shall have at least the values shown by it. The circumstances aid in answering this question. If the sample has been drawn from an existing bulk, it must be regarded as describing values of the goods contracted for unless it is accompanied by an unmistakable denial of such responsibility. If, on the other hand, a model of merchandise not on hand is offered, the mercantile presumption that it has become a literal description of the subject matter is not so strong, and particularly so if modification on the buyer's initiative impairs any feature of the model.

7. The precise time when words of description or affirmation are made or samples are shown is not material. The sole question is whether the language or samples or models are fairly to be regarded as part of the contract. If language is used after the closing of the deal (as when the buyer when taking delivery asks and receives an additional assurance), the warranty becomes a modification, and need not be supported by consideration if it is otherwise reasonable and in order (Section 2-209).

8. Concerning affirmations of value or a seller's opinion or commendation under subsection (2), the basic question remains the same: What statements of the seller have in the circumstances and in objective judgment become part of the basis of the bargain? As indicated above, all of the statements of the seller do so unless good reason is shown to the contrary. The provisions of subsection (2) are included, however, since common experience discloses that some statements or predictions cannot fairly be viewed as entering into the bargain. Even as to false statements of value, however, the possibility is left open that a remedy may be provided by the law relating to fraud or misrepresentation.

Cross References:
   Point 1: Section 2-316.
   Point 2: Sections 1-102(3) and 2-318.
   Point 3: Section 2-316(2)(b).
   Point 4: Section 2-316.
   Point 5: Sections 1-205(4) and 2-314.
   Point 6: Section 2-316.
   Point 7: Section 2-209.
   Point 8: Section 1-103.

Definitional Cross References:
   "Buyer." Section 2-103.

"Conforming." Section 2-106.
"Goods." Section 2-105.
"Seller." Section 2-103.

§2-314. Implied Warranty: Merchantability; Usage of Trade

(1) Unless excluded or modified (Section 2-316), a warranty that the goods shall be merchantable is implied in a contract for their sale if the seller is a merchant with respect to goods of that kind. Under this section the serving for value of food or drink to be consumed either on the premises or elsewhere is a sale.

(2) Goods to be merchantable must be at least such as

[handwritten margin note: Cone up the most often]

(a) pass without objection in the trade under the contract description; and
(b) in the case of fungible goods, are of fair average quality within the description; and
(c) are fit for the ordinary purposes for which such goods are used; and
(d) run, within the variations permitted by the agreement, of even kind, quality and quantity within each unit and among all units involved; and
(e) are adequately contained, packaged, and labeled as the agreement may require; and
(f) conform to the promises or affirmations of fact made on the container or label if any.

(3) Unless excluded or modified (Section 2-316) other implied warranties may arise from course of dealing or usage of trade.

Official Comment

Prior Uniform Statutory Provision: Section 15(2), Uniform Sales Act.

Changes: Completely rewritten.

Purposes of Changes: This section, drawn in view of the steadily developing case law on the subject, is intended to make it clear that:

1. The seller's obligation applies to present sales as well as to contracts to sell subject to the effects of any examination of specific goods. (Subsection (2) of Section 2-316.) Also, the warranty of merchantability applies to sales for use as well as to sales for resale.

2. The question when the warranty is imposed turns basically on the meaning of the terms of the agreement as recognized in the trade. Goods delivered under an agreement made by a merchant in a given line of trade must be of a quality comparable to that generally acceptable in that line of trade under the description or other designation of the goods used in the agreement. The responsibility imposed rests on any merchant-seller, and the absence of the words "grower or manufacturer or not" which appeared in Section 15(2) of the Uniform Sales Act does not restrict the applicability of this section.

3. A specific designation of goods by the buyer does not exclude the seller's obligation that they be fit for the general purposes appropriate to such goods. A contract for the sale of second-hand goods, however, involves only such obligation as is appropriate to such goods for that is their contract description.

A person making an isolated sale of goods is not a "merchant" within the meaning of the full scope of this section and, thus, no warranty of merchantability would apply. His knowledge of any defects not apparent on inspection would, however, without need for express agreement and in keeping with the underlying reason of the present section and the provisions on good faith, impose an obligation that known material but hidden defects be fully disclosed.

4. Although a seller may not be a "merchant" as to the goods in question, if he states generally that they are "guaranteed" the provisions of this section may furnish a guide to the content of the resulting express warranty. This has particular significance in the case of second-hand sales, and has further significance in limiting the effect of fine-print disclaimer clauses where their effect would be inconsistent with large-print assertions of "guarantee."

5. The second sentence of subsection (1) covers the warranty with respect to food and drink. Serving food or drink for value is a sale, whether to be consumed on the premises or elsewhere. Cases to the contrary are rejected. The principal warranty is that stated in subsections (1) and (2)(c) of this section.

6. Subsection (2) does not purport to exhaust the meaning of "merchantable" nor to negate any of its attributes not specifically mentioned in the text of the statute, but arising by usage of trade or through case law. The language used is "must be at least such as . . . ," and the intention is to leave open other possible attributes of merchantability.

7. Paragraphs (a) and (b) of subsection (2) are to be read together. Both refer, as indicated above, to the standards of that line of the trade which fits the transaction and the seller's business. "Fair average" is a term directly appropriate to agricultural bulk products and means goods centering around the middle belt of quality, not the least or the worst that can be understood in the particular trade by the designation, but such as can pass "without objection." Of course a fair percentage of the least is permissible but the goods are not "fair average" if they are all of the least or worst quality possible under the description. In cases of doubt as to what quality is intended, the price at which a merchant closes a contract is an excellent index of the nature and scope of his obligation under the present section.

8. Fitness for the ordinary purposes for which goods of the type are used is a fundamental concept of the present section and is covered in paragraph (c). As stated above, merchantability is also a part of the obligation owing to the purchaser for use. Correspondingly, protection, under this aspect of the warranty, of the person buying for resale to the ultimate consumer is equally necessary, and merchantable goods must therefore be "honestly" resalable in the normal course of business because they are what they purport to be.

9. Paragraph (d) on evenness of kind, quality and quantity follows case law. But precautionary language has been added as a reminder of the frequent usages of trade which permit substantial variations both with and without an allowance or an obligation to replace the varying units.

10. Paragraph (e) applies only where the nature of the goods and of the transaction require a certain type of container, package or label. Paragraph (f) applies, on the other hand, wherever there is a label or container on which representations are made, even though the original contract, either by express terms or usage of trade, may not have required either the labeling or the representation. This follows from the general obligation of good faith which

requires that a buyer should not be placed in the position of reselling or using goods delivered under false representations appearing on the package or container. No problem of extra consideration arises in this connection since, under this Article, an obligation is imposed by the original contract not to deliver mislabeled articles, and the obligation is imposed where mercantile good faith so requires and without reference to the doctrine of consideration.

11. Exclusion or modification of the warranty of merchantability, or of any part of it, is dealt with in the section to which the text of the present section makes explicit precautionary references. That section must be read with particular reference to its subsection (4) on limitation of remedies. The warranty of merchantability, wherever it is normal, is so commonly taken for granted that its exclusion from the contract is a matter threatening surprise and therefore requiring special precaution.

12. Subsection (3) is to make explicit that usage of trade and course of dealing can create warranties and that they are implied rather than express warranties and thus subject to exclusion or modification under Section 2-316. A typical instance would be the obligation to provide pedigree papers to evidence conformity of the animal to the contract in the case of a pedigreed dog or blooded bull.

13. In an action based on breach of warranty, it is of course necessary to show not only the existence of the warranty but the fact that the warranty was broken and that the breach of the warranty was the proximate cause of the loss sustained. In such an action an affirmative showing by the seller that the loss resulted from some action or event following his own delivery of the goods can operate as a defense. Equally, evidence indicating that the seller exercised care in the manufacture, processing or selection of the goods is relevant to the issue of whether the warranty was in fact broken. Action by the buyer following an examination of the goods which ought to have indicated the defect complained of can be shown as matter bearing on whether the breach itself was the cause of the injury.

Cross References:
    Point 1: Section 2-316.
    Point 3: Sections 1-203 and 2-104.
    Point 5: Section 2-315.
    Point 11: Section 2-316.
    Point 12: Sections 1-201, 1-205 and 2-316.

Definitional Cross References:
    "Agreement." Section 1-201.
    "Contract." Section 1-201.
    "Contract for sale." Section 2-106.
    "Goods." Section 2-105.
    "Merchant." Section 2-104.
    "Seller." Section 2-103.

§2-315. Implied Warranty: Fitness for Particular Purpose

Where the seller at the time of contracting has reason to know any particular purpose for which the goods are required and that the buyer is relying on the seller's skill or judgment to select or furnish suitable goods, there is unless excluded or modified under the next section an implied warranty that the goods shall be fit for such purpose.

Official Comment

Prior Uniform Statutory Provision: Section 15(1), (4), (5), Uniform Sales Act.

Changes: Rewritten.

Purposes of Changes:

1. Whether or not this warranty arises in any individual case is basically a question of fact to be determined by the circumstances of the contracting. Under this section the buyer need not bring home to the seller actual knowledge of the particular purpose for which the goods are intended or of his reliance on the seller's skill and judgment, if the circumstances are such that the seller has reason to realize the purpose, intended or that the reliance exists. The buyer, of course, must actually be relying on the seller.

2. A "particular purpose" differs from the ordinary purpose for which the goods are used in that it envisages a specific use by the buyer which is peculiar to the nature of his business whereas the ordinary purposes for which goods are used are those envisaged in the concept of merchantability and go to uses which are customarily made of the goods in question. For example, shoes are generally used for the purpose of walking upon ordinary ground, but a seller may know that a particular pair was selected to be used for climbing mountains.

A contract may of course include both a warranty of merchantability and one of fitness for a particular purpose.

The provisions of this Article on the cumulation and conflict of express and implied warranties must be considered on the question of inconsistency between or among warranties. In such a case any question of fact as to which warranty was intended by the parties to apply must be resolved in favor of the warranty of fitness for particular purpose as against all other warranties except where the buyer has taken upon himself the responsibility of furnishing the technical specifications.

3. In connection with the warranty of fitness for a particular purpose the provisions of this Article on the allocation or division of risks are particularly applicable in any transaction in which the purpose for which the goods are to be used combines requirements both as to the quality of the goods themselves and compliance with certain laws or regulations. How the risks are divided is a question of fact to be determined, where not expressly contained in the agreement, from the circumstances of contracting, usage of trade, course of performance and the like, matters which may constitute the "otherwise agreement" of the parties by which they may divide the risk or burden.

4. The absence from this section of the language used in the Uniform Sales Act in referring to the seller, "whether he be the grower or manufacturer or not," is not intended to impose any requirement that the seller be a grower or manufacturer. Although normally the warranty will arise only where the seller is

a merchant with the appropriate "skill or judgment," it can arise as to non-merchants where this is justified by the particular circumstances.

5. The elimination of the "patent or other trade name" exception constitutes the major extension of the warranty of fitness which has been made by the cases and continued in this Article. Under the present section the existence of a patent or other trade name and the designation of the article by that name, or indeed in any other definite manner, is only one of the facts to be considered on the question of whether the buyer actually relied on the seller, but it is not of itself decisive of the issue. If the buyer himself is insisting on a particular brand he is not relying on the seller's skill and judgment and so no warranty results. But the mere fact that the article purchased has a particular patent or trade name is not sufficient to indicate nonreliance if the article has been recommended by the seller as adequate for the buyer's purposes.

6. The specific reference forward in the present section to the following section on exclusion or modification of warranties is to call attention to the possibility of eliminating the warranty in any given case. However it must be noted that under the following section the warranty of fitness for a particular purpose must be excluded or modified by a conspicuous writing.

Cross References:
Point 2: Sections 2-314 and 2-317.
Point 3: Section 2-303.
Point 6: Section 2-316.

Definitional Cross References:
"Buyer." Section 2-103.
"Goods." Section 2-105.
"Seller." Section 2-103.

§2-316. Exclusion or Modification of Warranties

(1) Words or conduct relevant to the creation of an express warranty and words or conduct tending to negate or limit warranty shall be construed wherever reasonable as consistent with each other; but subject to the provisions of this Article on parol or extrinsic evidence (Section 2-202) negation or limitation is inoperative to the extent that such construction is unreasonable.

(2) Subject to subsection (3), to exclude or modify the implied warranty of merchantability or any part of it the language must mention merchantability and in case of a writing must be conspicuous, and to exclude or modify any implied warranty of fitness the exclusion must be by a writing and conspicuous. Language to exclude all implied warranties of fitness is sufficient if it states, for example, that "There are no warranties which extend beyond the description on the face hereof."

(3) Notwithstanding subsection (2)

    (a) unless the circumstances indicate otherwise, all implied warranties are excluded by expressions like "as is," "with all faults" or other language which in common understanding calls the buyer's attention to the exclusion of warranties and makes plain that there is no implied warranty; and

(b) when the buyer before entering into the contract has examined the goods or the sample or model as fully as he desired or has refused to examine the goods there is no implied warranty with regard to defects which an examination ought in the circumstances to have revealed to him; and

(c) an implied warranty can also be excluded or modified by course of dealing or course of performance or usage of trade.

(4) Remedies for breach of warranty can be limited in accordance with the provisions of this Article on liquidation or limitation of damages and on contractual modification of remedy (Sections 2-718 and 2-719).

Official Comment

Prior Uniform Statutory Provision: None. See sections 15 and 71, Uniform Sales Act.

Purposes:

1. This section is designed principally to deal with those frequent clauses in sales contracts which seek to exclude "all warranties, express or implied." It seeks to protect a buyer from unexpected and unbargained language of disclaimer by denying effect to such language when inconsistent with language of express warranty and permitting the exclusion of implied warranties only by conspicuous language or other circumstances which protect the buyer from surprise.

2. The seller is protected under this Article against false allegations of oral warranties by its provisions on parol and extrinsic evidence and against unauthorized representations by the customary "lack of authority" clauses. This Article treats the limitation or avoidance of consequential damages as a matter of limiting remedies for breach, separate from the matter of creation of liability under a warranty. If no warranty exists, there is of course no problem of limiting remedies for breach of warranty. Under subsection (4) the question of limitation of remedy is governed by the sections referred to rather than by this section.

3. Disclaimer of the implied warranty of merchantability is permitted under subsection (2), but with the safeguard that such disclaimers must mention merchantability and in case of a writing must be conspicuous.

4. Unlike the implied warranty of merchantability, implied warranties of fitness for a particular purpose may be excluded by general language, but only if it is in writing and conspicuous.

5. Subsection (2) presupposes that the implied warranty in question exists unless excluded or modified. Whether or not language of disclaimer satisfies the requirements of this section, such language may be relevant under other sections to the question whether the warranty was ever in fact created. Thus, unless the provisions of this Article on parol and extrinsic evidence prevent, oral language of disclaimer may raise issues of fact as to whether reliance by the buyer occurred and whether the seller had "reason to know" under the section on implied warranty of fitness for a particular purpose.

6. The exceptions to the general rule set forth in paragraphs (a), (b) and (c) of subsection (3) are common factual situations in which the circumstances

surrounding the transaction are in themselves sufficient to call the buyer's attention to the fact that no implied warranties are made or that a certain implied warranty is being excluded.

7. Paragraph (a) of subsection (3) deals with general terms such as "as is," "as they stand," "with all faults," and the like. Such terms in ordinary commercial usage are understood to mean that the buyer takes the entire risk as to the quality of the goods involved. The terms covered by paragraph (a) are in fact merely a particularization of paragraph (c) which provides for exclusion or modification of implied warranties by usage of trade.

8. Under paragraph (b) of subsection (3) warranties may be excluded or modified by the circumstances where the buyer examines the goods or a sample or model of them before entering into the contract. "Examination" as used in this paragraph is not synonymous with inspection before acceptance or at any other time after the contract has been made. It goes rather to the nature of the responsibility assumed by the seller at the time of the making of the contract. Of course if the buyer discovers the defect and uses the goods anyway, or if he unreasonably fails to examine the goods before he uses them, resulting injuries may be found to result from his own action rather than proximately from a breach of warranty. See Sections 2-314 and 2-715 and comments thereto.

In order to bring the transaction within the scope of "refused to examine" in paragraph (b), it is not sufficient that the goods are available for inspection. There must in addition be a demand by the seller that the buyer examine the goods fully. The seller by the demand puts the buyer on notice that he is assuming the risk of defects which the examination ought to reveal. The language "refused to examine" in this paragraph is intended to make clear the necessity for such demand.

Application of the doctrine of "caveat emptor" in all cases where the buyer examines the goods regardless of statements made by the seller is, however, rejected by this Article. Thus, if the offer of examination is accompanied by words as to their merchantability or specific attributes and the buyer indicates clearly that he is relying on those words rather than on his examination, they give rise to an "express" warranty. In such cases the question is one of fact as to whether a warranty of merchantability has been expressly incorporated in the agreement. Disclaimer of such an express warranty is governed by subsection (1) of the present section.

The particular buyer's skill and the normal method of examining goods in the circumstances determine what defects are excluded by the examination. A failure to notice defects which are obvious cannot excuse the buyer. However, an examination under circumstances which do not permit chemical or other testing of the goods would not exclude defects which could be ascertained only by such testing. Nor can latent defects be excluded by a simple examination. A professional buyer examining a product in his field will be held to have assumed the risk as to all defects which a professional in the field ought to observe, while a nonprofessional buyer will be held to have assumed the risk only for such defects as a layman might be expected to observe.

9. The situation in which the buyer gives precise and complete specifications to the seller is not explicitly covered in this section, but this is a frequent circumstance by which the implied warranties may be excluded. The warranty of fitness for a particular purpose would not normally arise since in such a

situation there is usually no reliance on the seller by the buyer. The warranty of merchantability in such a transaction, however, must be considered in connection with the next section on the cumulation and conflict of warranties. Under paragraph (c) of that section in case of such an inconsistency the implied warranty of merchantability is displaced by the express warranty that the goods will comply with the specifications. Thus, where the buyer gives detailed specifications as to the goods, neither of the implied warranties as to quality will normally apply to the transaction unless consistent with the specifications.

Cross References:
> Point 2: Sections 2-202, 2-718 and 2-719.
> Point 7: Sections 1-205 and 2-208.

Definitional Cross References:
> "Agreement." Section 1-201.
> "Buyer." Section 2-103.
> "Contract." Section 1-201.
> "Course of dealing." Section 1-205.
> "Goods." Section 2-105.
> "Remedy." Section 1-201.
> "Seller." Section 2-103.
> "Usage of trade." Section 1-205.

§2-317. Cumulation and Conflict of Warranties Express or Implied

Warranties whether express or implied shall be construed as consistent with each other and as cumulative, but if such construction is unreasonable the intention of the parties shall determine which warranty is dominant. In ascertaining that intention the following rules apply:
> (a) Exact or technical specifications displace an inconsistent sample or model or general language of description.
> (b) A sample from an existing bulk displaces inconsistent general language of description.
> (c) Express warranties displace inconsistent implied warranties other than an implied warranty of fitness for a particular purpose.

§2-318. Third Party Beneficiaries of Warranties Express or Implied

[**Note:** *If this Act is introduced in the Congress of the United States this section should be omitted. (States to select one alternative.)*]

ALTERNATIVE A

A seller's warranty whether express or implied extends to any natural person who is in the family or household of his buyer or who is a guest in his home if it is reasonable to expect that such person may use, consume or be affected by the goods and who is injured in person by breach of the warranty. A seller may not exclude or limit the operation of this section.

ALTERNATIVE B

A seller's warranty whether express or implied extends to any natural person who may reasonably be expected to use, consume or be affected by the goods and who is injured in person by breach of the warranty. A seller may not exclude or limit the operation of this section.

ALTERNATIVE C

A seller's warranty whether express or implied extends to any person who may reasonably be expected to use, consume or be affected by the goods and who is injured by breach of the warranty. A seller may not exclude or limit the operation of this section with respect to injury to the person of an individual to whom the warranty extends.

§2-319. F.O.B. and F.A.S. Terms

(1) Unless otherwise agreed the term F.O.B. (which means "free on board") at a named place, even though used only in connection with the stated price, is a delivery term under which

(a) when the term is F.O.B. the place of shipment, the seller must at that place ship the goods in the manner provided in this Article (Section 2-504) and bear the expense and risk of putting them into the possession of the carrier; or

(b) when the term is F.O.B. the place of destination, the seller must at his own expense and risk transport the goods to that place and there tender delivery of them in the manner provided in this Article (Section 2-503);

(c) when under either (a) or (b) the term is also F.O.B. vessel, car or other vehicle, the seller must in addition at his own expense and risk load the goods on board. If the term is F.O.B. vessel the buyer must name the vessel and in an appropriate case the seller must comply with the provisions of this Article on the form of bill of lading (Section 2-323).

(2) Unless otherwise agreed the term F.A.S. vessel (which means "free along-side") at a named port, even though used only in connection with the stated price, is a delivery term under which the seller must

(a) at his own expense and risk deliver the goods alongside the vessel in the manner usual in that port or on a dock designated and provided by the buyer; and

(b) obtain and tender a receipt for the goods in exchange for which the carrier is under a duty to issue a bill of lading.

(3) Unless otherwise agreed in any case falling within subsection (1)(a) or (c) or subsection (2) the buyer must seasonably give any needed instructions for making delivery, including when the term is F.A.S. or F.O.B. the loading berth of the vessel and in an appropriate case its name and sailing date. The seller may treat the failure of needed instructions as a failure of cooperation under this Article (Section 2-311). He may also at his option move the goods in any reasonable manner preparatory to delivery or shipment.

(4) Under the term F.O.B. vessel or F.A.S. unless otherwise agreed the buyer must make payment against tender of the required documents and the seller may not tender nor the buyer demand delivery of the goods in substitution for the documents.

§2-320.   C.I.F. and C. & F. Terms

(1) The term C.I.F. means that the price includes in a lump sum the cost of the goods and the insurance and freight to the named destination. The term C. & F. or C.F. means that the price so includes cost and freight to the named destination.

(2) Unless otherwise agreed and even though used only in connection with the stated price and destination, the term C.I.F. destination or its equivalent requires the seller at his own expense and risk to

(a) put the goods into the possession of a carrier at the port for shipment and obtain a negotiable bill or bills of lading covering the entire transportation to the named destination; and

(b) load the goods and obtain a receipt from the carrier (which may be contained in the bill of lading) showing that the freight has been paid or provided for; and

(c) obtain a policy or certificate of insurance, including any war risk insurance, of a kind and on terms then current at the port of shipment in the usual amount, in the currency of the contract, shown to cover the same goods covered by the bill of lading and providing for payment of loss to the order of the buyer or for the account of whom it may concern; but the seller may add to the price the amount of the premium for any such war risk insurance; and

(d) prepare an invoice of the goods and procure any other documents required to effect shipment or to comply with the contract; and

(e) forward and tender with commercial promptness all the documents in due form and with any indorsement necessary to perfect the buyer's rights.

(3) Unless otherwise agreed the term C. & F. or its equivalent has the same effect and imposes upon the seller the same obligations and risks as a C.I.F. term except the obligation as to insurance.

(4) Under the term C.I.F. or C. & F. unless otherwise agreed the buyer must make payment against tender of the required documents and the seller may not tender nor the buyer demand delivery of the goods in substitution for the documents.

§2-326.   Sale on Approval and Sale or Return; Rights of Creditors

(1) Unless otherwise agreed, if delivered goods may be returned by the buyer even though they conform to the contract, the transaction is

(a) a "sale on approval" if the goods are delivered primarily for use, and

(b) a "sale or return" if the goods are delivered primarily for resale.

(2) Goods held on approval are not subject to the claims of the buyer's creditors until acceptance; goods held on sale or return are subject to such claims while in the buyer's possession.

(3) Any "or return" term of a contract for sale is to be treated as a separate contract for sale within the statute of frauds section of this Article (Section 2-201) and as contradicting the sale aspect of the contract within the provisions of this Article on parol or extrinsic evidence (Section 2-202).

[As amended in 1999 to conform to Revised Article 9 (2000) of the Code.]

§2-327. Special Incidents of Sale on Approval and Sale or Return

(1) Under a sale on approval unless otherwise agreed

(a) although the goods are identified to the contract the risk of loss and the title do not pass to the buyer until acceptance; and

(b) use of the goods consistent with the purpose of trial is not acceptance but failure seasonably to notify the seller of election to return the goods is acceptance, and if the goods conform to the contract acceptance of any part is acceptance of the whole; and

(c) after due notification of election to return, the return is at the seller's risk and expense but a merchant buyer must follow any reasonable instructions.

(2) Under a sale or return unless otherwise agreed

(a) the option to return extends to the whole or any commercial unit of the goods while in substantially their original condition, but must be exercised seasonably; and

(b) the return is at the buyer's risk and expense.

§2-328. Sale by Auction

(1) In a sale by auction if goods are put up in lots each lot is the subject of a separate sale.

(2) A sale by auction is complete when the auctioneer so announces by the fall of the hammer or in other customary manner. Where a bid is made while the hammer is falling in acceptance of a prior bid the auctioneer may in his discretion reopen the bidding or declare the goods sold under the bid on which the hammer was falling.

(3) Such a sale is with reserve unless the goods are in explicit terms put up without reserve. In an auction with reserve the auctioneer may withdraw the goods at any time until he announces completion of the sale. In an auction without reserve, after the auctioneer calls for bids on an article or lot, that article or lot cannot be withdrawn unless no bid is made within a reasonable time. In either case a bidder may retract his bid until the auctioneer's announcement of completion of the sale, but a bidder's retraction does not revive any previous bid.

(4) If the auctioneer knowingly receives a bid on the seller's behalf or the seller makes or procures such a bid, and notice has not been given that liberty for such bidding is reserved, the buyer may at his option avoid the sale or take the goods at the price of the last good faith bid prior to the completion of the sale. This subsection shall not apply to any bid at a forced sale.

Part 4. Title, Creditors and Good Faith Purchasers

§2-401. Passing of Title; Reservation for Security; Limited Application of This Section

Each provision of this Article with regard to the rights, obligations and remedies of the seller, the buyer, purchasers or other third parties applies irrespective of title to the goods except where the provision refers to such title. Insofar as situations are not covered by the other provisions of this Article and matters concerning title become material the following rules apply:

(1) Title to goods cannot pass under a contract for sale prior to their identification to the contract (Section 2-501), and unless otherwise explicitly agreed the buyer acquires by their identification a special property as limited by this Act. Any retention or reservation by the seller of the title (property) in goods shipped or delivered to the buyer is limited in effect to a reservation of a security interest. Subject to these provisions and to the provisions of the Article on Secured Transactions (Article 9), title to goods passes from the seller to the buyer in any manner and on any conditions explicitly agreed on by the parties.

(2) Unless otherwise explicitly agreed title passes to the buyer at the time and place at which the seller completes his performance with reference to the physical delivery of the goods, despite any reservation of a security interest and even though a document of title is to be delivered at a different time or place; and in particular and despite any reservation of a security interest by the bill of lading

(a) if the contract requires or authorizes the seller to send the goods to the buyer but does not require him to deliver them at destination, title passes to the buyer at the time and place of shipment; but

(b) if the contract requires delivery at destination, title passes on tender there.

(3) Unless otherwise explicitly agreed where delivery is to be made without moving the goods,

(a) if the seller is to deliver a document of title, title passes at the time when and the place where he delivers such documents; or

(b) if the goods are at the time of contracting already identified and no documents are to be delivered, title passes at the time and place of contracting.

(4) A rejection or other refusal by the buyer to receive or retain the goods, whether or not justified, or a justified revocation of acceptance revests title to the goods in the seller. Such revesting occurs by operation of law and is not a "sale."

§2-402. Rights of Seller's Creditors Against Sold Goods

(1) Except as provided in subsections (2) and (3), rights of unsecured creditors of the seller with respect to goods which have been identified to a contract for sale are subject to the buyer's rights to recover the goods under this Article (Sections 2-502 and 2-716).

(2) A creditor of the seller may treat a sale or an identification of goods to a contract for sale as void if as against him a retention of possession by the seller is fraudulent under any rule of law of the state where the goods are situated, except

that retention of possession in good faith and current course of trade by a merchant-seller for a commercially reasonable time after a sale or identification is not fraudulent.

(3) Nothing in this Article shall be deemed to impair the rights of creditors of the seller

(a) under the provisions of the Article on Secured Transactions (Article 9); or

(b) where identification to the contract or delivery is made not in current course of trade but in satisfaction of or as security for a pre-existing claim for money, security or the like and is made under circumstances which under any rule of law of the state where the goods are situated would apart from this Article constitute the transaction a fraudulent transfer or voidable preference.

§2-403.   Power to Transfer; Good Faith Purchase of Goods; "Entrusting"

(1) A purchaser of goods acquires all title which his transferor had or had power to transfer except that a purchaser of a limited interest acquires rights only to the extent of the interest purchased. A person with voidable title has power to transfer a good title to a good faith purchaser for value. When goods have been delivered under a transaction of purchase the purchaser has such power even though

(a) the transferor was deceived as to the identify of the purchaser, or

(b) the delivery was in exchange for a check which is later dishonored, or

(c) it was agreed that the transaction was to be a "cash sale," or

(d) the delivery was procured through fraud punishable as larcenous under the criminal law.

(2) Any entrusting of possession of goods to a merchant who deals in goods of that kind gives him power to transfer all rights of the entruster to a buyer in ordinary course of business.

(3) "Entrusting" includes any delivery and any acquiescence in retention of possession regardless of any condition expressed between the parties to the delivery or acquiescence and regardless of whether the procurement of the entrusting or the possessor's disposition of the goods have been such as to be larcenous under the criminal law.

(4) The rights of other purchasers of goods and of lien creditors are governed by the Articles on Secured Transactions (Article 9), Bulk Transfers (Article 6) and Documents of Title (Article 7).

Part 5.   Performance

§2-501.   Insurable Interest in Goods; Manner of Identification of Goods

(1) The buyer obtains a special property and an insurable interest in goods by identification of existing goods as goods to which the contract refers even though the goods so identified are non-conforming and he has an option to return or reject them. Such identification can be made at any time and in any manner

explicitly agreed to by the parties. In the absence of explicit agreement identification occurs

(a) when the contract is made if it is for the sale of goods already existing and identified;

(b) if the contract is for the sale of future goods other than those described in paragraph (c), when goods are shipped, marked or otherwise designated by the seller as goods to which the contract refers;

(c) when the crops are planted or otherwise become growing crops or the young are conceived if the contract is for the sale of unborn young to be born within twelve months after contracting or for the sale of crops to be harvested within twelve months or the next normal harvest season after contracting whichever is longer.

(2) The seller retains an insurable interest in goods so long as title to or any security interest in the goods remains in him and where the identification is by the seller alone he may until default or insolvency or notification to the buyer that the identification is final substitute other goods for those identified.

(3) Nothing in this section impairs any insurable interest recognized under any other statute or rule of law.

§2-502. Buyer's Right to Goods on Seller's Repudiation, Failure to Deliver, or Insolvency

(1) Subject to subsections (2) and (3) and even though the goods have not been shipped a buyer who has paid a part or all of the price of goods in which he has a special property under the provisions of the immediately preceding section may on making and keeping good a tender of any unpaid portion of their price recover them from the seller if:

(a) in the case of goods bought for personal, family, or household purposes, the seller repudiates or fails to deliver as required by the contract; or

(b) in all cases, the seller becomes insolvent within ten days after receipt of the first installment on their price.

(2) The buyer's right to recover the goods under subsection (1)(a) vests upon acquisition of a special property, even if the seller had not then repudiated or failed to deliver.

(3) If the identification creating his special property has been made by the buyer he acquires the right to recover the goods only if they conform to the contract for sale.

[As amended in 1999 to conform to Revised Article 9 (2000) of the Code.]

§2-503. Manner of Seller's Tender of Delivery

(1) Tender of delivery requires that the seller put and hold conforming goods at the buyer's disposition and give the buyer any notification reasonably necessary to enable him to take delivery. The manner, time and place for tender are determined by the agreement and this Article, and in particular

(a) tender must be at a reasonable hour, and if it is of goods they must be kept available for the period reasonably necessary to enable the buyer to take possession; but

(b) unless otherwise agreed the buyer must furnish facilities reasonably suited to the receipt of the goods.

(2) Where the case is within the next section respecting shipment tender requires that the seller comply with its provisions.

(3) Where the seller is required to deliver at a particular destination tender requires that he comply with subsection (1) and also in any appropriate case tender documents as described in subsections (4) and (5) of this section.

(4) Where goods are in the possession of a bailee and are to be delivered without being moved

(a) tender requires that the seller either tender a negotiable document of title covering such goods or procure acknowledgment by the bailee of the buyer's right to possession of the goods; but

(b) tender to the buyer of a non-negotiable document of title or of a written direction to the bailee to deliver is sufficient tender unless the buyer seasonably objects, and receipt by the bailee of notification of the buyer's rights fixes those rights as against the bailee and all third persons; but risk of loss of the goods and of any failure by the bailee to honor the non-negotiable document of title or to obey the direction remains on the seller until the buyer has had a reasonable time to present the document or direction, and a refusal by the bailee to honor the document or to obey the direction defeats the tender.

(5) Where the contract requires the seller to deliver documents

(a) he must tender all such documents in correct form, except as provided in this Article with respect to bills of lading in a set (subsection (2) of Section 2-323); and

(b) tender through customary banking channels is sufficient and dishonor of a draft accompanying the documents constitutes non-acceptance or rejection.

§2-504. Shipment by Seller

Where the seller is required or authorized to send the goods to the buyer and the contract does not require him to deliver them at a particular destination, then unless otherwise agreed he must

(a) put the goods in the possession of such a carrier and make such a contract for their transportation as may be reasonable having regard to the nature of the goods and other circumstances of the case; and

(b) obtain and promptly deliver or tender in due form any document necessary to enable the buyer to obtain possession of the goods or otherwise required by the agreement or by usage of trade; and

(c) promptly notify the buyer of the shipment.

Failure to notify the buyer under paragraph (c) or to make a proper contract under paragraph (a) is a ground for rejection only if material delay or loss ensues.

§2-507.   Effect of Seller's Tender; Delivery on Condition

(1) Tender of delivery is a condition to the buyer's duty to accept the goods and, unless otherwise agreed, to his duty to pay for them. Tender entitles the seller to acceptance of the goods and to payment according to the contract.

(2) Where payment is due and demanded on the delivery to the buyer of goods or documents of title, his right as against the seller to retain or dispose of them is conditional upon his making the payment due.

§2-508.   Cure by Seller of Improper Tender or Delivery; Replacement

(1) Where any tender or delivery by the seller is rejected because non-conforming and the time for performance has not yet expired, the seller may seasonably notify the buyer of his intention to cure and may then within the contract time make a conforming delivery.

(2) Where the buyer rejects a non-conforming tender which the seller had reasonable grounds to believe would be acceptable with or without money allowance the seller may if he seasonably notifies the buyer have a further reasonable time to substitute a conforming tender.

Official Comment

Prior Uniform Statutory Provision: None

Purposes:

1. Subsection (1) permits a seller who has made a non-conforming tender in any case to make a conforming delivery within the contract time upon seasonable notification to the buyer. It applies even where the seller has taken back the non-conforming goods and refunded the purchase price. He may still make a good tender within the contract period. The closer, however, it is to the contract date, the greater is the necessity for extreme promptness on the seller's part in notifying of his intention to cure, if such notification is to be "seasonable" under this subsection.

The rule of this subsection, moreover, is qualified by its underlying reasons. Thus if, after contracting for June delivery, a buyer later makes known to the seller his need for shipment early in the month and the seller ships accordingly, the "contract time" has been cut down by the supervening modification and the time for cure of tender must be referred to this modified time term.

2. Subsection (2) seeks to avoid injustice to the seller by reason of a surprise rejection by the buyer. However, the seller is not protected unless he had "reasonable grounds to believe" that the tender would be acceptable. Such reasonable grounds can lie in prior course of dealing, course of performance or usage of trade as well as in the particular circumstances surrounding the making of the contract. The seller is charged with commercial knowledge of any factors in a particular sales situation which require him to comply strictly with his obligations under the contract as, for example, strict conformity of documents in an overseas shipment or the sale of precision parts or chemicals

for use in manufacture. Further, if the buyer gives notice either implicitly, as by a prior course of dealing involving rigorous inspections, or expressly, as by the deliberate inclusion of a "no replacement" clause in the contract, the seller is to be held to rigid compliance. If the clause appears in a "form" contract evidence that it is out of line with trade usage or the prior course of dealing and was not called to the seller's attention may be sufficient to show that the seller had reasonable grounds to believe that the tender would be acceptable.

3. The words "a further reasonable time to substitute a conforming tender" are intended as words of limitation to protect the buyer. What is a "reasonable time" depends upon the attending circumstances. Compare Section 2-511 on the comparable case of a seller's surprise demand for legal tender.

4. Existing trade usages permitting variations without rejection but with price allowance enter into the agreement itself as contractual limitations of remedy and are not covered by this section.

Cross References:
  Point 2: Section 2-302.
  Point 3: Section 2-511.
  Point 4: Sections 1-205 and 2-721.

Definitional Cross References:
  "Buyer." Section 2-103.
  "Conforming." Section 2-106.
  "Contract." Section 1-201.
  "Money." Section 1-201.
  "Reasonable time." Section 1-204.
  "Seasonably." Section 1-204.
  "Seller." Section 2-103.

§2-509.   Risk of Loss in the Absence of Breach

(1) Where the contract requires or authorizes the seller to ship the goods by carrier

  (a) if it does not require him to deliver them at a particular destination, the risk of loss passes to the buyer when the goods are duly delivered to the carrier even though the shipment is under reservation (Section 2-505); but

  (b) if it does require him to deliver them at a particular destination and the goods are there duly tendered while in the possession of the carrier, the risk of loss passes to the buyer when the goods are there duly so tendered as to enable the buyer to take delivery.

(2) Where the goods are held by a bailee to be delivered without being moved, the risk of loss passes to the buyer

  (a) on his receipt of a negotiable document of title covering the goods; or

  (b) on acknowledgment by the bailee of the buyer's right to possession of the goods; or

  (c) after his receipt of a non-negotiable document of title or other written direction to deliver, as provided in subsection (4) (b) of Section 2-503.

(3) In any case not within subsection (1) or (2), the risk of loss passes to the buyer on his receipt of the goods if the seller is a merchant; otherwise the risk passes to the buyer on tender of delivery.

(4) The provisions of this section are subject to contrary agreement of the parties and to the provisions of this Article on sale on approval (Section 2-327) and on effect of breach on risk of loss (Section 2-510).

§2-510. Effect of Breach on Risk of Loss

(1) Where a tender or delivery of goods so fails to conform to the contract as to give a right of rejection the risk of their loss remains on the seller until cure or acceptance.

(2) Where the buyer rightfully revokes acceptance he may to the extent of any deficiency in his effective insurance coverage treat the risk of loss as having rested on the seller from the beginning.

(3) Where the buyer as to conforming goods already identified to the contract for sale repudiates or is otherwise in breach before risk of their loss has passed to him, the seller may to the extent of any deficiency in his effective insurance coverage treat the risk of loss as resting on the buyer for a commercially reasonable time.

§2-511. Tender of Payment by Buyer; Payment by Check

(1) Unless otherwise agreed tender of payment is a condition to the seller's duty to tender and complete any delivery.

(2) Tender of payment is sufficient when made by any means or in any manner current in the ordinary course of business unless the seller demands payment in legal tender and gives any extension of time reasonably necessary to procure it.

(3) Subject to the provisions of this Act on the effect of an instrument on an obligation (Section 3-802), payment by check is conditional and is defeated as between the parties by dishonor of the check on due presentment.

§2-512. Payment by Buyer Before Inspection

(1) Where the contract requires payment before inspection non-conformity of goods does not excuse the buyer from so making payment unless

(a) the non-conformity appears without inspection; or

(b) despite tender of the required documents the circumstances would justify injunction against honor under the provisions of this Act (Section 5-114).

(2) Payment pursuant to subsection (1) does not constitute an acceptance of goods or impair the buyer's right to inspect or any of his remedies.

§2-513. Buyer's Right to Inspection of Goods

(1) Unless otherwise agreed and subject to subsection (3), where goods are tendered or delivered or identified to the contract for sale, the buyer has a right before payment or acceptance to inspect them at any reasonable place and time and in any reasonable manner. When the seller is required or authorized to send the goods to the buyer, the inspection may be after their arrival.

(2) Expenses of inspection must be borne by the buyer but may be recovered from the seller if the goods do not conform and are rejected.

(3) Unless otherwise agreed and subject to the provisions of this Article on C.I.F. contracts (subsection (3) of Section 2-321), the buyer is not entitled to inspect the goods before payment of the price when the contract provides

(a) for delivery "C.O.D." or on other like terms; or

(b) for payment against documents of title, except where such payment is due only after the goods are to become available for inspection.

(4) A place or method of inspection fixed by the parties is presumed to be exclusive but unless otherwise expressly agreed it does not postpone identification or shift the place for delivery or for passing the risk of loss. If compliance becomes impossible, inspection shall be as provided in this section unless the place or method fixed was clearly intended as an indispensable condition failure of which avoids the contract.

Part 6. Breach, Repudiation and Excuse

§2-601. Buyer's Rights on Improper Delivery

Subject to the provisions of this Article on breach in installment contracts (Section 2-612) and unless otherwise agreed under the sections on contractual limitations of remedy (Section 2-718 and 2-719), if the goods or the tender of delivery fail in any respect to conform to the contract, the buyer may

(a) reject the whole; or

(b) accept the whole; or

(c) accept any commercial unit or units and reject the rest.

§2-602. Manner and Effect of Rightful Rejection

(1) Rejection of goods must be within a reasonable time after their delivery or tender. It is ineffective unless the buyer seasonably notifies the seller.

(2) Subject to the provisions of the two following sections on rejected goods (Sections 2-603 and 2-604),

(a) after rejection any exercise of ownership by the buyer with respect to any commercial unit is wrongful as against the seller; and

(b) if the buyer has before rejection taken physical possession of goods in which he does not have a security interest under the provisions of this Article (subsection (3) of Section 2-711), he is under a duty after rejection to hold them with reasonable care at the seller's disposition for a time sufficient to permit the seller to remove them; but

(c) the buyer has no further obligations with regard to goods rightfully rejected.

(3) The seller's rights with respect to goods wrongfully rejected are governed by the provisions of this Article on Seller's remedies in general (Section 2-703).

Official Comment

Prior Uniform Statutory Provision: Section 50, Uniform Sales Act.

Changes: Rewritten.

Purposes of Changes: To make it clear that:

1. A tender or delivery of goods made pursuant to a contract of sale, even though wholly non-conforming, requires affirmative action by the buyer to avoid acceptance. Under subsection (1), therefore, the buyer is given a reasonable time to notify the seller of his rejection, but without such seasonable notification his rejection is ineffective. The sections of this Article dealing with inspection of goods must be read in connection with the buyer's reasonable time for action under this subsection. Contract provisions limiting the time for rejection fall within the rule of the section on "Time" and are effective if the time set gives the buyer a reasonable time for discovery of defects. What constitutes a due "notifying" of rejection by the buyer to the seller is defined in Section 1-201.

2. Subsection (2) lays down the normal duties of the buyer upon rejection, which flow from the relationship of the parties. Beyond his duty to hold the goods with reasonable care for the buyer's [seller's] disposition, this section continues the policy of prior uniform legislation in generally relieving the buyer from any duties with respect to them, except when the circumstances impose the limited obligation of salvage upon him under the next section.

3. The present section applies only to rightful rejection by the buyer. If the seller has made a tender which in all respects conforms to the contract, the buyer has a positive duty to accept and his failure to do so constitutes a "wrongful rejection" which gives the seller immediate remedies for breach. Subsection (3) is included here to emphasize the sharp distinction between the rejection of an improper tender and the non-acceptance which is a breach by the buyer.

4. The provisions of this section are to be appropriately limited or modified when a negotiation is in process.

Cross References:
   Point 1: Sections 1-201, 1-204(1) and (3), 2-512(2), 2-513(1) and 2-606(1) (b).
   Point 2: Section 2-603(1).
   Point 3: Section 2-703.

Definitional Cross References:
   "Buyer." Section 2-103.
   "Commercial unit." Section 2-105.
   "Goods." Section 2-105.
   "Merchant." Section 2-104.
   "Notifies." Section 1-201.
   "Reasonable time." Section 1-204.
   "Remedy." Section 1-201.
   "Rights." Section 1-201.
   "Seasonably." Section 1-204.
   "Security interest." Section 1-201.
   "Seller." Section 2-103.

§2-603. Merchant Buyer's Duties as to Rightfully Rejected Goods

(1) Subject to any security interest in the buyer (subsection (3) of Section 2-711), when the seller has no agent or place of business at the market of rejection a merchant buyer is under a duty after rejection of goods in his possession or control to follow any reasonable instructions received from the seller with respect to the goods and in the absence of such instructions to make reasonable efforts to sell them for the seller's account if they are perishable or threaten to decline in value speedily. Instructions are not reasonable if on demand indemnity for expenses is not forthcoming.

(2) When the buyer sells goods under subsection (1), he is entitled to reimbursement from the seller or out of the proceeds for reasonable expenses of caring for the selling them, and if the expenses include no selling commission then to such commission as is usual in the trade or if there is none to a reasonable sum not exceeding ten per cent on the gross proceeds.

(3) In complying with this section the buyer is held only to good faith and good faith conduct hereunder is neither acceptance nor conversion nor the basis of an action for damages.

§2-604. Buyer's Options as to Salvage of Rightfully Rejected Goods

Subject to the provisions of the immediately preceding section on perishables if the seller gives no instructions within a reasonable time after notification of rejection the buyer may store the rejected goods for the seller's account or reship them to him or re-sell them for the seller's account with reimbursement as provided in the preceding section. Such action is not acceptance or conversion.

§2-605. Waiver of Buyer's Objections by Failure to Particularize

(1) The buyer's failure to state in connection with rejection a particular defect which is ascertainable by reasonable inspection precludes him from relying on the unstated defect to justify rejection or to establish breach
(a) where the seller could have cured it if stated seasonally; or
(b) between merchants when the seller has after rejection made a request in writing for a full and final written statement of all defects on which the buyer proposes to rely.

(2) Payment against documents made without reservation of rights precludes recovery of the payment for defects apparent on the face of the documents.

§2-606. What Constitutes Acceptance of Goods

(1) Acceptance of goods occurs when the buyer

(a) after a reasonable opportunity to inspect the goods signifies to the seller that the goods are conforming or that he will take or retain them in spite of their non-conformity; or

(b) fails to make an effective rejection (subsection (1) of Section 2-602), but such acceptance does not occur until the buyer has had a reasonable opportunity to inspect them; or

(c) does any act inconsistent with the seller's ownership; but if such act is wrongful as against the seller it is an acceptance only if ratified by him.

(2) Acceptance of a part of any commercial unit is acceptance of that entire unit.

§2-607. Effect of Acceptance; Notice of Breach; Burden of Establishing Breach After Acceptance; Notice of Claim or Litigation to Person Answerable Over

(1) The buyer must pay at the contract rate for any goods accepted.

(2) Acceptance of goods by the buyer precludes rejection of the goods accepted and if made with knowledge of a non-conformity cannot be revoked because of it unless the acceptance was on the reasonable assumption that the non-conformity would be seasonably cured but acceptance does not of itself impair any other remedy provided by this Article for non-conformity.

(3) Where a tender has been accepted

(a) the buyer must within a reasonable time after he discovers or should have discovered any breach notify the seller of breach or be barred from any remedy; and

(b) if the claim is one for infringement or the like (subsection (3) of Section 2-312) and the buyer is sued as a result of such a breach he must so notify the seller within a reasonable time after he receives notice of the litigation or be barred from any remedy over for liability established by the litigation.

(4) The burden is on the buyer to establish any breach with respect to the goods accepted.

(5) Where the buyer is sued for breach of a warranty or other obligation for which his seller is answerable over

(a) he may give his seller written notice of the litigation. If the notice states that the seller may come in and defend and that if the seller does not do so he will be bound in any action against him by his buyer by any determination of fact common to the two litigations, then unless the seller after seasonable receipt of the notice does come in and defend he is so bound.

(b) if the claim is one for infringement or the like (subsection (3) of Section 2-312) the original seller may demand in writing that his buyer turn over to him control of the litigation including settlement or else be barred from any remedy over and if he also agrees to bear all expense and to satisfy any adverse judgment, then unless the buyer after seasonable receipt of the demand does turn over control the buyer is so barred.

(6) The provisions of subsections (3), (4) and (5) apply to any obligation of a buyer to hold the seller harmless against infringement or the like (subsection (3) of Section 2-312).

Official Comment

Prior Uniform Statutory Provision: Subsection (1)—Section 41, Uniform Sales Act; Subsections (2) and (3)—Sections 49 and 69, Uniforms Sales Act.

Changes: Rewritten.

Purposes of Changes: To continue the prior basic policies with respect to acceptance of goods while making a number of minor though material changes in the interest of simplicity and commercial convenience so that:

1. Under subsection (1), once the buyer accepts a tender the seller acquires a right to its price on the contract terms. In cases of partial acceptance, the price of any part accepted is, if possible, to be reasonably apportioned, using the type of apportionment familiar to the courts in quantum valebat cases, to be determined in terms of "the contract rate," which is the rate determined from the bargain in fact (the agreement) after the rules and policies of this Article have been brought to bear.

2. Under subsection (2) acceptance of goods precludes their subsequent rejection. Any return of the goods thereafter must be by way of revocation of acceptance under the next section. Revocation is unavailable for a non-conformity known to the buyer at the time of acceptance, except where the buyer has accepted on the reasonable assumption that the non-conformity would be seasonably cured.

3. All other remedies of the buyer remain unimpaired under subsection (2). This is intended to include the buyer's full rights with respect to future installments despite his acceptance of any earlier non-conforming installment.

4. The time of notification is to be determined by applying commercial standards to a merchant buyer. "A reasonable time" for notification from a retail consumer is to be judged by different standards so that in his case it will be extended, for the rule of requiring notification is designed to defeat commercial bad faith, not to deprive a good faith consumer of his remedy.

The content of the notification need merely be sufficient to let the seller know that the transaction is still troublesome and must be watched. There is no reason to require that the notification which saves the buyer's rights under this section must include a clear statement of all the objections that will be relied on by the buyer, as under the section covering statements of defects upon rejection (Section 2-605). Nor is there reason for requiring the notification to be a claim for damages or of any threatened litigation or other resort to a remedy. The notification which saves the buyer's rights under this Article need only be such as informs the seller that the transaction is claimed to involve a breach, and thus opens the way for normal settlement through negotiation.

5. Under this Article various beneficiaries are given rights for injuries sustained by them because of the seller's breach of warranty. Such a beneficiary does not fall within the reason of the present section in regard to discovery of defects and the giving of notice within a reasonable time after acceptance, since he has nothing to do with acceptance. However, the reason of this section does extend to requiring the beneficiary to notify the seller that an injury has occurred. What is said above, with regard to the extended time for reasonable notification from the lay consumer after the injury is also applicable here; but

even a beneficiary can be properly held to the use of good faith in notifying, once he has had time to become aware of the legal situation.

6. Subsection (4) unambiguously places the burden of proof to establish breach on the buyer after acceptance. However, this rule becomes one purely of procedure when the tender accepted was non-conforming and the buyer has given the seller notice of breach under subsection (3). For subsection (2) makes it clear that acceptance leaves unimpaired the buyer's right to be made whole, and that right can be exercised by the buyer not only by way of cross-claim for damages, but also by way of recoupment in diminution or extinction of the price.

7. Subsections (3)(b) and (5)(b) give a warrantor against infringement an opportunity to defend or compromise third-party claims or be relieved of his liability. Subsection (5)(a) codifies for all warranties the practice of voucher to defend. Compare Section 3-803. Subsection (6) makes these provisions applicable to the buyer's liability for infringement under Section 2-312.

8. All of the provisions of the present section are subject to any explicit reservation of rights.

Cross References:
   Point 1: Section 1-201.
   Point 2: Section 2-608.
   Point 4: Sections 1-204 and 2-605.
   Point 5: Section 2-318.
   Point 6: Section 2-717.
   Point 7: Sections 2-312 and 3-803.
   Point 8: Section 1-207.

Definitional Cross References:
   "Burden of establishing." Section 1-201.
   "Buyer." Section 2-103.
   "Conform." Section 2-106.
   "Contract." Section 1-201.
   "Goods." Section 2-105.
   "Notifies." Section 1-201.
   "Reasonable time." Section 1-204.
   "Remedy." Section 1-201.
   "Seasonably." Section 1-204.

§2-608.   Revocation of Acceptance in Whole or in Part

(1) The buyer may revoke his acceptance of a lot or commercial unit whose non-conformity substantially impairs its value to him if he has accepted it
   (a) on the reasonable assumption that its non-conformity would be cured and it has not been seasonably cured; or
   (b) without discovery of such non-conformity if his acceptance was reasonably induced either by the difficulty of discovery before acceptance or by the seller's assurances.

(2) Revocation of acceptance must occur within a reasonable time after the buyer discovers or should have discovered the ground for it and before any substantial change in condition of the goods which is not caused by their own defects. It is not effective until the buyer notifies the seller of it.

(3) A buyer who so revokes has the same rights and duties with regard to the goods involved as if he had rejected them.

§2-609. Right to Adequate Assurance of Performance

(1) A contract for sale imposes an obligation on each party that the other's expectation of receiving due performance will not be impaired. When reasonable grounds for insecurity arise with respect to the performance of either party the other may in writing demand adequate assurance of due performance and until he receives such assurance may if commercially reasonable suspend any performance for which he has not already received the agreed return.

(2) Between merchants the reasonableness of grounds for insecurity and the adequacy of any assurance offered shall be determined according to commercial standards.

(3) Acceptance of any improper delivery or payment does not prejudice the aggrieved party's right to demand adequate assurance of future performance.

(4) After receipt of a justified demand failure to provide within a reasonable time not exceeding thirty days such assurance of due performance as is adequate under the circumstances of the particular case is a repudiation of the contract.

Official Comment

Prior Uniform Statutory Provision: See Sections 53, 54(1)(b), 55 and 63(2), Uniform Sales Act.

Purposes:
1. The section rests on the recognition of the fact that the essential purpose of a contract between commercial men is actual performance and they do not bargain merely for a promise, or for a promise plus the right to win a lawsuit and that a continuing sense of reliance and security that the promised performance will be forthcoming when due, is an important feature of the bargain. If either the willingness or the ability of a party to perform declines materially between the time of contracting and the time for performance, the other party is threatened with the loss of a substantial part of what he has bargained for. A seller needs protection not merely against having to deliver on credit to a shaky buyer, but also against having to procure and manufacture the goods, perhaps turning down other customers. Once he has been given reason to believe that the buyer's performance has become uncertain, it is an undue hardship to force him to continue his own performance. Similarly, a buyer who believes that the seller's deliveries have become uncertain cannot safely wait for the due date of performance when he has been buying to assure himself of materials for his current manufacturing or to replenish his stock of merchandise.

2. Three measures have been adopted to meet the needs of commercial men in such situations. First, the aggrieved party is permitted to suspend his own performance and any preparation therefore, with excuse for any resulting necessary delay, until the situation has been clarified. "Suspend performance" under this section means to hold up performance pending the outcome of the demand, and includes also the holding up of any preparatory action. This is the same principle which governs the ancient law of stoppage and seller's lien, and also of excuse of a buyer from prepayment if the seller's actions manifest that he cannot or will not perform. (Original Act, Section 63(2).)

Secondly, the aggrieved party is given the right to require adequate assurance that the other party's performance will be duly forthcoming. This principle is reflected in the familiar clauses permitting the seller to curtail deliveries if the buyer's credit becomes impaired, which when held within the limits of reasonableness and good faith actually express no more than the fair business meaning of any commercial contract.

Third, and finally, this section provides the means by which the aggrieved party may treat the contract as broken if his reasonable grounds for insecurity are not cleared up within a reasonable time. This is the principle underlying the law of anticipatory breach, whether by way of defective part performance or by repudiation. The present section merges these three principles of law and commercial practice into a single theory of general application to all sales agreements looking to future performance.

3. Subsection (2) of the present section requires that "reasonable" grounds and "adequate" assurance as used in subsection (1) be defined by commercial rather than legal standards. The express reference to commercial standards carries no connotation that the obligation of good faith is not equally applicable here.

Under commercial standards and in accord with commercial practice, a ground for insecurity need not arise from or be directly related to the contract in question. The law as to "dependence" or "independence" of promises within a single contract does not control the application of the present section.

Thus a buyer who falls behind in "his account" with the seller, even though the items involved have to do with separate and legally distinct contracts, impairs the seller's expectation of due performance. Again, under the same test, a buyer who requires precision parts which he intends to use immediately upon delivery, may have reasonable grounds for insecurity if he discovers that his seller is making defective deliveries of such parts to other buyers with similar needs. Thus, too, in a situation such as arose in Jay Dreher Corporation v. Delco Appliance Corporation, 93 F.2d 275 (C.C.A.2, 1937), where a manufacturer gave a dealer an exclusive franchise for the sale of his product but on two or three occasions breached the exclusive dealing clause, although there was no default in orders, deliveries or payments under the separate sales contract between the parties, the aggrieved dealer would be entitled to suspend his performance of the contract for sale under the present section and to demand assurance that the exclusive dealing contract would be lived up to. There is no need for an explicit clause tying the exclusive franchise into the contract for the sale of goods since the situation itself ties the agreements together.

The nature of the sales contract enters also into the question of reasonableness. For example, a report from an apparently trustworthy source that the seller had shipped defective goods or was planning to ship them would normally give the buyer reasonable grounds for insecurity. But when the buyer has assumed the risk of payment before inspection of the goods, as in a sales contract on C.I.F. or similar cash against documents terms, that risk is not to be evaded by a demand for assurance. Therefore no ground for insecurity would exist under this section unless the report went to a ground which would excuse payment by the buyer.

4. What constitutes "adequate" assurance of due performance is subject to the same test of factual conditions. For example, where the buyer can make use of a defective delivery, a mere promise by a seller of good repute that he is giving the matter his attention and that the defect will not be repeated, is normally sufficient. Under the same circumstances, however, a similar statement by a known corner-cutter might well be considered insufficient without the posting of a guaranty or, if so demanded by the buyer, a speedy replacement of the delivery involved. By the same token where a delivery has defects, even though easily curable, which interfere with easy use by the buyer, no verbal assurance can be deemed adequate which is not accompanied by replacement, repair, money-allowance, or other commercially reasonable cure.

A fact situation such as arose in Corn Products Refining Co. v. Fasola, 94 N.J.L. 181, 109 A. 505 (1920) offers illustration both of reasonable grounds for insecurity and "adequate" assurance. In that case a contract for the sale of oils on 30 days' credit, 2% off for payment within 10 days, provided that credit was to be extended to the buyer only if his financial responsibility was satisfactory to the seller. The buyer had been in the habit of taking advantage of the discount but at the same time that he failed to make his customary 10 day payment, the seller heard rumors, in fact false, that the buyer's financial condition was shaky. Thereupon, the seller demanded cash before shipment or security satisfactory to him. The buyer sent a good credit report from his banker, expressed willingness to make payments when due on the 30 day terms and insisted on further deliveries under the contract. Under this Article the rumors, although false, were enough to make the buyer's financial condition "unsatisfactory" to the seller under the contract clause. Moreover, the buyer's practice of taking the cash discounts is enough, apart from the contract clause, to lay a commercial foundation for suspicion when the practice is suddenly stopped. These matters, however, go only to the justification of the seller's demand for security, or his "reasonable grounds for insecurity."

The adequacy of the assurance given is not measured as in the type of "satisfaction" situation affected with intangibles, such as in personal service cases, cases involving a third party's judgment as final, or cases in which the whole contract is dependent on one party's satisfaction, as in a sale on approval. Here, the seller must exercise good faith and observe commercial standards. This Article thus approves the statement of the court in James B. Berry's Sons Co. of Illinois v. Monark Gasoline & Oil Co., Inc., 32 F.2d 74 (C.C.A.8, 1929), that the seller's satisfaction under such a clause must be based upon reason and must not be arbitrary or capricious; and rejects the purely personal "good faith" test of the Corn Products Refining Co. case, which held that in the seller's sole judgment, if for *any* reason he was dissatisfied, he was entitled to revoke the credit. In the absence of the buyer's failure to take the 2% discount as was his custom, the banker's report given in that case would have been "adequate" assurance under this Act, regardless of the language of the "satisfaction" clause.

However, the seller is reasonably entitled to feel insecure at a sudden expansion of the buyer's use of a credit term, and should be entitled either to security or to a satisfactory explanation.

The entire foregoing discussion as to adequacy of assurance by way of explanation is subject to qualification when repeated occasions for the application of this section arise. This Act recognizes that repeated delinquencies must be viewed as cumulative. On the other hand, commercial sense also requires that if repeated claims for assurance are made under this section, the basis for these claims must be increasingly obvious.

5. A failure to provide adequate assurance of performance and thereby to reestablish the security of expectation, results in a breach only "by repudiation" under subsection (4). Therefore, the possibility is continued of retraction of the repudiation under the section dealing with that problem, unless the aggrieved party has acted on the breach in some manner.

The thirty day limit on the time to provide assurance is laid down to free the question of reasonable time from uncertainty in later litigation.

6. Clauses seeking to give the protected party exceedingly wide powers to cancel or readjust the contract when ground for insecurity arises must be read against the fact that good faith is a part of the obligation of the contract and not subject to modification by agreement and includes, in the case of a merchant, the reasonable observance of commercial standards of fair dealing in the trade. Such clauses can thus be effective to enlarge the protection given by the present section to a certain extent, to fix the reasonable time within which requested assurance must be given, or to define adequacy of the assurance in any commercially reasonable fashion. But any clause seeking to set up arbitrary standards for action is ineffective under this Article. Acceleration clauses are treated similarly in the Articles on Commercial Paper and Secured Transactions.

Cross References:
Point 3: Section 1-203.
Point 5: Section 2-611.
Point 6: Sections 1-203 and 1-208 and Articles 3 and 9.

Definitional Cross References:
"Aggrieved party." Section 1-201.
"Between merchants." Section 2-104.
"Contract." Section 1-201.
"Contract for sale." Section 2-106.
"Party." Section 1-201.
"Reasonable time." Section 1-204.
"Rights." Section 1-201.
"Writing." Section 1-201.

§2-610. Anticipatory Repudiation

When either party repudiates the contract with respect to a performance not yet due the loss of which will substantially impair the value of the contract to the other, the aggrieved party may

(a) for a commercially reasonable time await performance by the repudiating party; or

(b) resort to any remedy for breach (Section 2-703 or Section 2-711), even though he has notified the repudiating party that he would await the latter's performance and has urged retraction; and

(c) in either case suspend his own performance or proceed in accordance with the provisions of this Article on the seller's right to identify goods to the contract notwithstanding breach or to salvage unfinished goods (Section 2-704).

Official Comment

Prior Uniform Statutory Provision: See Sections 63(2) and 65, Uniform Sales Act.

Purposes: To make it clear that:

1. With the problem of insecurity taken care of by the preceding section and with provision being made in this Article as to the effect of a defective delivery under an installment contract, anticipatory repudiation centers upon an overt communication of intention or an action which renders performance impossible or demonstrates a clear determination not to continue with performance.

Under the present section when such a repudiation substantially impairs the value of the contract, the aggrieved party may at any time resort to his remedies for breach, or he may suspend his own performance while he negotiates with, or awaits performance by, the other party. But if he awaits performance beyond a commercially reasonable time he cannot recover resulting damages which he should have avoided.

2. It is not necessary for repudiation that performance be made literally and utterly impossible. Repudiation can result from action which reasonably indicates a rejection of the continuing obligation. And, a repudiation automatically results under the preceding section on insecurity when a party fails to provide adequate assurance of due future performance within thirty days after a justifiable demand therefore has been made. Under the language of this section, a demand by one or both parties for more than the contract calls for in the way of counter-performance is not in itself a repudiation nor does it invalidate a plain expression of desire for future performance. However, when under a fair reading it amounts to a statement of intention not to perform except on conditions which go beyond the contract, it becomes a repudiation.

3. The test chosen to justify an aggrieved party's action under this section is the same as that in the section on breach in installment contracts — namely the substantial value of the contract. The most useful test of substantial value is to determine whether material inconvenience or injustice will result if the aggrieved party is forced to wait and receive an ultimate tender minus the part or aspect repudiated.

4. After repudiation, the aggrieved party may immediately resort to any remedy he chooses provided he moves in good faith (see Section 1-203). Inaction and silence by the aggrieved party may leave the matter open but it cannot be regarded as misleading the repudiating party. Therefore the

aggrieved party is left free to proceed at any time with his options under this section, unless he has taken some positive action which in good faith requires notification to the other party before the remedy is pursued.

Cross References:
   Point 1: Sections 2-609 and 2-612.
   Point 2: Section 2-609.
   Point 3: Section 2-612.
   Point 4: Section 1-203.

Definitional Cross References:
   "Aggrieved party." Section 1-201.
   "Contract." Section 1-201.
   "Party." Section 1-201.
   "Remedy." Section 1-201.

§2-611. Retraction of Anticipatory Repudiation

(1) Until the repudiating party's next performance is due he can retract his repudiation unless the aggrieved party has since the repudiation cancelled or materially changed his position or otherwise indicated that he considers the repudiation final.

(2) Retraction may be by any method which clearly indicates to the aggrieved party that the repudiating party intends to perform, but must include any assurance justifiably demanded under the provisions of this Article (Section 2-609).

(3) Retraction reinstates the repudiating party's rights under the contract with due excuse and allowance to the aggrieved party for any delay occasioned by the repudiation.

§2-612. "Installment Contract"; Breach

(1) An "installment contract" is one which requires or authorizes the delivery of goods in separate lots to be separately accepted, even though the contract contains a clause "each delivery is a separate contract" or its equivalent.

(2) The buyer may reject any installment which is non-conforming if the non-conformity substantially impairs the value of that installment and cannot be cured or if the non-conformity is a defect in the required documents; but if the non-conformity does not fall within subsection (3) and the seller gives adequate assurance of its cure the buyer must accept that installment.

(3) Whenever non-conformity or default with respect to one or more installments substantially impairs the value of the whole contract there is a breach of the whole. But the aggrieved party reinstates the contract if he accepts a non-conforming installment without seasonably notifying of cancellation or if he brings an action with respect only to past installments or demands performance as to future installments.

§2-613.   Casualty to Identified Goods

Where the contract requires for its performance goods identified when the contract is made, and the goods suffer casualty without fault of either party before the risk of loss passes to the buyer, or in a proper case under a "no arrival, no sale" term (Section 2-324) then

(a) if the loss is total the contract is avoided; and

(b) if the loss is partial or the goods have so deteriorated as no longer to conform to the contract the buyer may nevertheless demand inspection and at his option either treat the contract as avoided or accept the goods with due allowance from the contract price for the deterioration or the deficiency in quantity but without further right against the seller.

§2-614.   Substituted Performance

(1) Where without fault of either party the agreed berthing, loading, or unloading facilities fail or an agreed type of carrier becomes unavailable or the agreed manner of delivery otherwise becomes commercially impracticable but a commercially reasonable substitute is available, such substitute performance must be tendered and accepted.

(2) If the agreed means or manner of payment fails because of domestic or foreign governmental regulation, the seller may withhold or stop delivery unless the buyer provides a means or manner of payment which is commercially a substantial equivalent. If delivery has already been taken, payment by the means or in the manner provided by the regulation discharges the buyer's obligation unless the regulation is discriminatory, oppressive or predatory.

§2-615.   Excuse by Failure of Presupposed Conditions

Except so far as a seller may have assumed a greater obligation and subject to the preceding section on substituted performance:

(a) Delay in delivery or non-delivery in whole or in part by a seller who complies with paragraphs (b) and (c) is not a breach of his duty under a contract for sale if performance as agreed has been made impracticable by the occurrence of a contingency the non-occurrence of which was a basic assumption on which the contract was made or by compliance in good faith with any applicable foreign or domestic governmental regulation or order whether or not it later proves to be invalid.

(b) Where the causes mentioned in paragraph (a) affect only a part of the seller's capacity to perform, he must allocate production and deliveries among his customers but may at his option include regular customers not then under contract as well as his own requirements for further manufacture. He may so allocate in any manner which is fair and reasonable.

(c) The seller must notify the buyer seasonably that there will be delay or non-delivery and, when allocation is required under paragraph (b), of the estimated quota thus made available for the buyer.

Official Comment

Prior Uniform Statutory Provision: None.

Purposes:

1. This section excuses a seller from timely delivery of goods contracted for, where his performance has become commercially impracticable because of unforeseen supervening circumstances not within the contemplation of the parties at the time of contracting. The destruction of specific goods and the problem of the use of substituted performance on points other than delay or quantity, treated elsewhere in this Article, must be distinguished from the matter covered by this section.

2. The present section deliberately refrains from any effort at an exhaustive expression of contingencies and is to be interpreted in all cases sought to be brought within its scope in terms of its underlying reason and purpose.

3. The first test for excuse under this Article in terms of basic assumption is a familiar one. The additional test of commercial impracticability (as contrasted with "impossibility," "frustration of performance" or "frustration of the venture") has been adopted in order to call attention to the commercial character of the criterion chosen by this Article.

4. Increased cost alone does not excuse performance unless the rise in cost is due to some unforeseen contingency which alters the essential nature of the performance. Neither is a rise or a collapse in the market in itself a justification, for that is exactly the type of business risk which business contracts made at fixed prices are intended to cover. But a severe shortage of raw materials or of supplies due to a contingency such as war, embargo, local crop failure, unforeseen shutdown of major sources of supply or the like, which either causes a marked increase in cost or altogether prevents the seller from securing supplies necessary to his performance, is within the contemplation of this section. (See Ford & Sons, Ltd. v. Henry Leetham & Sons, Ltd., 21 Com. Cas. 55 (1915, K.B.D.).)

5. Where a particular source of supply is exclusive under the agreement and fails through casualty, the present section applies rather than the provision on destruction or deterioration of specific goods. The same holds true where a particular source of supply is shown by the circumstances to have been contemplated or assumed by the parties at the time of contracting. (See Davis Co. v. Hoffmann-LaRoche Chemical Works, 178 App. Div. 855, 166 N.Y.S. 179 (1917) and International Paper Co. v. Rockefeller, 161 App. Div. 180, 146 N.Y.S. 371 (1914).) There is no excuse under this section, however, unless the seller has employed all due measures to assure himself that his source will not fail. (See Canadian Industrial Alcohol Co., Ltd. v. Dunbar Molasses Co., 258 N.Y. 194, 179 N.E. 383, 80 A.L.R. 1173 (1932) and Washington Mfg. Co. v. Midland Lumber Co., 113 Wash. 593, 194 P. 777 (1921).)

In the case of failure of production by an agreed source for causes beyond the seller's control, the seller should, if possible, be excused since production by an agreed source is without more a basic assumption of the contract. Such excuse should not result in relieving the defaulting supplier from liability nor in dropping into the seller's lap an unearned bonus of damages over. The flexible adjustment machinery of this Article provides the solution under the provision on the obligation of good faith. A condition to his making good the claim of excuse is the turning over to the buyer of his rights against the defaulting source of supply to the extent of the buyer's contract in relation to which excuse is being claimed.

6. In situations in which neither sense nor justice is served by either answer when the issue is posed in flat terms of "excuse" or "no excuse," adjustment under the various provisions of this Article is necessary, especially the sections on good faith, on insecurity and assurance and on the reading of all provisions in the light of their purposes, and the general policy of this Act to use equitable principles in furtherance of commercial standards and good faith.

7. The failure of conditions which go to convenience or collateral values rather than to the commercial practicability of the main performance does not amount to a complete excuse. However, good faith and the reason of the present section and of the preceding one may properly be held to justify and even to require any needed delay involved in a good faith inquiry seeking a readjustment of the contract terms to meet the new conditions.

8. The provisions of this section are made subject to assumption of greater liability by agreement and such agreement is to be found not only in the expressed terms of the contract but in the circumstances surrounding the contracting, in trade usage and the like. Thus the exemptions of this section do not apply when the contingency in question is sufficiently foreshadowed at the time of contracting to be included among the business risks which are fairly to be regarded as part of the dickered terms, either consciously or as a matter of reasonable, commercial interpretation from the circumstances. (See Madeirense Do Brasil, S. A. v. Stulman-Emrick Lumber Co., 147 F.2d 399 (C.C.A., 2 Cir., 1945).) The exemption otherwise present through usage of trade under the present section may also be expressly negated by the language of the agreement. Generally, express agreements as to exemptions designed to enlarge upon or supplant the provisions of this section are to be read in the light of mercantile sense and reason, for this section itself sets up the commercial standard for normal and reasonable interpretation and provides a minimum beyond which agreement may not go.

Agreement can also be made in regard to the consequences of exemption as laid down in paragraphs (b) and (c) and the next section on procedure on notice claiming excuse.

9. The case of a farmer who has contracted to sell crops to be grown on designated land may be regarded as falling either within the section on casualty to identified goods or this section, and he may be excused, when there is a failure of the specific crop, either on the basis of the destruction of identified goods or because of the failure of a basic assumption of the contract.

Exemption of the buyer in the case of a "requirements" contract is covered by the "Output and Requirements" section both as to assumption and allocation of the relevant risks. But when a contract by a manufacturer to buy fuel or raw material makes no specific reference to a particular venture and no such reference may be drawn from the circumstances, commercial understanding views it as a general deal in the general market and not conditioned on any assumption of the continuing operation of the buyer's plant. Even when notice is given by the buyer that the supplies are needed to fill a specific contract of a normal commercial kind, commercial understanding does not see such a supply contract as conditioned on the continuance of the buyer's further contract for outlet. On the other hand, where the buyer's contract is in reasonable commercial understanding conditioned on a definite and specific venture or assumption as, for instance, a war procurement subcontract known to be based on a prime contract which is subject to termination, or a supply contract for a particular construction venture, the reason of the present section may well apply and entitle the buyer to the exemption.

10. Following its basic policy of using commercial practicability as a test for excuse, this section recognizes as of equal significance either a foreign or domestic regulation and disregards any technical distinctions between "law," "regulation," "order" and the like. Nor does it make the present action of the seller depend upon the eventual judicial determination of the legality of the particular governmental action. The seller's good faith belief in the validity of the regulation is the test under this Article and the best evidence of his good faith is the general commercial acceptance of the regulation. However, governmental intereference cannot excuse unless it truly "supervenes" in such a manner as to be beyond the seller's assumption of risk. And any action by the party claiming excuse which causes or colludes in inducing the governmental action preventing his performance would be in breach of good faith and would destroy his exemption.

11. An excused seller must fulfil his contract to the extent which the supervening contingency permits, and if the situation is such that his customers are generally affected he must take account of all in supplying one. Subsections (a) and (b), therefore, explicitly permit in any proration a fair and reasonable attention to the needs of regular customers who are probably relying on spot orders for supplies. Customers at different stages of the manufacturing process may be fairly treated by including the seller's manufacturing requirements. A fortiori, the seller may also take account of contracts later in date than the one in question. The fact that such spot orders may be closed at an advanced price causes no difficulty, since any allocation which exceeds normal past requirements will not be reasonable. However, good faith requires, when prices have advanced, that the seller exercise real care in making his allocations, and in case of doubt his contract customers should be favored and supplies prorated evenly among them regardless of price. Save for the extra care thus required by changes in the market, this section seeks to leave every reasonable business leeway to the seller.

Cross References:
    Point 1: Sections 2-613 and 2-614.
    Point 2: Section 1-102.
    Point 5: Sections 1-203 and 2-613.
    Point 6: Sections 1-102, 1-203 and 2-609.
    Point 7: Section 2-614.
    Point 8: Sections 1-201, 2-302 and 2-616.
    Point 9: Sections 1-102, 2-306 and 2-613.

Definitional Cross References:
    "Between merchants." Section 2-104.
    "Buyer." Section 2-103.
    "Contract." Section 1-201.
    "Contract for sale." Section 2-106.

"Good faith." Section 1-201.
"Merchant." Section 2-104.
"Notifies." Section 1-201.
"Seasonably." Section 1-204.
"Seller." Section 2-103.

§2-616. Procedure on Notice Claiming Excuse

(1) Where the buyer receives notification of a material or indefinite delay or an allocation justified under the preceding section he may by written notification to the seller as to any delivery concerned, and where the prospective deficiency substantially impairs the value of the whole contract under the provisions of this Article relating to breach of installment contracts (Section 2-612), then also as to the whole.

(a) terminate and thereby discharge any unexecuted portion of the contract; or

(b) modify the contract by agreeing to take his available quota in substitution.

(2) If after receipt of such notification from the seller the buyer fails so to modify the contract within a reasonable time not exceeding thirty days the contract lapses with respect to any deliveries affected.

(3) The provisions of this section may not be negated by agreement except in so far as the seller has assumed a greater obligation under the preceding section.

Part 7.   Remedies

§2-702. Seller's Remedies on Discovery of Buyer's Insolvency

(1) Where the seller discovers the buyer to be insolvent he may refuse delivery except for cash including payment for all goods theretofore delivered under the contract, and stop delivery under this Article (Section 2-705).

(2) Where the seller discovers that the buyer has received goods on credit while insolvent he may reclaim the goods upon demand made within ten days after the receipt, but if misrepresentation of solvency has been made to the particular seller in writing within three months before delivery the ten day limitation does not apply. Except as provided in this subsection the seller may not base a right to reclaim goods on the buyer's fraudulent or innocent misrepresentation of solvency or of intent to pay.

(3) The seller's right to reclaim under subsection (2) is subject to the rights of a buyer in ordinary course or other good faith purchaser under this Article (Section 2-403). Successful reclamation of goods excludes all other remedies with respect to them.

§2-703. Seller's Remedies in General

Where the buyer wrongfully rejects or revokes acceptance of goods or fails to make a payment due on or before delivery or repudiates with respect to a part or the whole, then with respect to any goods directly affected and, if the breach is of the whole contract (Section 2-612), then also with respect to the whole undelivered balance, the aggrieved seller may

> (a) withhold delivery of such goods;
>
> (b) stop delivery by any bailee as hereafter provided (Section 2-705);
>
> (c) proceed under the next section respecting goods still unidentified to the contract;
>
> (d) resell and recover damages as hereafter provided (Section 2-706);
>
> (e) recover damages for non-acceptance (Section 2-708) or in a proper case the price (Section 2-709);
>
> (f) cancel.

§2-704. Seller's Right to Identify Goods to the Contract Notwithstanding Breach or to Salvage Unfinished Goods

(1) An aggrieved seller under the preceding section may

> (a) identify to the contract conforming goods not already identified if at the time he learned of the breach they are in his possession or control;
>
> (b) treat as the subject of resale goods which have demonstrably been intended for the particular contract even though those goods are unfinished.

(2) Where the goods are unfinished an aggrieved seller may in the exercise of reasonable commercial judgment for the purposes of avoiding loss and of effective realization either complete the manufacture and wholly identify the goods to the contract or cease manufacture and resell for scrap or salvage value or proceed in any other reasonable manner.

§2-705. Seller's Stoppage of Delivery in Transit or Otherwise

(1) The seller may stop delivery of goods in the possession of a carrier or other bailee when he discovers the buyer to be insolvent (Section 2-702) and may stop delivery of carload, truckload, planeload or larger shipments of express or freight when the buyer repudiates or fails to make a payment due before delivery or if for any other reason the seller has a right to withhold or reclaim the goods.

(2) As against such buyer the seller may stop delivery until

> (a) receipt of the goods by the buyer; or
>
> (b) acknowledgment to the buyer by any bailee of the goods except a carrier that the bailee holds the goods for the buyer; or
>
> (c) such acknowledgment to the buyer by a carrier by reshipment or as warehouseman; or
>
> (d) negotiation to the buyer of any negotiable document of title covering the goods.

(3)(a) To stop delivery the seller must so notify as to enable the bailee by reasonable diligence to prevent delivery of the goods.

> (b) After such notification the bailee must hold and deliver the goods according to the directions of the seller but the seller is liable to the bailee for any ensuing charges or damages.

(c) If a negotiable document of title has been issued for goods the bailee is not obliged to obey a notification to stop until surrender of the document.

(d) A carrier who has issued a non-negotiable bill of lading is not obliged to obey a notification to stop received from a person other than the consignor.

§2-706. Seller's Resale Including Contract for Resale

(1) Under the conditions stated in Section 2-703 on seller's remedies, the seller may resell the goods concerned or the undelivered balance thereof. Where the resale is made in good faith and in a commercially reasonable manner the seller may recover the difference between the resale price and the contract price together with any incidental damages allowed under the provisions of this Article (Section 2-710), but less expenses saved in consequence of the buyer's breach.

(2) Except as otherwise provided in subsection (3) or unless otherwise agreed resale may be at public or private sale including sale by way of one or more contracts to sell or of identification to an existing contract of the seller. Sale may be as a unit or in parcels and at any time and place and on any terms but every aspect of the sale including the method, manner, time, place and terms must be commercially reasonable. The resale must be reasonably identified as referring to the broken contract, but it is not necessary that the goods be in existence or that any or all of them have been identified to the contract before the breach.

(3) Where the resale is at private sale the seller must give the buyer reasonable notification of his intention to resell.

(4) Where the resale is at public sale

(a) only identified goods can be sold except where there is a recognized market for a public sale of futures in goods of the kind; and

(b) it must be made at a usual place or market for public sale if one is reasonably available and except in the case of goods which are perishable or threaten to decline in value speedily the seller must give the buyer reasonable notice of the time and place of the resale; and

(c) if the goods are not to be within the view of those attending the sale the notification of sale must state the place where the goods are located and provide for their reasonable inspection by prospective bidders; and

(d) the seller may buy.

(5) A purchaser who buys in good faith at a resale takes the goods free of any rights of the original buyer even though the seller fails to comply with one or more of the requirements of this section.

(6) The seller is not accountable to the buyer for any profit made on any resale. A person in the position of a seller (Section 2-707) or a buyer who has rightfully rejected or justifiably revoked acceptance must account for any excess over the amount of his security interest, as hereinafter defined (subsection (3) of Section 2-711).

§2-708. Seller's Damages for Non-acceptance or Repudiation

(1) Subject to subsection (2) and to the provisions of this Article with respect to proof of market price (Section 2-723), the measure of damages for non-acceptance or repudiation by the buyer is the difference between the market price at the

time and place for tender and the unpaid contract price together with any incidental damages provided in this Article (Section 2-710), but less expenses saved in consequence of the buyer's breach.

(2) If the measure of damages provided in subsection (1) is inadequate to put the seller in as good a position as performance would have done then the measure of damages is the profit (including reasonable overhead) which the seller would have made from full performance by the buyer, together with any incidental damages provided in this Article (Section 2-710), due allowance for costs reasonably incurred and due credit for payments or proceeds of resale.

§2-709. Action for the Price

(1) When the buyer fails to pay the price as it becomes due the seller may recover, together with any incidental damages under the next section, the price
　(a) of goods accepted or of conforming goods lost or damaged within a commercially reasonable time, after risk of their loss has passed to the buyer; and
　(b) of goods identified to the contract if the seller is unable after reasonable effort to resell them at a reasonable price or the circumstances reasonably indicate that such effort will be unavailing.

(2) Where the seller sues for the price he must hold for the buyer any goods which have been identified to the contract and are still in his control except that if resale becomes possible he may resell them at any time prior to the collection of the judgment. The net proceeds of any such resale must be credited to the buyer and payment of the judgment entitles him to any goods not resold.

(3) After the buyer has wrongfully rejected or revoked acceptance of the goods or has failed to make a payment due or has repudiated (Section 2-610), a seller who is held not entitled to the price under this section shall nevertheless be awarded damages for non-acceptance under the preceding section.

§2-710. Seller's Incidental Damages

Incidental damages to an aggrieved seller include any commercially reasonable charges, expenses or commissions incurred in stopping delivery, in the transportation, care and custody of goods after the buyer's breach, in connection with return or resale of the goods or otherwise resulting from the breach.

§2-711. Buyer's Remedies in General; Buyer's Security Interest in Rejected Goods

(1) Where the seller fails to make delivery or repudiates or the buyer rightfully rejects or justifiably revokes acceptance then with respect to any goods involved, and with respect to the whole if the breach goes to the whole contract (Section 2-612), the buyer may cancel and whether or not he has done so may in addition to recovering so much of the price as has been paid

(a) "cover" and have damages under the next section as to all the goods affected whether or not they have been identified to the contract; or

(b) recover damages for non-delivery as provided in this Article (Section 2-713).

(2) Where the seller fails to deliver or repudiates the buyer may also

(a) if the goods have been identified recover them as provided in this Article (Section 2-502); or

(b) in a proper case obtain specific performance or replevy the goods as provided in this Article (Section 2-716).

(3) On rightful rejection or justifiable revocation of acceptance a buyer has a security interest in goods in his possession or control for any payments made on their price and any expenses reasonably incurred in their inspection, receipt, transportation, care and custody and may hold such goods and resell them in like manner as an aggrieved seller (Section 2-706).

§2-712. "Cover"; Buyer's Procurement of Substitute Goods

(1) After a breach within the preceding section the buyer may "cover" by making in good faith and without unreasonable delay any reasonable purchase of or contract to purchase goods in substitution for those due from the seller.

(2) The buyer may recover from the seller as damages the difference between the cost of cover and the contract price together with any incidental or consequential damages as hereinafter defined (Section 2-715), but less expenses saved in consequence of the seller's breach.

(3) Failure of the buyer to effect cover within this section does not bar him from any other remedy.

Official Comment

Prior Uniform Statutory Provision: None.

Purposes:

1. This section provides the buyer with a remedy aimed at enabling him to obtain the goods he needs thus meeting his essential need. This remedy is the buyer's equivalent of the seller's right to resell.

2. The definition of "cover" under subsection (1) envisages a series of contracts or sales, as well as a single contract or sale; goods not identical with those involved but commercially usable as reasonable substitutes under the circumstances of the particular case; and contracts on credit or delivery terms differing from the contract in breach, but again reasonable under the circumstances. The test of proper cover is whether at the time and place the buyer acted in good faith and in a reasonable manner, and it is immaterial that hindsight may later prove that the method of cover used was not the cheapest or most effective.

The requirement that the buyer must cover "without unreasonable delay" is not intended to limit the time necessary for him to look around and decide as to how he may best effect cover. The test here is similar to that generally used in this Article as to reasonable time and seasonable action.

3. Subsection (3) expresses the policy that cover is not a mandatory remedy for the buyer. The buyer is always free to choose between cover and damages for non-delivery under the next section.

However, this subsection must be read in conjunction with the section which limits the recovery of consequential damages to such as could not have been obviated by cover. Moreover, the operation of the section on specific performance of contracts for "unique" goods must be considered in this connection for availability of the goods to the particular buyer for his particular needs is the test for that remedy and inability to cover is made an express condition to the right of the buyer to replevy the goods.

4. This section does not limit cover to merchants, in the first instance. It is the vital and important remedy for the consumer buyer as well. Both are free to use cover: the domestic or non-merchant consumer is required only to act in normal good faith while the merchant buyer must also observe all reasonable commercial standards of fair dealing in the trade, since this falls within the definition of good faith on his part.

Cross References:
Point 1: Section 2-706.
Point 2: Section 1-204.
Point 3: Sections 2-713, 2-715 and 2-716.
Point 4: Section 1-203.

Definitional Cross References:
"Buyer." Section 2-103.
"Contract." Section 1-201.
"Good faith." Section 2-103.
"Goods." Section 2-105.
"Purchase." Section 1-201.
"Remedy." Section 1-201.
"Seller." Section 2-103.

§2-713. Buyer's Damages for Non-Delivery or Repudiation

(1) Subject to the provisions of this Article with respect to proof of market price (Section 2-723), the measure of damages for non-delivery or repudiation by the seller is the difference between the market price at the time when the buyer learned of the breach and the contract price together with any incidental and consequential damages provided in this Article (Section 2-715), but less expenses saved in consequence of the seller's breach.

(2) Market price is to be determined as of the place for tender or, in cases of rejection after arrival or revocation of acceptance, as of the place of arrival.

§2-714. Buyer's Damages for Breach in Regard to Accepted Goods

(1) Where the buyer has accepted goods and given notification (subsection (3) of Section 2-607) he may recover as damages for any non-conformity of tender the

loss resulting in the ordinary course of events from the seller's breach as determined in any manner which is reasonable.

(2) The measure of damages for breach of warranty is the difference at the time and place of acceptance between the value of the goods accepted and the value they would have had if they had been as warranted, unless special circumstances show proximate damages of a different amount.

(3) In a proper case any incidental and consequential damages under the next section may also be recovered.

§2-715. Buyer's Incidental and Consequential Damages

(1) Incidental damages resulting from the seller's breach include expenses reasonably incurred in inspection, receipt, transportation and care and custody of goods rightfully rejected, any commercially reasonable charges, expenses or commissions in connection with effecting cover and any other reasonable expense incident to the delay or other breach.

(2) Consequential damages resulting from the seller's breach include

(a) any loss resulting from general or particular requirements and needs of which the seller at the time of contracting had reason to know and which could not reasonably be prevented by cover or otherwise; and

(b) injury to person or property proximately resulting from any breach of warranty.

Official Comment

Prior Uniform Statutory Provisions: Subsection (2)(b)—Sections 69(7) and 70, Uniform Sales Act.

Changes: Rewritten.

Purposes of Changes and New Matter:

1. Subsection (1) is intended to provide reimbursement for the buyer who incurs reasonable expenses in connection with the handling of rightfully rejected goods or goods whose acceptance may be justifiably revoked, or in connection with effecting cover where the breach of the contract lies in non-conformity or non-delivery of the goods. The incidental damages listed are not intended to be exhaustive but are merely illustrative of the typical kinds of incidental damage.

2. Subsection (2) operates to allow the buyer, in an appropriate case, any consequential damages which are the result of the seller's breach. The "tacit agreement" test for the recovery of consequential damages is rejected. Although the older rule at common law which made the seller liable for all consequential damages of which he had "reason to know" in advance is followed, the liberality of that rule is modified by refusing to permit recovery unless the buyer could not reasonably have prevented the loss by cover or otherwise. Subparagraph (2) carries forward the provisions of the Prior Uniform statutory provision as to consequential damages resulting from breach of warranty, but modifies the rule by requiring first that the buyer attempt to minimize his damages in good faith, either by cover or otherwise.

3. In the absence of excuse under the section on merchant's excuse by failure of presupposed conditions, the seller is liable for consequential damages in all cases where he had reason to know of the buyer's general or particular requirements at the time of contracting. It is not necessary that there be a conscious acceptance of an insurer's liability on the seller's part, nor is his obligation for consequential damages limited to cases in which he fails to use due effort in good faith.

Particular needs of the buyer must generally be made known to the seller while general needs must rarely be made known to charge the seller with knowledge.

Any seller who does not wish to take the risk of consequential damages has available the section on contractual limitation of remedy.

4. The burden of proving the extent of loss incurred by way of consequential damage is on the buyer, but the section on liberal administration of remedies rejects any doctrine of certainty which requires almost mathematical precision in the proof of loss. Loss may be determined in any manner which is reasonable under the circumstances.

5. Subsection (2)(b) states the usual rule as to breach of warranty, allowing recovery for injuries "proximately" resulting from the breach. Where the injury involved follows the use of goods without discovery of the defect causing the damage, the question of "proximate" cause turns on whether it was reasonable for the buyer to use the goods without such inspection as would have revealed the defects. If it was not reasonable for him to do so, or if he did in fact discover the defect prior to his use, the injury would not proximately result from the breach of warranty.

6. In the case of sale of wares to one in the business of reselling them, resale is one of the requirements of which the seller has reason to know within the meaning of subsection (2)(a).

Cross References:
> Point 1: Section 2-608.
> Point 3: Sections 1-203, 2-615 and 2-719.
> Point 4: Section 1-106.

Definitional Cross References:
> "Cover." Section 2-712.
> "Goods." Section 1-201.
> "Person." Section 1-201.
> "Receipt" of goods. Section 2-103.
> "Seller." Section 2-103.

§2-716. Buyer's Right to Specific Performance or Replevin

(1) Specific performance may be decreed where the goods are unique or in other proper circumstances.

(2) The decree for specific performance may include such terms and conditions as to payment of the price, damages, or other relief as the court may deem just.

(3) The buyer has a right of replevin for goods identified to the contract if after reasonable effort he is unable to effect cover for such goods or the circumstances reasonably indicate that such effort will be unavailing or if the goods have been shipped under reservation and satisfaction of the security interest in them has been made or tendered. In the case of goods bought for personal, family, or household purposes, the buyer's right of replevin vests upon acquisition of a special property, even if the seller had not then repudiated or failed to deliver.

[As amended in 1999 to conform to Revised Article 9 (2000) of the Code.]

§2-717.   Deduction of Damages from the Price

The buyer on notifying the seller of his intention to do so may deduct all or any part of the damages resulting from any breach of the contract from any part of the price still due under the same contract.

§2-718.   Liquidation or Limitation of Damages; Deposits

(1) Damages for breach by either party may be liquidated in the agreement but only at an amount which is reasonable in the light of the anticipated or actual harm caused by the breach, the difficulties of proof of loss, and the inconvenience or nonfeasibility of otherwise obtaining an adequate remedy. A term fixing unreasonably large liquidated damages is void as a penalty.

(2) Where the seller justifiably withholds delivery of goods because of the buyer's breach, the buyer is entitled to restitution of any amount by which the sum of his payments exceeds

(a) the amount to which the seller is entitled by virtue of terms liquidating the seller's damages in accordance with subsection (1), or

(b) in the absence of such terms, twenty per cent of the value of the total performance for which the buyer is obligated under the contract or $500, whichever is smaller.

(3) The buyer's right to restitution under subsection (2) is subject to offset to the extent that the seller establishes

(a) a right to recover damages under the provisions of this Article other than subsection (1), and

(b) the amount or value of any benefits received by the buyer directly or indirectly by reason of the contract.

(4) Where a seller has received payment in goods their reasonable value or the proceeds of their resale shall be treated as payments for the purposes of subsection (2); but if the seller has notice of the buyer's breach before reselling goods received in part performance, his resale is subject to the conditions laid down in this Article on resale by an aggrieved seller (Section 2-706).

Official Comment

Prior Uniform Statutory Provision: None.

Purposes:

1. Under subsection (1) liquidated damage clauses are allowed where the amount involved is reasonable in the light of the circumstances of the case. The subsection sets forth explicitly the elements to be considered in determining the reasonableness of a liquidated damage clause. A term fixing unreasonably large liquidated damages is expressly made void as a penalty. An unreasonably small amount would be subject to similar criticism and might be stricken under the section on unconscionable contracts or clauses.

2. Subsection (2) refuses to recognize a forfeiture unless the amount of the payment so forfeited represents a reasonable liquidation of damages as determined under subsection (1). A special exception is made in the case of small amounts (20% of the price or $500, whichever is smaller) deposited as security. No distinction is made between cases in which the payment is to be applied on the price and those in which it is intended as security for performance. Subsection (2) is applicable to any deposit or down or part payment. In the case of a deposit or turn in of goods resold before the breach, the amount actually received on the resale is to be viewed as the deposit rather than the amount allowed the buyer for the trade in. However, if the seller knows of the breach prior to the resale of the goods turned in, he must make reasonable efforts to realize their true value, and this is assured by requiring him to comply with the conditions laid down in the section on resale by an aggrieved seller.

Cross References:

Point 1: Section 2-302.
Point 2: Section 2-706.

Definitional Cross References:

"Aggrieved party." Section 1-201.
"Agreement." Section 1-201.
"Buyer." Section 2-103.
"Goods." Section 2-105.
"Notice." Section 1-201.
"Party." Section 1-201.
"Remedy." Section 1-201.
"Seller." Section 2-103.
"Term." Section 1-201.

§2-719. Contractual Modification or Limitation of Remedy

(1) Subject to the provisions of subsections (2) and (3) of this section and of the preceding section on liquidation and limitation of damages,

(a) the agreement may provide for remedies in addition to or in substitution for those provided in this Article and may limit or alter the measure of damages recoverable under this Article, as by limiting the buyer's remedies to return of the goods and repayment of the price or to repair and replacement of non-conforming goods or parts; and

(b) resort to a remedy as provided is optional unless the remedy is expressly agreed to be exclusive, in which case it is the sole remedy.

(2) Where circumstances cause an exclusive or limited remedy to fail of its essential purpose, remedy may be had as provided in this Act.

(3) Consequential damages may be limited or excluded unless the limitation or exclusion is unconscionable. Limitation of consequential damages for injury to the person in the case of consumer goods is prima facie unconscionable but limitation of damages where the loss is commercial is not.

§2-721.   Remedies for Fraud

Remedies for material misrepresentation or fraud include all remedies available under this Article for non-fraudulent breach. Neither rescission or a claim for rescission of the contract for sale nor rejection or return of the goods shall bar or be deemed inconsistent with a claim for damages or other remedy.

§2-723.   Proof of Market Price: Time and Place

(1) If an action based on anticipatory repudiation comes to trial before the time for performance with respect to some or all of the goods, any damages based on market price (Section 2-708 or Section 2-713) shall be determined according to the price of such goods prevailing at the time when the aggrieved party learned of the repudiation.

(2) If evidence of a price prevailing at the times or places described in this Article is not readily available the price prevailing within any reasonable time before or after the time described or at any other place which in commercial judgment or under usage of trade would serve as a reasonable substitute for the one described may be used, making any proper allowance for the cost of transporting the goods to or from such other place.

(3) Evidence of a relevant price prevailing at a time or place other than the one described in this Article offered by one party is not admissible unless and until he has given the other party such notice as the court finds sufficient to prevent unfair surprise.

§2-725.   Statute of Limitations in Contracts for Sale

(1) An action for breach of any contract for sale must be commenced within four years after the cause of action has accrued. By the original agreement the parties may reduce the period of limitation to not less than one year but may not extend it.

(2) A cause of action accrues when the breach occurs, regardless of the aggrieved party's lack of knowledge of the breach. A breach of warranty occurs when tender of delivery is made, except that where a warranty explicitly extends to future performance of the goods and discovery of the breach must await the time of such performance the cause of action accrues when the breach is or should have been discovered.

(3) Where an action commenced within the time limited by subsection (1) is so terminated as to leave available a remedy by another action for the same breach such other action may be commenced after the expiration of the time limited and within six months after the termination of the first action unless the termination resulted from voluntary discontinuance or from dismissal for failure or neglect to prosecute.

(4) This section does not alter the law on tolling of the statute of limitations nor does it apply to causes of action which have accrued before this Act becomes effective.

ARTICLE 3. NEGOTIABLE INSTRUMENTS

Part 1. General Provisions and Definitions

§3-104. Negotiable Instrument

(a) Except as provided in subsections (c) and (d), "negotiable instrument" means an unconditional promise or order to pay a fixed amount of money, with or without interest or other charges described in the promise or order, if it:

(1) is payable to bearer or to order at the time it is issued or first comes into possession of a holder;

(2) is payable on demand or at a definite time; and

(3) does not state any other undertaking or instruction by the person promising or ordering payment to do any act in addition to the payment of money, but the promise or order may contain

(i) an undertaking or power to give, maintain, or protect collateral to secure payment,

(ii) an authorization or power to the holder to confess judgment or realize on or dispose of collateral, or

(iii) a waiver of the benefit of any law intended for the advantage or protection of an obligor.

(b) "Instrument" means a negotiable instrument.

(c) An order that meets all of the requirements of subsection (a), except paragraph (1), and otherwise falls within the definition of "check" in subsection (f) is a negotiable instrument and a check.

(d) A promise or order other than a check is not an instrument if, at the time it is issued or first comes into possession of a holder, it contains a conspicuous statement, however expressed, to the effect that the promise or order is not negotiable or is not an instrument governed by this Article.

(e) An instrument is a "note" if it is a promise and is a "draft" if it is an order. If an instrument falls within the definition of both "note" and "draft," a person entitled to enforce the instrument may treat it as either.

(f) "Check" means (i) a draft, other than a documentary draft, payable on demand and drawn on a bank or (ii) a cashier's check or teller's check. An instrument may be a check even though it is described on its face by another term, such as "money order."

(g) "Cashier's check" means a draft with respect to which the drawer and drawee are the same bank or branches of the same bank.

(h) "Teller's check" means a draft drawn by a bank (i) on another bank, or (ii) payable at or through a bank.

(i) "Traveler's check" means an instrument that (i) is payable on demand, (ii) is drawn on or payable at or through a bank, (iii) is designated by the term "traveler's check" or by a substantially similar term, and (iv) requires, as a condition to payment, a countersignature by a person whose specimen signature appears on the instrument.

(j) "Certificate of deposit" means an instrument containing an acknowledgment by a bank that a sum of money has been received by the bank and a promise by the bank to repay the sum of money. A certificate of deposit is a note of the bank.

Part 3.   Enforcement of Instruments

§3-302.   Holder in Due Course

(a) Subject to subsection (c) and Section 3-106(d), "holder in due course" means the holder of an instrument if:

(1) the instrument when issued or negotiated to the holder does not bear such apparent evidence of forgery or alteration or is not otherwise so irregular or incomplete as to call into question its authenticity; and

(2) the holder took the instrument

(i) for value,

(ii) in good faith,

(iii) without notice that the instrument is overdue or has been dishonored or that there is an uncured default with respect to payment of another instrument issued as part of the same series,

(iv) without notice that the instrument contains an unauthorized signature or has been altered,

(v) without notice of any claim to the instrument described in Section 3-306, and

(vi) without notice that any party has a defense or claim in recoupment described in Section 3-305(a).

(b) Notice of discharge of a party, other than discharge in an insolvency proceeding, is not notice of a defense under subsection (a), but discharge is effective against a person who became a holder in due course with notice of the discharge. Public filing or recording of a document does not of itself constitute notice of a defense, claim in recoupment, or claim to the instrument.

(c) Except to the extent a transferor or predecessor in interest has rights as a holder in due course, a person does not acquire rights of a holder in due course of an instrument taken

(i) by legal process or by purchase in an execution, bankruptcy, or creditor's sale or similar proceeding,

(ii) by purchase as part of a bulk transaction not in ordinary course of business of the transferor, or

(iii) as the successor in interest to an estate or other organization.

(d) If, under Section 3-303(a)(1), the promise of performance that is the consideration for an instrument has been partially performed, the holder may assert rights as a holder in due course of the instrument only to the fraction of the amount payable under the instrument equal to the value of the partial performance divided by the value of the promised performance.

(e) If (i) the person entitled to enforce an instrument has only a security interest in the instrument and (ii) the person obliged to pay the instrument has a defense, claim in recoupment, or claim to the instrument that may be asserted against the person who granted the security interest, the person entitled to enforce the instrument may assert rights as a holder in due course only to an amount payable under the instrument which, at the time of enforcement of the instrument, does not exceed the amount of the unpaid obligation secured.

(f) To be effective, notice must be received at a time and in a manner that gives a reasonable opportunity to act on it.

(g) This section is subject to any law limiting status as a holder in due course in particular classes of transactions.

§3-305. Defenses and Claims in Recoupment

(a) Except as otherwise provided in this section, the right to enforce the obligation of a party to pay an instrument is subject to the following:

(1) a defense of the obligor based on (i) infancy of the obligor to the extent it is a defense to a simple contract, (ii) duress, lack of legal capacity, or illegality of the transaction, which under other law, nullifies the obligation of the obligor, (iii) fraud that induced the obligor to sign the instrument with neither knowledge nor reasonable opportunity to learn of its character or its essential terms, or (iv) discharge of the obligor in insolvency proceedings;

(2) a defense of the obligor stated in another section of this Article or a defense of the obligor that would be available if the person entitled to enforce the instrument were enforcing a right to payment under a simple contract; and

(3) a claim in recoupment of the obligor against the original payee of the instrument if the claim arose from the transaction that gave rise to the instrument; but the claim of the obligor may be asserted against a transferee of the instrument only to reduce the amount owing on the instrument at the time the action is brought.

(b) The right of a holder in due course to enforce the obligation of a party to pay the instrument is subject to defenses of the obligor stated in subsection (a)(1), but is not subject to defenses of the obligor stated in subsection (a)(2) or claims in recoupment stated in subsection (a)(3) against a person other than the holder.

(c) Except as stated in subsection (d), in an action to enforce the obligation of a party to pay the instrument, the obligor may not assert against the person entitled to enforce the instrument a defense, claim in recoupment, or claim to the instrument (Section 3-306) of another person, but the other person's claim to the instrument may be asserted by the obligor if the other person is joined in the action and personally asserts the claim against the person entitled to enforce the instrument. An obligor is not obliged to pay the instrument if the person seeking enforcement of the instrument does not have rights of a holder in due course and the obligor proves that the instrument is a lost or stolen instrument.

(d) In an action to enforce the obligation of an accommodation party to pay an instrument, the accommodation party may assert against the person entitled to enforce the instrument any defense or claim in recoupment under subsection (a) that the accommodated party could assert against the person entitled to enforce the instrument, except the defenses of discharge in insolvency proceedings, infancy, and lack of legal capacity.

(e) In a consumer transaction, if law other than this article requires that an instrument include a statement to the effect that the rights of a holder or transferee are subject to a claim or defense that the issuer could assert against the original payee, and the instrument does not include such a statement:

(1) the instrument has the same effect as if the instrument included such a statement;

(2) the issuer may assert against the holder or transferee all claims and defenses that would have been available if the instrument included such a statement; and

(3) the extent to which claims may be asserted against the holder or transferee is determined as if the instrument included such a statement.

(f) This section is subject to law other than this article that establishes a different rule for consumer transactions.

§3-306.   Claims to an Instrument

A person taking an instrument, other than a person having rights of a holder in due course, is subject to a claim of a property or possessory right in the instrument or its proceeds, including a claim to rescind a negotiation and to recover the instrument or its proceeds. A person having rights of a holder in due course takes free of the claim to the instrument.

§3-311.   Accord and Satisfaction by Use of Instrument

(a) If a person against whom a claim is asserted proves that

(i) that person in good faith tendered an instrument to the claimant as full satisfaction of the claim,

(ii) the amount of the claim was unliquidated or subject to a bona fide dispute, and

(iii) the claimant obtained payment of the instrument, the following subsections apply.

(b) Unless subsection (c) applies, the claim is discharged if the person against whom the claim is asserted proves that the instrument or an accompanying written communication contained a conspicuous statement to the effect that the instrument was tendered as full satisfaction of the claim.

(c) Subject to subsection (d), a claim is not discharged under subsection (b) if either of the following applies:

(1) The claimant, if an organization, proves that

(i) within a reasonable time before the tender, the claimant sent a conspicuous statement to the person against whom the claim is asserted that communications concerning disputed debts, including an instrument tendered as full satisfaction of a debt, are to be sent to a designated person, office, or place, and

(ii) the instrument or accompanying communication was not received by that designated person, office, or place.

(2) The claimant, whether or not an organization, proves that within 90 days after payment of the instrument, the claimant tendered repayment of the amount of the instrument to the person against whom the claim is asserted. This paragraph does not apply if the claimant is an organization that sent a statement complying with paragraph (1)(i).

(d) A claim is discharged if the person against whom the claim is asserted proves that within a reasonable time before collection of the instrument was initiated, the claimant, or an agent of the claimant having direct responsibility with respect to the disputed obligation, knew that the instrument was tendered in full satisfaction of the claim.

ARTICLE 9.   SECURED TRANSACTIONS

Part 1.   General Provisions

§9-109.   Scope

(a) [General scope of article.] Except as otherwise provided in subsections (c) and (d), this article applies to:

(1) a transaction, regardless of its form, that creates a security interest in personal property or fixtures by contract;

(2) an agricultural lien;

(3) a sale of accounts, chattel paper, payment intangibles, or promissory notes;

(4) a consignment;

(5) a security interest arising under Sections 2-401, 2-505, 2-711(3), or 2A-508(5), as provided in Section 9-110; and

(6) a security interest arising under Sections 4-210 or 5-118.

(b) [Security interest in secured obligation.] The application of this article to a security interest in a secured obligation is not affected by the fact that the obligation is itself secured by a transaction or interest to which this article does not apply.

(c) [Extent to which article does not apply.] This article does not apply to the extent that:

(1) a statute, regulation, or treaty of the United States preempts this article;

(2) another statute of this State expressly governs the creation, perfection, priority, or enforcement of a security interest created by this State or a governmental unit of this State;

(3) a statute of another State, a foreign country, or a governmental unit of another State or a foreign country, other than a statute generally applicable to security interests, expressly governs creation, perfection, priority, or enforcement of a security interest created by the State, country, or governmental unit; or

(4) the rights of a transferee beneficiary or nominated person under a letter of credit are independent and superior under Section 5-114.

(d) [Inapplicability of article.] This article does not apply to:

(1) a landlord's lien, other than an agricultural lien;

(2) a lien, other than an agricultural lien, given by statute or other rule of law for services or materials, but Section 9-333 applies with respect to priority of the lien;

(3) an assignment of a claim for wages, salary, or other compensation of an employee;

(4) a sale of accounts, chattel paper, payment intangibles, or promissory notes as part of a sale of the business out of which they arose;

(5) an assignment of accounts, chattel paper, payment intangibles, or promissory notes which is for the purpose of collection only;

(6) an assignment of a right to payment under a contract to an assignee that is also obligated to perform under the contract;

(7) an assignment of a single account, payment intangible, or promissory note to an assignee in full or partial satisfaction of a preexisting indebtedness;

(8) a transfer of an interest in or an assignment of a claim under a policy of insurance, other than an assignment by or to a health-care provider of a health-care-insurance receivable and any subsequent assignment of the right to payment, but Sections 9-315 and 9-322 apply with respect to proceeds and priorities in proceeds;

(9) an assignment of a right represented by a judgment, other than a judgment taken on a right to payment that was collateral;

(10) a right of recoupment or set-off, but:

(A) Section 9-340 applies with respect to the effectiveness of rights of recoupment or set-off against deposit accounts; and

(B) Section 9-404 applies with respect to defenses or claims of an account debtor;

(11) the creation or transfer of an interest in or lien on real property, including a lease or rents thereunder, except to the extent that provision is made for:

(A) liens on real property in Sections 9-203 and 9-308;

(B) fixtures in Section 9-334;

(C) fixture filings in Sections 9-501, 9-502, 9-512, 9-516, and 9-519; and

(D) security agreements covering personal and real property in Section 9-604;

(12) an assignment of a claim arising in tort, other than a commercial tort claim, but Sections 9-315 and 9-322 apply with respect to proceeds and priorities in proceeds; or

(13) an assignment of a deposit account in a consumer transaction, but Sections 9-315 and 9-322 apply with respect to proceeds and priorities in proceeds.

§9-110. Security Interests Arising Under Article 2 or 2A

A security interest arising under Section 2-401, 2-505, 2-711(3), or 2A-508(5) is subject to this article. However, until the debtor obtains possession of the goods:

(1) the security interest is enforceable, even if Section 9-203(b)(3) has not been satisfied;

(2) filing is not required to perfect the security interest;

(3) the rights of the secured party after default by the debtor are governed by Article 2 or 2A; and

(4) the security interest has priority over a conflicting security interest created by the debtor.

Part 4. Rights of Third Parties

§9-403. Agreement Not to Assert Defenses Against Assignee

(a) ["Value."] In this section, "value" has the meaning provided in Section 3-303(a).

(b) [Agreement not to assert claim or defense.] Except as otherwise provided in this section, an agreement between an account debtor and an assignor not to assert against an assignee any claim or defense that the account debtor may have against the assignor is enforceable by an assignee that takes an assignment:

(1) for value;

(2) in good faith;

(3) without notice of a claim of a property or possessory right to the property assigned; and

(4) without notice of a defense or claim in recoupment of the type that may be asserted against a person entitled to enforce a negotiable instrument under Section 3-305(a).

(c) [When subsection (b) not applicable.] Subsection (b) does not apply to defenses of a type that may be asserted against a holder in due course of a negotiable instrument under Section 3-305(b).

(d) [Omission of required statement in consumer transaction.] In a consumer transaction, if a record evidences the account debtor's obligation, law other than this article requires that the record include a statement to the effect that the rights of an assignee are subject to claims or defenses that the account debtor could assert against the original obligee, and the record does not include such a statement:

(1) the record has the same effect as if the record included such a statement; and

(2) the account debtor may assert against an assignee those claims and defenses that would have been available if the record included such a statement.

(e) [Rule for individual under other law.] This section is subject to law other than this article which establishes a different rule for an account debtor who is an individual and who incurred the obligation primarily for personal, family, or household purposes.

(f) [Other law not displaced.] Except as otherwise provided in subsection (d), this section does not displace law other than this article which gives effect to an agreement by an account debtor not to assert a claim or defense against an assignee.

§9-404. Rights Acquired by Assignee; Claims and Defenses Against Assignee

(a) [Assignee's rights subject to terms, claims, and defenses; exceptions.] Unless an account debtor has made an enforceable agreement not to assert defenses or claims, and subject to subsections (b) through (e), the rights of an assignee are subject to:

(1) all terms of the agreement between the account debtor and assignor and any defense or claim in recoupment arising from the transaction that gave rise to the contract; and

(2) any other defense or claim of the account debtor against the assignor which accrues before the account debtor receives a notification of the assignment authenticated by the assignor or the assignee.

(b) [Account debtor's claim reduces amount owed to assignee.] Subject to subsection (c) and except as otherwise provided in subsection (d), the claim of an account debtor against an assignor may be asserted against an assignee under subsection (a) only to reduce the amount the account debtor owes.

(c) [Rule for individual under other law.] This section is subject to law other than this article which establishes a different rule for an account debtor who is an individual and who incurred the obligation primarily for personal, family, or household purposes.

(d) [Omission of required statement in consumer transaction.] In a consumer transaction, if a record evidences the account debtor's obligation, law other than this article requires that the record include a statement to the effect that the account debtor's recovery against an assignee with respect to claims and defenses against the assignor may not exceed amounts paid by the account debtor under the record, and the record does not include such a statement, the extent to which a claim of an account debtor against the assignor may be asserted against an assignee is determined as if the record included such a statement.

(e) [Inapplicability to health-care-insurance receivable.] This section does not apply to an assignment of a health-care-insurance receivable.

§9-405. Modification of Assigned Contract

(a) [Effect of modification on assignee.] A modification of or substitution for an assigned contract is effective against an assignee if made in good faith. The assignee acquires corresponding rights under the modified or substituted contract. The assignment may provide that the modification or substitution is a breach of contract by the assignor. This subsection is subject to subsections (b) through (d).

(b) [Applicability of subsection (a).] Subsection (a) applies to the extent that:

(1) the right to payment or a part thereof under an assigned contract has not been fully earned by performance; or

(2) the right to payment or a part thereof has been fully earned by performance and the account debtor has not received notification of the assignment under Section 9-406(a).

(c) [Rule for individual under other law.] This section is subject to law other than this article which establishes a different rule for an account debtor who is an individual and who incurred the obligation primarily for personal, family, or household purposes.

(d) [Inapplicability to health-care-insurance receivable.] This section does not apply to an assignment of a health-care-insurance receivable.

§9-406. Discharge of Account Debtor; Notification of Assignment; Identification and Proof of Assignment; Restrictions on Assignment of Accounts, Chattel Paper, Payment Intangibles, and Promissory Notes Ineffective

(a) [Discharge of account debtor; effect of notification.] Subject to subsections (b) through (i), an account debtor on an account, chattel paper, or a payment intangible may discharge its obligation by paying the assignor until, but not after, the account debtor receives a notification, authenticated by the assignor or the assignee, that the amount due or to become due has been assigned and that payment is to be made to the assignee. After receipt of the notification, the account debtor may discharge its obligation by paying the assignee and may not discharge the obligation by paying the assignor.

(b) [When notification ineffective.] Subject to subsection (h), notification is ineffective under subsection (a):

(1) if it does not reasonably identify the rights assigned;

(2) to the extent that an agreement between an account debtor and a seller of a payment intangible limits the account debtor's duty to pay a person other than the seller and the limitation is effective under law other than this article; or

(3) at the option of an account debtor, if the notification notifies the account debtor to make less than the full amount of any installment or other periodic payment to the assignee, even if:

(A) only a portion of the account, chattel paper, or payment intangible has been assigned to that assignee;

(B) a portion has been assigned to another assignee; or

(C) the account debtor knows that the assignment to that assignee is limited.

(c) [Proof of assignment.] Subject to subsection (h), if requested by the account debtor, an assignee shall seasonably furnish reasonable proof that the assignment has been made. Unless the assignee complies, the account debtor may discharge its obligation by paying the assignor, even if the account debtor has received a notification under subsection (a).

(d) [Term restricting assignment generally ineffective.] Except as otherwise provided in subsection (e) and Sections 2A-303 and 9-407, and subject to subsection (h), a term in an agreement between an account debtor and an assignor or in a promissory note is ineffective to the extent that it:

(1) prohibits, restricts, or requires the consent of the account debtor or person obligated on the promissory note to the assignment or transfer of, or the creation, attachment, perfection, or enforcement of a security interest in, the account, chattel paper, payment intangible, or promissory note; or

(2) provides that the assignment or transfer or the creation, attachment, perfection, or enforcement of the security interest may give rise to a default, breach, right of recoupment, claim, defense, termination, right of termination, or remedy under the account, chattel paper, payment intangible, or promissory note.

(e) [Inapplicability of subsection (d) to certain sales.] Subsection (d) does not apply to the sale of a payment intangible or promissory note.

(f) [Legal restrictions on assignment generally ineffective.] Except as otherwise provided in Sections 2A-303 and 9-407 and subject to subsections (h) and (i), a rule of law, statute, or regulation that prohibits, restricts, or requires the consent of a government, governmental body or official, or account debtor to the assignment or transfer of, or creation of a security interest in, an account or chattel paper is ineffective to the extent that the rule of law, statute, or regulation:

(1) prohibits, restricts, or requires the consent of the government, governmental body or official, or account debtor to the assignment or transfer of, or the creation, attachment, perfection, or enforcement of a security interest in the account or chattel paper; or

(2) provides that the assignment or transfer or the creation, attachment, perfection, or enforcement of the security interest may give rise to a default, breach, right of recoupment, claim, defense, termination, right of termination, or remedy under the account or chattel paper.

(g) [Subsection (b)(3) not waivable.] Subject to subsection (h), an account debtor may not waive or vary its option under subsection (b)(3).

(h) [Rule for individual under other law.] This section is subject to law other than this article which establishes a different rule for an account debtor who is an individual and who incurred the obligation primarily for personal, family, or household purposes.

(i) [Inapplicability to health-care-insurance receivable.] This section does not apply to an assignment of a health-care-insurance receivable.

(j) [Section prevails over specified inconsistent law.] This section prevails over any inconsistent provisions of the following statutes, rules, and regulations:

[List here any statutes, rules, and regulations containing provisions inconsistent with this section.]

Legislative Note: States that amend statutes, rules, and regulations to remove provisions inconsistent with this section need not enact subsection (j).

Convention on Contracts for the International Sale of Goods

EDITORS' NOTE

On December 11, 1986, the United States ratified the United Nations Convention on Contracts for the International Sale of Goods (CISG). The Convention, which became effective on January 1, 1988, was the product of almost two decades of work by the United Nations Commission on International Trade Law (UNCITRAL). The Commission was itself the outgrowth of earlier efforts to unify the law of international trade, particularly the Hague Convention of 1964, which had approved a uniform law on the international sale of goods. For the history of these developments, see John Honnold, The Uniform Law for the International Sale of Goods: the Hague Convention of 1964, 30 Law & Contemp. Probs. 326 (1965).

Article 1(1)(a) of the Convention provides that the Convention applies to contracts for the sale of goods between parties whose "places of business" are in different "States" (in the Convention countries are referred as "States"), when the States are parties to the Convention. Article 1(1)(b) also provides that the Convention applies when "the rules of private international law lead to the application of the law of a Contracting State," but this provision is not effective in the United States because the United States has taken an exception to it pursuant to Article 95 of the Convention. Many of the major trading partners of the United States are parties to the CISG, including Canada, Mexico, France, Germany, Italy, Japan, and the People's Republic of China. The United Kingdom, however, is not a party to the Convention.[*]

---

[*] The website for the United Nations Commission on International Trade Law (UNCITRAL) (*www. uncitral.org/uncitral/en/index.html*) provides a regularly updated list of states that have become parties to UNCITRAL treaties. As of May 12, 2012, the following 78 states had signed or acceded to the UN Convention on Contracts for the International Sale of Goods: Albania, Argentina, Armenia, Australia, Austria, Belarus, Belgium, Benin, Bosnia and Herzegovina, Bulgaria, Burundi, Canada, Chile, China, Colombia, Croatia, Cuba, Cyprus, Czech Republic, Denmark, Dominican Republic, Ecuador, Egypt, El Salvador, Estonia, Finland, France, Gabon, Georgia, Germany, Ghana, Greece, Guinea, Honduras, Hungary, Iceland, Iraq, Israel, Italy, Japan, Kyrgyzstan, Latvia, Lebanon, Lesotho, Liberia, Lithuania, Luxembourg, Macedonia, Mauritania, Mexico, Mongolia, Montenegro, Netherlands, New Zealand, Norway,

In determining the application of the Convention, the places of business of the parties to the contract are determinative, rather than their nationality, residence, or place of incorporation. If a party has multiple places of business, the place of business that has the "closest relationship to the contract and its performance" controls. Article 10(a). If a party has no place of business, then the party's "habitual residence" controls. Article 10(b).

A number of transactions are excluded from the CISG. See Articles 2-6. In particular, note that the CISG does not apply to consumer transactions, Article 2(a); to contracts in which the predominant part of the sale involves services, Article 3(2); and to contracts involving real estate, Article 1(1). Unlike the UCC, the CISG does not apply to liability of the seller for death or personal injury caused by goods. Article 5. The Convention also governs only formation of a contract and the rights and obligations arising from the contract. It does not cover defenses against enforcement of the contract, such as duress, fraud, mistake, and unconscionability. Article 4(a). Because of this "gap" in the coverage of the CISG, other bodies of law must be consulted when such issues arise. In particular, the UNIDROIT Principles of International Commercial Contracts, which are also reprinted later in this supplement, deal with such issues and were drafted to supplement the CISG.

Article 6 of the Convention provides that the parties may exclude the application of the Convention or "derogate from or vary the effect of any of its provisions." If a buyer and seller with places of business in different countries that are parties to the Convention agree to a sales contract that is silent about the applicability of the Convention, the Convention applies. Thus, it is important for lawyers to be aware of the applicability of the Convention and to evaluate its substantive provisions to decide whether a contract of sale should exclude the applicability of the Convention entirely or modify any of its provisions.

The CISG is in many respects the international equivalent of Article 2 of the UCC. If a sale of goods takes place between businesses in the United States, Article 2 of the UCC applies. On the other hand, if the sale takes place between companies that have their places of business in countries that are parties to the Convention, then the CISG rather than the UCC applies. For example, if an Italian manufacturer of shoes has a contract dispute with an American retailer, the CISG applies unless the parties have excluded its application by contract.

While the CISG is analogous to the UCC, many significant differences exist. For example, the UCC places a greater emphasis on formality than the CISG. The UCC contains both a statute of frauds (UCC §2-201) and a parol evidence rule (UCC §2-202), while the CISG does not have either provision. A useful comparison of the provisions of the CISG with domestic law can be found in the Letter of Submittal of the CISG from the State Department to President Reagan, dated August 30, 1983, reprinted in 3B U.L.A. Appendix III (1992) (on Westlaw). See generally William S. Dodge, Teaching the CISG in Contracts, 50 J. Leg. Ed. 72 (2000); Henry D. Gabriel, A Primer on the United Nations Convention on the International Sale of Goods: From the Perspective of the Uniform Commercial Code, 7 Ind. Int'l & Comp. L. Rev. 279 (1997); Symposium, Celebrating the 25th Anniversary of the United Nations

Paraguay, Peru, Poland, Republic of Korea, Republic of Moldova, Romania, Russian Federation, Saint Vincent and the Grenadines, San Marino, Serbia, Singapore, Slovakia, Slovenia, Spain, Sweden, Switzerland, Syrian Arab Republic, Turkey, Uganda, Ukraine, United States, Uruguay, Uzbekistan, Venezuela, and Zambia. Two states, Ghana and Venezuela, had not taken action to bring the treaty into effect under their national law.

Convention on Contracts for the International Sale of Goods, 25 J.L. & Com. 1 (2005); Symposium—Ten Years of the United Nations Sales Convention, 17 J.L. & Com. 181 (1998).

The CISG has been in force for more than 20 years and the number of reported decisions applying the Convention, within the United States and in foreign states, has steadily grown. A database devoted to the CISG has been established by Pace University and it provides access to a large number of case opinions and arbitral decisions as well as many other materials related to the CISG.[**] The CISG is applied by the court in Zapata Hermanos Sucesores, S.A. v. Hearthside Baking Co., included in Chapter 11 of the editors' casebook, Problems in Contract Law. Other representative cases applying the CISG include Chateau des Charmes Wines Ltd. v. Sabate USA Inc., 328 F.3d 528 (9th Cir. 2003) (mere performance of obligations under contract by buyer was not enough to manifest assent to sellers' attempted modification of contract to include a forum selection clause); MCC-Marble Ceramic Center, Inc. v. Ceramica Nuova d'Agostino, S.p.A., 144 F.3d 1384 (11th Cir. 1998) (under CISG subjective intentions of contracting parties are relevant to interpretation of written contract and parol evidence rule does not apply); Delchi Carrier S.p.A. v. Rotorex Corp., 71 F.3d 1024 (2d Cir. 1995) (applying CISG principles dealing with fundamental breach and measure of damages).

PART I. SPHERE OF APPLICATION AND GENERAL PROVISIONS

Chapter I. Sphere of Application

Chapter II. General Provisions

PART II. FORMATION OF THE CONTRACT

[**] The Pace University database can be found at: *http://www.cisg.law.pace.edu/cisg/guide.html.* As of May 12, 2012, the database contained access to more than 2,600 case and arbitral decisions.

*** The titles of articles listed in this table have been prepared by the editors and are not part of the Convention.

Convention on Contracts for the International Sale of Goods

THE STATES PARTIES TO THIS CONVENTION,

BEARING IN MIND the broad objectives in the resolutions adopted by the sixth special session of the General Assembly of the United Nations on the establishment of a New International Economic Order,

CONSIDERING that the development of international trade on the basis of equality and mutual benefit is an important element in promoting friendly relations among States,

BEING OF THE OPINION that the adoption of uniform rules which govern contracts for the international sale of goods and take into account the different social, economic and legal systems would contribute to the removal of legal barriers in international trade and promote the development of international trade,

Have agreed as follows:

PART I.   SPHERE OF APPLICATION AND GENERAL PROVISIONS

Chapter I.   Sphere of Application

Article 1

(1) This Convention applies to contracts of sale of goods between parties whose places of business are in different States:

(a) When the States are Contracting States; or

(b) When the rules of private international law lead to the application of the law of a Contracting State.[*]

(2) The fact that the parties have their places of business in different States is to be disregarded whenever this fact does not appear either from the contract or

---

[*] The United States has declared a reservation under Article 95 and is not bound by §1(b). — Eds.

from any dealings between, or from information disclosed by, the parties at any time before or at the conclusion of the contract.

(3) Neither the nationality of the parties nor the civil or commercial character of the parties or of the contract is to be taken into consideration in determining the application of this Convention.

Article 2

This Convention does not apply to sales:

(a) Of goods bought for personal, family or household use, unless the seller, at any time before or at the conclusion of the contract, neither knew nor ought to have known that the goods were bought for any such use;

(b) By auction;

(c) On execution or otherwise by authority of law;

(d) Of stocks, shares, investment securities, negotiable instruments or money;

(e) Of ships, vessels, hovercraft or aircraft;

(f) Of electricity

Article 3

(1) Contracts for the supply of goods to be manufactured or produced are to be considered sales unless the party who order[s] the goods undertakes to supply a substantial part of the materials necessary for such manufacture or production.

(2) This Convention does not apply to contracts in which the prepronderant part of the obligations of the party who furnishes the goods consists in the supply of labour or other services.

Article 4

This Convention governs only the formation of the contract of sale and the rights and obligations of the seller and the buyer arising from such a contract. In particular, except as otherwise expressly provided in this Convention, it is not concerned with:

(a) The validity of the contract or of any of its provisions or of any usage;

(b) The effect which the contract may have on the property in the goods sold.

Article 5

This Convention does not apply to the liability of the seller for death or personal injury caused by the goods to any person.

Article 6

The parties may exclude the application of this Convention or, subject to article 12, derogate from or vary the effect of any of its provisions.

Chapter II.   General Provisions

Article 7

(1) In the interpretation of this Convention, regard is to be had to its international character and to the need to promote uniformity in its application and the observance of good faith in international trade.

(2) Questions concerning matters governed by this Convention which are not expressly settled in it are to be settled in conformity with the general principles on which it is based or, in the absence of such principles, in conformity with the law applicable by virtue of the rules of private international law.

Article 8

(1) For the purposes of this Convention statements made by and other conduct of a party are to be interpreted according to his intent where the other party knew or could not have been unaware what that intent was.

(2) If the preceding paragraph is not applicable, statements made by and other conduct of a party are to be interpreted according to the understanding that a reasonable person of the same kind as the other party would have had in the same circumstances.

(3) In determining the intent of a party or the understanding a reasonable person would have had, due consideration is to be given to all relevant circumstances of the case including the negotiations, any practices which the parties have established between themselves, usages and any subsequent conduct of the parties.

Article 9

(1) The parties are bound by any usages to which they have agreed and by any practices which they have established between themselves.

(2) The parties are considered, unless otherwise agreed, to have impliedly made applicable to their contract or its formation a usage of which the parties knew or ought to have known and which in international trade is widely known to, and regularly observed by, parties to contracts of the type involved in the particular trade concerned.

Article 10

For the purpose of this Convention:

(a) If a party has more than one place of business, the place of business is that which has the closest relationship to the contract and its performance, having regard to the circumstances known to or contemplated by the parties at any time before or at the conclusion of the contract;

(b) If a party does not have a place of business, reference is to be made to his habitual residence.

Article 11

A contract of sale need not be concluded in or evidenced by writing and is not subject to any other requirement as to form. It may be proved by any means, including witnesses.

Article 12

Any provision of article 11, article 29 or Part II of this Convention that allows a contract of sale or its modification or termination by agreement or any offer, acceptance or other indication of intention to be made in any form other than in writing does not apply where any party has his place of business in a Contracting State which has made a declaration under article 96 of this Convention. The parties may not derogate from or vary the effect of this article.

Article 13

For the purposes of this Convention "writing" includes telegram and telex.

PART II.   FORMATION OF THE CONTRACT

Article 14

(1) A Proposal for concluding a contract addressed to one or more specific persons constitutes an offer if it is sufficiently definite and indicates the intention of the offeror to be bound in case of acceptance. A proposal is sufficiently definite if it indicates the goods and expressly or implicitly fixes or makes provision for determining the quantity and the price.

(2) A proposal other than one addressed to one or more specific persons is to be considered merely as an invitation to make offers, unless the contrary is clearly indicated by the person making the proposal.

Article 15

(1) An offer becomes effective when it reaches the offeree.

(2) An offer, even if it is irrevocable, may be withdrawn if the withdrawal reaches the offeree before or at the same time as the offer.

Article 16

(1) Until a contract is concluded an offer may be revoked if the revocation reaches the offeree before he has dispatched an acceptance.

(2) However, an offer cannot be revoked:

(a) If it indicates, whether by stating a fixed time for acceptance or otherwise, that it is irrevocable; or

(b) If it was reasonable for the offeree to rely on the offer as being irrevocable and the offeree has acted in reliance on the offer.

Article 17

An offer, even if it is irrevocable, is terminated when a rejection reaches the offeror.

Article 18

(1) A statement made by or other conduct of the offeree indicating assent to an offer is an acceptance. Silence or inactivity does not in itself amount to acceptance.

(2) An acceptance of an offer becomes effective at the moment the indication of assent reaches the offeror. An acceptance is not effective if the indication of assent does not reach the offeror within the time he has fixed or, if no time is fixed, within a reasonable time, due account being taken of the circumstances of the transaction,

including the rapidity of the means of communication employed by the offeror. An oral offer must be accepted immediately unless the circumstances indicate otherwise.

(3) However, if, by virtue of the offer or as a result of practices which the parties have established between themselves or of usage, the offeree may indicate assent by performing an act, such as one relating to the dispatch of the goods or payment of the price, without notice to the offeror, the acceptance is effective at the moment the act is performed, provided that the act is performed within the period of time laid down in the preceding paragraph.

Article 19

(1) A reply to an offer which purports to be an acceptance but contains additions, limitations or other modifications is a rejection of the offer and constitutes a counter-offer.

(2) However, a reply to an offer which purports to be an acceptance but contains additional or different terms which do not materially alter the terms of the offer constitutes an acceptance, unless the offeror, without undue delay, objects orally to the discrepancy or dispatches a notice to that effect. If he does not so object, the terms of the contract are the terms of the offer with the modifications contained in the acceptance.

(3) Additional or different terms relating, among other things, to the price, payment, quality and quantity of the goods, place and time of delivery, extent of one party's liability to the other or the settlement of disputes are considered to alter the terms of the offer materially.

Article 20

(1) A period of time for acceptance fixed by the offeror in a telegram or a letter begins to run from the moment the telegram is handed in for dispatch or from the date shown on the letter or, if no such date is shown, from the date shown on the envelope. A period of time for acceptance fixed by the offeror by telephone, telex or other means of instantaneous communication, begins to run from the moment that the offer reaches the offeree.

(2) Official holidays or non-business days occurring during the period for acceptance are included in calculating the period. However, if a notice of acceptance cannot be delivered at the address of the offeror on the last day of the period because that day falls on an official holiday or a non-business day at the place of business of the offeror, the period is extended until the first business day which follows.

Article 21

(1) A late acceptance is nevertheless effective as an acceptance if without delay the offeror orally so informs the offeree or dispatches a notice to that effect.

(2) If a letter or other writing containing a late acceptance shows that it has been sent in such circumstances that if its transmission had been normal it would have reached the offeror in due time, the late acceptance is effective as an acceptance unless, without delay, the offeror orally informs the offeree that he considers his offer as having lapsed or dispatches a notice to that effect.

Article 22

An acceptance may be withdrawn if the withdrawal reaches the offeror before or at the same time as the acceptance would have become effective.

Article 23

A contract is concluded at the moment when an acceptance of an offer becomes effective in accordance with the provisions of this Convention.

Article 24

For the purposes of this Part of the Convention, an offer, declaration of acceptance or any other indication of intention "reaches" the addressee when it is made orally to him or delivered by any other means to him personally, to his place of business or mailing address or, if he does not have a place of business or mailing address, to his habitual residence.

PART III. SALE OF GOODS

Chapter I. General Provisions

Article 25

A breach of contract committed by one of the parties is fundamental if it results in such detriment to the other party as substantially to deprive him of what he is entitled to expect under the contract, unless the party in breach did not foresee, and a reasonable person of the same kind in the same circumstances would not have foreseen, such a result.

Article 26

A declaration of avoidance of the contract is effective only if made by notice to the other party.

Article 27

Unless otherwise expressly provided in this Part of the Convention, if any notice, request or other communication is given or made by a party in accordance with this Part and by means appropriate in the circumstances, a delay or error in the transmission of the communication or its failure to arrive does not deprive that party of the right to rely on the communication.

Article 28

If, in accordance with the provisions of this Convention, one party is entitled to require performance of any obligation by the other party, a court is not bound to enter a judgement for specific performance unless the court would do so under its own law in respect of similar contracts of sale not governed by this Convention.

Article 29

(1) A contract may be modified or terminated by the mere agreement of the parties.

(2) A contract in writing which contains a provision requiring any modification or termination by agreement to be in writing may not be otherwise modified or terminated by agreement. However, a party may be precluded by his conduct from asserting such a provision to the extent that the other party has relied on that conduct.

Chapter II.   Obligations of the Seller

Article 30

The seller must deliver the goods, hand over any documents relating to them and transfer the property in the goods, as required by the contract and this Convention.

Section I.   Delivery of the Goods and Handing Over of Documents

Article 31

If the seller is not bound to deliver the goods at any other particular place, his obligation to deliver consists:

(a) If the contract of sale involves carriage of the goods — in handing the goods over to the first carrier for transmission to the buyer;

(b) If, in cases not within the preceding subparagraph, the contract relates to specific goods, or unidentified goods to be drawn from a specific stock or to be manufactured or produced, and at the time of the conclusion of the contract the parties knew that the goods were at, or were to be manufactured or produced at, a particular place — in placing the goods at the buyer's disposal at that place;

(c) In other cases — in placing the goods at the buyer's disposal at the place where the seller had his place of business at the time of the conclusion of the contract.

Article 32

(1) If the seller in accordance with the contract or this Convention, hands the goods over to a carrier and if the goods are not clearly identified to the contract by markings on the goods, by shipping documents or otherwise, the seller must give the buyer notice of the consignment specifying the goods.

(2) If the seller is bound to arrange for carriage of the goods, he must make such contracts as are necessary for carrige to the place fixed by means of transportation appropriate in the circumstances and according to the usual terms for such transportation.

(3) If the seller is not bound to effect insurance in respect of the carriage of the goods, he must, at the buyer's request, provide him with all available information necessary to enable him to effect such insurance.

Article 33

The seller must deliver the goods:

    (a) If a date is fixed by or determinable from the contract, on that date;

    (b) If a period of time is fixed by or determinable from the contract, at any time within that period unless circumstances indicate that the buyer is to choose a date; or

    (c) In any other case, within a reasonable time after the conclusion of the contract.

Article 34

If the seller is bound to hand over documents relating to the goods, he must hand them over at the time and place and in the form required by the contract. If the seller has handed over documents before that time, he may, up to that time, cure any lack of conformity in the documents, if the exercise of this right does not cause the buyer unreasonable inconvenience or unreasonable expense. However, the buyer retains any right to claim damages as provided for in this Convention.

Section II.   Conformity of the Goods and Third Party Claims

Article 35

(1) The seller must deliver goods which are of the quantity, quality and description required by the contract and which are contained or packaged in the manner required by the contract.

(2) Except where the parties have agreed otherwise, the goods do not conform with the contract unless they:

    (a) Are fit for the purposes for which goods of the same description would ordinarily be used;

    (b) Are fit for any particular purpose expressly or impliedly made known to the seller at the time of the conclusion of the contract, except where the circumstances show that the buyer did not rely, or that it was unreasonable for him to rely, on the seller's skill and judgment;

    (c) Possess the qualities of goods which the seller has held out to the buyer as a sample or model;

    (d) Are contained or packaged in the manner usual for such goods or, where there is no such manner, in a manner adequate to preserve and protect the goods.

(3) The seller is not liable under subparagraphs (a) to (d) of the preceding paragraph for any lack of conformity of the goods if at the time of the conclusion of the contract the buyer knew or could not have been unaware of such lack of conformity.

Article 36

(1) The seller is liable in accordance with the contract and this Convention for any lack of conformity which exists at the time when the risk passes to the buyer, even though the lack of conformity becomes apparent only after that time.

(2) The seller is also liable for any lack of conformity which occurs after the time indicated in the preceding paragraph and which is due to a breach of any of his obligations, including a breach of any guarantee that for a period of time the goods will remain fit for their ordinary purpose or for some particular purpose or will retain specified qualities or characteristics.

Article 37

If the seller has delivered goods before the date for delivery, he may, up to that date, deliver any missing part or make up any deficiency in the quantity of the goods delivered, or deliver goods in replacement of any nonconforming goods delivered or remedy any lack of conformity in the goods delivered, provided that the exercise of this right does not cause the buyer unreasonable inconvenience or unreasonable expense. However, the buyer retains any right to claim damages as provided for in this Convention.

Article 38

(1) The buyer must examine the goods, or cause them to be examined, within as short a period as is practicable in the circumstances.

(2) If the contract involves carriage of the goods, examination my be deferred until after the goods have arrived at their destination.

(3) If the goods are redirected in transit or redispatched by the buyer without a reasonable opportunity for examination by him and at the time of the conclusion of the contract the seller knew or ought to have known of the possibility of such redirection or redispatch, examination may be deferred until after the goods have arrived at the new destination.

Article 39

(1) The buyer loses the right to rely on a lack of conformity of the goods if he does not give notice to the seller specifying the nature of the lack of conformity within a reasonable time after he has discovered it or ought to have discovered it.

(2) In any event, the buyer loses the right to rely on a lack of conformity of the goods if he does not give the seller notice thereof at the latest within a period of two years from the date on which the goods were actually handed over to the buyer, unless this time-limit is inconsistent with a contractual period of guarantee.

Article 40

The seller is not entitled to rely on the provisions of articles 38 and 39 if the lack of conformity relates to facts of which he knew or could not have been unaware and which he did not disclose to the buyer.

Article 41

The seller must deliver goods which are free from any right or claim of a third party, unless the buyer agreed to take the goods subject to that right or claim. However, if such right or claim is based on industrial property or other intellectual property, the seller's obligation is governed by article 42.

Article 42

(1) The seller must deliver goods which are free from any right or claim of a third party based on industrial property or other intellectual property, of which at the time of the conclusion of the contract the seller knew or could not have been unaware, provided that the right or claim is based on industrial property or other intellectual property:

(a) Under the law of the State where the goods will be resold or otherwise used, if it was contemplated by the parties at the time of the conclusion of the contract that the goods would be resold or otherwise used in that State; or

(b) In any other case, under the law of the State where the buyer has his place of business.

(2) The obligation of the seller under the preceding paragraph does not extend to cases where:

(a) At the time of the conclusion of the contract the buyer knew or could not have been unaware of the right or claim; or

(b) The right or claim results from the seller's compliance with technical drawings, designs, formulae or other such specifications furnished by the buyer.

Article 43

(1) The buyer loses the right to rely on the provisions of article 41 or article 42 if he does not give notice to the seller specifying the nature of the right or claim of the third party within a reasonable time after he has become aware or ought to have become aware of the right or claim.

(2) The seller is not entitled to rely on the provisions of the preceding paragraph if he knew of the right or claim of the third party and the nature of it.

Article 44

Notwithstanding the provisions of paragraph (1) of article 39 and paragraph (1) of article 43, the buyer may reduce the price in accordance with article 50 or claim damages, except for loss of profit, if he has a reasonable excuse for his failure to give the required notice.

Section III.   Remedies for Breach of Contract by the Seller

Article 45

(1) If the seller fails to perform any of his obligations under the contract or this Convention, the buyer may:

(a) Exercise the rights provided in articles 46 to 52;

(b) Claim damages as provided in articles 74 to 77.

(2) The buyer is not deprived of any right he may have to claim damages by exercising his right to other remedies.

(3) No period of grace may be granted to the seller by a court or arbitral tribunal when the buyer resorts to a remedy for breach of contract.

Article 46

(1) The buyer may require performance by the seller of his obligations unless the buyer has resorted to a remedy which is inconsistent with this requirement.

(2) If the goods do not conform with the contract, the buyer may require delivery of substitute goods only if the lack of conformity constitutes a fundamental breach of contract and a request for substitute goods is made either in conjunction with notice given under article 39 or within a reasonable time thereafter.

(3) If the goods do not conform with the contract, the buyer may require the seller to remedy the lack of conformity by repair, unless this is unreasonable having regard to all the circumstances. A request for repair must be made either in conjunction with notice given under article 39 or within a reasonable time thereafter.

Article 47

(1) The buyer may fix an additional period of time of reasonable length for performance by the seller of his obligations.

(2) Unless the buyer has received notice from the seller that he will not perform within the period so fixed, the buyer may not, during that period, resort to any remedy for breach of contract. However, the buyer is not deprived thereby of any right he may have to claim damages for delay in performance.

Article 48

(1) Subject to article 49, the seller may, even after the date for delivery, remedy at his own expense any failure to perform his obligations, if he can do so without unreasonable delay and without causing the buyer unreasonable inconvenience or uncertainty of reimbursement by the seller of expenses advanced by the buyer. However, the buyer retains any right to claim damages as provided for in this Convention.

(2) If the seller requests the buyer to make known whether he will accept performance and the buyer does not comply with the request within a reasonable time, the seller may perform within the time indicated in his request. The buyer may not, during that period of time, resort to any remedy which is inconsistent with performance by the seller.

(3) A notice by the seller that he will perform within a specified period of time is assumed to include a request, under the preceding paragraph, that the buyer make known his decision.

(4) A request or notice by the seller under paragraph (2) or (3) of this article is not effective unless received by the buyer.

Article 49

(1) The buyer may declare the contract avoided:

(a) If the failure by the seller to perform any of his obligations under the contract or this Convention amounts to a fundamental breach of contract; or

(b) In case of non-delivery, if the seller does not deliver the goods within the additional period of time fixed by the buyer in accordance with paragraph (1) of article 47 or declares that he will not deliver within the period so fixed.

(2) However, in cases where the seller has delivered the goods, the buyer loses the right to declare the contract avoided unless he does so:

(a) In respect of late delivery, within a reasonable time after he has become aware that delivery has been made:

(b) In respect of any breach other than late delivery, within a reasonable time:

(i) After he knew or ought to have known of the breach;

(ii) After the expiration of any additional period of time fixed by the buyer in accordance with paragraph (1) of article 47, or after the seller has declared that he will not perform his obligations within such an additional period; or

(iii) After the expiration of any additional period of time indicated by the seller in accordance with paragraph (2) of article 48, or after the buyer has declared that he will not accept performance.

Article 50

If the goods do not conform with the contract and whether or not the price has already been paid, the buyer may reduce the price in the same proportion as the value that the goods actually delivered had at the time of the delivery bears to the value that conforming goods would have had at that time. However, if the seller remedies any failure to perform his obligations in accordance with article 37 or article 48 or if the buyer refuses to accept performance by the seller in accordance with those articles, the buyer may not reduce the price.

Article 51

(1) If the seller delivers only a part of the goods or if only a part of the goods delivered is in conformity with the contract, articles 46 to 50 apply in respect of the part which is missing or which does not conform.

(2) The buyer may declare the contract avoided in its entirety only if the failure to make delivery completely or in conformity with the contract amounts to a fundamental breach of the contract.

Article 52

(1) If the seller delivers the goods before the date fixed, the buyer may take delivery or refuse to take delivery.

(2) If the seller delivers a quantity of goods greater than that provided for in the contract, the buyer may take delivery or refuse to take delivery of the excess quantity. If the buyer takes delivery of all or part of the excess quantity, he must pay for it at the contract rate.

Chapter III.   Obligations of the Buyer

Article 53

The buyer must pay the price for the goods and take delivery of them as required by the contract and this Convention.

Section I. Payment of the Price

Article 54

The buyer's obligation to pay the price includes taking such steps and complying with such formalities as may be required under the contract or any laws and regulations to enable payment to be made.

Article 55

Where a contract has been validly concluded but does not expressly or implicitly fix or make provision for determining the price, the parties are considered, in the absence of any indication to the contrary, to have impliedly made reference to the price generally charged at the time of the conclusion of the contract for such goods sold under comparable circumstances in the trade concerned.

Article 56

If the price is fixed according to the weight of the goods, in case of doubt it is to be determined by the net weight.

Article 57

(1) If the buyer is not bound to pay the price at any other particular place, he must pay it to the seller:

(a) At the seller's place of business; or

(b) If the payment is to be made against the handing over of the goods or of documents, at the place where the handing over takes place.

(2) The seller must bear any increase in the expenses incidental to payment which is caused by a change in his place of business subsequent to the conclusion of the contract.

Article 58

(1) If the buyer is not bound to pay the price at any other specific time, he must pay it when the seller places either the goods or documents controlling their disposition at the buyer's disposal in accordance with the contract and this Convention. The seller may make such payment a condition for handing over the goods or documents.

(2) If the contract involves carriage of the goods, the seller may dispatch the goods on terms whereby the goods, or documents controlling their disposition, will not be handed over to the buyer except against payment of the price.

(3) The buyer is not bound to pay the price until he has had an opportunity to examine the goods, unless the procedures for delivery or payment agreed upon by the parties are inconsistent with his having such an opportunity.

Article 59

The buyer must pay the price on the date fixed by or determinable from the contract and this Convention without the need for any request or compliance with any formality on the part of the seller.

Section II.   Taking Delivery

Article 60

The buyer's obligation to take delivery consists:
(a) In doing all the acts which could reasonably be expected of him in order to enable the seller to make delivery; and
(b) In taking over the goods.

Section III.   Remedies for Breach of Contract by the Buyer

Article 61

(1) If the buyer fails to perform any of his obligations under the contract or this Convention, the seller may:
(a) Exercise the rights provided in articles 62 to 65;
(b) Claim damages as provided in articles 74 to 77.
(2) The seller is not deprived of any rights he may have to claim damages by exercising his right to other remedies.
(3) No period of grace may be granted to the buyer by a court or arbitral tribunal when the seller resorts to a remedy for breach of contract.

Article 62

The seller may require the buyer to pay the price, take delivery or perform his other obligations, unless the seller has resorted to a remedy which is inconsistent with this requirement.

Article 63

(1) The seller may fix an additional period of time of reasonable length for performance by the buyer of his obligations.
(2) Unless the seller has received notice from the buyer that he will not perform within the period so fixed, the seller may not, during that period, resort to any remedy for breach of contract. However, the seller is not deprived thereby of any right he may have to claim damages for delay in performance.

Article 64

(1) The seller may declare the contract avoided:
(a) If the failure by the buyer to perform any of his obligations under the contract or this Convention amounts to a fundamental breach of contract; or
(b) If the buyer does not, within the additional period of time fixed by the seller in accordance with paragraph (1) of article 63, perform his obligation to pay the price or take delivery of the goods, or declares that he will not do so within the period so fixed.
(2) However, in cases where the buyer has paid the price, the seller loses the right to declare the contract avoided unless he does so:
(a) In respect of late performance by the buyer, before the seller has become aware that performance has been rendered; or

(b) In respect of any breach other than late performance by the buyer, within a reasonable time:

(i) After the seller knew or ought to have known of the breach; or

(ii) After the expiration of any additional period of time fixed by the seller in accordance with paragraph (1) of article 63, or after the buyer has declared that he will not perform his obligations within such an additional period.

Article 65

(1) If under the contract the buyer is to specify the form, measurement or other features of the goods and he fails to make such specification either on the date agreed upon or within a reasonable time after receipt of a request from the seller, the seller may, without prejudice to any other rights he may have, make the specification himself in accordance with the requirements of the buyer that may be known to him.

(2) If the seller makes the specification himself, he must inform the buyer of the details thereof and must fix a reasonable time within which the buyer may make a different specification. If, after receipt of such a communication, the buyer fails to do so within the time so fixed, the specification made by the seller is binding.

Chapter IV. Passing of Risk

Article 66

Loss of or damage to the goods after the risk has passed to the buyer does not discharge him from his obligation to pay the price, unless the loss or damage is due to an act or omission of the seller.

Article 67

(1) If the contract of sale involves carriage of the goods and the seller is not bound to hand them over at a particular place, the risk passes to the buyer when the goods are handed over to the first carrier for transmission to the buyer in accordance with the contract of sale. If the seller is bound to hand the goods over to a carrier at a particular place, the risk does not pass to the buyer until the goods are handed over the the carrier at that place. The fact that the seller is authorized to retain documents controlling the disposition of the goods does not affect the passage of the risk.

(2) Nevertheless, the risk does not pass to the buyer until the goods are clearly identified to the contract, whether by markings on the goods, by shipping documents, by notice given to the buyer or otherwise.

Article 68

The risk in respect of goods sold in transit passes to the buyer from the time of the conclusion of the contract. However, if the circumstances so indicate, the risk is assumed by the buyer from the time the goods were handed over to the carrier who issued the documents embodying the contract of carriage. Nevertheless, if at the time of the conclusion of the contract of sale the seller knew or ought to have known that the goods had been lost or damaged and did not disclose this to the buyer, the loss or damage is at the risk of the seller.

Article 69

(1) In cases not within articles 67 and 68, the risk passes to the buyer when he takes over the goods or, if he does not do so in due time, from the time when the goods are placed at his disposal and he commits a breach of contract by failing to take delivery.

(2) However, if the buyer is bound to take over the goods at a place other than a place of business of the seller, the risk passes when delivery is due and the buyer is aware of the fact that the goods are placed at his disposal at that place.

(3) If the contract relates to goods not then identified, the goods are considered not to be placed at the disposal of the buyer until they are clearly identified to the contract.

Article 70

If the seller has committed a fundamental breach of contract, articles 67, 68, and 69 do not impair the remedies available to the buyer on account of the breach.

Chapter V. *Provisions Common to the Obligations of the Seller and of the Buyer*

Section I. Anticipatory Breach and Installment Contracts

Article 71

(1) A party may suspend the performance of his obligations if, after the conclusion of the contract, it becomes apparent that the other party will not perform a substantial part of his obligations as a result of:

(a) A serious deficiency in his ability to perform or in his creditworthiness; or

(b) His conduct in preparing to perform or in performing the contract.

(2) If the seller has already dispatched the goods before the grounds described in the preceding paragraph become evident, he may prevent the handing over of the goods to the buyer even though the buyer holds a document which entitles him to obtain them. The present paragraph relates only to the rights in the goods as between the buyer and the seller.

(3) A party suspending performance, whether before or after dispatch of the goods, must immediately give notice of the suspension to the other party and must continue with performance if the other party provides adequate assurance of his performance.

Article 72

(1) If prior to the date for performance of the contract it is clear that one of the parties will commit a fundamental breach of contract, the other party may declare the contract avoided.

(2) If time allows, the party intending to declare the contract avoided must give reasonable notice to the other party in order to permit him to provide adequate assurance of his performance.

(3) The requirements of the preceding paragraph do not apply if the other party has declared that he will not perform his obligations.

Article 73

(1) In the case of a contract for delivery of goods by installments, if the failure of one party to perform any of his obligations in respect of any instalment constitutes a fundamental breach of contract with respect to that instalment, the other party may declare the contract avoided with respect to that instalment.

(2) If one party's failure to perform any of his obligations in respect of any instalment gives the other party good grounds to conclude that a fundamental breach of contract will occur with respect to future instalments, he may declare the contract avoided for the future, provided that he does so within a reasonable time.

(3) A buyer who declares the contract avoided in respect of any delivery may, at the same time, declare it avoided in respect of deliveries already made or of future deliveries if, by reason of their interdependence, those deliveries could not be used for the purpose contemplated by the parties at the time of the conclusion of the contract.

Section II. Damages

Article 74

Damages for breach of contract by one party consist of a sum equal to the loss, including loss of profit, suffered by the other party as a consequence of the breach. Such damages may not exceed the loss which the party in breach foresaw or ought to have foreseen at the time of the conclusion of the contract, in the light of the facts and matters of which he then knew or ought to have known, as a possible consequence of the breach of contract.

Article 75

If the contract is avoided and if, in a reasonable manner and within a reasonable time after avoidance, the buyer has bought goods in replacement or the seller has resold the goods, the party claiming damages may recover the difference between the contract price and the price in the substitute transaction as well as any further damages recoverable under article 74.

Article 76

(1) If the contract is avoided and there is a current price for the goods, the party claiming damages may, if he has not made a purchase or resale under article 75, recover the difference between the price fixed by the contract and the current price at the time of avoidance as well as any further damages recoverable under article 74. If, however, the party claiming damages has avoided the contract after

taking over the goods, the current price at the time of such taking over shall be applied instead of the current price at the time of avoidance.

(2) For the purposes of the preceding paragraph, the current price is the price prevailing at the place where delivery of the goods should have been made or, if there is no current price at that place, the price at such other place serves as a reasonable substitute, making due allowance for differences in the cost of transporting the goods.

Article 77

A party who relies on a breach of contract must take such measures as are reasonable in the circumstances to mitigate the loss, including loss of profit, resulting from the breach. If he fails to take such measures, the party in breach may claim a reduction in the damages in the amount by which the loss should have been mitigated.

Section III.   Interest

Article 78

If a party fails to pay the price or any other sum that is in arrears, the other party is entitled to interest on it, without prejudice to any claim for damages recoverable under article 74.

Section IV.   Exemptions

Article 79

(1) A party is not liable for a failure to perform any of his obligations if he proves that the failure was due to an impediment beyond his control and that he could not reasonably be expected to have taken the impediment into account at the time of the conclusion of the contract or to have avoided or overcome it or its consequences.

(2) If the party's failure is due to the failure by a third person whom he has engaged to perform the whole or a part of the contract, that party is exempt from liability only if:

(a) He is exempt under the preceding paragraph; and

(b) The person whom he has so engaged would be so exempt if the provisions of that paragraph were applied to him.

(3) The exemption provided by this article has effect for the period during which the impediment exists.

(4) The party who fails to perform must give notice to the other party of the impediment and its effect on his ability to perform. If the notice is not received by the other party within a reasonable time after the party who fails to perform knew or ought to have known of the impediment, he is liable for damages resulting from such non-receipt.

(5) Nothing in this article prevents either party from exercising any right other than to claim damages under this Convention.

Article 80

A party may not rely on a failure of the other party to perform, to the extent that such failure was caused by the first party's act or omission.

Section V.   Effects of Avoidance

Article 81

(1) Avoidance of the contract releases both parties from their obligations under it, subject to any damages which may be due. Avoidance does not affect any provision of the contract for the settlement of disputes or any other provision of the contract governing the rights and obligations of the parties consequent upon the avoidance of the contract.

(2) A party who has performed the contract either wholly or in part may claim restitution from the other party of whatever the first party has supplied or paid under the contract. If both parties are bound to make restitution, they must do so concurrently.

Article 82

(1) The buyer loses the right to declare the contract avoided or to require the seller to deliver substitute goods if it is impossible for him to make restitution of the goods substantially in the condition in which he received them.

(2) The preceding paragraph does not apply:

(a) If the impossibility of making restitution of the goods or of making restitution of the goods substantially in the condition in which the buyer received them is not due to his act or omission;

(b) If the goods or part of the goods have perished or deteriorated as a result of the examination provided for in article 38; or

(c) If the goods or part of the goods have been sold in the normal course of business or have been consumed or transformed by the buyer in the course of normal use before he discovered or ought to have discovered the lack of conformity.

Article 83

A buyer who has lost the right to declare the contract avoided or to require the seller to deliver substitute goods in accordance with article 82 retains all other remedies under the contract and this Convention.

Article 84

(1) If the seller is bound to refund the price, he must also pay interest on it, from the date on which the price was paid.

(2) The buyer must account to the seller for all benefits which he has derived from the goods or part of them:

(a) If he must make restitution of the goods or part of them; or

(b) If it is impossible for him to make restitution of all or part of the goods or to make restitution of all or part of the goods substantially in the condition in which he received them, but he has nevertheless declared the contract avoided or required the seller to deliver substitute goods.

Section VI. Preservation of the Goods

Article 85

If the buyer is in delay in taking delivery of the goods or, where payment of the price and delivery of the goods are to be made concurrently, if he fails to pay the price, and the seller is either in possession of the goods or otherwise able to control their disposition, the seller must take such steps as are reasonable in the circumstances to preserve them. He is entitled to retain them until he has been reimbursed his reasonable expenses by the buyer.

Article 86

(1) If the buyer has received the goods and intends to exercise any right under the contract or this Convention to reject them, he must take such steps to preserve them as are reasonable in the circumstances. He is entitled to retain them until he has been reimbursed his reasonable expenses by the seller.

(2) If the goods dispatched to the buyer have been placed at his disposal at their destination and he exercises the right to reject them, he must take possession of them on behalf of the seller, provided that this can be done without payment of the price and without unreasonable inconvenience or unreasonable expense. This provision does not apply if the seller or a person authorized to take charge of the goods on his behalf is present at the destination. If the buyer takes possession of the goods under this paragraph, his rights and obligations are governed by the preceding paragraph.

Article 87

A party who is bound to take steps to preserve the goods may deposit them in a warehouse of a third person at the expense of the other party provided that the expense incurred is not unreasonable.

Article 88

(1) A party who is bound to preserve the goods in accordance with article 85 or 86 may sell them by any appropriate means if there has been an unreasonable delay by the other party in taking possession of the goods or in taking them back or in paying the price or the cost of preservation, provided that reasonable notice of the intention to sell has been given to the other party.

(2) If the goods are subject to rapid deterioration or their preservation would involve unreasonable expense, a party who is bound to preserve the goods in accordance with article 85 or 86 must take reasonable measures to sell them. To the extent possible he must give notice to the other party of this intention to sell.

(3) A party selling the goods has the right to retain out of the proceeds of sale an amount equal to the reasonable expenses of preserving the goods and of selling them. He must account to the other party for the balance.

PART IV.   FINAL PROVISIONS

Article 96

A Contracting State whose legislation requires contracts of sale to be concluded in or evidenced by writing may at any time make a declaration in accordance with article 12 that any provision of article 11, article 29, or Part II of this Convention, that allows a contract of sale or its modification or termination by agreement or any offer, acceptance, or other indication of intention to be made in any form other than in writing, does not apply where any party has his place of business in that State.

Restatement (Second) of Contracts

EDITORS' NOTE[1]

For centuries critics of the legal system have complained of its delay, uncertainty, and complexity, and each generation has attempted to devise solutions to these problems. In the early part of the twentieth century, prominent members of the legal profession created an institution to study the legal system and to offer proposals for reform. Formed in 1923, this organization, the American Law Institute (ALI), remains today a private, nonprofit corporation, funded by grants principally from foundations.

While the Institute has undertaken a variety of projects since its formation, its best-known work has been the preparation of "Restatements" of the common law. Begun in the 1920s and 1930s, the Restatements are black-letter pronouncements, in statute-like form, of the rules of the major common law subjects, such as contracts, property, torts, and agency. The ALI appointed Professor Samuel Williston of Harvard Law School, the best-known contracts scholar of his day, as Chief Reporter for the first Restatement of Contracts. Professor Arthur Corbin of Yale Law School acted as a special advisor for the Remedies section of that Restatement.

Adopted by the ALI in 1932, the first Restatement of Contracts has generated both respect and ridicule. Thousands of courts have cited provisions of the Restatement to support their decisions. Yet some scholars, particularly those associated with the movement in law known as "legal realism," have attacked the Restatements. Writing in 1933, one year after the publication of the first Restatement of Contracts, Dean Charles Clark of the Yale Law School remarked that the drafters of the Restatement had tried to simplify contract law by preparing an authoritative statement of rules. He was extremely critical of this approach:

> Actually the resulting statement is the law nowhere and in its unreality only deludes and misleads. It is either a generality so obvious as immediately to be accepted, or so vague

---

1. For further material on the history of the Restatements, see Grant Gilmore, The Death of Contract (1974); John Honnold, The Life of the Law 144-180 (1964); Nathan M. Crystal, Codification and the Rise of the Restatement Movement, 54 Wash. L. Rev. 239 (1979).

as not to offend, or of such antiquity as to be unchallenged as a statement of past history.

... There are a large number of purely bromidic sections, such as section 3 ("An agreement is a manifestation of mutual assent by two or more persons to one another."). . . . No one would wish to dissent from them. They cannot be used in deciding cases; nor are they now useful in initiating students into contract law, for the present teaching mode is to start with case study, not abstract definition. They may afford convenient citations to a court, but that is all.

Charles E. Clark, The Restatement of the Law of Contracts, 42 Yale L.J. 643, 654-655 (1933).

When the American Law Institute began preparing the Restatements, it recognized that the project would be a continuing one, requiring periodic reexamination. In the 1950s and 1960s the Institute began work on the second generation of Restatements. The ALI chose Professor Robert Braucher of Harvard Law School as Chief Reporter for the Restatement (Second) of Contracts. After Professor Braucher's appointment to the Supreme Judicial Court of Massachusetts in 1971, Professor Allan Farnsworth of Columbia Law School was designated Chief Reporter. Originally issued in 14 installments labeled "tentative drafts," the final version (revised and renumbered) was adopted by the ALI in 1979.

While the revised Restatement continues the black-letter approach of the first Restatement, it also represents a shift in several respects. Stylistically, the black-letter text has been rewritten and supplemented with extensive commentary and case citations. Substantively, influenced by the publication of the Uniform Commercial Code, the drafters of the Restatement (Second) have added a number of new provisions not found in the first Restatement. These include §205, which imposes on each party to a contract a duty of good faith and fair dealing, and §208, which provides that a court may refuse to enforce an agreement or any of its terms that the court finds to be unconscionable. Many other rules carried forward from the original Restatement have been modified to reflect the Code's influence. E.g., Restatement (Second) §33 (requirement of certainty of contractual terms reformulated based on UCC §2-204); Restatement (Second) §222 (concept of usage of trade modeled on UCC §1-303, formerly UCC §1-205).

Unlike a statute or a court decision, the provisions of the Restatements do not have the force of law. They are generally regarded, however, as authoritative by courts and commentators. Judge Herbert Goodrich, former Director of the Institute, characterized the Restatements as "common law 'persuasive authority' with a high degree of persuasion." Restatement and Codification, in John Honnold, The Life of the Law at 173 (1964). Indeed, many cases have used the Restatement (Second) provisions as the framework for analysis of contract problems. See, e.g., Alaska Democratic Party v. Rice, 934 P.2d 1313 (Alaska 1997) (applying provisions of Restatement (Second) §139 to determine when oral promise is enforceable under doctrine of promissory estoppel notwithstanding statute of frauds); Lenawee County Board of Health v. Messerly, 331 N.W.2d 203 (Mich. 1982) (adopting Restatement (Second) §152 to analyze issue of mutual mistake). Courts are zealous in protecting their independence, however, and may sometimes bristle at the suggestion that they should blindly follow the Restatement. For example, in Rowe v. Montgomery Ward & Co., 473 N.W.2d 268 (Mich. 1991), the Michigan Supreme Court (the court that nine years earlier in *Lenawee* had relied on the Restatement) had this to say in response to the argument that it should follow the provisions of Restatement (Second) §33, which deals with contractual certainty:

> While we acknowledge the Restatement as persuasive authority on the subject of contracts, this Court is not, nor is any other court, bound to follow any of the rules set out in the Restatement. Moreover, even assuming . . . that our ruling is inconsistent with the Restatement, the writings of the American Law Institute do not control the rulings of this Court, nor is the contract law of this state necessarily written to be consistent with the Restatement.

Id. at 278.

The selections from the Restatement (Second) contained in this supplement consist only of the black-letter provisions. In the unabridged version of the Restatement published by the American Law Institute, each section is followed by comments and illustrations. Some of these are cited or quoted in the Editors' casebook, Problems in Contract Law. In addition, Reporter's Notes, which follow the comments and illustrations in the Restatement, refer the reader to cases and commentary. The most complete treatment of the revised Restatement to date can be found in E. Allan Farnsworth, Contracts (4th ed. 2004).

The following provisions are copyright 1981 by the American Law Institute. Reprinted with permission. All rights reserved.

CHAPTER 1.   MEANING OF TERMS

CHAPTER 2.   FORMATION OF CONTRACTS — PARTIES AND CAPACITY

CHAPTER 3.   FORMATION OF CONTRACTS — MUTUAL ASSENT

Topic 1.   In General

Topic 2.   Manifestation of Assent in General

Topic 3.   Making of Offers

CHAPTER 9.   THE SCOPE OF CONTRACTUAL OBLIGATIONS

Topic 1.   The Meaning of Agreements

Topic 2.   Considerations of Fairness and the Public Interest

Topic 3.   Effect of Adoption of a Writing

Topic 4.   Scope as Affected by Usage

Topic 5.   Conditions and Similar Events

CHAPTER 10.   PERFORMANCE AND NON-PERFORMANCE

Topic 1.   Performances to Be Exchanged Under an Exchange of Promises

Topic 2.   Effect of Performance and Non-Performance

CHAPTER 1.   MEANING OF TERMS

§1.   Contract Defined

A contract is a promise or a set of promises for the breach of which the law gives a remedy or the performance of which the law in some way recognizes as a duty.

§2. Promise; Promisor; Promisee; Beneficiary

(1) A promise is a manifestation of intention to act or refrain from acting in a specified way, so made as to justify a promisee in understanding that a commitment has been made.

(2) The person manifesting the intention is the promisor.

(3) The person to whom the manifestation is addressed is the promisee.

(4) Where performance will benefit a person other than the promisee, that person is a beneficiary.

§4. How a Promise May Be Made

A promise may be stated in words either oral or written, or may be inferred wholly or partly from conduct.

CHAPTER 2. FORMATION OF CONTRACTS — PARTIES AND CAPACITY

§14. Infants

Unless a statute provides otherwise, a natural person has the capacity to incur only voidable contractual duties until the beginning of the day before the person's eighteenth birthday.

§15. Mental Illness or Defect

(1) A person incurs only voidable contractual duties by entering into a transaction if by reason of mental illness or defect

(a) he is unable to understand in a reasonable manner the nature and consequences of the transaction, or

(b) he is unable to act in a reasonable manner in relation to the transaction and the other party has reason to know of his condition.

(2) Where the contract is made on fair terms and the other party is without knowledge of the mental illness or defect, the power of avoidance under Subsection (1) terminates to the extent that the contract has been so performed in whole or in part or the circumstances have so changed that avoidance would be unjust. In such a case a court may grant relief as justice requires.

§16. Intoxicated Persons

A person incurs only voidable contractual duties by entering into a transaction if the other party has reason to know that by reason of intoxication

(a) he is unable to understand in a reasonable manner the nature and consequences of the transaction, or

(b) he is unable to act in a reasonable manner in relation to the transaction.

CHAPTER 3. FORMATION OF CONTRACTS — MUTUAL ASSENT

Topic 1. In General

§17. Requirement of a Bargain

(1) Except as stated in Subsection (2) the formation of a contract requires a bargain in which there is a manifestation of mutual assent to the exchange and a consideration.

(2) Whether or not there is a bargain a contract may be formed under special rules applicable to formal contracts or under the rules stated §§82-94.

Topic 2. Manifestation of Assent in General

§20. Effect of Misunderstanding

(1) There is no manifestation of mutual assent to an exchange if the parties attach materially different meanings to their manifestations and

(a) neither party knows or has reason to know the meaning attached by the other; or

(b) each party knows or each party has reason to know the meaning attached by the other.

(2) The manifestations of the parties are operative in accordance with the meaning attached to them by one of the parties if

(a) that party does not know of any different meaning attached by the other, and the other knows the meaning attached by the first party; or

(b) that party has no reason to know of any different meaning attached by the other, and the other has reason to know the meaning attached by the first party.

§21. Intention to Be Legally Bound

Neither real nor apparent intention that a promise be legally binding is essential to the formation of a contract, but a manifestation of intention that a promise shall not affect legal relations may prevent the formation of a contract.

§22. Mode of Assent: Offer and Acceptance

(1) The manifestation of mutual assent to an exchange ordinarily takes the form of an offer or proposal by one party followed by an acceptance by the other party or parties.

(2) A manifestation of mutual assent may be made even though neither offer nor acceptance can be identified and even though the moment of formation cannot be determined.

Topic 3. Making of Offers

§24. Offer Defined

An offer is the manifestation of willingness to enter into a bargain, so made as to justify another person in understanding that his assent to that bargain is invited and will conclude it.

§25. Option Contracts

An option contract is a promise which meets the requirements for the formation of a contract and limits the promisor's power to revoke an offer.

§26. Preliminary Negotiations

A manifestation of willingness to enter into a bargain is not an offer if the person to whom it is addressed knows or has reason to know that the person making it does not intend to conclude a bargain until he has made a further manifestation of assent.

§27. Existence of Contract Where Written Memorial Is Contemplated

Manifestations of assent that are in themselves sufficient to conclude a contract will not be prevented from so operating by the fact that the parties also manifest an intention to prepare and adopt a written memorial thereof; but the circumstances may show that the agreements are preliminary negotiations.

§32. Invitation of Promise or Performance

In case of doubt an offer is interpreted as inviting the offeree to accept either by promising to perform what the offer requests or by rendering the performance, as the offeree chooses.

§33. Certainty

(1) Even though a manifestation of intention is intended to be understood as an offer, it cannot be accepted so as to form a contract unless the terms of the contract are reasonably certain.

(2) The terms of a contract are reasonably certain if they provide a basis for determining the existence of a breach and for giving an appropriate remedy.

(3) The fact that one or more terms of a proposed bargain are left open or uncertain may show that a manifestation of intention is not intended to be understood as an offer or as an acceptance.

Topic 4. Duration of the Offeree's Power of Acceptance

§36. Methods of Termination of the Power of Acceptance

(1) An offeree's power of acceptance may be terminated by
    (a) rejection or counter-offer by the offeree, or
    (b) lapse of time, or
    (c) revocation by the offeror, or
    (d) death or incapacity of the offeror or offeree.

(2) In addition, an offeree's power of acceptance is terminated by the non-occurrence of any condition of acceptance under the terms of the offer.

§38. Rejection

(1) An offeree's power of acceptance is terminated by his rejection of the offer, unless the offeror has manifested a contrary intention.

(2) A manifestation of intention not to accept an offer is a rejection unless the offeree manifests an intention to take it under further advisement.

§39. Counter-Offers

(1) A counter-offer is an offer made by an offeree to his offeror relating to the same matter as the original offer and proposing a substituted bargain differing from that proposed by the original offer.

(2) An offeree's power of acceptance is terminated by his making of a counter-offer, unless the offeror has manifested a contrary intention or unless the counter-offer manifests a contrary intention of the offeree.

§40. Time When Rejection or Counter-Offer Terminates the Power of Acceptance

Rejection or counter-offer by mail or telegram does not terminate the power of acceptance until received by the offeror, but limits the power so that a letter or telegram of acceptance started after the sending of an otherwise effective rejection or counter-offer is only a counter-offer unless the acceptance is received by the offeror before he receives the rejection or counter-offer.

§43. Indirect Communication of Revocation

An offeree's power of acceptance is terminated when the offeror takes definite action inconsistent with an intention to enter into the proposed contract and the offeree acquires reliable information to that effect.

§45. Option Contract Created by Part Performance or Tender

(1) Where an offer invites an offeree to accept by rendering a performance and does not invite a promissory acceptance, an option contract is created when the offeree tenders or begins the invited performance or tenders a beginning of it.

(2) The offeror's duty of performance under any option contract so created is conditional on completion or tender of the invited performance in accordance with the terms of the offer.

Topic 5. Acceptance of Offers

§50. Acceptance of Offer Defined; Acceptance by Performance; Acceptance by Promise

(1) Acceptance of an offer is a manifestation of assent to the terms thereof made by the offeree in a manner invited or required by the offer.

(2) Acceptance by performance requires that at least part of what the offer requests be performed or tendered and includes acceptance by a performance which operates as a return promise.

(3) Acceptance by a promise requires that the offeree complete every act essential to the making of the promise.

§58. Necessity of Acceptance Complying with Terms of Offer

An acceptance must comply with the requirements of the offer as to the promise to be made or the performance to be rendered.

§59. Purported Acceptance Which Adds Qualifications

A reply to an offer which purports to accept it but is conditional on the offeror's assent to terms additional to or different from those offered is not an acceptance but is a counter-offer.

§60. Acceptance of Offer Which States Place, Time, or Manner of Acceptance

If an offer prescribes the place, time or manner of acceptance its terms in this respect must be complied with in order to create a contract. If an offer merely suggests a permitted place, time or manner of acceptance, another method of acceptance is not precluded.

§63.   Time When Acceptance Takes Effect

Unless the offer provides otherwise,

(a) an acceptance made in a manner and by a medium invited by an offer is operative and completes the manifestation of mutual assent as soon as put out of the offeree's possession, without regard to whether it ever reaches the offeror; but

(b) an acceptance under an option contract is not operative until received by the offeror.

§69.   Acceptance by Silence or Exercise of Dominion

(1) Where an offeree fails to reply to an offer his silence and inaction operate as an acceptance in the following cases only:

(a) Where an offeree takes the benefit of offered services with reasonable opportunity to reject them and reason to know that they were offered with the expectation of compensation.

(b) Where the offeror has stated or given the offeree reason to understand that assent may be manifested by silence or inaction, and the offeree in remaining silent and inactive intends to accept the offer.

(c) Where because of previous dealings or otherwise it is reasonable that the offeree should notify the offeror if he does not intend to accept.

(2) An offeree who does any act inconsistent with the offeror's ownership of offered property is bound in accordance with the offered terms unless they are manifestly unreasonable. But if the act is wrongful as against the offeror it is an acceptance only if ratified by him.

CHAPTER 4.   FORMATION OF CONTRACTS — CONSIDERATION

Topic 1.   The Requirement of Consideration

§71.   Requirement of Exchange; Types of Exchange

(1) To constitute consideration, a performance or a return promise must be bargained for.

(2) A performance or return promise is bargained for if it is sought by the promisor in exchange for his promise and is given by the promisee in exchange for that promise.

(3) The performance may consist of

(a) an act other than a promise, or

(b) a forbearance, or

(c) the creation, modification, or destruction of a legal relation.

(4) The performance or return promise may be given to the promisor or to some other person. It may be given by the promisee or by some other person.

§73. Performance of Legal Duty

Performance of a legal duty owed to a promisor which is neither doubtful nor the subject of honest dispute is not consideration; but a similar performance is consideration if it differs from what was required by the duty in a way which reflects more than a pretense of bargain.

§74. Settlement of Claims

(1) Forbearance to assert or the surrender of a claim or defense which proves to be invalid is not consideration unless
    (a) the claim or defense is in fact doubtful because of uncertainty as to the facts or the law, or
    (b) the forbearing or surrendering party believes that the claim or defense may be fairly determined to be valid.

(2) The execution of a written instrument surrendering a claim or defense by one who is under no duty to execute it is consideration if the execution of the written instrument is bargained for even though he is not asserting the claim or defense and believes that no valid claim or defense exists.

§77. Illusory and Alternative Promises

A promise or apparent promise is not consideration if by its terms the promisor or purported promisor reserves a choice of alternative performances unless
    (a) each of the alternative performances would have been consideration if it alone had been bargained for; or
    (b) one of the alternative performances would have been consideration and there is or appears to the parties to be a substantial possibility that before the promisor exercises his choice events may eliminate the alternatives which would not have been consideration.

§79. Adequacy of Consideration; Mutuality of Obligation

If the requirement of consideration is met, there is no additional requirement of
    (a) a gain, advantage, or benefit to the promisor or a loss, disadvantage, or detriment to the promisee; or
    (b) equivalence in the values exchanged; or
    (c) "mutuality of obligation."

§81. Consideration as Motive or Inducing Cause

(1) The fact that what is bargained for does not of itself induce the making of a promise does not prevent it from being consideration for the promise.

(2) The fact that a promise does not of itself induce a performance or return promise does not prevent the performance or return promise from being consideration for the promise.

Topic 2.   *Contracts Without Consideration*

§82.   Promise to Pay Indebtedness; Effect on the Statute of Limitations

(1) A promise to pay all or part of an antecedent contractual or quasi-contractual indebtedness owed by the promisor is binding if the indebtedness is still enforceable or would be except for the effect of a statute of limitations.

(2) The following facts operate as such a promise unless other facts indicate a different intention:

(a) A voluntary acknowledgement to the obligee, admitting the present existence of the antecedent indebtedness; or

(b) A voluntary transfer of money, a negotiable instrument, or other thing by the obligor to the obligee, made as interest on or part payment of or collateral security for the antecedent indebtedness; or

(c) A statement to the obligee that the statute of limitations will not be pleaded as a defense.

§83.   Promise to Pay Indebtedness Discharged in Bankruptcy

An express promise to pay all or part of an indebtedness of the promisor, discharged or dischargeable in bankruptcy proceedings begun before the promise is made, is binding.

§84.   Promise to Perform a Duty in Spite of Non-Occurrence of a Condition

(1) Except as stated in Subsection (2), a promise to perform all or part of a conditional duty under an antecedent contract in spite of the non-occurrence of the condition is binding, whether the promise is made before or after the time for the condition to occur, unless

(a) occurrence of the condition was a material part of the agreed exchange for the performance of the duty and the promisee was under no duty that it occur; or

(b) uncertainty of the occurrence of the condition was an element of the risk assumed by the promisor.

(2) If such a promise is made before the time for the occurrence of the condition has expired and the condition is within the control of the promisee or a beneficiary, the promisor can make his duty again subject to the condition by notifying the promisee or beneficiary of his intention to do so if

(a) the notification is received while there is still a reasonable time to cause the condition to occur under the antecedent terms or an extension given by the promisor; and

(b) reinstatement of the requirement of the condition is not unjust because of a material change of position by the promisee or beneficiary; and

(c) the promise is not binding apart from the rule stated in Subsection (1).

§85. Promise to Perform a Voidable Duty

Except as stated in §93, a promise to perform all or part of an antecedent contract of the promisor, previously voidable by him, but not avoided prior to the making of the promise, is binding.

§86. Promise for Benefit Received

(1) A promise made in recognition of a benefit previously received by the promisor from the promisee is binding to the extent necessary to prevent injustice.
(2) A promise is not binding under Subsection (1)
(a) if the promisee conferred the benefit as a gift or for other reasons the promisor has not been unjustly enriched; or
(b) to the extent that its value is disproportionate to the benefit.

§87. Option Contract

(1) An offer is binding as an option contract if it
(a) is in writing and signed by the offeror, recites a purported consideration for the making of the offer, and proposes an exchange on fair terms within a reasonable time; or
(b) is made irrevocable by statute.
(2) An offer which the offeror should reasonably expect to induce action or forbearance of a substantial character on the part of the offeree before acceptance and which does induce such action or forbearance is binding as an option contract to the extent necessary to avoid injustice.

§89. Modification of Executory Contract

A promise modifying a duty under a contract not fully performed on either side is binding
(a) if the modification is fair and equitable in view of circumstances not anticipated by the parties when the contract was made; or
(b) to the extent provided by statute; or
(c) to the extent that justice requires enforcement in view of material change of position in reliance on the promise.

§90. Promise Reasonably Inducing Action or Forbearance

(1) A promise which the promisor should reasonably expect to induce action or forbearance on the part of the promisee or a third person and which does induce such action or forbearance is binding if injustice can be avoided only by enforcement of the promise. The remedy granted for breach may be limited as justice requires.
(2) A charitable subscription or a marriage settlement is binding under Subsection (1) without proof that the promise induced action or forbearance.

courts don't always use this language

CHAPTER 5.   THE STATUTE OF FRAUDS

§110.   Classes of Contracts Covered

(1) The following classes of contracts are subject to a statute, commonly called the Statute of Frauds, forbidding enforcement unless there is a written memorandum or an applicable exception:

(a) a contract of an executor or administrator to answer for a duty of his decedent (the executor-administrator provision);

(b) a contract to answer for the duty of another (the suretyship provision);

(c) a contract made upon consideration of marriage (the marriage provision);

(d) a contract for the sale of an interest in land (the land contract provision);

(e) a contract that is not to be performed within one year from the making thereof (the one-year provision).

(2) The following classes of contracts, which were traditionally subject to the Statute of Frauds, are now governed by Statute of Frauds provisions of the Uniform Commercial Code:

(a) a contract for the sale of goods for the price of $500 or more (Uniform Commercial Code §2-201);

(b) a contract for the sale of securities (Uniform Commercial Code §8-319);

(c) a contract for the sale of personal property not otherwise covered, to the extent of enforcement by way of action or defense beyond $5,000 in amount of value of remedy (Uniform Commercial Code §1-206).

(3) In addition the Uniform Commercial Code requires a writing signed by the debtor for an agreement which creates or provides for a security interest in personal property or fixtures not in the possession of the secured party.

(4) Statutes in most states provide that no acknowledgment or promise is sufficient evidence of a new or continuing contract to take a case out of the operation of a statute of limitations unless made in some writing signed by the party to be charged, but that the statute does not alter the effect of any payment of principal or interest.

(5) In many states other classes of contracts are subject to a requirement of a writing.

Topic 4.   The Land Contract Provision

§129.   Action in Reliance; Specific Performance

A contract for the transfer of an interest in land may be specifically enforced notwithstanding failure to comply with the Statute of Frauds if it is established that the party seeking enforcement, in reasonable reliance on the contract and on the continuing assent of the party against whom enforcement is sought, has so changed his position that injustice can be avoided only by specific enforcement.

Topic 5.   The One-Year Provision

§130.   Contract Not to Be Performed Within a Year

(1) Where any promise in a contract cannot be fully performed within a year from the time the contract is made, all promises in the contract are within the Statute of Frauds until one party to the contract completes his performance.

(2) When one party to a contract has completed his performance, the one-year provision of the Statute does not prevent enforcement of the promises of other parties.

Topic 6. Satisfaction of the Statute by a Memorandum

§131. General Requisites of a Memorandum

Unless additional requirements are prescribed by the particular statute, a contract within the Statute of Frauds is enforceable if it is evidenced by any writing, signed by or on behalf of the party to be charged, which
    (a) reasonably identifies the subject matter of the contract,
    (b) is sufficient to indicate that a contract with respect thereto has been made between the parties or offered by the signer to the other party, and
    (c) states with reasonable certainty the essential terms of the unperformed promises in the contract.

§132. Several Writings

The memorandum may consist of several writings if one of the writings is signed and the writings in the circumstances clearly indicate that they relate to the same transaction.

§133. Memorandum Not Made as Such

Except in the case of a writing evidencing a contract upon consideration of marriage, the Statute may be satisfied by a signed writing not made as a memorandum of a contract.

§134. Signature

The signature to a memorandum may be any symbol made or adopted with an intention, actual or apparent, to authenticate the writing as that of the signer.

Topic 7. Consequences of Non-Compliance

§139. Enforcement by Virtue of Action in Reliance

(1) A promise which the promisor should reasonably expect to induce action or forbearance on the part of the promisee or a third person and which does induce the action or forbearance is enforceable notwithstanding the Statute of Frauds if injustice can be avoided only by enforcement of the promise. The remedy granted for breach is to be limited as justice requires.

(2) In determining whether injustice can be avoided only by enforcement of the promise, the following circumstances are significant:

(a) the availability and adequacy of other remedies, particularly cancellation and restitution;

(b) the definite and substantial character of the action or forbearance in relation to the remedy sought;

(c) the extent to which the action or forbearance corroborates evidence of the making and terms of the promise, or the making and terms are otherwise established by clear and convincing evidence;

(d) the reasonableness of the action or forbearance;

(e) the extent to which the action or forbearance was foreseeable by the promisor.

§144. Effect of Unenforceable Contract as to Third Parties

Only a party to a contract or a transferee or successor of a party to the contract can assert that the contract is unenforceable under the Statute of Frauds.

§150. Reliance on Oral Modification

Where the parties to an enforceable contract subsequently agree that all or part of a duty need not be performed or if a condition need not occur, the Statute of Frauds does not prevent enforcement of the subsequent agreement if reinstatement of the original terms would be unjust in view of a material change of position in reliance on the subsequent agreement.

CHAPTER 6. MISTAKE

§151. Mistake Defined

A mistake is a belief that is not in accord with the facts.

§152. When Mistake of Both Parties Makes a Contract Voidable

(1) Where a mistake of both parties at the time a contract was made as to a basic assumption on which the contract was made has a material effect on the agreed exchange of performances, the contract is voidable by the adversely affected party unless he bears the risk of the mistake under the rule stated in §154.

(2) In determining whether the mistake has a material effect on the agreed exchange of performances, account is taken of any relief by way of reformation, restitution, or otherwise.

§153. When Mistake of One Party Makes a Contract Voidable

Where a mistake of one party at the time a contract was made as to a basic assumption on which he made the contract has a material effect on the agreed exchange of performances that is adverse to him, the contract is voidable by him if he does not bear the risk of the mistake under the rule stated in §154, and

(a) the effect of the mistake is such that enforcement of the contract would be unconscionable, or

(b) the other party had reason to know of the mistake or his fault caused the mistake.

§154. When a Party Bears the Risk of a Mistake

A party bears the risk of a mistake when

(a) the risk is allocated to him by agreement of the parties, or

(b) he is aware, at the time the contract is made, that he has only limited knowledge with respect to the facts to which the mistake relates but treats his limited knowledge as sufficient, or

(c) the risk is allocated to him by the court on the ground that it is reasonable in the circumstances to do so.

§157. Effect of Fault of Party Seeking Relief

A mistaken party's fault in failing to know or discover the facts before making the contract does not bar him from avoidance or reformation under the rules stated in this Chapter, unless his fault amounts to a failure to act in good faith and in accordance with reasonable standards of fair dealing.

§158. Relief Including Restitution

(1) In any case governed by the rules stated in this Chapter, either party may have a claim for relief including restitution under the rules stated in §§240 and 376.

(2) In any case governed by the rules stated in this Chapter, if those rules together with the rules stated in Chapter 16 will not avoid injustice, the court may grant relief on such terms as justice requires including protection of the parties' reliance interests.

CHAPTER 7. MISREPRESENTATION, DURESS AND UNDUE INFLUENCE

Topic 1. Misrepresentation

§161. When Non-Disclosure Is Equivalent to an Assertion

A person's non-disclosure of a fact known to him is equivalent to an assertion that the fact does not exist in the following cases only:

(a) where he knows that disclosure of the fact is necessary to prevent some previous assertion from being a misrepresentation or from being fraudulent or material.

(b) where he knows that disclosure of the fact would correct a mistake of the other party as to a basic assumption on which that party is making the contract and if non-disclosure of the fact amounts to a failure to act in good faith and in accordance with reasonable standards of fair dealing.

(c) where he knows that disclosure of the fact would correct a mistake of the other party as to the contents or effect of a writing, evidencing or embodying an agreement in whole or in part.

(d) where the other person is entitled to know the fact because of a relation of trust and confidence between them.

§162. When a Misrepresentation Is Fraudulent or Material

(1) A misrepresentation is fraudulent if the maker intends his assertion to induce a party to manifest his assent and the maker

(a) knows or believes that the assertion is not in accord with the facts, or

(b) does not have the confidence that he states or implies in the truth of the assertion, or

(c) knows that he does not have the basis that he states or implies for the assertion.

(2) A misrepresentation is material if it would be likely to induce a reasonable person to manifest his assent, or if the maker knows that it would be likely to induce the recipient to do so.

§163. When a Misrepresentation Prevents Formation of a Contract

If a misrepresentation as to the character or essential terms of a proposed contract induces conduct that appears to be a manifestation of assent by one who neither knows nor has reasonable opportunity to know of the character or essential terms of the proposed contract, his conduct is not effective as a manifestation of assent.

§164. When a Misrepresentation Makes a Contract Voidable

(1) If a party's manifestation of assent is induced by either a fraudulent or a material misrepresentation by the other party upon which the recipient is justified in relying, the contract is voidable by the recipient.

(2) If a party's manifestation of assent is induced by either a fraudulent or a material misrepresentation by one who is not a party to the transaction upon which the recipient is justified in relying, the contract is voidable by the recipient, unless the other party to the transaction in good faith and without reason to know of the misrepresentation either gives value or relies materially on the transaction.

§166. When a Misrepresentation as to a Writing Justifies Reformation

If a party's manifestation of assent is induced by the other party's fraudulent misrepresentation as to the contents or effect of a writing evidencing or embodying in whole or in part an agreement, the court at the request of the recipient may reform the writing to express the terms of the agreement as asserted,

(a) if the recipient was justified in relying on the misrepresentation, and

(b) except to the extent that rights of third parties such as good faith purchasers for value will be unfairly affected.

§168. Reliance on Assertions of Opinion

(1) An assertion is one of opinion if it expresses only a belief, without certainty, as to the existence of a fact or expresses only a judgment as to quality, value, authenticity, or similar matters.

(2) If it is reasonable to do so, the recipient of an assertion of a person's opinion as to facts not disclosed and not otherwise known to the recipient may properly interpret it as an assertion

(a) that the facts known to that person are not incompatible with his opinion, or

(b) that he knows facts sufficient to justify him in forming it.

§169. When Reliance on an Assertion of Opinion Is Not Justified

To the extent that an assertion is one of opinion only, the recipient is not justified in relying on it unless the recipient

(a) stands in such a relation of trust and confidence to the person whose opinion is asserted that the recipient is reasonable in relying on it, or

(b) reasonably believes that, as compared with himself, the person whose opinion is asserted has special skill, judgment or objectivity with respect to the subject matter, or

(c) is for some other special reason particularly susceptible to a misrepresentation of the type involved.

§173. When Abuse of a Fiduciary Relation Makes a Contract Voidable

If a fiduciary makes a contract with his beneficiary relating to matters within the scope of the fiduciary relation, the contract is voidable by the beneficiary, unless

(a) it is on fair terms, and

(b) all parties beneficially interested manifest assent with full understanding of their legal rights and of all relevant facts that the fiduciary knows or should know.

Topic 2. Duress and Undue Unfluence

§174. When Duress by Physical Compulsion Prevents Formation of a Contract

If conduct that appears to be a manifestation of assent by a party who does not intend to engage in that conduct is physically compelled by duress, the conduct is not effective as a manifestation of assent.

§175. When Duress by Threat Makes a
Contract Voidable

(1) If a party's manifestation of assent is induced by an improper threat by the other party that leaves the victim no reasonable alternative, the contract is voidable by the victim.

(2) If a party's manifestation of assent is induced by one who is not a party to the transaction, the contract is voidable by the victim unless the other party to the transaction in good faith and without reason to know of the duress either gives value or relies materially on the transaction.

§176. When a Threat Is Improper

(1) A threat is improper if
    (a) what is threatened is a crime or a tort, or the threat itself would be a crime or a tort if it resulted in obtaining property,
    (b) what is threatened is a criminal prosecution,
    (c) what is threatened is the use of civil process and the threat is made in bad faith, or
    (d) the threat is a breach of the duty of good faith and fair dealing under a contract with the recipient.

(2) A threat is improper if the resulting exchange is not on fair terms, and
    (a) the threatened act would harm the recipient and would not significantly benefit the party making the threat,
    (b) the effectiveness of the threat in inducing the manifestation of assent is significantly increased by prior unfair dealing by the party making the threat, or
    (c) what is threatened is otherwise a use of power for illegitimate ends.

§177. When Undue Influence Makes a
Contract Voidable

(1) Undue influence is unfair persuasion of a party who is under the domination of the person exercising the persuasion or who by virtue of the relation between them is justified in assuming that that person will not act in a manner inconsistent with his welfare.

(2) If a party's manifestation of assent is induced by undue influence by the other party, the contract is voidable by the victim.

(3) If a party's manifestation of assent is induced by one who is not a party to the transaction, the contract is voidable by the victim unless the other party to the transaction in good faith and without reason to know of the undue influence either gives value or relies materially on the transaction.

CHAPTER 8. UNENFORCEABILITY ON GROUNDS OF PUBLIC POLICY

Topic 1. Unenforceability in General

§178. When a Term Is Unenforceable on Grounds of Public Policy

(1) A promise or other term of an agreement is unenforceable on grounds of public policy if legislation provides that it is unenforceable or the interest in its enforcement is clearly outweighed in the circumstances by a public policy against the enforcement of such terms.

(2) In weighing the interest in the enforcement of a term, account is taken of
(a) the parties' justified expectations,
(b) any forfeiture that would result if enforcement were denied, and
(c) any special public interest in the enforcement of the particular term.

(3) In weighing a public policy against enforcement of a term, account is taken of
(a) the strength of that policy as manifested by legislation or judicial decisions,
(b) the likelihood that a refusal to enforce the term will further that policy,
(c) the seriousness of any misconduct involved and the extent to which it was deliberate, and
(d) the directness of the connection between that misconduct and the term.

§181. Effect of Failure to Comply with Licensing or Similar Requirement

If a party is prohibited from doing an act because of his failure to comply with a licensing, registration or similar requirement, a promise in consideration of his doing that act or of his promise to do so it is unenforceable on grounds of public policy if
(a) the requirements has a regulatory purpose, and
(b) the interest in the enforcement of the promise is clearly outweighed by the public policy behind the requirement.

Topic 2. Restraint of Trade

§187. Non-Ancillary Restraints on Competition

A promise to refrain from competition that imposes a restraint that is not ancillary to an otherwise valid transaction or relationship is unreasonably in restraint of trade.

§188. Ancillary Restraints on Competition

(1) A promise to refrain from competition that imposes a restraint that is ancillary to an otherwise valid transaction or relationship is unreasonably in restraint of trade if

(a) the restraint is greater than is needed to protect the promisee's legitimate interest, or

(b) the promisee's need is outweighed by the hardship to the promisor and the likely injury to the public.

(2) Promises imposing restraints that are ancillary to a valid transaction or relationship include the following:

(a) a promise by the seller of a business not to compete with the buyer in such a way as to injure the value of the business sold;

(b) a promise by an employee or other agent not to compete with his employer or other principal;

(c) a promise by a partner not to compete with the partnership.

Topic 3. Impairment of Family Relations

§191. Promise Affecting Custody

A promise affecting the right of custody of a minor child is unenforceable on grounds of public policy unless the disposition as to custody is consistent with the best interest of the child.

Topic 5. Restitution

§198. Restitution in Favor of Party Who Is Excusably Ignorant or Is Not Equally in the Wrong

A party has a claim in restitution for performance that he has rendered under or in return for a promise that is unenforceable on grounds of public policy if

(a) he was excusably ignorant of the facts or of legislation of a minor character, in the absence of which the promise would be enforceable, or

(b) he was not equally in the wrong with the promisor.

CHAPTER 9. THE SCOPE OF CONTRACTUAL OBLIGATIONS

Topic 1. The Meaning of Agreements

§201. Whose Meaning Prevails

(1) Where the parties have attached the same meaning to a promise or agreement or a term thereof; it is interpreted in accordance with that meaning.

(2) Where the parties have attached different meanings to a promise or agreement or a term thereof, it is interpreted in accordance with the meaning attached by one of them if at the time the agreement was made

(a) that party did not know of any different meaning attached by the other, and the other knew the meaning attached by the first party; or

(b) that party had no reason to know of any different meaning attached by the other, and the other had reason to know the meaning attached by the first party.

(3) Except as stated in this Section, neither party is bound by the meaning attached by the other, even though the result may be a failure of mutual assent.

§202. Rules in Aid of Interpretation

(1) Words and other conduct are interpreted in the light of all the circumstances, and if the principal purpose of the parties is ascertainable it is given great weight.

(2) A writing is interpreted as a whole, and all writings that are part of the same transaction are interpreted together.

(3) Unless a different intention is manifested,

(a) where language has a generally prevailing meaning, it is interpreted in accordance with that meaning;

(b) technical terms and words of art are given their technical meaning when used in a transaction within their technical field.

(4) Where an agreement involves repeated occasions for performance by either party with knowledge of the nature of the performance and opportunity for objection to it by the other, any course of performance accepted or acquiesced in without objection is given great weight in the interpretation of the agreement.

(5) Wherever reasonable, the manifestations of intention of the parties to a promise or agreement are interpreted as consistent with each other and with any relevant course of performance, course of dealing, or usage of trade.

§203. Standards of Preference in Interpretation

In the interpretation of a promise or agreement or a term thereof, the following standards of preference are generally applicable:

(a) an interpretation which gives a reasonable, lawful, and effective meaning to all the terms is preferred to an interpretation which leaves a part unreasonable, unlawful, or of no effect;

(b) express terms are given greater weight than course of performance, course of dealing, and usage of trade, course of performance is given greater weight than course of dealing or usage of trade, and course of dealing is given greater weight than usage of trade;

(c) specific terms and exact terms are given greater weight than general language;

(d) separately negotiated or added terms are given greater weight than standardized terms or other terms not separately negotiated.

§204. Supplying an Omitted Essential Term

When the parties to a bargain sufficiently defined to be a contract have not agreed with respect to a term which is essential to a determination of their rights and duties, a term which is reasonable in the circumstances is supplied by the court.

Topic 2.   Considerations of Fairness and the Public Interest

§205. Duty of Good Faith and Fair Dealing

Every contract imposes upon each party a duty of good faith and fair dealing in its performance and its enforcement.

§206. Interpretation Against the Draftsman

In choosing among the reasonable meanings of a promise or agreement or a term thereof, that meaning is generally preferred which operates against the party who supplies the words or from whom a writing otherwise proceeds.

§207. Interpretation Favoring the Public

In choosing among the reasonable meanings of a promise or agreement or a term thereof, a meaning that serves the public interest is generally preferred.

§208. Unconscionable Contract or Term

If a contract or term thereof is unconscionable at the time the contract is made a court may refuse to enforce the contract, or may enforce the remainder of the contract without the unconscionable term, or may so limit the application of any unconscionable term as to avoid any unconscionable result.

Topic 3.   Effect of Adoption of a Writing

§209. Integrated Agreements

    (1) An integrated agreement is a writing or writings constituting a final expression of one or more terms of an agreement.

    (2) Whether there is an integrated agreement is to be determined by the court as a question preliminary to determination of a question of interpretation or to application of the parol evidence rule.

    (3) Where the parties reduce an agreement to a writing which in view of its completeness and specificity reasonably appears to be a complete agreement, it is taken to be an integrated agreement unless it is established by other evidence that the writing did not constitute a final expression.

§210. Completely and Partially Integrated Agreements

    (1) A completely integrated agreement is an integrated agreement adopted by the parties as a complete and exclusive statement of the terms of the agreement.

(2) A partially integrated agreement is an integrated agreement other than a completely integrated agreement.

(3) Whether an agreement is completely or partially integrated is to be determined by the court as a question preliminary to determination of a question of interpretation or to application of the parol evidence rule.

§211. Standardized Agreements

(1) Except as stated in Subsection (3), where a party to an agreement signs or otherwise manifests assent to a writing and has reason to believe that like writings are regularly used to embody terms of agreements of the same type, he adopts the writing as an integrated agreement with respect to the terms included in the writing.

(2) Such a writing is interpreted wherever reasonable as treating alike all those similarly situated, without regard to their knowledge or understanding of the standard terms of the writing.

(3) Where the other party has reason to believe that the party manifesting such assent would not do so if he knew that the writing contained a particular term, the term is not part of the agreement.

§213. Effect of Integrated Agreement on Prior Agreements (Parol Evidence Rule)

(1) A binding integrated agreement discharges prior agreements to the extent that it is inconsistent with them.

(2) A binding completely integrated agreement discharges prior agreements to the extent that they are within its scope.

(3) An integrated agreement that is not binding or that is voidable and avoided does not discharge a prior agreement. But an integrated agreement, even though not binding, may be effective to render inoperative a term which would have been part of the agreement if it had not been integrated.

§214. Evidence of Prior or Contemporaneous Agreements and Negotiations

Agreements and negotiations prior to or contemporaneous with the adoption of a writing are admissible in evidence to establish

(a) that the writing is or is not an integrated agreement;

(b) that the integrated agreement, if any, is completely or partially integrated;

(c) the meaning of the writing, whether or not integrated;

(d) illegality, fraud, duress, mistake, lack of consideration, or other invalidating cause;

(e) ground for granting or denying rescission, reformation, specific performance, or other remedy.

§215. Contradiction of Integrated Terms

Except as stated in the preceding Section, where there is a binding agreement, either completely or partially integrated, evidence of prior or contemporaneous agreements or negotiations is not admissible in evidence to contradict a term of the writing.

§216. Consistent Additional Terms

(1) Evidence of a consistent additional term is admissible to supplement an integrated agreement unless the court finds that the agreement was completely integrated.

(2) An agreement is not completely integrated if the writing omits a consistent additional agreed term which is

(a) agreed to for separate consideration, or

(b) such a term as in the circumstances might naturally be omitted from the writing.

§217. Integrated Agreement Subject to Oral Requirement of a Condition

Where the parties to a written agreement agree orally that performance of the agreement is subject to the occurrence of a stated condition, the agreement is not integrated with respect to the oral condition.

Topic 4. Scope as Affected by Usage

§222. Usage of Trade

(1) A usage of trade is a usage having such regularity of observance in a place, vocation, or trade as to justify an expectation that it will be observed with respect to a particular agreement. It may include a system of rules regularly observed even though particular rules are changed from time to time.

(2) The existence and scope of a usage of trade are to be determined as questions of fact. If a usage is embodied in a written trade code or similar writing the interpretation of the writing is to be determined by the court as a question of law.

(3) Unless otherwise agreed, a usage of trade in the vocation or trade in which the parties are engaged or a usage of trade of which they know or have reason to know gives meaning to or supplements or qualifies their agreement.

§223. Course of Dealing

(1) A course of dealing is a sequence of previous conduct between the parties to an agreement which is fairly to be regarded as establishing a common basis of understanding for interpreting their expressions and other conduct.

(2) Unless otherwise agreed, a course of dealing between the parties gives meaning to or supplements or qualifies their agreement.

Topic 5. *Conditions and Similar Events*

§224. Condition Defined

A condition is an event, not certain to occur, which must occur, unless its non-occurrence is excused, before performance under a contract becomes due.

§225. Effects of the Non-Occurrence of a Condition

(1) Performance of a duty subject to a condition cannot become due unless the condition occurs or its non-occurrence is excused.

(2) Unless it has been excused, the non-occurrence of a condition discharges the duty when the condition can no longer occur.

(3) Non-occurrence of a condition is not a breach by a party unless he is under a duty that the condition occur.

§226. How an Event May Be Made a Condition

An event may be made a condition either by the agreement of the parties or by a term supplied by the court.

§227. Standards of Preference with Regard to Conditions

(1) In resolving doubts as to whether an event is made a condition of an obligor's duty, and as to the nature of such an event, an interpretation is preferred that will reduce the obligee's risk of forfeiture, unless the event is within the obligee's control or the circumstances indicate that he has assumed the risk.

(2) Unless the contract is of a type under which only one party generally undertakes duties, when it is doubtful whether

(a) a duty is imposed on an obligee that an event occur, or

(b) the event is made a condition of the obligor's duty, or

(c) the event is made a condition of the obligor's duty and a duty is imposed on the obligee that the event occur, the first interpretation is preferred if the event is within the obligee's control.

(3) In case of doubt, an interpretation under which an event is a condition of an obligor's duty is preferred over an interpretation under which the non-occurrence of the event is a ground for discharge of that duty after it has become a duty to perform.

§228. Satisfaction of the Obligor as a Condition

When it is a condition of an obligor's duty that he be satisfied with respect to the obligee's performance or with respect to something else, and it is practicable to determine whether a reasonable person in the position of the obligor would be satisfied, an interpretation is preferred under which the condition occurs if such a reasonable person in the position of the obligor would be satisfied.

§229. Excuse of a Condition to Avoid Forfeiture

To the extent that the non-occurrence of a condition would cause disproportionate forfeiture, a court may excuse the non-occurrence of that condition unless its occurrence was a material part of the agreed exchange.

CHAPTER 10. PERFORMANCE AND NON-PERFORMANCE

Topic 1. Performances to Be Exchanged Under an Exchange of Promises

§234. Order of Performances

(1) Where all or part of the performances to be exchanged under an exchange of promises can be rendered simultaneously, they are to that extent due simultaneously, unless the language or the circumstances indicate the contrary.

(2) Except to the extent stated in Subsection (1), where the performance of only one party under such an exchange requires a period of time, his performance is due at an earlier time than that of the other party, unless the language or the circumstances indicate the contrary.

Topic 2. Effect of Performance and Non-Performance

§235. Effect of Performance as Discharge and of Non-Performance as Breach

(1) Full performance of a duty under a contract discharges the duty.

(2) When performance of a duty under a contract is due any non-performance is a breach.

§237. Effect on Other Party's Duties of a Failure to Render Performance

Except as stated in §240, it is a condition of each party's remaining duties to render performances to be exchanged under an exchange of promises that there be no uncured material failure by the other party to render any such performance due at an earlier time.

§238. Effect on Other Party's Duties of a Failure to Offer Performance

Where all or part of the performances to be exchanged under an exchange of promises are due simultaneously, it is a condition of each party's duties to render such performance that the other party either render or, with manifested present ability to do so, offer performance of his part of the simultaneous exchange.

§240. Part Performances as Agreed Equivalents

If the performances to be exchanged under an exchange of promises can be apportioned into corresponding pairs of part performances so that the parts of each pair are properly regarded as agreed equivalents, a party's performance of his part of such a pair has the same effect on the other's duties to render performance of the agreed equivalent as it would have if only that pair of performances had been promised.

§241. Circumstances Significant in Determining Whether a Failure Is Material

In determining whether a failure to render or to offer performance is material, the following circumstances are significant:

(a) the extent to which the injured party will be deprived of the benefit which he reasonably expected;

(b) the extent to which the injured party can be adequately compensated for the part of that benefit of which he will be deprived;

(c) the extent to which the party failing to perform or to offer to perform will suffer forfeiture;

(d) the likelihood that the party failing to perform or to offer to perform will cure his failure, taking account of all the circumstances including any reasonable assurances;

(e) the extent to which the behavior of the party failing to perform or to offer to perform comports with standards of good faith and fair dealing.

§242. Circumstances Significant in Determining When Remaining Duties Are Discharged

In determining the time after which a party's uncured material failure to render or to offer performance discharges the other party's remaining duties to render performance under the rules stated in §§237 and 238, the following circumstances are significant:

(a) those stated in §241;

(b) the extent to which it reasonably appears to the injured party that delay may prevent or hinder him in making reasonable substitute arrangements;

(c) the extent to which the agreement provides for performance without delay, but a material failure to perform or to offer to perform on a stated day does not of itself discharge the other party's remaining duties unless the circumstances, including the language of the agreement, indicate that performance or an offer to perform by that day is important.

§243. Effect of a Breach by Non-Performance as Giving Rise to a Claim for Damages for Total Breach

(1) With respect to performances to be exchanged under an exchange of promises, a breach by non-performance gives rise to a claim for damages for total breach only if it discharges the injured party's remaining duties to render such performance, other than a duty to render an agreed equivalent under §240.

(2) Except as stated in Subsection (3), a breach by non-performance accompanied or followed by a repudiation gives rise to a claim for damages for total breach.

(3) Where at the time of the breach the only remaining duties of performance are those of the party in breach and are for the payment of money in installments not related to one another, his breach by non-performance as to less than the whole, whether or not accompanied or followed by a repudiation, does not give rise to a claim for damages for total breach.

(4) In any case other than those stated in the preceding subsections, a breach by non-performance gives rise to a claim for total breach only if it so substantially impairs the value of the contract to the injured party at the time of the breach that it is just in the circumstances to allow him to recover damages based on all his remaining rights to performance.

§245. Effect of a Breach by Non-Performance as Excusing the Non-Occurrence of a Condition

Where a party's breach by non-performance contributes materially to the non-occurrence of a condition of one of his duties, the non-occurrence is excused.

§246. Effect of Acceptance as Excusing the Non-Occurrence of a Condition

(1) Except as stated in Subsection (2), an obligor's acceptance or his retention for an unreasonable time of the obligee's performance, with knowledge of or reason to know of the non-occurrence of a condition of the obligor's duty, operates as a promise to perform in spite of that non-occurrence, under the rules stated in §84.

(2) If at the time of its acceptance or retention the obligee's performance involves such attachment to the obligor's property that removal would cause material loss, the obligor's acceptance or retention of that performance operates as a promise to perform in spite of the non-occurrence of the condition, under the

rules stated in §84, only if the obligor with knowledge of or reason to know of the defects manifests assent to the performance.

§247. Effect of Acceptance of Part Performance as Excusing the Subsequent Non-Occurrence of a Condition

An obligor's acceptance of part of the obligee's performance, with knowledge or reason to know of the non-occurrence of a condition of the obligor's duty, operates as a promise to perform in spite of a subsequent non-occurrence of the condition under the rules stated in §84 to the extent that it justifies the obligee in believing that subsequent performances will be accepted in spite of that non-occurrence.

§248. Effect of Insufficient Reason for Rejection as Excusing the Non-Occurrence of a Condition

Where a party rejecting a defective performance or offer of performance gives an insufficient reason for rejection, the non-occurrence of a condition of his duty is excused only if he knew or had reason to know of that non-occurrence and then only to the extent that the giving of an insufficient reason substantially contributes to a failure by the other party to cure.

Topic 3. Effect of Prospective Non-Performance

§250. When a Statement or an Act Is a Repudiation

A repudiation is
> (a) a statement by the obligor to the obligee indicating that the obligor will commit a breach that would of itself give the obligee a claim for damages for total breach under §243, or
> (b) a voluntary affirmative act which renders the obligor unable or apparently unable to perform without such a breach.

§251. When a Failure to Give Assurance May Be Treated as a Repudiation

(1) Where reasonable grounds arise to believe that the obligor will commit a breach by non-performance that would of itself give the obligee a claim for damages for total breach under §243, the obligee may demand adequate assurance of due performance and may, if reasonable, suspend any performance for which he has not already received the agreed exchange until he receives such assurance.

(2) The obligee may treat as a repudiation the obligor's failure to provide within a reasonable time such assurance of due performance as is adequate in the circumstances of the particular case.

§253. Effect of a Repudiation as a Breach and on Other Party's Duties

(1) Where an obligor repudiates a duty before he has committed a breach by non-performance and before he has received all of the agreed exchange for it, his repudiation alone gives rise to a claim for damages for total breach.

(2) Where performances are to be exchanged under an exchange of promises, one party's repudiation of a duty to render performance discharges the other party's remaining duties to render performance.

§256. Nullification of Repudiation or Basis for Repudiation

(1) The effect of a statement as constituting a repudiation under §250 or the basis for a repudiation under §251 is nullified by a retraction of the statement if notification of the retraction comes to the attention of the injured party before he materially changes his position in reliance on the repudiation or indicates to the other party that he considers the repudiation to be final.

(2) The effect of events other than a statement as constituting a repudiation under §250 or the basis for a repudiation under §251 is nullified if, to the knowledge of the injured party, those events have ceased to exist before he materially changes his position in reliance on the repudiation or indicates to the other party that he considers the repudiation to be final.

CHAPTER 11. IMPRACTICABILITY OF PERFORMANCE AND FRUSTRATION OF PURPOSE

§261. Discharge by Supervening Impracticability

Where, after a contract is made, a party's performance is made impracticable without his fault by the occurrence of an event the non-occurrence of which was a basic assumption on which the contract was made, his duty to render that performance is discharged, unless the language or the circumstances indicate the contrary.

§262. Death or Incapacity of Person Necessary for Performance

If the existence of a particular person is necessary for the performance of a duty, his death or such incapacity as makes performance impracticable is an event the non-occurrence of which was a basic assumption on which the contract was made.

§263. Destruction, Deterioration or Failure to Come into Existence of Thing Necessary for Performance

If the existence of a specific thing is necessary for the performance of a duty, its failure to come into existence, destruction, or such deterioration as makes performance impracticable is an event the non-occurrence of which was a basic assumption on which the contract was made.

§264. Prevention by Governmental Regulation or Order

If the performance of a duty is made impracticable by having to comply with a domestic or foreign governmental regulation or order, that regulation or order is an event the non-occurrence of which was a basic assumption on which the contract was made.

§265. Discharge by Supervening Frustration

Where, after a contract is made, a party's principal purpose is substantially frustrated without his fault by the occurrence of an event the non-occurrence of which was a basic assumption on which the contract was made, his remaining duties to render performance are discharged, unless the language or the circumstances indicate the contrary.

§271. Impracticability as Excuse for Non-Occurrence of a Condition

Impracticability excuses the non-occurrence of a condition if the occurrence of the condition is not a material part of the agreed exchange and forfeiture would otherwise result.

§272. Relief Including Restitution

(1) In any case governed by the rules stated in this Chapter, either party may have a claim for relief including restitution under the rules stated in §§240 and 377.

(2) In any case governed by the rules stated in this Chapter, if those rules together with the rules stated in Chapter 16 will not avoid injustice, the court may grant relief on such terms as justice requires including protection of the parties' reliance interests.

CHAPTER 12.   DISCHARGE BY ASSENT OR ALTERATION

Topic 2.   Substituted Performance, Substituted Contract, Accord and Account Stated

§279. Substituted Contract

(1) A substituted contract is a contract that is itself accepted by the obligee in satisfaction of the obligor's existing duty.

(2) The substituted contract discharges the original duty and breach of the substituted contract by the obligor does not give the obligee a right to enforce the original duty.

§280. Novation

A novation is a substituted contract that includes as a party one who was neither the obligor nor the obligee of the original duty.

§281. Accord and Satisfaction

(1) An accord is a contract under which an obligee promises to accept a stated performance in satisfaction of the obligor's existing duty. Performance of the accord discharges the original duty.

(2) Until performance of the accord, the original duty is suspended unless there is such a breach of the accord by the obligor as discharges the new duty of the obligee to accept the performance in satisfaction. If there is such a breach, the obligee may enforce either the original duty or any duty under the accord.

(3) Breach of the accord by the obligee does not discharge the original duty, but the obligor may maintain a suit for specific performance of the accord, in addition to any claim for damages for partial breach.

CHAPTER 14. CONTRACT BENEFICIARIES

§302. Intended and Incidental Beneficiaries

(1) Unless otherwise agreed between promisor and promisee, a beneficiary of a promise is an intended beneficiary if recognition of a right to performance in the beneficiary is appropriate to effectuate the intention of the parties and either

(a) the performance of the promise will satisfy an obligation of the promisee to pay money to the beneficiary; or

(b) the circumstances indicate that the promisee intends to give the beneficiary the benefit of the promised performance.

(2) An incidental beneficiary is a beneficiary who is not an intended beneficiary.

§309. Defenses Against the Beneficiary

(1) A promise creates no duty to a beneficiary unless a contract is formed between the promisor and the promisee; and if a contract is voidable or unenforceable at the time of its formation the right of any beneficiary is subject to the infirmity.

(2) If a contract ceases to be binding in whole or in part because of impracticability, public policy, non-occurrence of a condition, or present or prospective failure of performance, the right of any beneficiary is to that extent discharged or modified.

(3) Except as stated in Subsections (1) and (2) and in §311 or as provided by the contract, the right of any beneficiary against the promisor is not subject to the

promisor's claims or defenses against the promisee or to the promisee's claims or defenses against the beneficiary.

(4) A beneficiary's right against the promisor is subject to any claim or defense arising from his own conduct or agreement.

§311. Variation of a Duty to a Beneficiary

(1) Discharge or modification of a duty to an intended beneficiary by conduct of the promisee or by a subsequent agreement between promisor and promisee is ineffective if a term of the promise creating the duty so provides.

(2) In the absence of such a term, the promisor and promisee retain power to discharge or modify the duty by subsequent agreement.

(3) Such a power terminates when the beneficiary, before he receives notification of the discharge or modification, materially changes his position in justifiable reliance on the promise or brings suit on it or manifests assent to it at the request of the promisor or promisee.

(4) If the promisee receives consideration for an attempted discharge or modification of the promisor's duty which is ineffective against the beneficiary, the beneficiary can assert a right to the consideration so received. The promisor's duty is discharged to the extent of the amount received by the beneficiary.

§313. Government Contracts

(1) The rules stated in this Chapter apply to contracts with a government or governmental agency except to the extent that application would contravene the policy of the law authorizing the contract or prescribing remedies for its breach.

(2) In particular, a promisor who contracts with a government or governmental agency to do an act for or render a service to the public is not subject to contractual liability to a member of the public for consequential damages resulting from performance or failure to perform unless

(a) the terms of the promise provide for such liability; or

(b) the promisee is subject to liability to the member of the public for the damages and a direct action against the promisor is consistent with the terms of the contract and with the policy of the law authorizing the contract and prescribing remedies for its breach.

CHAPTER 15. ASSIGNMENT AND DELEGATION

Topic 1.   What Can Be Assigned or Delegated

§317.   Assignment of a Right

(1) An assignment of a right is a manifestation of the assignor's intention to transfer it by virtue of which the assignor's right to performance by the obligor is

extinguished in whole or in part and the assignee acquires a right to such performance.

(2) A contractual right can be assigned unless

(a) the substitution of a right of the assignee for the right of the assignor would materially change the duty of the obligor, or materially increase the burden or risk imposed on him by his contract, or materially impair his chance of obtaining return performance, or materially reduce its value to him, or

(b) the assignment is forbidden by statute or is otherwise inoperative on grounds of public policy, or

(c) assignment is validly precluded by contract.

§318. Delegation of Performance of Duty

(1) An obligor can properly delegate the performance of his duty to another unless the delegation is contrary to public policy or the terms of his promise.

(2) Unless otherwise agreed, a promise requires performance by a particular person only to the extent that the obligee has a substantial interest in having that person perform or control the acts promised.

(3) Unless the obligee agrees otherwise, neither delegation of performance nor a contract to assume the duty made with the obligor by the person delegated discharges any duty or liability of the delegating obligor.

§321. Assignment of Future Rights

(1) Except as otherwise provided by statute, an assignment of a right to payment expected to arise out of an existing employment or other continuing business relationship is effective in the same way as an assignment of an existing right.

(2) Except as otherwise provided by statute and as stated in Subsection (1), a purported assignment of a right expected to arise under a contract not in existence operates only a promise to assign the right when it arises and as a power to enforce it.

§322. Contractual Prohibition of Assignment

(1) Unless the circumstances indicate the contrary, a contract term prohibiting assignment of "the contract" bars only the delegation to an assignee of the performance by the assignor of a duty or condition.

(2) A contract term prohibiting assignment of rights under the contract, unless a different intention is manifested,

(a) does not forbid assignment of a right to damages for breach of the whole contract or a right arising out of the assignor's due performance of his entire obligation;

(b) gives the obligor a right to damages for breach of the terms forbidding assignment but does not render the assignment ineffective;

(c) is for the benefit of the obligor, and does not prevent the assignee from acquiring rights against the assignor or the obligor from discharging his duty as if there were no such prohibition.

Topic 2. Mode of Assignment or Delegation

§326. Partial Assignment

(1) Except as stated in Subsection (2), an assignment of a part of a right, whether the part is specified as a fraction, as an amount, or otherwise, is operative as to that part to the same extent and in the same manner as if the part had been a separate right.

(2) If the obligor has not contracted to perform separately the assigned part of a right, no legal proceeding can be maintained by the assignor or assignee against the obligor over his objection, unless all the persons entitled to the promised performance are joined in the proceeding, or unless joinder is not feasible and it is equitable to proceed without joinder.

§328. Interpretation of Words of Assignment; Effect of Acceptance of Assignment

(1) Unless the language or the circumstances indicate the contrary, as in an assignment for security, an assignment of "the contract" or of "all my rights under the contract" on an assignment in similar general terms is an assignment of the assignor's rights and a delegation of his unperformed duties under the contract.

(2) Unless the language or the circumstances indicate the contrary, the acceptance by an assignee of such an assignment operates as a promise to the assignor to perform the assignor's unperformed duties, and the obligor of the assigned rights is an intended beneficiary of the promise.

Caveat: The Institute expresses no opinion as to whether the rule stated in Subsection (2) applies to an assignment by a purchaser of his rights under a contract for the sale of land.

Topic 4. Effect on the Obligor's Duty

§336. Defenses Against an Assignee

(1) By an assignment the assignee acquires a right against the obligor only to the extent that the obligor is under a duty to the assignor; and if the right of the assignor would be voidable by the obligor or unenforceable against him if no assignment had been made, the right of the assignee is subject to the infirmity.

(2) The right of an assignee is subject to any defense or claim of the obligor which accrues before the obligor receives notification of the assignment, but not to defenses or claims which accrue thereafter except as stated in this Section or as provided by statute.

(3) Where the right of an assignor is subject to discharge or modification in whole or in part by impracticability, public policy, non-occurrence of a condition, or present or prospective failure of performance by an obligee, the right of the assignee is to that extent subject to discharge or modification even after the obligor receives notification of the assignment.

(4) An assignee's right against the obligor is subject to any defense or claim arising from his conduct or to which he was subject as a party or a prior assignee because he had notice.

CHAPTER 16.　REMEDIES

Topic 1.　In General

⭐ §344.　Purposes of Remedies

Judical remedies under the rules stated in this Restatement serve to protect one or more of the following interests of a promisee:

1st Beast　(a) his "expectation interest," which is his interest in having the benefit of his bargain by being put in as good a position as he would have been in had the contract been performed,

2nd Beast　(b) his "reliance interest," which is his interest in being reimbursed for loss caused by reliance on the contract by being put in as good a position as he would have been in had the contract not been made, or

3rd Beast　(c) his "restitution interest," which is his interest in having restored to him any benefit that he has conferred on the other party.

Topic 2.　Enforcement by Award of Damages

§347.　Measure of Damages in General

Subject to the limitations stated in §§350-53, the injured party has a right to damages based on his expectation interest as measured by
(a) the loss in the value to him of the other party's performance caused by its failure or deficiency, plus
(b) any other loss, including incidental or consequential loss, caused by the breach, less
(c) any cost or other loss that he has avoided by not having to perform.

§348.　Alternatives to Loss in Value of Performance

(1) If a breach delays the use of property and the loss in value to the injured party is not proved with reasonable certainty, he may recover damages based on the rental value of the property or on interest on the value of the property.
(2) If a breach results in defective or unfinished construction and the loss in value to the injured party is not proved with sufficient certainty, he may recover damages based on
(a) the diminution in the market price of the property caused by the breach, or
(b) the reasonable cost of completing performance or of remedying the defects if that cost is not clearly disproportionate to the probable loss in value to him.

(3) If a breach is of a promise conditioned on a fortuitous event and it is uncertain whether the event would have occurred had there been no breach, the injured party may recover damages based on the value of the conditional right at the time of breach.

§349. Damages Based on Reliance Interest

As an alternative to the measure of damages stated in §347, the injured party has a right to damages based on his reliance interest, including expenditures made in preparation for performance or in performance, less any loss that the party in breach can prove with reasonable certainty the injured party would have suffered had the contract been performed.

§350. Avoidability as a Limitation on Damages

(1) Except as stated in Subsection (2), damages are not recoverable for loss that the injured party could have avoided without undue risk, burden or humiliation.

(2) The injured party is not precluded from recovery by the rule stated in Subsection (1) to the extent that he has made reasonable but unsuccessful efforts to avoid loss.

§351. Unforeseeability and Related Limitations on Damages

(1) Damages are not recoverable for loss that the party in breach did not have reason to foresee as a probable result of the breach when the contract was made.

(2) Loss may be foreseeable as a probable result of a breach because it follows from the breach

(a) in the ordinary course of events, or

(b) as a result of special circumstances, beyond the ordinary course of events, that the party in breach had reason to know.

(3) A court may limit damages for foreseeable loss by excluding recovery for loss of profits, by allowing recovery only for loss incurred in reliance, or otherwise if it concludes that in the circumstances justice so requires in order to avoid disproportionate compensation.

§352. Uncertainty as a Limitation on Damages

Damages are not recoverable for loss beyond an amount that the evidence permits to be established with reasonable certainty.

§353. Loss Due to Emotional Disturbance

Recovery for emotional disturbance will be excluded unless the breach also caused bodily harm or the contract or the breach is of such a kind that serious emotional disturbance was a particularly likely result.

§355.   Punitive Damages

Punitive damages are not recoverable for a breach of contract unless the conduct constituting the breach is also a tort for which punitive damages are recoverable.

§356.   Liquidated Damages and Penalties

(1) Damages for breach by either party may be liquidated in the agreement but only at an amount that is reasonable in the light of the anticipated or actual loss caused by the breach and the difficulties of proof of loss. A term fixing unreasonably large liquidated damages is unenforceable on grounds of public policy as a penalty.

(2) A term in a bond providing for an amount of money as a penalty for non-occurrence of the condition of the bond is unenforceable on grounds of public policy to the extent that the amount exceeds the loss caused by such non-occurrence.

Topic 3.   *Enforcement by Specific Performance and Injunction*

§359.   Effect of Adequacy of Damages

(1) Specific performance or an injunction will not be ordered if damages would be adequate to protect the expectation interest of the injured party.

(2) The adequacy of the damage remedy for failure to render one part of the performance due does not preclude specific performance or injunction as to the contract as a whole.

(3) Specific performance or an injunction will not be refused merely because there is a remedy for breach other than damages, but such a remedy may be considered in exercising discretion under the rule stated in §357.

§360.   Factors Affecting Adequacy of Damages

In determining whether the remedy in damages would be adequate, the following circumstances are significant:

(a) the difficulty of proving damages with reasonable certainty,

(b) the difficulty of procuring a suitable substitute performance by means of money awarded as damages, and

(c) the likelihood that an award of damages could not be collected.

§361.   Effect of Provision for Liquidated Damages

Specific performance or an injunction may be granted to enforce a duty even though there is a provision for liquidated damages for breach of that duty.

§362. Effect of Uncertainty of Terms

Specific performance or an injunction will not be granted unless the terms of the contract are sufficiently certain to provide a basis for an appropriate order.

§364. Effect of Unfairness

(1) Specific performance or an injunction will be refused if such relief would be unfair because
    (a) the contract was induced by mistake or by unfair practices,
    (b) the relief would cause unreasonable hardship or loss to the party in breach or to third persons, or
    (c) the exchange is grossly inadequate or the terms of the contract are otherwise unfair.

(2) Specific performance or an injunction will be granted in spite of a term of the agreement if denial of such relief would be unfair because it would cause unreasonable hardship or loss to the party seeking relief or to third persons.

§365. Effect of Public Policy

Specific performance or an injunction will not be granted if the act or forbearance that would be compelled or the use of compulsion is contrary to public policy.

§366. Effect of Difficulty in Enforcement or Supervision

A promise will not be specifically enforced if the character and magnitude of the performance would impose on the court burdens in enforcement or supervision that are disproportionate to the advantages to be gained from enforcement and to the harm to be suffered from its denial.

§367. Contracts for Personal Service or Supervision

(1) A promise to render personal service will not be specifically enforced.

(2) A promise to render personal service exclusively for one employer will not be enforced by an injunction against serving another if its probable result will be to compel a performance involving personal relations the enforced continuance of which is undesirable or will be to leave the employee without other reasonable means of making a living.

Topic 4. Restitution

§370. Requirement That Benefit Be Conferred

A party is entitled to restitution under the rules stated in this Restatement only to the extent that he has conferred a benefit on the other party by way of part performance or reliance.

§371. Measure of Restitution Interest

If a sum of money is awarded to protect a party's restitution interest, it may as justice requires be measured by either

(a) the reasonable value to the other party of what he received in terms of what it would have cost him to obtain it from a person in the claimant's position, or

(b) the extent to which the other party's property has been increased in value or his other interests advanced.

§373. Restitution When Other Party Is in Breach

(1) Subject to the rule stated in Subsection (2), on a breach by non-performance that gives rise to a claim for damages for total breach or on a repudiation, the injured party is entitled to restitution for any benefit that he has conferred on the other party by way of part performance or reliance.

(2) The injured party has no right to restitution if he has performed all of his duties under the contract and no performance by the other party remains due other than payment of a definite sum of money for that performance.

§374. Restitution in Favor of Party in Breach

(1) Subject to the rule stated in Subsection (2), if a party justifiably refuses to perform on the ground that his remaining duties of performance have been discharged by the other party's breach, the party in breach is entitled to restitution for any benefit that he has conferred by way of part performance or reliance in excess of the loss that he has caused by his own breach.

(2) To the extent that, under the manifested assent of the parties, a party's performance is to be retained in the case of breach, that party is not entitled to restitution if the value of the performance as liquidated damages is reasonable in the light of the anticipated or actual loss caused by the breach and the difficulties of proof of loss.

§375. Restitution When Contract Is Within Statute of Frauds

A party who would otherwise have a claim in restitution under a contract is not barred from restitution for the reason that the contract is unenforceable by him because of the Statute of Frauds unless the Statute provides otherwise or its purpose would be frustrated by allowing restitution.

§376. Restitution When Contract Is Voidable

A party who has avoided a contract on the ground of lack of capacity, mistake, misrepresentation, duress, undue influence or abuse of a fiduciary relation is entitled to restitution for any benefit that he has conferred on the other party by way of part performance or reliance.

§377. Restitution in Cases of Impracticability, Frustration, Non-Occurrence of Condition or Disclaimer by Beneficiary

A party whose duty of performance does not arise or is discharged as a result of impracticability of performance, frustration of purpose, non-occurrence of a condition or disclaimer by a beneficiary is entitled to restitution for any benefit that he has conferred on the other party by way of part performance or reliance.

Topic 5. Preclusion by Election and Affirmance

§384. Requirement That Party Seeking Restitution Return Benefit

(1) Except as stated in Subsection (2), a party will not be granted restitution unless

(a) he returns or offers to return, conditional on restitution, any interest in property that he has received in exchange in substantially as good condition as when it was received by him, or

(b) the court can assure such return in connection with the relief granted.

(2) The requirement stated in Subsection (1) does not apply to property

(a) that was worthless when received or that has been destroyed or lost by the other party or as a result of its own defects,

(b) that either could not from the time of receipt have been returned or has been used or disposed or without knowledge of the grounds for restitution if justice requires that compensation be accepted in its place and the payment of such compensation can be assured, or

(c) as to which the contract apportions the price if that part of the price is not included in the claim for restitution.

Principles of International Commercial Contracts (2010)

EDITORS' NOTE

The International Institute for the Unification of Private Law (UNIDROIT) has been working since the 1920s to promote harmonization and modernization of rules governing international transactions. In 1994, after more than a decade of work, the Institute published the Principles of International Commercial Contracts. UNIDROIT published new editions of the Principles in 2004 and in 2011, with additional chapters, revisions of some provisions, and updating of the text to adapt to the growth in electronic contracting. The most recent version of the UNIDROIT Principles is reprinted following this introductory note.*

Just as there is a similarity between the UCC and the Convention for the International Sale of Goods (CISG) in that both have the force of law, so there is a parallel between the Restatement of Contracts and the UNIDROIT Principles. The UNIDROIT Principles, like the Restatements, have been prepared by a respected private organization and do not have the force of law. But a striking difference exists. While the Restatements are based on the common law, the UNIDROIT Principles represent a blend of legal traditions, drawing heavily on both the civil law and the common law. As a result, a common law lawyer reading the principles will find much that is familiar, only to be jarred by an encounter with a foreign concept. See E. Allan Farnsworth, An International Restatement: The UNIDROIT Principles of International Commercial Contracts, 26 U. Balt. L. Rev. 1 (1997).

At the inception, commentators identified a number of roles that the UNIDROIT Principles could play in international commercial transactions. First, the UNIDROIT Principles may be an important resource for drafters of international commercial

---

* Adopted by the UNIDROIT Governing Council at its 90th Session held in Rome, Italy, May 9-11, 2011, the newest edition was given the "2010" publication date in its title. Only the black letter rules of these Principles are reproduced hereunder—by kind permission of UNIDROIT—but it should be recalled that the comments on the Articles are an integral part of the UNIDROIT Principles. The integral version may be ordered from: *publications@unidroit.org*.

contracts. Parties to such contracts often include a "choice of law" provision to avoid uncertainty about the law that governs a cross-border transaction. Because parties in different countries may be reluctant to agree to apply the law of the country of the other party to the contract, the UNIDROIT Principles may provide a neutral source of law for incorporation in the contract. Second, the Principles can play a significant role in dispute resolution. If the UNIDROIT Principles have been incorporated in a contract, they will provide the rules of decision. If the contract is silent on choice of law, or if it has a general choice of law provision ("*lex mercatoria,*" "general commercial law," or similar provision), the dispute resolution body (whether an arbitration panel or a court) could turn to the UNIDROIT Principles to resolve the dispute. In those cases in which the CISG applies because the contracting parties have places of business in states that are parties to the Convention, the UNIDROIT Principles could still play a role to supplement the CISG when the Convention does not deal with a particular issue. Finally, the UNIDROIT Principles have the potential to be an influential source for law reform. By drawing on what the drafters consider the best rules of the civil and common law, they have provided a set of standards to which legislatures in various countries can turn when considering modernization of their law. See Joseph M. Perillo, Essay, UNIDROIT Principles of International Commercial Contracts: The Black Letter Text and a Review, 63 Fordham L. Rev. 281, 283-284 (1994). See generally Michael J. Bonell, UNIDROIT Symposium: Soft Law and Party Autonomy: The Case of the UNIDROIT Principles, 51 Loy. L. Rev. 229 (2005); Symposium: The UNIDROIT Principles of International Commercial Contracts, 69 Tul. L. Rev. 1121 (1995).

The UNIDROIT Principles have made considerable progress toward these goals. The UNIDROIT Principles have been cited by many arbitral tribunals and several courts, received substantial attention from scholars, and have even had influence on states engaged in reform of commercial law. See Sandeep Gopalan, New Trends in the Making of International Commercial Law, 23 J.L. & Com. 117, 159-164 (2004) (citing positive effect of the UNIDROIT Principles in arbitral proceedings and noting they have influenced law reform in Russia, Estonia, and Lithuania); Fabrizio Marrella, International Commercial Arbitration: Choice of Law in Third-Millennium Arbitrations: The Relevance of the UNIDROIT Principles of International Commercial Contracts, 36 Vand. J. Transnat'l L. 1137 (2003) (stating that the UNIDROIT Principles have played a positive role in international commercial arbitration). A database on the UNIDROIT Principles, as well as the CISG, has been established by the Rome-based Centre for Comparative and Foreign Law Studies and allows access to arbitral and court decisions which cite the UNIDROIT Principles.**

Another project that has paralleled the emergence of the UNIDROIT Principles has been the work of the Commission on European Contract Law in preparing the Principles of European Contract Law (PECL). The Commission on European Contract Law is an independent body of experts from each Member State of the European Union that began its work in 1982. An introduction to the PECL prepared by the Commission on European Contract Law reflects that one primary anticipated purpose of the Principles is to play an important role in the possible development of a code of common European contract law.*** The Principles of European Contract

---

** See *http://www.unilex.info.*
*** The introduction and full text of the Principles of European Contract Law can be found at the Commission's website: *http://frontpage.cbs.dk/law/commission_on_european_contract_law.* See also Ole Lando,

Law are stated in the form of articles with a detailed commentary explaining the purpose and operation of each article. While there was some reciprocal influence during the drafting of the UNIDROIT Principles and the PECL, one important difference between the two publications is that the former applies only to commercial transactions while the latter also applies to consumer contracts. See Sandeep Gopolan, New Trends in the Making of International Commercial Law, 23 J.L. & Com. 117, 164-167 (2004). Ultimately, the future impact of the PECL remains uncertain. See generally Michael J. Bonell, The CISG, European Contract Law and the Development of a World Contract Law, 56 AM. J. Comp. L. 1 (2008).

PREAMBLE

CHAPTER 1.   GENERAL PROVISIONS

CHAPTER 2.   FORMATION AND AUTHORITY OF AGENTS

Section 1:   Formation

The Common Core of European Private Law and the Principles of European Contract Law, 21 Hastings Int'l & Comp. L. Rev. 809 (1998) (stating hoped-for goal of providing framework for a European Code of Contracts).

CHAPTER 4.   INTERPRETATION

CHAPTER 5.   CONTENT AND THIRD PARTY RIGHTS

Section 1:   Content

Section 2:   Third Party Rights

Section 3:   Conditions

CHAPTER 6.   PERFORMANCE

Section 1:   Performance in General

CHAPTER 11.   PLURALITY OF OBLIGORS AND OF OBLIGEES

Section 1:   Plurality of Obligors

Section 2:   Plurality of Obligees

PREAMBLE

(Purpose of the Principles)

These Principles set forth general rules for international commercial contracts.

They shall be applied when the parties have agreed that their contract be governed by them.*

They may be applied when the parties have agreed that their contract be governed by general principles of law, the *lex mercatoria* or the like.

---

* Parties wishing to provide that their agreement be governed by the Principles might use the following words, adding any desired exceptions or modifications: "This contract shall be governed by the UNIDROIT Principles (2010) [except as to Articles . . .]". Parties wishing to provide in addition for the application of the law of a particular jurisdiction might use the following words: "This contract shall be governed by the UNIDROIT Principles (2010) [except as to Articles . . .], supplemented when necessary by the law of [jurisdiction X]."

They may be applied when the parties have not chosen any law to govern their contract. They may be used to interpret or supplement international uniform law instruments.

They may be used to interpret or supplement domestic law.

They may serve as a model for national and international legislators.

CHAPTER 1.   GENERAL PROVISIONS

Article 1.1   Freedom of Contract

The parties are free to enter into a contract and to determine its content.

Article 1.2   No Form Required

Nothing in these Principles requires a contract, statement or any other act to be made in or evidenced by a particular form. It may be proved by any means, including witnesses.

Article 1.3   Binding Character of Contract

A contract validly entered into is binding upon the parties. It can only be modified or terminated in accordance with its terms or by agreement or as otherwise provided in these Principles.

Article 1.4   Mandatory Rules

Nothing in these Principles shall restrict the application of mandatory rules, whether of national, international or supranational origin, which are applicable in accordance with the relevant rules of private international law.

Article 1.5   Exclusion or Modification by the Parties

The parties may exclude the application of these Principles or derogate from or vary the effect of any of their provisions, except as otherwise provided in the Principles.

Article 1.6   Interpretation and Supplementation of the Principles

(1) In the interpretation of these Principles, regard is to be had to their international character and to their purposes including the need to promote uniformity in their application.

(2) Issues within the scope of these Principles but not expressly settled by them are as far as possible to be settled in accordance with their underlying general principles.

Article 1.7   Good Faith and Fair Dealing

(1) Each party must act in accordance with good faith and fair dealing in international trade.

(2) The parties may not exclude or limit this duty.

Article 1.8   Inconsistent Behaviour

A party cannot act inconsistently with an understanding it has caused the other party to have and upon which that other party reasonably has acted in reliance to its detriment.

Article 1.9   Usages and Practices

(1) The parties are bound by any usage to which they have agreed and by any practices which they have established between themselves.

(2) The parties are bound by a usage that is widely known to and regularly observed in international trade by parties in the particular trade concerned except where the application of such a usage would be unreasonable.

Article 1.10   Notice

(1) Where notice is required it may be given by any means appropriate to the circumstances.

(2) A notice is effective when it reaches the person to whom it is given.

(3) For the purpose of paragraph (2) a notice "reaches" a person when given to that person orally or delivered at that person's place of business or mailing address.

(4) For the purpose of this article "notice" includes a declaration, demand, request or any other communication of intention.

Article 1.11   Definitions

In these Principles

"court" includes an arbitral tribunal;

where a party has more than one place of business the relevant "place of business" is that which has the closest relationship to the contract and its performance, having regard to the circumstances known to or contemplated by the parties at any time before or at the conclusion of the contract;

"obligor" refers to the party who is to perform an obligation and "obligee" refers to the party who is entitled to performance of that obligation.

"writing" means any mode of communication that preserves a record of the information contained therein and is capable of being reproduced in tangible form.

Article 1.12   Computation of Time Set by Parties

(1) Official holidays or non-business days occurring during a period set by parties for an act to be performed are included in calculating the period.

(2) However, if the last day of the period is an official holiday or a non-business day at the place of business of the party to perform the act, the period is extended until the first business day which follows, unless the circumstances indicate otherwise.

(3) The relevant time zone is that of the place of business of the party setting the time, unless the circumstances indicate otherwise.

CHAPTER 2.   FORMATION AND AUTHORITY OF AGENTS

Section 1:   Formation

Article 2.1.1   Manner of Formation

A contract may be concluded either by the acceptance of an offer or by conduct of the parties that is sufficient to show agreement.

Article 2.1.2   Definition of Offer

A proposal for concluding a contract constitutes an offer if it is sufficiently definite and indicates the intention of the offeror to be bound in case of acceptance.

Article 2.1.3   Withdrawal of Offer

(1) An offer becomes effective when it reaches the offeree.

(2) An offer, even if it is irrevocable, may be withdrawn if the withdrawal reaches the offeree before or at the same time as the offer.

Article 2.1.4   Revocation of Offer

(1) Until a contract is concluded an offer may be revoked if the revocation reaches the offeree before it has dispatched an acceptance.

(2) However, an offer cannot be revoked

(a) if it indicates, whether by stating a fixed time for acceptance or otherwise, that it is irrevocable; or

(b) if it was reasonable for the offeree to rely on the offer as being irrevocable and the offeree has acted in reliance on the offer.

Article 2.1.5   Rejection of Offer

An offer is terminated when a rejection reaches the offeror.

Article 2.1.6   Mode of Acceptance

(1) A statement made by or other conduct of the offeree indicating assent to an offer is an acceptance. Silence or inactivity does not in itself amount to acceptance.

(2) An acceptance of an offer becomes effective when the indication of assent reaches the offeror.

(3) However, if, by virtue of the offer or as a result of practices which the parties have established between themselves or of usage, the offeree may indicate assent by performing an act without notice to the offeror, the acceptance is effective when the act is performed.

Article 2.1.7   Time of Acceptance

An offer must be accepted within the time the offeror has fixed or, if no time is fixed, within a reasonable time having regard to the circumstances, including the rapidity of the means of communication employed by the offeror. An oral offer must be accepted immediately unless the circumstances indicate otherwise.

Article 2.1.8   Acceptance Within a Fixed Period of Time

A period of acceptance fixed by the offeror begins to run from the time that the offer is dispatched. A time indicated in the offer is deemed to be the time of dispatch unless the circumstances indicate otherwise.

Article 2.1.9   Late Acceptance. Delay in Transmission

(1) A late acceptance is nevertheless effective as an acceptance if without undue delay the offeror so informs the offeree or gives notice to that effect.

(2) If a communication containing a late acceptance shows that it has been sent in such circumstances that if its transmission had been normal it would have reached the offeror in due time, the late acceptance is effective as an acceptance unless, without undue delay, the offeror informs the offeree that it considers the offer as having lapsed.

Article 2.1.10   Withdrawal of Acceptance

An acceptance may be withdrawn if the withdrawal reaches the offeror before or at the same time as the acceptance would have become effective.

Article 2.1.11   Modified Acceptance

(1) A reply to an offer which purports to be an acceptance but contains additions, limitations or other modifications is a rejection of the offer and constitutes a counter-offer.

(2) However, a reply to an offer which purports to be an acceptance but contains additional or different terms which do not materially alter the terms of the offer constitutes an acceptance, unless the offeror, without undue delay, objects to the discrepancy. If the offeror does not object, the terms of the contract are the terms of the offer with the modifications contained in the acceptance.

Article 2.1.12   Writings in Confirmation

If a writing which is sent within a reasonable time after the conclusion of the contract and which purports to be a confirmation of the contract contains additional or different terms, such terms become part of the contract, unless they materially alter the contract or the recipient, without undue delay, objects to the discrepancy.

Article 2.1.13   Conclusion of Contract Dependent on Agreement on Specific Matters or in a Particular Form

Where in the course of negotiations one of the parties insists that the contract is not concluded until there is agreement on specific matters or in a particular form, no contract is concluded before agreement is reached on those matters or in that form.

Article 2.1.14   Contract with Terms Deliberately Left Open

(1) If the parties intend to conclude a contract, the fact that they intentionally leave a term to be agreed upon in further negotiations or to be de-

termined by a third person does not prevent a contract from coming into existence.

(2) The existence of the contract is not affected by the fact that subsequently

(a) the parties reach no agreement on the term; or

(b) the third person does not determine the term, provided that there is an alternative means of rendering the term definite that is reasonable in the circumstances, having regard to the intention of the parties.

Article 2.1.15   Negotiations in Bad Faith

(1) A party is free to negotiate and is not liable for failure to reach an agreement.

(2) However, a party who negotiates or breaks off negotiations in bad faith is liable for the losses caused to the other party.

(3) It is bad faith, in particular, for a party to enter into or continue negotiations when intending not to reach an agreement with the other party.

Article 2.1.16   Duty of Confidentiality

Where information is given as confidential by one party in the course of negotiations, the other party is under a duty not to disclose that information or to use it improperly for its own purposes, whether or not a contract is subsequently concluded. Where appropriate, the remedy for breach of that duty may include compensation based on the benefit received by the other party.

Article 2.1.17   Merger Clauses

A contract in writing which contains a clause indicating that the writing completely embodies the terms on which the parties have agreed cannot be contradicted or supplemented by evidence of prior statements or agreements. However, such statements or agreements may be used to interpret the writing.

Article 2.1.18   Modification in a Particular Form

A contract in writing which contains a clause requiring any modification or termination by agreement to be in a particular form may not be otherwise modified or terminated. However, a party may be precluded by its conduct from asserting such a clause to the extent that the other party has reasonably acted in reliance on that conduct.

Article 2.1.19   Contracting Under Standard Terms

(1) Where one party or both parties use standard terms in concluding a contract, the general rules on formation apply, subject to Articles 2.1.20-2.1.22.

(2) Standard terms are provisions which are prepared in advance for general and repeated use by one party and which are actually used without negotiation with the other party.

Article 2.1.20   Surprising Terms

(1) No term contained in standard terms which is of such a character that the other party could not reasonably have expected it, is effective unless it has been expressly accepted by that party.

(2) In determining whether a term is of such a character regard shall be had to its content, language and presentation.

Article 2.1.21 Conflict Between Standard Terms and Non-Standard Terms

In case of conflict between a standard term and a term which is not a standard term the latter prevails.

Article 2.1.22 Battle of Forms

Where both parties use standard terms and reach agreement except on those terms, a contract is concluded on the basis of the agreed terms and of any standard terms which are common in substance unless one party clearly indicates in advance, or later and without undue delay informs the other party, that it does not intend to be bound by such a contract.

Section 2: Authority of Agents

Article 2.2.1 Scope of the Section

(1) This Section governs the authority of a person ("the agent"), to affect the legal relations of another person ("the principal"), by or with respect to a contract with a third party, whether the agent acts in its own name or in that of the principal.

(2) It governs only the relations between the principal or the agent on the one hand, and the third party on the other.

(3) It does not govern an agent's authority conferred by law or the authority of an agent appointed by a public or judicial authority.

Article 2.2.2 Establishment and Scope of the Authority of the Agent

(1) The principal's grant of authority to an agent may be express or implied.

(2) The agent has authority to perform all acts necessary in the circumstances to achieve the purposes for which the authority was granted.

Article 2.2.3 Agency Disclosed

(1) Where an agent acts within the scope of its authority and the third party knew or ought to have known that the agent was acting as an agent, the acts of the agent shall directly affect the legal relations between the principal and the third party and no legal relation is created between the agent and the third party.

(2) However, the acts of the agent shall affect only the relations between the agent and the third party, where the agent with the consent of the principal undertakes to become the party to the contract.

Article 2.2.4   Agency Undisclosed

(1) Where an agent acts within the scope of its authority and the third party neither knew nor ought to have known that the agent was acting as an agent, the acts of the agent shall affect only the relations between the agent and the third party.

(2) However, where such an agent, when contracting with the third party on behalf of a business, represents itself to be the owner of that business, the third party, upon discovery of the real owner of the business, may exercise also against the latter the rights it has against the agent.

Article 2.2.5   Agent Acting Without or Exceeding Its Authority

(1) Where an agent acts without authority or exceeds its authority, its acts do not affect the legal relations between the principal and the third party.

(2) However, where the principal causes the third party reasonably to believe that the agent has authority to act on behalf of the principal and that the agent is acting within the scope of that authority, the principal may not invoke against the third party the lack of authority of the agent.

Article 2.2.6   Liability of Agent Acting Without or Exceeding Its Authority

(1) An agent that acts without authority or exceeds its authority is, failing ratification by the principal, liable for damages that will place the third party in the same position as if the agent had acted with authority and not exceeded its authority.

(2) However, the agent is not liable if the third party knew or ought to have known that the agent had no authority or was exceeding its authority.

Article 2.2.7   Conflict of Interests

(1) If a contract concluded by an agent involves the agent in a conflict of interests with the principal of which the third party knew or ought to have known, the principal may avoid the contract. The right to avoid is subject to Articles 3.12 and 3.14 to 3.17.

(2) However, the principal may not avoid the contract
    (a) if the principal had consented to, or knew or ought to have known of, the agent's involvement in the conflict of interests; or
    (b) if the agent had disclosed the conflict of interests to the principal and the latter had not objected within a reasonable time.

Article 2.2.8   Sub-Agency

An agent has implied authority to appoint a sub-agent to perform acts which it is not reasonable to expect the agent to perform itself. The rules of this Section apply to the sub-agency.

Article 2.2.9   Ratification

(1) An act by an agent that acts without authority or exceeds its authority may be ratified by the principal. On ratification the act produces the same effects as if it had initially been carried out with authority.

(2) The third party may by notice to the principal specify a reasonable period of time for ratification. If the principal does not ratify within that period of time it can no longer do so.

(3) If, at the time of the agent's act, the third party neither knew nor ought to have known of the lack of authority, it may, at any time before ratification, by notice to the principal indicate its refusal to become bound by a ratification.

Article 2.2.10   Termination of Authority

(1) Termination of authority is not effective in relation to the third party unless the third party knew or ought to have known of it.

(2) Notwithstanding the termination of its authority, an agent remains authorised to perform the acts that are necessary to prevent harm to the principal's interests.

CHAPTER 3.   VALIDITY

Section 1:   General Provisions

Article 3.1.1   Matters Not Covered

This Chapter does not deal with lack of capacity.

Article 3.1.2   Validity of Mere Agreement

A contract is concluded, modified or terminated by the mere agreement of the parties, without any further requirement.

Article 3.1.3   Initial Impossibility

(1) The mere fact that at the time of the conclusion of the contract the performance of the obligation assumed was impossible does not affect the validity of the contract.

(2) The mere fact that at the time of the conclusion of the contract a party was not entitled to dispose of the assets to which the contract relates does not affect the validity of the contract.

Article 3.1.4   Mandatory Character of the Provisions

The provisions on fraud, threat, gross disparity and illegality contained in this Chapter are mandatory.

Section 2:   Grounds for Avoidance

Article 3.2.1   Definition of Mistake

Mistake is an erroneous assumption relating to facts or to law existing when the contract was concluded.

Article 3.2.2   Relevant Mistake

(1) A party may only avoid the contract for mistake if, when the contract was concluded, the mistake was of such importance that a reasonable person in the same situation as the party in error would only have concluded the contract on materially different terms or would not have concluded it at all if the true state of affairs had been known, and

    (a) the other party made the same mistake, or caused the mistake, or knew or ought to have known of the mistake and it was contrary to reasonable commercial standards of fair dealing to leave the mistaken party in error; or

    (b) the other party had not at the time of avoidance reasonably acted in reliance on the contract.

(2) However, a party may not avoid the contract if

    (a) it was grossly negligent in committing the mistake; or

    (b) the mistake relates to a matter in regard to which the risk of mistake was assumed or, having regard to the circumstances, should be borne by the mistaken party.

Article 3.2.3   Error in Expression or Transmission

An error occurring in the expression or transmission of a declaration is considered to be a mistake of the person from whom the declaration emanated.

Article 3.2.4   Remedies for Non-Performance

A party is not entitled to avoid the contract on the ground of mistake if the circumstances on which that party relies afford, or could have afforded, a remedy for non-performance.

Article 3.2.5   Fraud

A party may avoid the contract when it has been led to conclude the contract by the other party's fraudulent representation, including language or practices, or fraudulent non-disclosure of circumstances which, according to reasonable commercial standards of fair dealing, the latter party should have disclosed.

Article 3.2.6   Threat

A party may avoid the contract when it has been led to conclude the contract by the other party's unjustified threat which, having regard to the circumstances, is so imminent and serious as to leave the first party no reasonable alternative. In particular, a threat is unjustified if the act or omission with which a party has been threatened is wrongful in itself, or it is wrongful to use it as a means to obtain the conclusion of the contract.

Article 3.2.7   Gross Disparity

(1) A party may avoid the contract or an individual term of it if, at the time of the conclusion of the contract, the contract or term unjustifiably gave the other party an excessive advantage. Regard is to be had, among other factors, to

(a) the fact that the other party has taken unfair advantage of the first party's dependence, economic distress or urgent needs, or of its improvidence, ignorance, inexperience or lack of bargaining skill, and

(b) the nature and purpose of the contract.

(2) Upon the request of the party entitled to avoidance, a court may adapt the contract or term in order to make it accord with reasonable commercial standards of fair dealing.

(3) A court may also adapt the contract or term upon the request of the party receiving notice of avoidance, provided that that party informs the other party of its request promptly after receiving such notice and before the other party has reasonably acted in reliance on it. Article 3.2.10(2) applies accordingly.

Article 3.2.8   Third Persons

(1) Where fraud, threat, gross disparity or a party's mistake is imputable to, or is known or ought to be known by, a third person for whose acts the other party is responsible, the contract may be avoided under the same conditions as if the behaviour or knowledge had been that of the party itself.

(2) Where fraud, threat or gross disparity is imputable to a third person for whose acts the other party is not responsible, the contract may be avoided if that party knew or ought to have known of the fraud, threat or disparity, or has not at the time of avoidance reasonably acted in reliance on the contract.

Article 3.2.9   Confirmation

If the party entitled to avoid the contract expressly or impliedly confirms the contract after the period of time for giving notice of avoidance has begun to run, avoidance of the contract is excluded.

Article 3.2.10   Loss of Right to Avoid

(1) If a party is entitled to avoid the contract for mistake but the other party declares itself willing to perform or performs the contract as it was understood by the party entitled to avoidance, the contract is considered to have been concluded as the latter party understood it. The other party must make such a declaration or render such performance promptly after having been informed of the manner in which the party entitled to avoidance had understood the contract and before that party has reasonably acted in reliance on a notice of avoidance.

(2) After such a declaration or performance the right to avoidance is lost and any earlier notice of avoidance is ineffective.

Article 3.2.11   Notice of Avoidance

The right of a party to avoid the contract is exercised by notice to the other party.

Article 3.2.12   Time Limits

(1) Notice of avoidance shall be given within a reasonable time, having regard to the circumstances, after the avoiding party knew or could not have been unaware of the relevant facts or became capable of acting freely.

(2) Where an individual term of the contract may be avoided by a party under Article 3.2.7, the period of time for giving notice of avoidance begins to run when that term is asserted by the other party.

Article 3.2.13   Partial Avoidance

Where a ground of avoidance affects only individual terms of the contract, the effect of avoidance is limited to those terms unless, having regard to the circumstances, it is unreasonable to uphold the remaining contract.

Article 3.2.14   Retroactive Effect of Avoidance

Avoidance takes effect retroactively.

Article 3.2.15   Restitution

(1) On avoidance either party may claim restitution of whatever it has supplied under the contract, or the part of it avoided, provided that the party concurrently makes restitution of whatever it has received under the contract, or the part of it avoided.

(2) If restitution in kind is not possible or appropriate, an allowance has to be made in money whenever reasonable.

(3) The recipient of the performance does not have to make an allowance in money if the impossibility to make restitution in kind is attributable to the other party.

(4) Compensation may be claimed for expenses reasonably required to preserve or maintain the performance received.

Article 3.2.16   Damages

Irrespective of whether or not the contract has been avoided, the party who knew or ought to have known of the ground for avoidance is liable for damages so as to put the other party in the same position in which it would have been if it had not concluded the contract.

Article 3.2.17   Unilateral Declarations

The provisions of this Chapter apply with appropriate adaptations to any communication of intention addressed by one party to the other.

Section 3:   Illegality

Article 3.3.1   Contracts Infringing Mandatory Rules

(1) Where a contract infringes a mandatory rule, whether of national, international or supranational origin, applicable under Article 1.4 of these Principles, the effects of that infringement upon the contract are the effects, if any, expressly prescribed by that mandatory rule.

(2) Where the mandatory rule does not expressly prescribe the effects of an infringement upon a contract, the parties have the right to exercise such remedies under the contract as in the circumstances are reasonable.

(3) In determining what is reasonable regard is to be had in particular to:

(a) the purpose of the rule which has been infringed;

(b) the category of persons for whose protection the rule exists;

(c) any sanction that may be imposed under the rule infringed;

(d) the seriousness of the infringement;

(e) whether one or both parties knew or ought to have known of the infringement;

(f) whether the performance of the contract necessitates the infringement; and

(g) the parties' reasonable expectations.

Article 3.3.2   Restitution

(1) Where there has been performance under a contract infringing a mandatory rule under Article 3.3.1, restitution may be granted where this would be reasonable in the circumstances.

(2) In determining what is reasonable, regard is to be had, with the appropriate adaptations, to the criteria referred to in Article 3.3.1(3).

(3) If restitution is granted, the rules set out in Article 3.2.15 apply with appropriate adaptations.

CHAPTER 4.   INTERPRETATION

Article 4.1   Intention of the Parties

(1) A contract shall be interpreted according to the common intention of the parties.

(2) If such an intention cannot be established, the contract shall be interpreted according to the meaning that reasonable persons of the same kind as the parties would give to it in the same circumstances.

Article 4.2   Interpretation of Statements and Other Conduct

(1) The statements and other conduct of a party shall be interpreted according to that party's intention if the other party knew or could not have been unaware of that intention.

(2) If the preceding paragraph is not applicable, such statements and other conduct shall be interpreted according to the meaning that a reasonable person of the same kind as the other party would give to it in the same circumstances.

Article 4.3   Relevant Circumstances

In applying Articles 4.1 and 4.2, regard shall be had to all the circumstances, including

(a) preliminary negotiations between the parties;

(b) practices which the parties have established between themselves;

(c) the conduct of the parties subsequent to the conclusion of the contract;

(d) the nature and purpose of the contract;

(e) the meaning commonly given to terms and expressions in the trade concerned;

(f) usages.

Article 4.4   Reference to Contract or Statement as a Whole

Terms and expressions shall be interpreted in the light of the whole contract or statement in which they appear.

Article 4.5   All Terms to Be Given Effect

Contract terms shall be interpreted so as to give effect to all the terms rather than to deprive some of them of effect.

Article 4.6   Contra Proferentem Rule

If contract terms supplied by one party are unclear, an interpretation against that party is preferred.

Article 4.7   Linguistic Discrepancies

Where a contract is drawn up in two or more language versions which are equally authoritative there is, in case of discrepancy between the versions, a preference for the interpretation according to a version in which the contract was originally drawn up.

Article 4.8   Supplying an Omitted Term

(1) Where the parties to a contract have not agreed with respect to a term which is important for a determination of their rights and duties, a term which is appropriate in the circumstances shall be supplied.

(2) In determining what is an appropriate term regard shall be had, among other factors, to

(a) the intention of the parties;

(b) the nature and purpose of the contract;

(c) good faith and fair dealing;

(d) reasonableness.

CHAPTER 5.   CONTENT AND THIRD PARTY RIGHTS

Section 1:   Content

Article 5.1.1   Express and Implied Obligations

The contractual obligations of the parties may be express or implied.

Article 5.1.2   Implied Obligations

Implied obligations stem from
 (a) the nature and purpose of the contract;
 (b) practices established between the parties and usages;
 (c) good faith and fair dealing;
 (d) reasonableness.

Article 5.1.3   Co-operation Between the Parties

Each party shall cooperate with the other party when such co-operation may reasonably be expected for the performance of that party's obligations.

Article 5.1.4   Duty to Achieve a Specific Result. Duty of Best Efforts

(1) To the extent that an obligation of a party involves a duty to achieve a specific result, that party is bound to achieve that result.

(2) To the extent that an obligation of a party involves a duty of best efforts in the performance of an activity, that party is bound to make such efforts as would be made by a reasonable person of the same kind in the same circumstances.

Article 5.1.5   Determination of Kind of Duty Involved

In determining the extent to which an obligation of a party involves a duty of best efforts in the performance of an activity or a duty to achieve a specific result, regard shall be had, among other factors, to
 (a) the way in which the obligation is expressed in the contract;
 (b) the contractual price and other terms of the contract;
 (c) the degree of risk normally involved in achieving the expected result;
 (d) the ability of the other party to influence the performance of the obligation.

Article 5.1.6   Determination of Quality of Performance

Where the quality of performance is neither fixed by, nor determinable from, the contract a party is bound to render a performance of a quality that is reasonable and not less than average in the circumstances.

Article 5.1.7   Price Determination

(1) Where a contract does not fix or make provision for determining the price, the parties are considered, in the absence of any indication to the contrary, to have made reference to the price generally charged at the time of the conclusion of the contract for such performance in comparable circumstances in the trade concerned or, if no such price is available, to a reasonable price.

(2) Where the price is to be determined by one party and that determination is manifestly unreasonable, a reasonable price shall be substituted notwithstanding any contract term to the contrary.

(3) Where the price is to be fixed by a third person, and that person cannot or will not do so, the price shall be a reasonable price.

(4) Where the price is to be fixed by reference to factors which do not exist or have ceased to exist or to be accessible, the nearest equivalent factor shall be treated as a substitute.

Article 5.1.8   Contract for an Indefinite Period

A contract for an indefinite period may be ended by either party by giving notice a reasonable time in advance.

Article 5.1.9   Release by Agreement

(1) An obligee may release its right by agreement with the obligor.

(2) An offer to release a right gratuitously shall be deemed accepted if the obligor does not reject the offer without delay after having become aware of it.

Section 2:   *Third Party Rights*

Article 5.2.1   Contracts in Favour of Third Parties

(1) The parties (the "promisor" and the "promisee") may confer by express or implied agreement a right on a third party (the "beneficiary").

(2) The existence and content of the beneficiary's right against the promisor are determined by the agreement of the parties and are subject to any conditions or other limitations under the agreement.

Article 5.2.2   Third Party Identifiable

The beneficiary must be identifiable with adequate certainty by the contract but need not be in existence at the time the contract is made.

Article 5.2.3   Exclusion and Limitation Clauses

The conferment of rights in the beneficiary includes the right to invoke a clause in the contract which excludes or limits the liability of the beneficiary.

Article 5.2.4   Defences

The promisor may assert against the beneficiary all defences which the promisor could assert against the promisee.

Article 5.2.5   Revocation

The parties may modify or revoke the rights conferred by the contract on the beneficiary until the beneficiary has accepted them or reasonably acted in reliance on them.

Article 5.2.6   Renunciation

The beneficiary may renounce a right conferred on it.

Section 3:   Conditions

Article 5.3.1   Types of Condition

A contract or a contractual obligation may be made conditional upon the occurrence of a future uncertain event, so that the contract or the contractual obligation only takes effect if the event occurs (suspensive condition) or comes to an end if the event occurs (resolutive condition).

Article 5.3.2   Effect of Conditions

Unless the parties otherwise agree:
(a) the relevant contract or contractual obligation takes effect upon fulfilment of a suspensive condition;
(b) the relevant contract or contractual obligation comes to an end upon fulfillment of a resolutive condition.

Article 5.3.3   Interference with Conditions

(1) If fulfilment of a condition is prevented by a party, contrary to the duty of good faith and fair dealing or the duty of co-operation, that party may not rely on the non-fulfilment of the condition.
(2) If fulfilment of a condition is brought about by a party, contrary to the duty of good faith and fair dealing or the duty of co-operation, that party may not rely on the fulfilment of the condition.

Article 5.3.4   Duty to Preserve Rights

Pending fulfilment of a condition, a party may not, contrary to the duty to act in accordance with good faith and fair dealing, act so as to prejudice the other party's rights in case of fulfilment of the condition.

Article 5.3.5   Restitution in Case of Fulfilment of a Resolutive Condition

(1) On fulfilment of a resolutive condition, the rules on restitution set out in Articles 7.3.6 and 7.3.7 apply with appropriate adaptations.
(2) If the parties have agreed that the resolutive condition is to operate retroactively, the rules on restitution set out in Article 3.2.15 apply with appropriate adaptations.

CHAPTER 6.   PERFORMANCE

Section 1:   Performance in General

Article 6.1.1   Time of Performance

A party must perform its obligations:
(a) if a time is fixed by or determinable from the contract, at that time;
(b) if a period of time is fixed by or determinable from the contract, at any time within that period unless circumstances indicate that the other party is to choose a time;

(c) in any other case, within a reasonable time after the conclusion of the contract.

Article 6.1.2 Performance at One Time or in Instalments

In cases under Article 6.1.1(b) or (c), a party must perform its obligations at one time if that performance can be rendered at one time and the circumstances do not indicate otherwise.

Article 6.1.3 Partial Performance

(1) The obligee may reject an offer to perform in part at the time performance is due, whether or not such offer is coupled with an assurance as to the balance of the performance, unless the obligee has no legitimate interest in so doing.

(2) Additional expenses caused to the obligee by partial performance are to be borne by the obligor without prejudice to any other remedy.

Article 6.1.4 Order of Performance

(1) To the extent that the performances of the parties can be rendered simultaneously, the parties are bound to render them simultaneously unless the circumstances indicate otherwise.

(2) To the extent that the performance of only one party requires a period of time, that party is bound to render its performance first, unless the circumstances indicate otherwise.

Article 6.1.5 Earlier Performance

(1) The obligee may reject an earlier performance unless it has no legitimate interest in so doing.

(2) Acceptance by a party of an earlier performance does not affect the time for the performance of its own obligations if that time has been fixed irrespective of the performance of the other party's obligations.

(3) Additional expenses caused to the obligee by earlier performance are to be borne by the obligor, without prejudice to any other remedy.

Article 6.1.6 Place of Performance

(1) If the place of performance is neither fixed by, nor determinable from, the contract, a party is to perform:

(a) a monetary obligation, at the obligee's place of business;

(b) any other obligation, at its own place of business.

(2) A party must bear any increase in the expenses incidental to performance which is caused by a change in its place of business subsequent to the conclusion of the contract.

Article 6.1.7 Payment by Cheque or Other Instrument

(1) Payment may be made in any form used in the ordinary course of business at the place for payment.

(2) However, an obligee who accepts, either by virtue of paragraph (1) or voluntarily, a cheque, any other order to pay or a promise to pay, is presumed to do so only on condition that it will be honoured.

Article 6.1.8   Payment by Funds Transfer

(1) Unless the obligee has indicated a particular account, payment may be made by a transfer to any of the financial institutions in which the obligee has made it known that it has an account.

(2) In case of payment by a transfer the obligation of the obligor is discharged when the transfer to the obligee's financial institution becomes effective.

Article 6.1.9   Currency of Payment

(1) If a monetary obligation is expressed in a currency other than that of the place for payment, it may be paid by the obligor in the currency of the place for payment unless

(a) that currency is not freely convertible; or

(b) the parties have agreed that payment should be made only in the currency in which the monetary obligation is expressed.

(2) If it is impossible for the obligor to make payment in the currency in which the monetary obligation is expressed, the obligee may require payment in the currency of the place for payment, even in the case referred to in paragraph (1)(b).

(3) Payment in the currency of the place for payment is to be made according to the applicable rate of exchange prevailing there when payment is due.

(4) However, if the obligor has not paid at the time when payment is due, the obligee may require payment according to the applicable rate of exchange prevailing either when payment is due or at the time of actual payment.

Article 6.1.10   Currency Not Expressed

Where a monetary obligation is not expressed in a particular currency, payment must be made in the currency of the place where payment is to be made.

Article 6.1.11   Costs of Performance

Each party shall bear the costs of performance of its obligations.

Article 6.1.12   Imputation of Payments

(1) An obligor owing several monetary obligations to the same obligee may specify at the time of payment the debt to which it intends the payment to be applied. However, the payment discharges first any expenses, then interest due and finally the principal.

(2) If the obligor makes no such specification, the obligee may, within a reasonable time after payment, declare to the obligor the obligation to which it imputes the payment, provided that the obligation is due and undisputed.

(3) In the absence of imputation under paragraphs (1) or (2), payment is imputed to that obligation which satisfies one of the following criteria in the order indicated:

    (a) an obligation which is due or which is the first to fall due;

    (b) the obligation for which the obligee has least security;

    (c) the obligation which is the most burdensome for the obligor;

    (d) the obligation which has arisen first.

If none of the preceding criteria applies, payment is imputed to all the obligations proportionally.

Article 6.1.13   Imputation of Non-Monetary Obligations

Article 6.1.12 applies with appropriate adaptations to the imputation of performance of non-monetary obligations.

Article 6.1.14   Application for Public Permission

Where the law of a State requires a public permission affecting the validity of the contract or its performance and neither that law nor the circumstances indicate otherwise

    (a) if only one party has its place of business in that State, that party shall take the measures necessary to obtain the permission;

    (b) in any other case the party whose performance requires permission shall take the necessary measures.

Article 6.1.15   Procedure in Applying for Permission

(1) The party required to take the measures necessary to obtain the permission shall do so without undue delay and shall bear any expenses incurred.

(2) That party shall whenever appropriate give the other party notice of the grant or refusal of such permission without undue delay.

Article 6.1.16   Permission Neither Granted Nor Refused

(1) If, notwithstanding the fact that the party responsible has taken all measures required, permission is neither granted nor refused within an agreed period or, where no period has been agreed, within a reasonable time from the conclusion of the contract, either party is entitled to terminate the contract.

(2) Where the permission affects some terms only, paragraph (1) does not apply if, having regard to the circumstances, it is reasonable to uphold the remaining contract even if the permission is refused.

Article 6.1.17   Permission Refused

(1) The refusal of a permission affecting the validity of the contract renders the contract void. If the refusal affects the validity of some terms only, only such terms are void if, having regard to the circumstances, it is reasonable to uphold the remaining contract.

(2) Where the refusal of a permission renders the performance of the contract impossible in whole or in part, the rules on non-performance apply.

Section 2:   Hardship

Article 6.2.1   Contract to Be Observed

Where the performance of a contract becomes more onerous for one of the parties, that party is nevertheless bound to perform its obligations subject to the following provisions on hardship.

Article 6.2.2   Definition of Hardship

There is hardship where the occurrence of events fundamentally alters the equilibrium of the contract either because the cost of a party's performance has increased or because the value of the performance a party receives has diminished, and

> (a) the events occur or become known to the disadvantaged party after the conclusion of the contract;
> (b) the events could not reasonably have been taken into account by the disadvantaged party at the time of the conclusion of the contract;
> (c) the events are beyond the control of the disadvantaged party; and
> (d) the risk of the events was not assumed by the disadvantaged party.

Article 6.2.3   Effects of Hardship

> (1) In case of hardship the disadvantaged party is entitled to request renegotiations. The request shall be made without undue delay and shall indicate the grounds on which it is based.
> (2) The request for renegotiation does not in itself entitle the disadvantaged party to withhold performance.
> (3) Upon failure to reach agreement within a reasonable time either party may resort to the court.
> (4) If the court finds hardship it may, if reasonable,
> > (a) terminate the contract at a date and on terms to be fixed, or
> > (b) adapt the contract with a view to restoring its equilibrium.

CHAPTER 7.   NON-PERFORMANCE

Section 1:   Non-Performance in General

Article 7.1.1   Non-Performance Defined

Non-performance is failure by a party to perform any of its obligations under the contract, including defective performance or late performance.

Article 7.1.2   Interference by the Other Party

A party may not rely on the non-performance of the other party to the extent that such non-performance was caused by the first party's act or omission or by another event as to which the first party bears the risk.

Article 7.1.3   Withholding Performance

(1) Where the parties are to perform simultaneously, either party may withhold performance until the other party tenders its performance.

(2) Where the parties are to perform consecutively, the party that is to perform later may withhold its performance until the first party has performed.

Article 7.1.4   Cure by Non-Performing Party

(1) The non-performing party may, at its own expense, cure any nonperformance, provided that

(a) without undue delay, it gives notice indicating the proposed manner and timing of the cure;

(b) cure is appropriate in the circumstances;

(c) the aggrieved party has no legitimate interest in refusing cure; and

(d) cure is effected promptly.

(2) The right to cure is not precluded by notice of termination.

(3) Upon effective notice of cure, rights of the aggrieved party that are inconsistent with the non-performing party's performance are suspended until the time for cure has expired.

(4) The aggrieved party may withhold performance pending cure.

(5) Notwithstanding cure, the aggrieved party retains the right to claim damages for delay as well as for any harm caused or not prevented by the cure.

Article 7.1.5   Additional Period for Performance

(1) In a case of non-performance the aggrieved party may by notice to the other party allow an additional period of time for performance.

(2) During the additional period the aggrieved party may withhold performance of its own reciprocal obligations and may claim damages but may not resort to any other remedy. If it receives notice from the other party that the latter will not perform within that period, or if upon expiry of that period due performance has not been made, the aggrieved party may resort to any of the remedies that may be available under this Chapter.

(3) Where in a case of delay in performance which is not fundamental the aggrieved party has given notice allowing an additional period of time of reasonable length, it may terminate the contract at the end of that period. If the additional period allowed is not of reasonable length it shall be extended to a reasonable length. The aggrieved party may in its notice provide that if the other party fails to perform within the period allowed by the notice the contract shall automatically terminate.

(4) Paragraph (3) does not apply where the obligation which has not been performed is only a minor part of the contractual obligation of the non-performing party.

Article 7.1.6   Exemption Clauses

A clause which limits or excludes one party's liability for non-performance or which permits one party to render performance substantially different from what the other party reasonably expected may not be invoked if it would be grossly unfair to do so, having regard to the purpose of the contract.

Article 7.1.7   Force Majeure

(1) Non-performance by a party is excused if that party proves that the nonperformance was due to an impediment beyond its control and that it could not reasonably be expected to have taken the impediment into account at the time of the conclusion of the contract or to have avoided or overcome it or its consequences.

(2) When the impediment is only temporary, the excuse shall have effect for such period as is reasonable having regard to the effect of the impediment on the performance of the contract.

(3) The party who fails to perform must give notice to the other party of the impediment and its effect on its ability to perform. If the notice is not received by the other party within a reasonable time after the party who fails to perform knew or ought to have known of the impediment, it is liable for damages resulting from such nonreceipt.

(4) Nothing in this article prevents a party from exercising a right to terminate the contract or to withhold performance or request interest on money due.

Section 2:   Right to Performance

Article 7.2.1   Performance of Monetary Obligation

Where a party who is obliged to pay money does not do so, the other party may require payment.

Article 7.2.2   Performance of Non-Monetary Obligation

Where a party who owes an obligation other than one to pay money does not perform, the other party may require performance, unless

(a) performance is impossible in law or in fact;

(b) performance or, where relevant, enforcement is unreasonably burdensome or expensive;

(c) the party entitled to performance may reasonably obtain performance from another source;

(d) performance is of an exclusively personal character; or

(e) the party entitled to performance does not require performance within a reasonable time after it has, or ought to have, become aware of the nonperformance.

Article 7.2.3   Repair and Replacement of Defective Performance

The right to performance includes in appropriate cases the right to require repair, replacement, or other cure of defective performance. The provisions of Articles 7.2.1 and 7.2.2 apply accordingly.

Article 7.2.4   Judicial Penalty

(1) Where the court orders a party to perform, it may also direct that this party pay a penalty if it does not comply with the order.

(2) The penalty shall be paid to the aggrieved party unless mandatory provisions of the law of the forum provide otherwise. Payment of the penalty to the aggrieved party does not exclude any claim for damages.

Article 7.2.5   Change of Remedy

(1) An aggrieved party who has required performance of a non-monetary obligation and who has not received performance within a period fixed or otherwise within a reasonable period of time may invoke any other remedy.

(2) Where the decision of a court for performance of a non-monetary obligation cannot be enforced, the aggrieved party may invoke any other remedy.

Section 3:   Termination

Article 7.3.1   Right to Terminate the Contract

(1) A party may terminate the contract where the failure of the other party to perform an obligation under the contract amounts to a fundamental non-performance.

(2) In determining whether a failure to perform an obligation amounts to a fundamental non-performance regard shall be had, in particular, to whether

(a) the non-performance substantially deprives the aggrieved party of what it was entitled to expect under the contract unless the other party did not foresee and could not reasonably have foreseen such result;

(b) strict compliance with the obligation which has not been performed is of essence under the contract;

(c) the non-performance is intentional or reckless;

(d) the non-performance gives the aggrieved party reason to believe that it cannot rely on the other party's future performance;

(e) the non-performing party will suffer disproportionate loss as a result of the preparation or performance if the contract is terminated.

(3) In the case of delay the aggrieved party may also terminate the contract if the other party fails to perform before the time allowed it under Article 7.1.5 has expired.

Article 7.3.2   Notice of Termination

(1) The right of a party to terminate the contract is exercised by notice to the other party.

(2) If performance has been offered late or otherwise does not conform to the contract the aggrieved party will lose its right to terminate the contract unless it gives notice to the other party within a reasonable time after it has or ought to have become aware of the offer or of the non-conforming performance.

Article 7.3.3   Anticipatory Non-Performance

Where prior to the date for performance by one of the parties it is clear that there will be a fundamental non-performance by that party, the other party may terminate the contract.

Article 7.3.4   Adequate Assurance of Due Performance

A party who reasonably believes that there will be a fundamental non-performance by the other party may demand adequate assurance of due performance and may meanwhile withhold its own performance. Where this assurance is not provided within a reasonable time the party demanding it may terminate the contract.

Article 7.3.5   Effects of Termination in General

(1) Termination of the contract releases both parties from their obligation to effect and to receive future performance.

(2) Termination does not preclude a claim for damages for non-performance.

(3) Termination does not affect any provision in the contract for the settlement of disputes or any other term of the contract which is to operate even after termination.

Article 7.3.6   Restitution with Respect to Contracts to Be Performed at One Time

(1) On termination of a contract to be performed at one time either party may claim restitution of whatever it has supplied under the contract, provided that such party concurrently makes restitution of whatever it has received under the contract.

(2) If restitution in kind is not possible or appropriate, an allowance has to be made in money whenever reasonable.

(3) The recipient of the performance does not have to make an allowance in money if the impossibility to make restitution in kind is attributable to the other party.

(4) Compensation may be claimed for expenses reasonably required to preserve or maintain the performance received.

Article 7.3.7   Restitution with Respect to Contracts to Be Performed over a Period of Time

(1) On termination of a contract to be performed over a period of time restitution can only be claimed for the period after termination has taken effect, provided the contract is divisible.

(2) As far as restitution has to be made, the provisions of Article 7.3.6 apply.

Section 4:   Damages

Article 7.4.1   Right to Damages

Any non-performance gives the aggrieved party a right to damages either exclusively or in conjunction with any other remedies except where the non-performance is excused under these Principles.

Article 7.4.2   Full Compensation

(1) The aggrieved party is entitled to full compensation for harm sustained as a result of the non-performance. Such harm includes both any loss which it suffered

and any gain of which it was deprived, taking into account any gain to the aggrieved party resulting from its avoidance of cost or harm.

(2) Such harm may be non-pecuniary and includes, for instance, physical suffering or emotional distress.

Article 7.4.3   Certainty of Harm

(1) Compensation is due only for harm, including future harm, that is established with a reasonable degree of certainty.

(2) Compensation may be due for the loss of a chance in proportion to the probability of its occurrence.

(3) Where the amount of damages cannot be established with a sufficient degree of certainty, the assessment is at the discretion of the court.

Article 7.4.4   Foreseeability of Harm

The non-performing party is liable only for harm which it foresaw or could reasonably have foreseen at the time of the conclusion of the contract as being likely to result from its non-performance.

Article 7.4.5   Proof of Harm in Case of Replacement Transaction

Where the aggrieved party has terminated the contract and has made a replacement transaction within a reasonable time and in a reasonable manner it may recover the difference between the contract price and the price of the replacement transaction as well as damages for any further harm.

Article 7.4.6   Proof of Harm by Current Price

(1) Where the aggrieved party has terminated the contract and has not made a replacement transaction but there is a current price for the performance contracted for, it may recover the difference between the contract price and the price current at the time the contract is terminated as well as damages for any further harm.

(2) Current price is the price generally charged for goods delivered or services rendered in comparable circumstances at the place where the contract should have been performed or, if there is no current price at that place, the current price at such other place that appears reasonable to take as a reference.

Article 7.4.7   Harm Due in Part to Aggrieved Party

Where the harm is due in part to an act or omission of the aggrieved party or to another event as to which that party bears the risk, the amount of damages shall be reduced to the extent that these factors have contributed to the harm, having regard to the conduct of each of the parties.

Article 7.4.8   Mitigation of Harm

(1) The non-performing party is not liable for harm suffered by the aggrieved party to the extent that the harm could have been reduced by the latter party's taking reasonable steps.

(2) The aggrieved party is entitled to recover any expenses reasonably incurred in attempting to reduce the harm.

Article 7.4.9   Interest for Failure to Pay Money

(1) If a party does not pay a sum of money when it falls due the aggrieved party is entitled to interest upon that sum from the time when payment is due to the time of payment whether or not the non-payment is excused.

(2) The rate of interest shall be the average bank short-term lending rate to prime borrowers prevailing for the currency of payment at the place for payment, or where no such rate exists at that place, then the same rate in the State of the currency of payment. In the absence of such a rate at either place the rate of interest shall be the appropriate rate fixed by the law of the State of the currency of payment.

(3) The aggrieved party is entitled to additional damages if the non-payment caused it a greater harm.

Article 7.4.10   Interest on Damages

Unless otherwise agreed, interest on damages for non-performance of non-monetary obligations accrues as from the time of non-performance.

Article 7.4.11   Manner of Monetary Redress

(1) Damages are to be paid in a lump sum. However, they may be payable in installments where the nature of the harm makes this appropriate.

(2) Damages to be paid in installments may be indexed.

Article 7.4.12   Currency in Which to Assess Damages

Damages are to be assessed either in the currency in which the monetary obligation was expressed or in the currency in which the harm was suffered, whichever is more appropriate.

Article 7.4.13   Agreed Payment for Non-Performance

(1) Where the contract provides that a party who does not perform is to pay a specified sum to the aggrieved party for such non-performance, the aggrieved party is entitled to that sum irrespective of its actual harm.

(2) However, notwithstanding any agreement to the contrary the specified sum may be reduced to a reasonable amount where it is grossly excessive in relation to the harm resulting from the non-performance and to the other circumstances.

CHAPTER 8.   SET-OFF

Article 8.1   Conditions of Set-Off

(1) Where two parties owe each other money or other performances of the same kind, either of them ("the first party") may set off its obligation against that of its obligee ("the other party") if at the time of set-off,

(a) the first party is entitled to perform its obligation;

(b) the other party's obligation is ascertained as to its existence and amount and performance is due.

(2) If the obligations of both parties arise from the same contract, the first party may also set off its obligation against an obligation of the other party which is not ascertained as to its existence or to its amount.

Article 8.2   Foreign Currency Set-Off

Where the obligations are to pay money in different currencies, the right of set-off may be exercised, provided that both currencies are freely convertible and the parties have not agreed that the first party shall pay only in a specified currency.

Article 8.3   Set-Off by Notice

The right of set-off is exercised by notice to the other party.

Article 8.4   Content of Notice

(1) The notice must specify the obligations to which it relates.

(2) If the notice does not specify the obligation against which set-off is exercised, the other party may, within a reasonable time, declare to the first party the obligation to which set-off relates. If no such declaration is made, the set-off will relate to all the obligations proportionally.

Article 8.5   Effect of Set-Off

(1) Set-off discharges the obligations.

(2) If obligations differ in amount, set-off discharges the obligations up to the amount of the lesser obligation.

(3) Set-off takes effect as from the time of notice.

CHAPTER 9.   ASSIGNMENT OF RIGHTS, TRANSFER OF OBLIGATIONS, ASSIGNMENT OF CONTRACTS

Section 1:   Assignment of Rights

Article 9.1.1   Definitions

"Assignment of a right" means the transfer by agreement from one person (the "assignor") to another person (the "assignee"), including transfer by way of security, of the assignor's right to payment of a monetary sum or other performance from a third person ("the obligor").

Article 9.1.2   Exclusions

This Section does not apply to transfers made under the special rules governing the transfers:

    (a) of instruments such as negotiable instruments, documents of title or financial instruments, or

    (b) of rights in the course of transferring a business.

Article 9.1.3   Assignability of Non-Monetary Rights

A right to non-monetary performance may be assigned only if the assignment does not render the obligation significantly more burdensome.

Article 9.1.4   Partial Assignment

    (1) A right to the payment of a monetary sum may be assigned partially.

    (2) A right to other performance may be assigned partially only if it is divisible, and the assignment does not render the obligation significantly more burdensome.

Article 9.1.5   Future Rights

A future right is deemed to be transferred at the time of the agreement, provided the right, when it comes into existence, can be identified as the right to which the assignment relates.

Article 9.1.6   Rights Assigned Without Individual Specification

A number of rights may be assigned without individual specification, provided such rights can be identified as rights to which the assignment relates at the time of the assignment or when they come into existence.

Article 9.1.7   Agreement Between Assignor and Assignee Sufficient

    (1) A right is assigned by mere agreement between the assignor and the assignee, without notice to the obligor.

    (2) The consent of the obligor is not required unless the obligation in the circumstances is of an essentially personal character.

Article 9.1.8   Obligor's Additional Costs

The obligor has a right to be compensated by the assignor or the assignee for any additional costs caused by the assignment.

Article 9.1.9   Non-Assignment Clauses

    (1) The assignment of a right to the payment of a monetary sum is effective notwithstanding an agreement between the assignor and the obligor limiting or prohibiting such an assignment. However, the assignor may be liable to the obligor for breach of contract.

    (2) The assignment of a right to other performance is ineffective if it is contrary to an agreement between the assignor and the obligor limiting or prohibiting the assignment. Nevertheless, the assignment is effective if the assignee, at the time of the assignment, neither knew nor ought to have known of the agreement. The assignor may then be liable to the obligor for breach of contract.

Article 9.1.10   Notice to the Obligor

(1) Until the obligor receives a notice of the assignment from either the assignor or the assignee, it is discharged by paying the assignor.

(2) After the obligor receives such a notice, it is discharged only by paying the assignee.

Article 9.1.11   Successive Assignments

If the same right has been assigned by the same assignor to two or more successive assignees, the obligor is discharged by paying according to the order in which the notices were received.

Article 9.1.12   Adequate Proof of Assignment

(1) If notice of the assignment is given by the assignee, the obligor may request the assignee to provide within a reasonable time adequate proof that the assignment has been made.

(2) Until adequate proof is provided, the obligor may withhold payment.

(3) Unless adequate proof is provided, notice is not effective.

(4) Adequate proof includes, but is not limited to, any writing emanating from the assignor and indicating that the assignment has taken place.

Article 9.1.13   Defences and Rights of Set-Off

(1) The obligor may assert against the assignee all defences that the obligor could assert against the assignor.

(2) The obligor may exercise against the assignee any right of set-off available to the obligor against the assignor up to the time notice of assignment was received.

Article 9.1.14   Rights Related to the Right Assigned

The assignment of a right transfers to the assignee:

(a) all the assignor's rights to payment or other performance under the contract in respect of the right assigned, and

(b) all rights securing performance of the right assigned.

Article 9.1.15   Undertakings of the Assignor

The assignor undertakes towards the assignee, except as otherwise disclosed to the assignee, that:

(a) the assigned right exists at the time of the assignment, unless the right is a future right;

(b) the assignor is entitled to assign the right;

(c) the right has not been previously assigned to another assignee, and it is free from any right or claim from a third party;

(d) the obligor does not have any defences;

(e) neither the obligor nor the assignor has given notice of set-off concerning the assigned right and will not give any such notice;

(f) the assignor will reimburse the assignee for any payment received from the obligor before notice of the assignment was given.

Section 2: Transfer of Obligations

Article 9.2.1   Modes of Transfer

An obligation to pay money or render other performance may be transferred from one person (the "original obligor") to another person (the "new obligor") either

> (a) by an agreement between the original obligor and the new obligor subject to Article 9.2.3, or
>
> (b) by an agreement between the obligee and the new obligor, by which the new obligor assumes the obligation.

Article 9.2.2   Exclusion

This Section does not apply to transfers of obligations made under the special rules governing transfers of obligations in the course of transferring a business.

Article 9.2.3   Requirement of Obligee's Consent to Transfer

The transfer of an obligation by an agreement between the original obligor and the new obligor requires the consent of the obligee.

Article 9.2.4   Advance Consent of Obligee

> (1) The obligee may give its consent in advance.
>
> (2) If the obligee has given its consent in advance, the transfer of the obligation becomes effective when a notice of the transfer is given to the obligee or when the obligee acknowledges it.

Article 9.2.5   Discharge of Original Obligor

> (1) The obligee may discharge the original obligor.
>
> (2) The obligee may also retain the original obligor as an obligor in case the new obligor does not perform properly.
>
> (3) Otherwise the original obligor and the new obligor are jointly and severally liable.

Article 9.2.6   Third Party Performance

> (1) Without the obligee's consent, the obligor may contract with another person that this person will perform the obligation in place of the obligor, unless the obligation in the circumstances has an essentially personal character.
>
> (2) The obligee retains its claim against the obligor.

Article 9.2.7   Defences and Rights of Set-Off

> (1) The new obligor may assert against the obligee all defences which the original obligor could assert against the obligee.
>
> (2) The new obligor may not exercise against the obligee any right of set-off available to the original obligor against the obligee.

Article 9.2.8   Rights Related to the Obligation Transferred

(1) The obligee may assert against the new obligor all its rights to payment or other performance under the contract in respect of the obligation transferred.

(2) If the original obligor is discharged under Article 9.2.5(1), a security granted by any person other than the new obligor for the performance of the obligation is discharged, unless that other person agrees that it should continue to be available to the obligee.

(3) Discharge of the original obligor also extends to any security of the original obligor given to the obligee for the performance of the obligation, unless the security is over an asset which is transferred as part of a transaction between the original obligor and the new obligor.

Section 3:   Assignment of Contracts

Article 9.3.1   Definitions

"Assignment of a contract" means the transfer by agreement from one person (the "assignor") to another person (the "assignee") of the assignor's rights and obligations arising out of a contract with another person (the "other party").

Article 9.3.2   Exclusion

This Section does not apply to the assignment of contracts made under the special rules governing transfers of contracts in the course of transferring a business.

Article 9.3.3   Requirement of Consent of the Other Party

The assignment of a contract requires the consent of the other party.

Article 9.3.4   Advance Consent of the Other Party

(1) The other party may give its consent in advance.

(2) If the other party has given its consent in advance, the assignment of the contract becomes effective when a notice of the assignment is given to the other party or when the other party acknowledges it.

Article 9.3.5   Discharge of the Assignor

(1) The other party may discharge the assignor.

(2) The other party may also retain the assignor as an obligor in case the assignee does not perform properly.

(3) Otherwise the assignor and the assignee are jointly and severally liable.

Article 9.3.6   Defences and Rights of Set-Off

(1) To the extent that the assignment of a contract involves an assignment of rights, Article 9.1.13 applies accordingly.

(2) To the extent that the assignment of a contract involves a transfer of obligations, Article 9.2.7 applies accordingly.

Article 9.3.7   Rights Transferred with the Contract

(1) To the extent that the assignment of a contract involves an assignment of rights, Article 9.1.14 applies accordingly.

(2) To the extent that the assignment of a contract involves a transfer of obligations, Article 9.2.8 applies accordingly.

CHAPTER 10.   LIMITATION PERIODS

Article 10.1   Scope of the Chapter

(1) The exercise of rights governed by these Principles is barred by the expiration of a period of time, referred to as "limitation period", according to the rules of this Chapter.

(2) This Chapter does not govern the time within which one party is required under these Principles, as a condition for the acquisition or exercise of its right, to give notice to the other party or to perform any act other than the institution of legal proceedings.

Article 10.2   Limitation Periods

(1) The general limitation period is three years beginning on the day after the day the obligee knows or ought to know the facts as a result of which the obligee's right can be exercised.

(2) In any event, the maximum limitation period is ten years beginning on the day after the day the right can be exercised.

Article 10.3   Modification of Limitation Periods by the Parties

(1) The parties may modify the limitation periods.

(2) However they may not
   (a) shorten the general limitation period to less than one year;
   (b) shorten the maximum limitation period to less than four years;
   (c) extend the maximum limitation period to more than fifteen years.

Article 10.4   New Limitation Period by Acknowledgement

(1) Where the obligor before the expiration of the general limitation period acknowledges the right of the obligee, a new general limitation period begins on the day after the day of the acknowledgement.

(2) The maximum limitation period does not begin to run again, but may be exceeded by the beginning of a new general limitation period under Art. 10.2(1).

Article 10.5   Suspension by Judicial Proceedings

(1) The running of the limitation period is suspended

(a) when the obligee performs any act, by commencing judicial proceedings or in judicial proceedings already instituted, that is recognised by the law of the court as asserting the obligee's right against the obligor;

(b) in the case of the obligor's insolvency when the obligee has asserted its rights in the insolvency proceedings; or

(c) in the case of proceedings for dissolution of the entity which is the obligor when the obligee has asserted its rights in the dissolution proceedings.

(2) Suspension lasts until a final decision has been issued or until the proceedings have been otherwise terminated.

Article 10.6   Suspension by Arbitral Proceedings

(1) The running of the limitation period is suspended when the obligee performs any act, by commencing arbitral proceedings or in arbitral proceedings already instituted, that is recognised by the law of the arbitral tribunal as asserting the obligee's right against the obligor. In the absence of regulations for arbitral proceedings or provisions determining the exact date of the commencement of arbitral proceedings, the proceedings are deemed to commence on the date on which a request that the right in dispute should be adjudicated reaches the obligor.

(2) Suspension lasts until a binding decision has been issued or until the proceedings have been otherwise terminated.

Article 10.7   Alternative Dispute Resolution

The provisions of Articles 10.5 and 10.6 apply with appropriate modifications to other proceedings whereby the parties request a third person to assist them in their attempt to reach an amicable settlement of their dispute.

Article 10.8   Suspension in Case of Force Majeure, Death or Incapacity

(1) Where the obligee has been prevented by an impediment that is beyond its control and that it could neither avoid nor overcome, from causing a limitation period to cease to run under the preceding articles, the general limitation period is suspended so as not to expire before one year after the relevant impediment has ceased to exist.

(2) Where the impediment consists of the incapacity or death of the obligee or obligor, suspension ceases when a representative for the incapacitated or deceased party or its estate has been appointed or a successor has inherited the respective party's position. The additional one-year period under paragraph (1) applies accordingly.

Article 10.9   The Effects of Expiration of Limitation Period

(1) The expiration of the limitation period does not extinguish the right.

(2) For the expiration of the limitation period to have effect, the obligor must assert it as a defence.

(3) A right may still be relied on as a defence even though the expiration of the limitation period for that right has been asserted.

Article 10.10   Right of Set-Off

The obligee may exercise the right of set-off until the obligor has asserted the expiration of the limitation period.

Article 10.11   Restitution

Where there has been performance in order to discharge an obligation, there is no right of restitution merely because the limitation period has expired.

CHAPTER 11.   PLURALITY OF OBLIGORS AND OF OBLIGEES

Section 1:   Plurality of Obligors

Article 11.1.1   Definitions

When several obligors are bound by the same obligation towards an obligee:
   (a) the obligations are joint and several when each obligor is bound for the whole obligation;
   (b) the obligations are separate when each obligor is bound only for its share.

Article 11.1.2   Presumption of Joint and Several Obligations

When several obligors are bound by the same obligation towards an obligee, they are presumed to be jointly and severally bound, unless the circumstances indicate otherwise.

Article 11.1.3   Obligee's Rights Against Joint and Several Obligors

When obligors are jointly and severally bound, the obligee may require performance from any one of them, until full performance has been received.

Article 11.1.4   Availability of Defences and Rights of Set-Off

A joint and several obligor against whom a claim is made by the obligee may assert all the defences and rights of set-off that are personal to it or that are common to all the co-obligors, but may not assert defences or rights of set-off that are personal to one or several of the other co-obligors.

Article 11.1.5   Effect of Performance or Set-Off

Performance or set-off by a joint and several obligor or set-off by the obligee against one joint and several obligor discharges the other obligors in relation to the obligee to the extent of the performance or set-off.

Article 11.1.6   Effect of Release or Settlement

   (1) Release of one joint and several obligor, or settlement with one joint and several obligor, discharges all the other obligors for the share of the released or settling obligor, unless the circumstances indicate otherwise.

(2) When the other obligors are discharged for the share of the released obligor, they no longer have a contributory claim against the released obligor under Article 11.1.10.

Article 11.1.7   Effect of Expiration or Suspension of Limitation Period

(1) Expiration of the limitation period of the obligee's rights against one joint and several obligor does not affect:

(a) the obligations to the obligee of the other joint and several obligors; or

(b) the rights of recourse between the joint and several obligors under Article 11.1.10.

(2) If the obligee initiates proceedings under Articles 10.5, 10.6 or 10.7 against one joint and several obligor, the running of the limitation period is also suspended against the other joint and several obligors.

Article 11.1.8   Effect of Judgment

(1) A decision by a court as to the liability to the obligee of one joint and several obligor does not affect:

(a) the obligations to the obligee of the other joint and several obligors; or

(b) the rights of recourse between the joint and several obligors under Article 11.1.10.

(2) However, the other joint and several obligors may rely on such a decision, except if it was based on grounds personal to the obligor concerned. In such a case, the rights of recourse between the joint and several obligors under Article 11.1.10 are affected accordingly.

Article 11.1.9   Apportionment Among Joint and Several Obligors

As among themselves, joint and several obligors are bound in equal shares, unless the circumstances indicate otherwise.

Article 11.1.10   Extent of Contributory Claim

A joint and several obligor who has performed more than its share may claim the excess from any of the other obligors to the extent of each obligor's unperformed share.

Article 11.1.11   Rights of the Obligee

(1) A joint and several obligor to whom Article 11.1.10 applies may also exercise the rights of the obligee, including all rights securing their performance, to recover the excess from all or any of the other obligors to the extent of each obligor's unperformed share.

(2) An obligee who has not received full performance retains its rights against the co-obligors to the extent of the unperformed part, with precedence over co-obligors exercising contributory claims.

Article 11.1.12   Defences in Contributory Claims

A joint and several obligor against whom a claim is made by the co-obligor who has performed the obligation :

(a) may raise any common defences and rights of set-off that were available to be asserted by the co-obligor against the obligee ;

(b) may assert defences which are personal to itself ;

(c) may not assert defences and rights of set-off which are personal to one or several of the other co-obligors.

Article 11.1.13   Inability to Recover

If a joint and several obligor who has performed more than that obligor's share is unable, despite all reasonable efforts, to recover contribution from another joint and several obligor, the share of the others, including the one who has performed, is increased proportionally.

Section 2:   *Plurality of Obligees*

Article 11.2.1   Definitions

When several obligees can claim performance of the same obligation from an obligor:

(a) the claims are separate when each obligee can only claim its share;

(b) the claims are joint and several when each obligee can claim the whole performance;

(c) the claims are joint when all obligees have to claim performance together.

Article 11.2.2   Effects of Joint and Several Claims

Full performance of an obligation in favour of one of the joint and several obliges discharges the obligor towards the other obligees.

Article 11.2.3   Availability of Defences Against Joint and Several Obligees

(1) The obligor may assert against any of the joint and several obligees all the defences and rights of set-off that are personal to its relationship to that obligee or that it can assert against all the co-obligees, but may not assert defences and rights of set-off that are personal to its relationship to one or several of the other co-obligees.

(2) The provisions of Articles 11.1.5, 11.1.6, 11.1.7 and 11.1.8 apply, with appropriate adaptations, to joint and several claims.

Article 11.2.4   Allocation Between Joint and Several Obligees

(1) As among themselves, joint and several obligees are entitled to equal shares, unless the circumstances indicate otherwise.

(2) An obligee who has received more than its share must transfer the excess to the other obligees to the extent of their respective shares.

Materials on Electronic Contracting

COMMENT: UNIFORM COMPUTER INFORMATION TRANSACTIONS ACT

The origins of the Uniform Computer Information Transactions Act (UCITA) are intertwined with the revision process of the Uniform Commercial Code — Article 2 on the Sale of Goods.[1] The entities responsible for the systematic review of the Uniform Commercial Code, the National Conference of Commissioners on Uniform State Laws (NCCUSL)[2] and the American Law Institute (ALI), began revisions of Article 2 in the late 1980s. At the same time, a consensus emerged that a new commercial statute was needed to address the fact that the U.S. economy had made a significant shift from an economy based largely on buying and selling tangible items of goods at the time Article 2 was drafted to an economy increasingly dominated by intangible information products and services. Moreover, the distribution mechanisms for all sales transactions often utilize some form of computer technology. While courts applied Article 2 provisions to answer some of the growing number of questions raised by computer- and software-related transactions, its provisions predictably did not address many information-transaction issues, and its application was likely to produce uncertain and nonuniform results.[3] For these reasons, the relevant organizations decided that an article should be added to the Uniform Commercial Code to specifically address the

---

1. For general discussion of UCITA and its drafting history, see John A. Chanin, The Uniform Computer Information Transactions Act: A Practitioner's View, 18 John Marshall J. Computer & Info. L. 279 (Winter 1999); Maureen A. O'Rourke, An Essay on the Challenges of Drafting a Uniform Law of Software Contracting, 10 Lewis & Clark L. Rev. 925 (2006); Carlyle C. Ring, Jr., Uniform Rules for Internet Information Transactions: An Overview of Proposed UCITA, 38 Duq. L. Rev. 319 (Winter 2000).

2. NCCUSL is now also known as the Uniform Law Commission or ULC.

3. See, e.g., Specht v. Netscape Communications Corp., 306 F.3d 17, 30 n.13 (2d Cir. 2002) (discussing application of Article 2 to software and information transactions in earlier cases); Advent Systems Ltd. v. Unisys Corp., 925 F.2d 670 (3d Cir. 1991) (holding that computer software falls within definition of "goods" under U.C.C. Article 2); I. Lan Sys., Inc. v. Nextpoint Networks, Inc., 183 F. Supp. 2d 328 (D. Mass. 2002) (noting that earlier decisions have applied Article 2 to software licenses but expressing doubt about the correctness of that approach).

contract issues arising in software licensing and other computer information transactions. As recounted below, however, UCITA ultimately took the form of a proposed uniform state law outside the ambit of the Uniform Commercial Code.

Precedent existed for expansion of the Uniform Commercial Code to address evolving segments of the marketplace. Uniform Commercial Code Article 2A on Personal Property Leasing was promulgated in 1989 to address the increasing significance of lease transactions in goods. Prior to the promulgation of Article 2A, courts were divided on the question of whether Article 2 applied to lease transactions. Some courts held that leases were indeed "transactions in goods" under Section 2-102 and governed by Article 2 as a matter of law. Courts more frequently decided that leases were not strictly subject to Article 2, but that the provisions of Article 2 could be applied by analogy to leases when appropriate. The Uniform Commercial Code editorial board resolved the question by promulgating Article 2A to specifically address lease transactions. The provisions of Article 2A closely follow many provisions of Article 2 with the adaptations necessary to regulate lease transactions. Article 2A has now been adopted in the District of Columbia and every state except Louisiana.

With Articles 2 and 2A before them and arguably in need of revision, the editorial board of the UCC appointed a drafting committee in the early 1990s that began work on an article that would be designed to address sale and licensing of intangible products. During an early phase of the process, the drafters pursued a "hub and spoke" concept for the Articles 2 and 2A revisions and the new computer information article. The essence of this proposal was that Article 2 would serve as a "hub," containing provisions relevant to all types of transactions; provisions that related specifically to a particular type of transaction would be placed in separate "spoke" articles on sales, leases, and computer information transactions. Over time, however, the "hub and spoke" concept lost support and the drafters reverted to a more traditional format, with separate committees working to revise Articles 2 and 2A and to write a new Article 2B on "computer information" transactions.

During the course of Article 2B's drafting, the draft proposals drew substantial criticism from many quarters, including academics, consumer advocates, governmental agencies, the entertainment industry, and others. At the same time, the position eventually emerged that a uniform law on computer information transfers would not match the framework of Articles 2 and 2A on the sales and leases of goods properly. Ultimately, in spring 1999, the ALI withdrew its support of proposed 2B. Subsequently, the drafters and supporters of Article 2B tendered the proposed statute as a uniform law that would stand apart from the Uniform Commercial Code, with the new name of the Uniform Computer Information Transactions Act, or "UCITA." NCCUSL adopted UCITA in July 1999. Each state then faced the question of whether to adopt the law. Ultimately, Maryland and Virginia were the only states to enact UCITA.[4] The controversy over UCITA is reflected by the fact that a few states have actually adopted laws that preclude application of its provisions by the courts within those states.[5] Moreover, the ALI has declined to endorse or otherwise take a formal position on the Act.[6]

---

4. The status of state enactments or pending legislation can be obtained from the NCCUSL website, *http://www.uniformlaws.org*.

5. See Amelia H. Boss, Taking UCITA on the Road: What Lessons Have We Learned?, 7 Roger Williams U. L. Rev. 167, 175 n.19 (2001) (discussing opposition to UCITA and citing Iowa, West Virginia, and North Carolina as states that have adopted anti-UCITA laws).

6. See Letter from Michael Traynor, ALI President, to ALI membership (February 4, 2003) (published in ALI Reporter, Winter 2003 at p. 3) (stating that ALI discontinued work on UCITA because of

After UCITA's initial promulgation in 1999, a NCCUSL "Standby Committee" continued to study issues raised by the Act's supporters and opponents. A number of recommendations for amending UCITA also resulted from the efforts of an American Bar Association (ABA) Working Group. In response to the commentary from all parties, NCCUSL approved a number of amendments to UCITA at its 2002 Annual Meeting. The amendments clarified a number of issues, such as the prohibition on vendors engaging in a self-help remedy for a licensee's breach by electronically disabling software, and the requirement that UCITA provisions yield to applicable federal or state consumer protection laws.[7]

The scope provision of UCITA, Section 103(a), states that it applies to "computer information transactions," which are defined in Section 102(11) as agreements "to create, modify, transfer, or license computer information or informational rights in computer information." The definitional provisions further reveal that the Act applies to "information in electronic form which is obtained from or through the use of a computer or which is in a form capable of being processed by a computer." Section 102(10). Thus, UCITA applies to transactions that include the use of computer software, computer databases, and Internet and online information. As set out in the text and explained in the comments, Section 103(d) excludes a number of transactions from UCITA's scope, including contracts for personal services (except computer information development and support agreements); employment contracts; contracts where computer information is insignificant (de minimis); computers, televisions, VCRs, DVD players, or similar goods; financial services transactions; contracts for sound recordings and musical works; and contracts for motion pictures and broadcast or cable programming. Commentators have generally recognized that the attempt to define computer information can be particularly difficult and that the formulation in UCITA may prove to be less than ideal.[8]

Transactions that involve a mixture of computer information and other subject matter raise questions of whether all or any part of the transactions should be governed UCITA or other law. The comments to UCITA explain that it should generally apply to the computer information part of a transaction, while common law or the UCC, including Article 2-Sales or 2A-Leases, may apply to another portion.[9] The comments take the position that there should be "no overlap between goods and computer information since computer information and informational rights are not goods."[10] The comments offer this example: "A diskette is a tangible object but the information on the diskette does not become goods simply because it is copied on tangible medium, any more than the information in a book is governed by the law of goods because the book binding and paper may be Article 2 goods." Thus, if a transaction involves goods and computer information (e.g., a computer and software), Article 2 or Article 2A applies to the aspect of the transaction pertaining to the sale or lease of goods, but UCITA applies to the computer information aspects. Adopting what is often called the "gravamen of the

---

expectation that the product would not "meet the ALI's standards of legal coherence, appropriate co-ordination with existing legal doctrine, and fairness to all parties").

7. The amendments are explained in a NCCUSL document, UCITA 2002 Revisions—Memorandum and Chart, August 23, 2002, available at the NCCUSL website (*http://www.uniformlaws.org*).

8. See John A. Chanin, The Uniform Computer Information Transactions Act: A Practitioner's View, 18 John Marshall J. Computer & Info. L. 279 (Winter 1999).

9. Section 103, comment 4.

10. Id.

action" standard, the comment provides that the "law applicable to an issue depends on whether the issue pertains to goods or to computer information."[11]

Section 115 of the 2002 version of UCITA (previously Section 113 in the 1999 version of UCITA) grants parties a broad right to vary by agreement any provision of the Act except for a limited number of mandatory provisions, such as the obligation of good faith and the rule limiting enforceability of unconscionable terms. Comment 2 to Section 115 explains that the "fundamental policy of this Act is freedom of contract." As perhaps the ultimate manifestation of that freedom of contract theme, Section 104 in the 1999 version of the Act allowed parties to opt into or opt out of the statute. The general ability under pre-revision Section 104 to opt into or opt out of UCITA was limited by mandatory provisions — in UCITA or other law, such as certain consumer protection requirements — that cannot be avoided or varied by the agreement of the parties. Nevertheless, the "opt out" provision could lend itself to use by licensors to obtain applicable law that would be less favorable to consumers. In the 2002 amendments, Section 104 was deleted from the official version of UCITA on the ground that Section 115 effectively allows the same ability to opt in or out of UCITA provisions and that original Section 104 was redundant.[12]

Section 109 of UCITA allows the parties to choose the applicable state law, subject only to the limitation that the agreement may not avoid mandatory consumer protection rules. The comments explain that a primary motive for the section is that it allows a small company to engage in dealings with remote parties "spanning multiple jurisdictions and in circumstances that do not depend on physical location of either party or the information" without being subject to the law of all 50 States and all countries in the world.[13] The comments indicate that allowing such small companies to choose the applicable law would avoid barriers to entry.[14] In a companion provision, Section 110 allows parties to choose a judicial forum, with few restrictions. Section 110 provides that "[t]he parties in their agreement may choose an exclusive judicial forum unless the choice is unreasonable and unjust." Such a choice of forum, however, will not be exclusive unless the agreement expressly so provides.

Notably, contract transactions relating to computer information will also be subject to copyright or intellectual property law, which protects the rights of the creator or publisher of the information. As state law, UCITA would necessarily yield to federal copyright law on such issues. UCITA Section 105(a) recognizes the preemptive authority of federal law when there is a conflict between its provisions and federal law, such as the Copyright Act.

A UCITA transaction may be the grant of a license permitting limited use of the information technology, or it may be a more general sale of the rights pertinent to the information.[15] The "license" concept departs substantially from the transfer of rights attendant to a sale or lease. UCITA drafters note that a license may contain a variety of rights and restrictions that limit or govern commercial use, the right to access the information, the computers on which the information can be used, the ability to share use with others, the ability to distribute copies, and the ability to

---

11. Section 103, comment 4(b)(1).
12. See UCITA 2002 Annual Meeting Draft, available at the NCCUSL website (*http://www.uniformlaws. org*).
13. Section 109, comment 2.
14. Id.
15. See Section 102(a)(41) (definition of license); 102(a)(65)(B) (definition of transfer of computer information, a sale).

modify the computer information.[16] UCITA also recognizes that some licenses will be sold by mass marketing to consumers at large, addressing this issue by creation of the concept of a "mass market license" in Sections 102(a)(44) and (45), and facilitating the use of a standard form contract as an efficient manner to handle such transactions.[17] Mass-market licenses include retail transactions directed to the general public offering the license on substantially similar terms.

In addressing the mass market license, Section 209 offers limited consumer protection by providing a consumer is not bound by the contract unless he has consented to the contract after an opportunity to review during initial use or access to the information, or has the right to return, with an allowance for reasonable expense involved, if the terms of the agreement are not available until after the initial agreement has been made. The section also limits the enforceability of the terms of the standard license by denying enforcement to unconscionable terms and any terms conflicting with ones on which the parties have expressly agreed. Section 209, however, must be read together with Section 208, which specifically allows that the parties may adopt terms "after beginning performance or use if the parties had reason to know that their agreement would be represented in whole or part by a later record to be agreed on and there would not be an opportunity to review the record or a copy of it before performance or use begins."

As noted above, the transformation of the proposed legislation from Article 2B to UCITA did not silence its critics.[18] Those who continued to voice concerns about UCITA included the Federal Trade Commission, consumer groups, library associations, entertainment industry groups (motion pictures, recording industry, and writers), academics, and state attorneys general. Perhaps the most frequently heard complaint was that UCITA favors software producers to the detriment of software users. More specifically, the most controversial provisions in UCITA are those that allow licensors to use "shrinkwrap" or "clickwrap" agreements to establish terms governing the licensing or transfer of the computer information.[19] The shrinkwrap license includes terms that are not discovered by the licensee until after payment has been made, the wrapping on the product has been opened, and use of the information has begun. Additionally, the licensor may provide that the failure to return the product within a specified time period will mean that the licensee agrees to all of the licensor's terms in such a license. (The Hines v. Overstock.com and DeFontes v. Dell, Inc. cases in the editors' casebook, Problems in Contract Law, both raise clickwrap, shrinkwrap or later-added terms issues.) The effect of Sections 208 and 209, as indicated above, is to allow the terms to be added after the initial agreement between the parties in mass market licenses, subject to the opportunity to review before final assent and the right of return if the later added terms are

16. See UCITA, Prefatory Note.

17. See Holly K. Towle, Mass Market Transactions in the Uniform Computer Information Transactions Act, 38 Duq. L. Rev. 371 (Winter 2000).

18. See Amelia H. Boss, Taking UCITA on the Road: What Lessons Have We Learned?, 7 Roger Williams U. L. Rev. 167, 174-176 (2001) (discussing opposition to UCITA); Jean Braucher. The Failed Promise of the UCITA Mass-Market Concept and Its Lessons for Policing Standard Form Contracts, 7 J. Small & Emerging Bus. L. 393 (2003).

19. See Brian D. McDonald, Contract Enforceability: The Uniform Computer Information Transactions Act, 16 Berkeley Tech. L.J. 461, 463 (2001) (describing criticism of the UCITA related to power given to computer information industry over consumers); Robert E. Scott, The Rise and Fall of Article 2, 62 La. L. Rev. 1009, 1049-1050 (2002) (summarizing difficulties arising in UCITA drafting process concerning its "seller-friendly" nature).

rejected.[20] The "clickwrap" (or "clickthrough") concept applies to Internet transactions in which the customer must click on "I accept" options to be able to complete the transaction, thus indicating assent to the vendor's terms whether actually read or not.[21] Significantly, however, the clickwrap scenario appears to present the terms of the agreement *before* the licensee gives apparent assent to the terms of the contract.[22]

UCITA makes an attempt to adapt concepts of assent from the Restatement (Second) of Contracts to the computer-information context. More specifically, Section 112 of the Act builds on the basic concept that terms are proposed and then the parties to the contract must manifest assent to those terms in some meaningful way. The comments to the section cite the Restatement (Second) Contracts §19 for the proposition that assent may be given by "written or spoken words or by other acts or by failure to act."[23] The Act does differentiate between situations in which there is a question of manifestation of assent to a particular term as compared with a contract as a whole. Thus, as explained by the comments to Section 112, there may be occasions when the Act or an agreement contemplates that a party will manifest assent to a particular term in a manner analogous to the initialing of a term in a paper agreement.[24] Section 112 ostensibly offers some safeguards against vendor or licensor abuse by requiring that the person manifesting assent have the opportunity to review the terms before accepting proposed terms. The complementary provision of Section 113 (as added in the 2002 amendments to UCITA), defines the "right to return" required by Section 209 when additional terms are disclosed by the vendor after the initial agreement has been made. Sections 112 and 113 are reprinted following this comment.

In the electronic contracting context, assent is typically not reflected by a "signature" in the traditional sense. Instead, UCITA envisions a "record" that is "authenticated" in some form by the parties as a manifestation of assent. Authentication may take various forms that suggest that the party should reasonably be understood as agreeing to the proposed terms. As noted above, in some cases such manifestation of assent may take the form of the failure to return computer information after being chargeable with knowledge of the terms. A person may also authenticate a record, as specified in Section 102(a)(6)(B), by executing or adopting "an electronic symbol, sound, message, or process referring to, attached to, included in, or logically associated or linked with, that record." Section 112(b) also recognizes that the manifestation of assent may be made by an "electronic agent" without need for human intervention with regard to the transaction.

The recognition of the shrinkwrap approach to assent takes on even greater significance in light of the warranty provisions of UCITA. While UCITA adopts several warranties similar to those in Article 2 and adds additional warranties

---

20. Sean F. Crotty, Note: The How and Why of Shrinkwrap License Validation Under the Uniform Computer Information Transactions Act, 33 Rutgers L.J. 745 (2002) (describing and defending enforceability of shrinkwrap licenses under UCITA).

21. See Jennifer Femminella, Note: Online Terms and Conditions Agreements: Bound by the Web, 17 St. John's J. Legal Comment. 87 (2003) (discussing "shrink-wrap," "click-wrap," and "web-wrap" agreements, with the latter presenting the license agreement terms on the vendor's website home page or some other site that must be visited through a "link").

22. For a general defense of shrinkwrap and similar methods of assent, see Dan Streeter, Comment: Into Contract's Undiscovered Country: A Defense of Browse-Wrap Licenses, 39 S.D. L. Rev. 1363 (2002).

23. Section 112, comment 2.

24. Section 112, comment 3(d).

tailored to computer information transactions,[25] Section 406 also allows for disclaimer of all implied warranties, provided the disclaimer is conspicuous as defined by Section 102(a)(14), which generally requires that language be in a heading or contrasting type from the surrounding text. The official comment states that the test for conspicuousness of a term depends on whether "the attention of an ordinary person reasonably ought to have been called to it."[26] The specific provisions of the section, particularly in classifying a heading of the same size as surrounding text as being conspicuous, suggest that the test may be more lenient than in cases decided under Section 2-316 of the UCC.[27] Therefore, the later-added terms in a shrinkwrap agreement, or the unread pre-assent terms in a clickwrap agreement, may well include a disclaimer of warranty liability or limitation on the remedy available for breach.

UCITA includes an unconscionability provision intended to allow courts to police against unfair contracts or behavior, Section 111. The provisions of UCC Section 2-302 are repeated almost verbatim in Section 111 and the accompanying comments to Section 111 make it clear that UCITA fully embraces UCC Section 2-302 and cases decided thereunder. One innovation in the comments to Section 111, however, is a reflection that the unconscionability section may be used to guard against oppression that might result from automated contracting through electronic agents. Similarly, UCITA Section 116(b) (Section 114(b) under the 1999 version of UCITA) incorporates the principle that the duty of good faith inures in the performance and enforcement of all contracts in language identical to UCC Article §1-304. These provisions may have particular relevance to issues of assent to or enforcement of contract terms.

At the same time that NCCUSL promulgated UCITA, it also issued the Uniform Electronic Transactions Act (UETA) for introduction to state legislatures.[28] The comments to UETA state that its fundamental directive is to "enable electronic commerce" while maintaining "technological neutrality." UETA seeks to provide basic guidance regarding the validity and evidentiary acceptability of electronic records and signatures despite many uncertainties in the area.[29] UETA will apply only if each party to a transaction has agreed to conduct the transaction electronically as "determined from the context and surrounding circumstances, including the parties' conduct."[30] The essential effect of UETA is to provide that a record or signature will not be found invalid solely because of its electronic form, nor will a contract be unenforceable merely because an electronic record was used in its formation. This result will be true even if the law otherwise would require a writing or signature. Congress has also taken steps to promote uniformity of the law regarding electronic signatures and records by passing the Electronic Signatures in Global and National Commerce Act, reproduced later in this section.

---

25. See Section 402 on express warranty, Section 403 on implied warranty of merchantability of computer program, Section 404 on implied warranty of informational content, and Section 405 on implied warranty related to licensee's purpose.

26. Section 102, comment 12.

27. Section 102(a)(14)(A)(i).

28. For a comparison of UCITA and UETA, and their relative merits, see Cem Kaner, E-Commerce Provisions in the UCITA and UETA, *http://www.badsoftware.com/uetaanducitauccbull.htm* (visited May 12, 2012).

29. See generally Shea C. Meehan, Consumer Protection Law and the Uniform Electronic Transactions Act (UETA): Why States Should Adopt UETA as Drafted, 36 Idaho L. Rev. 563 (2000).

30. Section 5(b).

UNIFORM COMPUTER INFORMATION TRANSACTIONS ACT

Section 112. Manifesting Assent

(a) **[How person manifests assent.]** A person manifests assent to a record or term if the person, acting with knowledge of, or after having an opportunity to review the record or term or a copy of it:

(1) authenticates the record or term with intent to adopt or accept it; or

(2) intentionally engages in conduct or makes statements with reason to know that the other party or its electronic agent may infer from the conduct or statement that the person assents to the record or term.

(b) **[How electronic agent manifests assent.]** An electronic agent manifests assent to a record or term if, after having an opportunity to review it, the electronic agent:

(1) authenticates the record or term; or

(2) engages in operations that in the circumstances indicate acceptance of the record or term.

(c) **[Assent to specific term.]** If this [Act] or other law requires assent to a specific term, a manifestation of assent must relate specifically to the term.

(d) **[Proof of assent.]** Conduct or operations manifesting assent may be proved in any manner, including a showing that a person or an electronic agent obtained or used the information or informational rights and that a procedure existed by which a person or an electronic agent must have engaged in the conduct or operations in order to do so. Proof of compliance with subsection (a)(2) is sufficient if there is conduct that assents and subsequent conduct that reaffirms assent by electronic means.

(e) **[Agreement for future transactions.]** The effect of this section may be modified by an agreement setting out standards applicable to future transactions between the parties.

(f) **[Online services, network access, and telecommunications services.]** Providers of online services, network access, and telecommunications services, or the operators of facilities thereof, do not manifest assent to a contractual relationship simply by their provision of those services to other parties, including, without limitation, transmission, routing, or providing connections; linking; caching; hosting; information location tools; and storage of materials, at the request or initiation of a person other than the service provider.

Uniform Law Source: Restatement (Second) of Contracts §19.

Definitional Cross References: Section 102: "Agreement"; "Authenticate"; "Copy"; "Electronic"; "Electronic agent"; "Delivery"; "Information"; "Informational Rights"; "Knowledge"; "Mass-market license"; "Personal"; "Record"; "Return"; "Term". Section 117: "Reason to know".

Comment

1. Scope of Section. This section provides standards for "manifestation of assent." Section 113 deals with the related, important concept of an "opportunity to review." In this Act, having an opportunity to review a record is a precondition to manifesting assent.

2. General Theme. The term "manifesting assent" comes from *Restatement (Second) of Contracts* §19. This section corresponds to *Restatement* §19, but more fully explicates the concept. Codification establishes uniformity that is lacking in common law.

Restatement (Second) of Contracts §19(1) provides: "The manifestation of assent may be made wholly or partly by written or spoken words or by other acts or by failure to act." This section adopts that view. Conduct can convey assent as clearly as words. This rule is important in electronic commerce, where most interactions involve conduct rather than words. Subsection (b) adapts that principle to electronic agent contracting.

"Manifesting assent" has several roles: 1) a method by which a party agrees to a contract; 2) a method by which a party adopts terms of a record as the terms of a contract; and 3) if required by this Act, a means of assenting to a particular term. In most cases, the same act accomplishes the results under 1 and 2.

Manifesting assent does not require any specific formality of language or conduct. In this Act, however, to manifest assent to a record or term requires meeting three conditions:

First, the person must have knowledge of the record or term or an opportunity to review it before assenting. An opportunity to review requires that the record be available in a manner that ought to call it to the attention of a reasonable person and that readily permits review. Section 113 may also require a right of return if the opportunity to review comes after a person becomes obligated to pay or begins performance.

Second, having had an opportunity to review, the person must manifest assent. The person may authenticate the record or term, express assent verbally, or intentionally engage in conduct with reason to know that the conduct indicates assent. *Restatement (Second) of Contracts* §19. As in the *Restatement* this can include a failure to action if the circumstances so indicate.

Third, the conduct, statement, or authentication must be attributable in law to the person. General agency law and Section 212 provide standards for attribution.

3. Manifesting Assent.

a. Assent by Statements or Authentication. A person can assent to a record or term by stating or otherwise indicating its assent or by "authenticating" the record or term. Authentication occurs if a party signs a record or does an electronic equivalent. Section 102 (a)(6).

b. Assent by Conduct. Assent occurs if a person acts or fails to act having reason to know its behavior will be viewed by the other party as indicating assent. Whether this occurs depends on the circumstances. As in common law, proof of assent does not require proof of a person's subjective intent or purpose, but focuses on objective indicia, including whether there was an act or a failure to act voluntarily engaged in with reason to know that an inference of assent would be drawn. Actions objectively indicating assent are assent. This follows modern contract law doctrines of objective assent. Doctrines of mistake, fraud, and duress apply in appropriate cases.

Assent does not require that a party be able to negotiate or modify terms, but the assenting behavior must be intentional (voluntary). This same rule prevails in all other contract law. Intentional conduct is satisfied if the alternative of refusing to act exists, even if refusing leaves no alternative source for the computer information. On the other hand, conduct is not assent if it is conduct which the assenting party cannot avoid doing, such as blinking one's eyes. Courts use common sense in applying this standard in common law and will do so under this Act. Actions in a context of a mutual reservation of the right to defer agreement to a contract do not manifest assent; neither party has any reason to believe that its conduct will suggest assent to the other party. . . .

5. Proof of Assent. Many different acts can establish assent to a contract or a contract term. It is not possible to state them in a statute. In electronic commerce, one important method is by showing that a procedure existed that required an authentication or other assent in order to proceed in an automated system. This is recognized in subsection (d).

Subsection (d) also encourages use of double assent procedures as a reconfirmation showing intentional assent ("intentionally engages in conduct . . . with reason to know"). It makes clear that if the assenting party has an opportunity to confirm or deny assent before proceeding to obtain or use information, confirmation meets the requirement of subsection (a)(2). This does not alter the effectiveness of a single indication of assent. When properly set out with an opportunity to review terms and to make clear that an act such as clicking assent on-screen is assent, a single indication of assent suffices. See Caspi v. Microsoft Network, L.L.C., 323 N.J. Super. 118, 732 A.2d 528 (N.J. A.D. 1999), *cert. den.*, 162 N.J. 199, 743 A.2d 851 (1999); Register.com, Inc. v. Verio, Inc., 126 F. Supp. 2d 238 (S.D.N.Y. 2000).

> **Illustration 1:** The registration screen for NY Online prominently states: "Please read the License. It contains important terms about your use and our obligations. If you agree to the license, indicate this by clicking the 'I agree' button. If you do not agree, click 'I decline'." The on-screen buttons are clearly identified. The underlined text is a hypertext link that, if selected, promptly displays the license. A party that indicates "I agree" assents to the license and adopts its terms. . . .

Section 113. Opportunity to Review

(a) **[Manner of availability generally.]** A person has an opportunity to review a record or term only if it is made available in a manner that ought to call it to the attention of a reasonable person and permit review.

(b) **[Manner of availability by electronic agent.]** An electronic agent has an opportunity to review a record or term only if it is made available in a manner that would enable a reasonably configured electronic agent to react to the record or term.

(c) **[When right of return required.]** If a record or term is available for review only after a person becomes obligated to pay or begins its performance, the person has an opportunity to review only if it has a right to a return if it rejects the record. However, a right to a return is not required if:

(1) the record proposes a modification of contract or provides particulars of performance under Section 305; or

(2) the primary performance is other than delivery or acceptance of a copy, the agreement is not a mass-market transaction, and the parties at the time of contracting had reason to know that a record or term would be presented after performance, use, or access to the information began.

(d) **[Right of return created.]** The right to a return under this section may arise by law or agreement.

(e) **[Agreement for future transactions.]** The effect of this section may be modified by an agreement setting out standards applicable to future transactions between the parties.

Definitional Cross References: Section 102: "Agreement"; "Copy"; "Information"; "Mass-market transaction"; "Record"; "Term".

Comments

1. Scope of This Section. This section sets out the basic standards for when a party has been given an opportunity to review the terms of a record. Unless there is an opportunity to review the record, under Section 112 the party cannot manifest assent to it.

2. Opportunity to Review. A manifestation of assent to a record or term under this Act cannot occur unless there was an opportunity to review the record or term. Common law does not clearly establish this requirement, but the requirement of an opportunity to review terms reasonably made available reflects simple fairness and establishes concepts that curtail procedural aspects of unconscionability. Section 111. For a person, an opportunity to review requires that a record be made available in a manner that ought to call it to the attention of a reasonable person and permit review. See Specht v. Netscape Communications Corp., [306 F.3d 17, 28-29 n. 13 (2d Cir. 2002)]. This requirement is met if the person knows of the record or has reason to know that the record or term exists in a form and location that in the circumstances permit review of it or a copy of it. For an electronic agent, an opportunity to review exists only if the record is one to which a reasonably configured electronic agent could respond. Terms made available for review during an over-the-counter transaction or otherwise in a manner required under federal law give an opportunity to review.

a. Declining to Use the Opportunity to Review. An opportunity to review does not require that the person use that opportunity. The condition is met even if the person does not read or actually review the record. This is not changed because the party desires to complete the transaction rapidly, is under pressure to do so, or because the party has other demands on its attention, unless the one party actively manipulates circumstances to induce the other party not to review the record. Such manipulation may vitiate the alleged opportunity to review.

b. Permits Review. How a record is made available for review may differ for electronic and paper records. In both, however, a record is not available for review if access to it is so time-consuming or cumbersome, or if its presentation is so obscure or oblique, as to make it difficult to review. It must be presented in a way as to reasonably permit review. In an electronic system, a record promptly accessible through an electronic link ordinarily qualifies. Actions that comply with federal or other applicable consumer laws that require making contract terms or disclosure available, or that provide standards for doing so, satisfy this requirement.

c. Right to Return. If terms in a record are not available until after there is an initial commitment to the transaction, subsection (c) indicates that ordinarily there is no opportunity to review unless the party can return the product (or for a vendor that refuses the other party's terms, recover the product) and receive appropriate reimbursement of payments if it rejects the terms. The return right creates a situation where meaningful assent can occur. The right exists only for the first licensee. If the right to a return is created only by agreement or by an offer from the one party, rather than by law, the right must be communicated to the other person so that the person ought to become aware of it. . . .

E-SIGN ACT AND UNIFORM ELECTRONIC TRANSACTIONS ACT

EDITORS' NOTE

More than 20 years ago American businesses began engaging in electronic transactions on a large scale.[1] In 1994 Utah became the first state to enact a law regulating electronic contracting and other states soon adopted legislation, but their approaches varied widely.[2] In 1997 the National Conference of Commissioners on Uniform State Laws (NCCUSL)[3] decided to prepare a uniform law on the subject and approved the Uniform Electronic Transactions Act (UETA) in July 1999. UETA should not be confused with the Uniform Computer Information Transactions Act (UCITA), discussed in another section of this supplement.

After the promulgation of UETA, there was concern that states were not moving quickly enough to adopt the uniform law and that inconsistencies persisted among the various state laws. Only 22 states had adopted a version of UETA by the year 2000.[4] Congress chose to act in the area of electronic contracting at the urging of high tech and financial services industries, which were concerned about the pace of enactment at the state level and the likelihood that some states would adopt nonuniform versions of UETA.[5] On June 30, 2000, President Clinton signed the Electronic Signatures in Global and National Commerce Act (E-Sign Act).

The relationship between UETA and the E-Sign Act is somewhat complex. With certain exceptions, the E-Sign Act preempts state laws and regulations.[6] However, Congress authorized states to supersede the E-Sign Act if they adopt the 1999 version of UETA. See E-Sign Act §102(a)(1). A state that does not adopt UETA can opt out of the E-Sign Act if it adopts other legislation that is not inconsistent with the

---

1. See Robert A. Wittie & Jane K. Winn, Electronic Records and Signatures under the Federal E-Sign Legislation and the UETA, 56 Bus. Law. 293, 295 (Nov. 2000).

2. Id. at 294-295.

3. NCCUSL is now also referred to as the Uniform Law Commission or ULC.

4. See Anda Lincoln, Comment: Electronic Signature Laws and the Need for Uniformity in the Global Market, 8 J. Small & Emerging Bus. L. 67, 72-73 (2004).

5. See Robert A. Wittie & Jane K. Winn, Electronic Records and Signatures under the Federal E-Sign Legislation and the UETA, 56 Bus. Law. at 296.

6. See Jean Braucher, Rent-Seeking and Risk-Fixing in the New Statutory Law of Electronic Commerce: Difficulties in Moving Consumer Protection Online, 2001 Wis. L. Rev. 527 (analyzing and comparing effect of UETA and Electronic Signatures in Global and National Commerce Act).

requirements of the E-Sign Act. See E-Sign Act §102(a)(2). Thus, if a state has adopted UETA without amendments, the state law rather than the E-Sign Act will control a transaction. If a state has not adopted any legislation, the E-Sign Act provides the governing rules. If a state has adopted some legislation on electronic contracting other than UETA, the validity of such legislation will depend on its consistency with the E-Sign Act.

As explained by the Official Comments to Section 7 of UETA, the fundamental premise of the Act is that the use of an electronic medium should not preclude the satisfaction of requirements for contract formation. UETA Section 7 (a) provides that: "A record or signature may not be denied legal effect or enforceability solely because it is in electronic form." Similarly, Section 7(c) provides that an electronic record satisfies any legal requirement that a record be in writing, and 7(d) states that an electronic signature will satisfy any requirement under the law for a signature. Thus, UETA does not change the substantive law of contracts, but rather provides that electronic communications may be used to satisfy any requirements for a writing or a signature.[7]

Another basic principle of UETA is that it depends on the free agreement of the parties to conduct a transaction electronically, as stated in Section 5. The test of whether the parties have reached such an agreement, however, is rather liberally construed with the goal of promoting broader application of UETA. Section 5(b) states, "Whether the parties agree to conduct a transaction by electronic means is determined from the context and surrounding circumstances, including the parties' conduct." Thus, an agreement to conduct a transaction electronically need not be explicit and it may be found in the parties' conduct. This latter point is emphasized by the Official Comment to Section 5. The full text of UETA is available online at the NCCUSL or ULC website.[8] As of May 2012, 47 states and the District of Columbia had adopted UETA.[9]

The E-Sign Act has three core provisions. First, section 101(a)(1) authorizes the use of electronic signatures. The Act provides for technological innovation and diversity by a broad definition of what constitutes an electronic signature: "The term 'electronic signature' means an electronic sound, symbol, or process, attached to or logically associated with a contract or other record and executed or adopted by a person with the intent to sign the record." Section 106(5). The Act does not require businesses or consumers to use electronic signatures and it preserves other rights and obligations. See §101(b). Second, section 101(a)(2) validates the use of electronic records of transactions and states that a contract may not be denied legal effect solely because an electronic signature or electronic record was used in its formation. The Act prohibits states from giving greater legal status to any specific technology used to make an electronic signature or record. See §102(a)(2)(A)(ii). Finally, the Act contains various consumer protection measures. See §§101(c)(1) (disclosure and consent) and 101(c)(2) (preservation of consumer rights granted under other law). Some transactions are specifically exempted from the E-Sign Act. These include execution of wills, codicils, and trusts; documents affecting family matters such as divorce decrees or separation agreements; and foreclosure notices. See §103.

---

7. See Valerie Watnick, The Electronic Formation of Contracts and the Common Law "Mailbox Rule," 56 Baylor L. Rev. 175, 189-190 (2004).

8. The address for the NCCUSL website is *http://www.uniformlaws.org* (visited May 12, 2012).

9. The state adoptions of UETA are reported at the NCCUSL website [*http://www.uniformlaws.org/ LegislativeFactSheet.aspx?title=Electronic%20Transactions%20Act*] (visited May 12, 2012). The states that have yet to adopt UETA are Illinois, New York, and Washington.

While the E-Sign Act authorizes use of electronic signatures and electronic recordkeeping, the extent and form that such transactions take will vary widely depending on market considerations. See Bill Zoellick, Wide Use of Electronic Signatures Awaits Market Decisions about Their Risks and Benefits, 72-DEC N.Y. St. B.J. 10 (Nov./Dec. 2000). For further discussions of the E-Sign Act see Holly K. Towle, E-Signatures — Basics of the U.S. Struture, 38 Hous. L. Rev. 921(2001); Scott R. Zemnick, Note, The E-Sign Act: The Means to Effectively Facilitate the Growth and Development of E-Commerce, 76 Chi.-Kent L. Rev. 1965 (2001).

The E-sign Act is reprinted below, followed by many sections and some comments from UETA.

ELECTRONIC SIGNATURES IN GLOBAL AND NATIONAL COMMERCE ACT

PL 106-229, 114 Stat 464, June 30, 2000

An Act to facilitate the use of electronic records and signatures in interstate or foreign commerce.

Be it enacted by the Senate and House of Representatives of the United States of America in Congress assembled,

Section 1. Short Title

This Act may be cited as the "Electronic Signatures in Global and National Commerce Act".

TITLE I — ELECTRONIC RECORDS AND SIGNATURES IN COMMERCE

SEC. 101. GENERAL RULE OF VALIDITY. [15 USCA §7001]

(a) IN GENERAL. — Notwithstanding any statute, regulation, or other rule of law (other than this title and title II), with respect to any transaction in or affecting interstate or foreign commerce —

(1) a signature, contract, or other record relating to such transaction may not be denied legal effect, validity, or enforceability solely because it is in electronic form; and

(2) a contract relating to such transaction may not be denied legal effect, validity, or enforceability solely because an electronic signature or electronic record was used in its formation.

(b) PRESERVATION OF RIGHTS AND OBLIGATIONS. — This title does not —

(1) limit, alter, or otherwise affect any requirement imposed by a statute, regulation, or rule of law relating to the rights and obligations of persons under such statute, regulation, or rule of law other than a requirement that contracts or other records be written, signed, or in nonelectronic form; or

(2) require any person to agree to use or accept electronic records or electronic signatures, other than a governmental agency with respect to a record other than a contract to which it is a party.

(c) CONSUMER DISCLOSURES. —

(1) CONSENT TO ELECTRONIC RECORDS. — Notwithstanding subsection (a), if a statute, regulation, or other rule of law requires that information relating to a transaction or transactions in or affecting interstate or foreign commerce be provided or made available to a consumer in writing, the use of an electronic record to provide or make available (whichever is required) such information satisfies the requirement that such information be in writing if—

(A) the consumer has affirmatively consented to such use and has not withdrawn such consent;

(B) the consumer, prior to consenting, is provided with a clear and conspicuous statement—

(i) informing the consumer of (I) any right or option of the consumer to have the record provided or made available on paper or in nonelectronic form, and (II) the right of the consumer to withdraw the consent to have the record provided or made available in an electronic form and of any conditions, consequences (which may include termination of the parties' relationship), or fees in the event of such withdrawal;

(ii) informing the consumer of whether the consent applies (I) only to the particular transaction which gave rise to the obligation to provide the record, or (II) to identified categories of records that may be provided or made available during the course of the parties' relationship;

(iii) describing the procedures the consumer must use to withdraw consent as provided in clause (i) and to update information needed to contact the consumer electronically; and

(iv) informing the consumer (I) how, after the consent, the consumer may, upon request, obtain a paper copy of an electronic record, and (II) whether any fee will be charged for such copy;

(C) the consumer—

(i) prior to consenting, is provided with a statement of the hardware and software requirements for access to and retention of the electronic records; and

(ii) consents electronically, or confirms his or her consent electronically, in a manner that reasonably demonstrates that the consumer can access information in the electronic form that will be used to provide the information that is the subject of the consent; and

(D) after the consent of a consumer in accordance with subparagraph (A), if a change in the hardware or software requirements needed to access or retain electronic records creates a material risk that the consumer will not be able to access or retain a subsequent electronic record that was the subject of the consent, the person providing the electronic record—

(i) provides the consumer with a statement of (I) the revised hardware and software requirements for access to and retention of the electronic records, and (II) the right to withdraw consent without the imposition of any fees for such withdrawal and without the imposition of any condition or consequence that was not disclosed under subparagraph (B)(i); and

(ii) again complies with subparagraph (C).

(2) OTHER RIGHTS. —

(A) PRESERVATION OF CONSUMER PROTECTIONS. — Nothing in this title affects the content or timing of any disclosure or other record required to be provided or made available to any consumer under any statute, regulation, or other rule of law.

(B) VERIFICATION OR ACKNOWLEDGMENT.—If a law that was enacted prior to this Act expressly requires a record to be provided or made available by a specified method that requires verification or acknowledgment of receipt, the record may be provided or made available electronically only if the method used provides verification or acknowledgment of receipt (whichever is required).

(3) EFFECT OF FAILURE TO OBTAIN ELECTRONIC CONSENT OR CONFIRMATION OF CONSENT.—The legal effectiveness, validity, or enforceability of any contract executed by a consumer shall not be denied solely because of the failure to obtain electronic consent or confirmation of consent by that consumer in accordance with paragraph (1)(C)(ii).

(4) PROSPECTIVE EFFECT.—Withdrawal of consent by a consumer shall not affect the legal effectiveness, validity, or enforceability of electronic records provided or made available to that consumer in accordance with paragraph (1) prior to implementation of the consumer's withdrawal of consent. A consumer's withdrawal of consent shall be effective within a reasonable period of time after receipt of the withdrawal by the provider of the record. Failure to comply with paragraph (1)(D) may, at the election of the consumer, be treated as a withdrawal of consent for purposes of this paragraph.

(5) PRIOR CONSENT.—This subsection does not apply to any records that are provided or made available to a consumer who has consented prior to the effective date of this title to receive such records in electronic form as permitted by any statute, regulation, or other rule of law.

(6) ORAL COMMUNICATIONS.—An oral communication or a recording of an oral communication shall not qualify as an electronic record for purposes of this subsection except as otherwise provided under applicable law.

(d) RETENTION OF CONTRACTS AND RECORDS.—

(1) ACCURACY AND ACCESSIBILITY.—If a statute, regulation, or other rule of law requires that a contract or other record relating to a transaction in or affecting interstate or foreign commerce be retained, that requirement is met by retaining an electronic record of the information in the contract or other record that—

(A) accurately reflects the information set forth in the contract or other record; and

(B) remains accessible to all persons who are entitled to access by statute, regulation, or rule of law, for the period required by such statute, regulation, or rule of law, in a form that is capable of being accurately reproduced for later reference, whether by transmission, printing, or otherwise.

(2) EXCEPTION.—A requirement to retain a contract or other record in accordance with paragraph (1) does not apply to any information whose sole purpose is to enable the contract or other record to be sent, communicated, or received.

(3) ORIGINALS.—If a statute, regulation, or other rule of law requires a contract or other record relating to a transaction in or affecting interstate or foreign commerce to be provided, available, or retained in its original form, or provides consequences if the contract or other record is not provided, available,

or retained in its original form, that statute, regulation, or rule of law is satisfied by an electronic record that complies with paragraph (1).

(4) CHECKS. — If a statute, regulation, or other rule of law requires the retention of a check, that requirement is satisfied by retention of an electronic record of the information on the front and back of the check in accordance with paragraph (1).

(e) ACCURACY AND ABILITY TO RETAIN CONTRACTS AND OTHER RECORDS. — Notwithstanding subsection (a), if a statute, regulation, or other rule of law requires that a contract or other record relating to a transaction in or affecting interstate or foreign commerce be in writing, the legal effect, validity, or enforceability of an electronic record of such contract or other record may be denied if such electronic record is not in a form that is capable of being retained and accurately reproduced for later reference by all parties or persons who are entitled to retain the contract or other record.

(f) PROXIMITY. — Nothing in this title affects the proximity required by any statute, regulation, or other rule of law with respect to any warning, notice, disclosure, or other record required to be posted, displayed, or publicly affixed.

(g) NOTARIZATION AND ACKNOWLEDGMENT. — If a statute, regulation, or other rule of law requires a signature or record relating to a transaction in or affecting interstate or foreign commerce to be notarized, acknowledged, verified, or made under oath, that requirement is satisfied if the electronic signature of the person authorized to perform those acts, together with all other information required to be included by other applicable statute, regulation, or rule of law, is attached to or logically associated with the signature or record.

(h) ELECTRONIC AGENTS. — A contract or other record relating to a transaction in or affecting interstate or foreign commerce may not be denied legal effect, validity, or enforceability solely because its formation, creation, or delivery involved the action of one or more electronic agents so long as the action of any such electronic agent is legally attributable to the person to be bound.

(i) INSURANCE. — It is the specific intent of the Congress that this title and title II apply to the business of insurance.

(j) INSURANCE AGENTS AND BROKERS. — An insurance agent or broker acting under the direction of a party that enters into a contract by means of an electronic record or electronic signature may not be held liable for any deficiency in the electronic procedures agreed to by the parties under that contract if —

(1) the agent or broker has not engaged in negligent, reckless, or intentional tortuous conduct;

(2) the agent or broker was not involved in the development or establishment of such electronic procedures; and

(3) the agent or broker did not deviate from such procedures.

SEC. 102.   EXEMPTION TO PREEMPTION. [15 USCA §7002]

(a) IN GENERAL. — A State statute, regulation, or other rule of law may modify, limit, or supersede the provisions of section 101 with respect to State law only if such statute, regulation, or rule of law —

(1) constitutes an enactment or adoption of the Uniform Electronic Transactions Act as approved and recommended for enactment in all the States by the National Conference of Commissioners on Uniform State Laws in 1999, except that any exception to the scope of such Act enacted by a State under

section 3(b)(4) of such Act shall be preempted to the extent such exception is inconsistent with this title or title II, or would not be permitted under paragraph (2)(A)(ii) of this subsection; or

(2) (A) specifies the alternative procedures or requirements for the use or acceptance (or both) of electronic records or electronic signatures to establish the legal effect, validity, or enforceability of contracts or other records, if —

(i) such alternative procedures or requirements are consistent with this title and title II; and

(ii) such alternative procedures or requirements do not require, or accord greater legal status or effect to, the implementation or application of a specific technology or technical specification for performing the functions of creating, storing, generating, receiving, communicating, or authenticating electronic records or electronic signatures; and

(B) if enacted or adopted after the date of the enactment of this Act, makes specific reference to this Act.

(b) EXCEPTIONS FOR ACTIONS BY STATES AS MARKET PARTICI-PANTS. — Subsection (a)(2)(A)(ii) shall not apply to the statutes, regulations, or other rules of law governing procurement by any State, or any agency or instrumentality thereof.

(c) PREVENTION OF CIRCUMVENTION. — Subsection (a) does not permit a State to circumvent this title or title II through the imposition of nonelectronic delivery methods under section 8(b)(2) of the Uniform Electronic Transactions Act.

SEC. 103.   SPECIFIC EXCEPTIONS. [15 USCA §7003]

(a) EXCEPTED REQUIREMENTS. — The provisions of section 101 shall not apply to a contract or other record to the extent it is governed by —

(1) a statute, regulation, or other rule of law governing the creation and execution of wills, codicils, or testamentary trusts;

(2) a State statute, regulation, or other rule of law governing adoption, divorce, or other matters of family law; or

(3) the Uniform Commercial Code, as in effect in any State, other than sections 1-107 and 1-206 and Articles 2 and 2A.

(b) ADDITIONAL EXCEPTIONS. — The provisions of section 101 shall not apply to —

(1) court orders or notices, or official court documents (including briefs, pleadings, and other writings) required to be executed in connection with court proceedings;

(2) any notice of —

(A) the cancellation or termination of utility services (including water, heat, and power);

(B) default, acceleration, repossession, foreclosure, or eviction, or the right to cure, under a credit agreement secured by, or a rental agreement for, a primary residence of an individual;

(C) the cancellation or termination of health insurance or benefits or life insurance benefits (excluding annuities); or

(D) recall of a product, or material failure of a product, that risks endangering health or safety; or

(3) any document required to accompany any transportation or handling of hazardous materials, pesticides, or other toxic or dangerous materials.

(c) REVIEW OF EXCEPTIONS. —

(1) EVALUATION REQUIRED. — The Secretary of Commerce, acting through the Assistant Secretary for Communications and Information, shall review the operation of the exceptions in subsections (a) and (b) to evaluate, over a period of 3 years, whether such exceptions continue to be necessary for the protection of consumers. Within 3 years after the date of enactment of this Act, the Assistant Secretary shall submit a report to the Congress on the results of such evaluation.

(2) DETERMINATIONS. — If a Federal regulatory agency, with respect to matter within its jurisdiction, determines after notice and an opportunity for public comment, and publishes a finding, that one or more such exceptions are no longer necessary for the protection of consumers and eliminating such exceptions will not increase the material risk of harm to consumers, such agency may extend the application of section 101 to the exceptions identified in such finding.

SEC. 104.   APPLICABILITY TO FEDERAL AND STATE GOVERNMENTS.
[15 USCA §7004]

(a) FILING AND ACCESS REQUIREMENTS. — Subject to subsection (c)(2), nothing in this title limits or supersedes any requirement by a Federal regulatory agency, self-regulatory organization, or State regulatory agency that records be filed with such agency or organization in accordance with specified standards or formats.

(b) PRESERVATION OF EXISTING RULEMAKING AUTHORITY. —

(1) USE OF AUTHORITY TO INTERPRET. — Subject to paragraph (2) and subsection (c), a Federal regulatory agency or State regulatory agency that is responsible for rulemaking under any other statute may interpret section 101 with respect to such statute through —

(A) the issuance of regulations pursuant to a statute; or

(B) to the extent such agency is authorized by statute to issue orders or guidance, the issuance of orders or guidance of general applicability that are publicly available and published (in the Federal Register in the case of an order or guidance issued by a Federal regulatory agency).

This paragraph does not grant any Federal regulatory agency or State regulatory agency authority to issue regulations, orders, or guidance pursuant to any statute that does not authorize such issuance.

(2) LIMITATIONS ON INTERPRETATION AUTHORITY. — Notwithstanding paragraph (1), a Federal regulatory agency shall not adopt any regulation, order, or guidance described in paragraph (1), and a State regulatory agency is preempted by section 101 from adopting any regulation, order, or guidance described in paragraph (1), unless —

(A) such regulation, order, or guidance is consistent with section 101;

(B) such regulation, order, or guidance does not add to the requirements of such section; and

(C) such agency finds, in connection with the issuance of such regulation, order, or guidance, that —

(i) there is a substantial justification for the regulation, order, or guidance;

(ii) the methods selected to carry out that purpose —

(I) are substantially equivalent to the requirements imposed on records that are not electronic records; and

(II) will not impose unreasonable costs on the acceptance and use of electronic records; and

(iii) the methods selected to carry out that purpose do not require, or accord greater legal status or effect to, the implementation or application of a specific technology or technical specification for performing the functions of creating, storing, generating, receiving, communicating, or authenticating electronic records or electronic signatures.

(3) PERFORMANCE STANDARDS. —

(A) ACCURACY, RECORD INTEGRITY, ACCESSIBILITY. — Notwithstanding paragraph (2)(C)(iii), a Federal regulatory agency or State regulatory agency may interpret section 101(d) to specify performance standards to assure accuracy, record integrity, and accessibility of records that are required to be retained. Such performance standards may be specified in a manner that imposes a requirement in violation of paragraph (2)(C)(iii) if the requirement (i) serves an important governmental objective; and (ii) is substantially related to the achievement of that objective. Nothing in this paragraph shall be construed to grant any Federal regulatory agency or State regulatory agency authority to require use of a particular type of software or hardware in order to comply with section 101(d).

(B) PAPER OR PRINTED FORM. — Notwithstanding subsection (c)(1), a Federal regulatory agency or State regulatory agency may interpret section 101(d) to require retention of a record in a tangible printed or paper form if —

(i) there is a compelling governmental interest relating to law enforcement or national security for imposing such requirement; and

(ii) imposing such requirement is essential to attaining such interest.

(4) EXCEPTIONS FOR ACTIONS BY GOVERNMENT AS MARKET PARTICIPANT. — Paragraph (2)(C)(iii) shall not apply to the statutes, regulations, or other rules of law governing procurement by the Federal or any State government, or any agency or instrumentality thereof.

(c) ADDITIONAL LIMITATIONS. —

(1) REIMPOSING PAPER PROHIBITED. — Nothing in subsection (b) (other than paragraph (3)(B) thereof) shall be construed to grant any Federal regulatory agency or State regulatory agency authority to impose or reimpose any requirement that a record be in a tangible printed or paper form.

(2) CONTINUING OBLIGATION UNDER GOVERNMENT PAPERWORK ELIMINATION ACT. — Nothing in subsection (a) or (b) relieves any Federal regulatory agency of its obligations under the Government Paperwork Elimination Act (title XVII of Public Law 105-277).

(d) AUTHORITY TO EXEMPT FROM CONSENT PROVISION. —

(1) IN GENERAL. — A Federal regulatory agency may, with respect to matter within its jurisdiction, by regulation or order issued after notice and an opportunity for public comment, exempt without condition a specified category or type of record from the requirements relating to consent in section 101(c) if such exemption is necessary to eliminate a substantial burden on electronic commerce and will not increase the material risk of harm to consumers.

(2) PROSPECTUSES. — Within 30 days after the date of enactment of this Act, the Securities and Exchange Commission shall issue a regulation or order

pursuant to paragraph (1) exempting from section 101(c) any records that are required to be provided in order to allow advertising, sales literature, or other information concerning a security issued by an investment company that is registered under the Investment Company Act of 1940, or concerning the issuer thereof, to be excluded from the definition of a prospectus under section 2(a)(10)(A) of the Securities Act of 1933.

(e) ELECTRONIC LETTERS OF AGENCY. — The Federal Communications Commission shall not hold any contract for telecommunications service or letter of agency for a preferred carrier change, that otherwise complies with the Commission's rules, to be legally ineffective, invalid, or unenforceable solely because an electronic record or electronic signature was used in its formation or authorization.

SEC. 105.   STUDIES. [15 USCA §7005]

(a) DELIVERY. — Within 12 months after the date of the enactment of this Act, the Secretary of Commerce shall conduct an inquiry regarding the effectiveness of the delivery of electronic records to consumers using electronic mail as compared with delivery of written records via the United States Postal Service and private express mail services. The Secretary shall submit a report to the Congress regarding the results of such inquiry by the conclusion of such 12-month period.

(b) STUDY OF ELECTRONIC CONSENT. — Within 12 months after the date of the enactment of this Act, the Secretary of Commerce and the Federal Trade Commission shall submit a report to the Congress evaluating any benefits provided to consumers by the procedure required by section 101(c)(1)(C)(ii); any burdens imposed on electronic commerce by that provision; whether the benefits outweigh the burdens; whether the absence of the procedure required by section 101(c)(1)(C)(ii) would increase the incidence of fraud directed against consumers; and suggesting any revisions to the provision deemed appropriate by the Secretary and the Commission. In conducting this evaluation, the Secretary and the Commission shall solicit comment from the general public, consumer representatives, and electronic commerce businesses.

SEC. 106.   DEFINITIONS. [15 USCA §7006]

For purposes of this title:

(1) CONSUMER. — The term "consumer" means an individual who obtains, through a transaction, products or services which are used primarily for personal, family, or household purposes, and also means the legal representative of such an individual.

(2) ELECTRONIC. — The term "electronic" means relating to technology having electrical, digital, magnetic, wireless, optical, electromagnetic, or similar capabilities.

(3) ELECTRONIC AGENT. — The term "electronic agent" means a computer program or an electronic or other automated means used independently to initiate an action or respond to electronic records or performances in whole or in part without review or action by an individual at the time of the action or response.

(4) ELECTRONIC RECORD. — The term "electronic record" means a contract or other record created, generated, sent, communicated, received, or stored by electronic means.

(5) ELECTRONIC SIGNATURE. — The term "electronic signature" means an electronic sound, symbol, or process, attached to or logically associated with

a contract or other record and executed or adopted by a person with the intent to sign the record.

(6) FEDERAL REGULATORY AGENCY. — The term "Federal regulatory agency" means an agency, as that term is defined in section 552(f) of title 5, United States Code.

(7) INFORMATION. — The term "information" means data, text, images, sounds, codes, computer programs, software, databases, or the like.

(8) PERSON. — The term "person" means an individual, corporation, business trust, estate, trust, partnership, limited liability company, association, joint venture, governmental agency, public corporation, or any other legal or commercial entity.

(9) RECORD. — The term "record" means information that is inscribed on a tangible medium or that is stored in an electronic or other medium and is retrievable in perceivable form.

(10) REQUIREMENT. — The term "requirement" includes a prohibition.

(11) SELF-REGULATORY ORGANIZATION. — The term "self-regulatory organization" means an organization or entity that is not a Federal regulatory agency or a State, but that is under the supervision of a Federal regulatory agency and is authorized under Federal law to adopt and administer rules applicable to its members that are enforced by such organization or entity, by a Federal regulatory agency, or by another self-regulatory organization.

(12) STATE. — The term "State" includes the District of Columbia and the territories and possessions of the United States.

(13) TRANSACTION. — The term "transaction" means an action or set of actions relating to the conduct of business, consumer, or commercial affairs between two or more persons, including any of the following types of conduct —

(A) the sale, lease, exchange, licensing, or other disposition of (i) personal property, including goods and intangibles, (ii) services, and (iii) any combination thereof; and

(B) the sale, lease, exchange, or other disposition of any interest in real property, or any combination thereof.

SEC. 107. EFFECTIVE DATE. [15 USCA §7001 NOTE]

(a) IN GENERAL. — Except as provided in subsection (b), this title shall be effective on October 1, 2000.

(b) EXCEPTIONS. —

(1) RECORD RETENTION. —

(A) IN GENERAL. — Subject to subparagraph (B), this title shall be effective on March 1, 2001, with respect to a requirement that a record be retained imposed by —

(i) a Federal statute, regulation, or other rule of law, or

(ii) a State statute, regulation, or other rule of law administered or promulgated by a State regulatory agency.

(B) DELAYED EFFECT FOR PENDING RULEMAKINGS. — If on March 1, 2001, a Federal regulatory agency or State regulatory agency has announced, proposed, or initiated, but not completed, a rulemaking proceeding to prescribe a regulation under section 104(b)(3) with respect to a requirement described in subparagraph (A), this title shall be effective on June 1, 2001, with respect to such requirement.

(2) CERTAIN GUARANTEED AND INSURED LOANS. — With regard to any transaction involving a loan guarantee or loan guarantee commitment (as those terms are defined in section 502 of the Federal Credit Reform Act of 1990), or involving a program listed in the Federal Credit Supplement, Budget of the United States, FY 2001, this title applies only to such transactions entered into, and to any loan or mortgage made, insured, or guaranteed by the United States Government thereunder, on and after one year after the date of enactment of this Act.

(3) STUDENT LOANS. — With respect to any records that are provided or made available to a consumer pursuant to an application for a loan, or a loan made, pursuant to title IV of the Higher Education Act of 1965, section 101(c) of this Act shall not apply until the earlier of —

(A) such time as the Secretary of Education publishes revised promissory notes under section 432(m) of the Higher Education Act of 1965; or

(B) one year after the date of enactment of this Act.

TITLE II — TRANSFERABLE RECORDS

SEC. 201. TRANSFERABLE RECORDS. [15 USCA §7021]

(a) DEFINITIONS. — For purposes of this section:

(1) TRANSFERABLE RECORD. — The term "transferable record" means an electronic record that —

(A) would be a note under Article 3 of the Uniform Commercial Code if the electronic record were in writing;

(B) the issuer of the electronic record expressly has agreed is a transferable record; and

(C) relates to a loan secured by real property.

A transferable record may be executed using an electronic signature.

(2) OTHER DEFINITIONS. — The terms "electronic record", "electronic signature", and "person" have the same meanings provided in section 106 of this Act.

(b) CONTROL. — A person has control of a transferable record if a system employed for evidencing the transfer of interests in the transferable record reliably establishes that person as the person to which the transferable record was issued or transferred.

(c) CONDITIONS. — A system satisfies subsection (b), and a person is deemed to have control of a transferable record, if the transferable record is created, stored, and assigned in such a manner that —

(1) a single authoritative copy of the transferable record exists which is unique, identifiable, and, except as otherwise provided in paragraphs (4), (5), and (6), unalterable;

(2) the authoritative copy identifies the person asserting control as —

(A) the person to which the transferable record was issued; or

(B) if the authoritative copy indicates that the transferable record has been transferred, the person to which the transferable record was most recently transferred;

(3) the authoritative copy is communicated to and maintained by the person asserting control or its designated custodian;

(4) copies or revisions that add or change an identified assignee of the authoritative copy can be made only with the consent of the person asserting control;

(5) each copy of the authoritative copy and any copy of a copy is readily identifiable as a copy that is not the authoritative copy; and

(6) any revision of the authoritative copy is readily identifiable as authorized or unauthorized.

(d) STATUS AS HOLDER.—Except as otherwise agreed, a person having control of a transferable record is the holder, as defined in section 1-201(20) of the Uniform Commercial Code, of the transferable record and has the same rights and defenses as a holder of an equivalent record or writing under the Uniform Commercial Code, including, if the applicable statutory requirements under section 3-302(a), 9-308, or revised section 9-330 of the Uniform Commercial Code are satisfied, the rights and defenses of a holder in due course or a purchaser, respectively. Delivery, possession, and endorsement are not required to obtain or exercise any of the rights under this subsection.

(e) OBLIGOR RIGHTS.—Except as otherwise agreed, an obligor under a transferable record has the same rights and defenses as an equivalent obligor under equivalent records or writings under the Uniform Commercial Code.

(f) PROOF OF CONTROL.—If requested by a person against which enforcement is sought, the person seeking to enforce the transferable record shall provide reasonable proof that the person is in control of the transferable record. Proof may include access to the authoritative copy of the transferable record and related business records sufficient to review the terms of the transferable record and to establish the identity of the person having control of the transferable record.

(g) UCC REFERENCES.—For purposes of this subsection, all references to the Uniform Commercial Code are to the Uniform Commercial Code as in effect in the jurisdiction the law of which governs the transferable record.

SEC. 202.   EFFECTIVE DATE. [15 USCA §7021 NOTE]
This title shall be effective 90 days after the date of enactment of this Act.

TITLE III—PROMOTION OF INTERNATIONAL ELECTRONIC COMMERCE

SEC. 301.   PRINCIPLES GOVERNING THE USE OF ELECTRONIC SIGNATURES IN INTERNATIONAL TRANSACTIONS. [15 USCA §7031]

(a) PROMOTION OF ELECTRONIC SIGNATURES.—

(1) REQUIRED ACTIONS.—The Secretary of Commerce shall promote the acceptance and use, on an international basis, of electronic signatures in accordance with the principles specified in paragraph (2) and in a manner consistent with section 101 of this Act. The Secretary of Commerce shall take all actions necessary in a manner consistent with such principles to eliminate or reduce, to the maximum extent possible, the impediments to commerce in electronic signatures, for the purpose of facilitating the development of interstate and foreign commerce.

(2) PRINCIPLES.—The principles specified in this paragraph are the following:

(A) Remove paper-based obstacles to electronic transactions by adopting relevant principles from the Model Law on Electronic Commerce adopted in 1996 by the United Nations Commission on International Trade Law.

(B) Permit parties to a transaction to determine the appropriate authentication technologies and implementation models for their transactions, with assurance that those technologies and implementation models will be recognized and enforced.

246

(C) Permit parties to a transaction to have the opportunity to prove in court or other proceedings that their authentication approaches and their transactions are valid.

(D) Take a nondiscriminatory approach to electronic signatures and authentication methods from other jurisdictions.

(b) CONSULTATION. — In conducting the activities required by this section, the Secretary shall consult with users and providers of electronic signature products and services and other interested persons.

(c) DEFINITIONS. — As used in this section, the terms "electronic record" and "electronic signature" have the same meanings provided in section 106 of this Act.

TITLE IV — COMMISSION ON ONLINE CHILD PROTECTION
[OMITTED]

UNIFORM ELECTRONIC TRANSACTIONS ACT
(1999)

TABLE OF CONTENTS

PREFATORY NOTE

With the advent of electronic means of communication and information transfer, business models and methods for doing business have evolved to take advantage of the speed, efficiencies, and cost benefits of electronic technologies. These developments have occurred in the face of existing legal barriers to the legal efficacy of records and documents which exist solely in electronic media. Whether the legal requirement that information or an agreement or contract must be contained or set forth in a pen and paper writing derives from a statute of frauds affecting the enforceability of an agreement, or from a record retention statute that calls for keeping the paper record of a transaction, such legal requirements raise real barriers to the effective use of electronic media.

One striking example of electronic barriers involves so called check retention statutes in every State. A study conducted by the Federal Reserve Bank of Boston identified more than 2500 different state laws which require the retention of canceled checks by the issuers of those checks. These requirements not only impose burdens on the issuers, but also effectively restrain the ability of banks handling the checks to automate the process. Although check truncation is validated under the Uniform Commercial Code, if the bank's customer must store the canceled paper check, the bank will not be able to deal with the item through electronic transmission of the information. By establishing the equivalence of an electronic record of the information, the Uniform Electronic Transactions Act (UETA) removes these barriers without affecting the underlying legal rules and requirements.

It is important to understand that the purpose of the UETA is to remove barriers to electronic commerce by validating and effectuating electronic records and signatures. It is NOT a general contracting statute—the substantive rules of contracts remain unaffected by UETA. Nor is it a digital signature statute. To the extent that a State has a Digital Signature Law, the UETA is designed to support and compliment that statute.

A. Scope of the Act and Procedural Approach. The scope of this Act provides coverage which sets forth a clear framework for covered transactions, and also avoids unwarranted surprises for unsophisticated parties dealing in this relatively new media. The clarity and certainty of the scope of the Act have been obtained while still providing a solid legal framework that allows for the continued development of innovative technology to facilitate electronic transactions.

With regard to the general scope of the Act, the Act's "coverage is inherently limited by the definition of transaction." The Act does not apply to *all* writings and signatures, but only to electronic records and signatures relating to a transaction, defined as those interactions between people relating to business, commercial and governmental affairs. In general, there are few writing or signature requirements imposed by law on many of the "standard" transactions that had been considered for exclusion. A good example relates to trusts, where the general rule on creation of a trust imposes no formal writing requirement. Further, the writing requirements in other contexts derived from governmental filing issues. For example, real estate transactions were considered potentially troublesome because of the need to file a deed or other instrument for protection against third parties. Since the efficacy of a real estate purchase contract, or even a deed, between the parties is not affected by any sort of filing, the question was raised why these transactions should not be validated by this Act if done via an electronic medium. No sound reason was found. Filing requirements fall within Sections 17-19 on governmental records. An exclusion of all real estate transactions would be particularly unwarranted in the event that a State chose to convert to an electronic recording system, as many have for Article 9 financing statement filings under the Uniform Commercial Code.

The exclusion of specific Articles of the Uniform Commercial Code reflects the recognition that, particularly in the case of Articles 5, 8 and revised Article 9, electronic transactions were addressed in the specific contexts of those revision processes. In the context of Articles 2 and 2A the UETA provides the vehicle for assuring that such transactions may be accomplished and effected via an electronic medium. At such time as Articles 2 and 2A are revised the extent of coverage in those Articles/Acts may make application of this Act as a gap-filling law desirable. Similar considerations apply to the recently promulgated Uniform Computer Information Transactions Act ("UCITA").

The need for certainty as to the scope and applicability of this Act is critical, and makes any sort of a broad, general exception based on notions of inconsistency with existing writing and signature requirements unwise at best. The uncertainty inherent in leaving the applicability of the Act to judicial construction of this Act with other laws is unacceptable if electronic transactions are to be facilitated.

Finally, recognition that the paradigm for the Act involves two willing parties conducting a transaction electronically, makes it necessary to expressly provide that some form of acquiescence or intent on the part of a person to conduct transactions electronically is necessary before the Act can be invoked. Accordingly, Section 5 specifically provides that the Act only applies between parties that have agreed to conduct transactions electronically. In this context, the construction of the term agreement must be broad in order to assure that the Act applies whenever the circumstances show the parties intention to transact electronically, regardless of whether the intent rises to the level of a formal agreement.

B. Procedural Approach. Another fundamental premise of the Act is that it be minimalist and procedural. The general efficacy of existing law in an electronic context, so long as biases and barriers to the medium are removed, validates this approach. The Act defers to existing substantive law. Specific areas of deference to other law in this Act include: (1) the meaning and effect of "sign" under existing law, (2) the method and manner of displaying, transmitting and formatting information in Section 8, (3) rules of attribution in Section 9, and (4) the law of mistake in Section 10.

The Act's treatment of records and signatures demonstrates best the minimalist approach that has been adopted. Whether a record is attributed to a person is left to law outside this Act. Whether an electronic signature has any effect is left to the surrounding circumstances and other law. These provisions are salutary directives to assure that records and signatures will be treated in the same manner, under currently existing law, as written records and manual signatures.

The deference of the Act to other substantive law does not negate the necessity of setting forth rules and standards for using electronic media. The Act expressly validates electronic records, signatures and contracts. It provides for the use of electronic records and information for retention purposes, providing certainty in an area with great potential in cost savings and efficiency. The Act makes clear that the actions of machines ("electronic agents") programmed and used by people will bind the user of the machine, regardless of whether human review of a particular transaction has occurred. It specifies the standards for sending and receipt of electronic records, and it allows for innovation in financial services through the implementation of transferable records. In these ways the Act permits electronic transactions to be accomplished with certainty under existing substantive rules of law.

§1. Short Title

This [Act] may be cited as the Uniform Electronic Transactions Act.

§2. Definitions

In this [Act]:

(1) "Agreement" means the bargain of the parties in fact, as found in their language or inferred from other circumstances and from rules, regulations, and procedures given the effect of agreements under laws otherwise applicable to a particular transaction.

(2) "Automated transaction" means a transaction conducted or performed, in whole or in part, by electronic means or electronic records, in which the acts or records of one or both parties are not reviewed by an individual in the ordinary course in forming a contract, performing under an existing contract, or fulfilling an obligation required by the transaction.

(3) "Computer program" means a set of statements or instructions to be used directly or indirectly in an information processing system in order to bring about a certain result.

(4) "Contract" means the total legal obligation resulting from the parties' agreement as affected by this [Act] and other applicable law.

(5) "Electronic" means relating to technology having electrical, digital, magnetic, wireless, optical, electromagnetic, or similar capabilities.

(6) "Electronic agent" means a computer program or an electronic or other automated means used independently to initiate an action or respond to electronic records or performances in whole or in part, without review or action by an individual.

(7) "Electronic record" means a record created, generated, sent, communicated, received, or stored by electronic means.

(8) "Electronic signature" means an electronic sound, symbol, or process attached to or logically associated with a record and executed or adopted by a person with the intent to sign the record.

(9) "Governmental agency" means an executive, legislative, or judicial agency, department, board, commission, authority, institution, or instrumentality of the federal government or of a State or of a county, municipality, or other political subdivision of a State.

(10) "Information" means data, text, images, sounds, codes, computer programs, software, databases, or the like.

(11) "Information processing system" means an electronic system for creating, generating, sending, receiving, storing, displaying, or processing information.

(12) "Person" means an individual, corporation, business trust, estate, trust, partnership, limited liability company, association, joint venture, governmental agency, public corporation, or any other legal or commercial entity.

(13) "Record" means information that is inscribed on a tangible medium or that is stored in an electronic or other medium and is retrievable in perceivable form.

(14) "Security procedure" means a procedure employed for the purpose of verifying that an electronic signature, record, or performance is that of a specific person or for detecting changes or errors in the information in an electronic record. The term includes a procedure that requires the use of algorithms or other codes, identifying words or numbers, encryption, or callback or other acknowledgment procedures.

(15) "State" means a State of the United States, the District of Columbia, Puerto Rico, the United States Virgin Islands, or any territory or insular possession subject to the jurisdiction of the United States. The term includes an Indian tribe or band, or Alaskan native village, which is recognized by federal law or formally acknowledged by a State.

(16) "Transaction" means an action or set of actions occurring between two or more persons relating to the conduct of business, commercial, or governmental affairs.

Sources: UNICTRAL Model Law on Electronic Commerce; Uniform Commercial Code; Uniform Computer Information Transactions Act; Restatement 2d Contracts.

Comments

1. **"Agreement."** Whether the parties have reached an agreement is determined by their express language and all surrounding circumstances. The Restatement 2d Contracts §3 provides that, "An agreement is a manifestation of mutual assent on the part of two or more persons." See also Restatement 2d Contracts, Section 2, Comment b. The Uniform Commercial Code specifically includes in the circumstances from which an agreement may be inferred "course of performance, course of dealing and usage of trade . . ." as defined in the UCC. Although the definition of agreement in this Act does not make specific reference to usage of trade and other party conduct, this definition is not intended to affect the construction of the parties' agreement under the substantive law applicable to a particular transaction. Where that law takes account of usage and conduct in informing the terms of the parties' agreement, the usage or conduct would be relevant as "other circumstances" included in the definition under this Act.

Where the law applicable to a given transaction provides that system rules and the like constitute part of the agreement of the parties, such rules will have the same effect in determining the parties agreement under this Act. For example, UCC Article 4 (Section 4-103(b)) provides that Federal Reserve regulations and operating circulars and clearinghouse rules have the effect of agreements. Such agreements by law properly would be included in the definition of agreement in this Act.

The parties' agreement is relevant in determining whether the provisions of this Act have been varied by agreement. In addition, the parties' agreement may establish the parameters of the parties' use of electronic records and signatures, security procedures and similar aspects of the transaction. See Model Trading Partner Agreement, 45 Business Lawyer Supp. Issue (June 1990). See Section 5(b) and Comments thereto.

. . .

5. "Electronic agent." This definition establishes that an electronic agent is a machine. As the term "electronic agent" has come to be recognized, it is limited to a tool function. The effect on the party using the agent is addressed in the operative provisions of the Act (e.g., Section 14)

An electronic agent, such as a computer program or other automated means employed by a person, is a tool of that person. As a general rule, the employer of a tool is responsible for the results obtained by the use of that tool since the tool has no independent volition of its own. However, an electronic agent, by definition, is capable within the parameters of its programming, of initiating, responding or interacting with other parties or their electronic agents once it has been activated by a party, without further attention of that party.

While this Act proceeds on the paradigm that an electronic agent is capable of performing only within the technical strictures of its preset programming, it is conceivable that, within the useful life of this Act, electronic agents may be created with the ability to act autonomously, and not just automatically. That is, through developments in artificial intelligence, a computer may be able to "learn through experience, modify the instructions in their own programs, and even devise new instructions." Allen and Widdison, "Can Computers Make Contracts?" *9 Harv. J.L. & Tech 25* (Winter, 1996). If such developments occur, courts may construe the definition of electronic agent accordingly, in order to recognize such new capabilities.

The examples involving Bookseller.com and Automaker in the Comment to the definition of Automated Transaction are equally applicable here. Bookseller acts through an electronic agent in processing an order for books. Automaker and the supplier each act through electronic agents in facilitating and effectuating the just-in-time inventory process through EDI.

6. "Electronic record." An electronic record is a subset of the broader defined term "record." It is any record created, used or stored in a medium other than paper (see definition of electronic). The defined term is also used in this Act as a limiting definition in those provisions in which it is used.

Information processing systems, computer equipment and programs, electronic data interchange, electronic mail, voice mail, facsimile, telex, telecopying, scanning, and similar technologies all qualify as electronic under this Act. Accordingly information stored on a computer hard drive or floppy disc, facsimiles, voice mail messages, messages on a telephone answering machine, audio and video tape recordings, among other records, all would be electronic records under this Act.

7. "Electronic signature." The idea of a signature is broad and not specifically defined. Whether any particular record is "signed" is a question of fact. Proof of that fact must be made under other applicable law. This Act simply assures that the signature may be accomplished through electronic means. No specific technology need be used in order to create a valid signature. One's voice on an answering machine may suffice if the requisite intention is present. Similarly, including one's name as part of an electronic mail communication also may suffice, as may the firm name on a facsimile. It also may be shown that the requisite intent was not present and accordingly the symbol, sound or process did not amount to a signature. One may use a digital signature with the requisite intention, or one may use the private key solely as an access device with no intention to sign, or otherwise accomplish a legally binding act. In any case the critical element is the intention to execute or adopt the sound or symbol or process for the purpose of signing the related record.

The definition requires that the signer execute or adopt the sound, symbol, or process with the intent to sign the record. The act of applying a sound, symbol or process to an electronic record could have differing meanings and effects. The consequence of the act and the effect of the act as a signature are determined under other applicable law. However, the essential attribute of a signature involves applying a sound, symbol or process with an intent to do a legally significant act. It is that intention that is understood in the law as a part of the word "sign", without the need for a definition.

This Act establishes, to the greatest extent possible, the equivalency of electronic signatures and manual signatures. Therefore the term "signature" has been used to connote and convey that equivalency. The purpose is to overcome unwarranted biases against electronic methods of signing and authenticating records. The term "authentication," used in other laws, often has a narrower meaning and purpose than an electronic signature as used in this Act. However, an authentication under any of those other laws constitutes an electronic signature under this Act.

The precise effect of an electronic signature will be determined based on the surrounding circumstances under Section 9(b).

This definition includes as an electronic signature the standard webpage click through process. For example, when a person orders goods or services through a vendor's website, the person will be required to provide information as part of a process which will result in receipt of the goods or services. When the customer ultimately gets to the last step and clicks "I agree," the person has adopted the process and has done so with the intent to associate the person with the record of that process. The actual effect of the electronic signature will be determined from all the surrounding circumstances, however, the person adopted a process which the circumstances indicate s/he intended to have the effect of getting the goods/services and being bound to pay for them. The adoption of the process carried the intent to do a legally significant act, the hallmark of a signature.

Another important aspect of this definition lies in the necessity that the electronic signature be linked or logically associated with the record. In the paper world, it is assumed that the symbol adopted by a party is attached to or located somewhere in the same paper that is intended to be authenticated, e.g., an allonge firmly attached to a promissory note, or the classic signature at the end of a long contract. These tangible manifestations do not exist in the electronic environment, and accordingly, this definition expressly provides that the symbol must in some way be linked to, or connected with, the electronic record being signed. This linkage is consistent with the regulations promulgated by the Food and Drug Administration. 21 CFR Part 11 (March 20, 1997).

A digital signature using public key encryption technology would qualify as an electronic signature, as would the mere inclusion of one's name as a part of an e-mail message so long as in each case the signer executed or adopted the symbol with the intent to sign.

. . .

10. "Record." This is a standard definition designed to embrace all means of communicating or storing information except human memory. It includes any method for storing or communicating information, including "writings." A record need not be indestructible or permanent, but the term does not include oral or other communications which are not stored or preserved by some means. Information that has not been retained other than through human memory does not qualify as a record. As in the case of the terms "writing" or "written," the term "record" does not establish the purposes, permitted uses or legal effect which a record may have under any particular provision of substantive law. ABA Report on Use of the Term "Record," October 1, 1996.

. . .

§3. Scope

(a) Except as otherwise provided in subsection (b), this [Act] applies to electronic records and electronic signatures relating to a transaction.

(b) This [Act] does not apply to a transaction to the extent it is governed by:

(1) a law governing the creation and execution of wills, codicils, or testamentary trusts;

(2) [The Uniform Commercial Code other than Sections 1-107 and 1-206, Article 2, and Article 2A];

(3) [the Uniform Computer Information Transactions Act]; and

(4) [other laws, if any, identified by State].

(c) This [Act] applies to an electronic record or electronic signature otherwise excluded from the application of this [Act] under subsection (b) to the extent it is governed by a law other than those specified in subsection (b).

(d) A transaction subject to this [Act] is also subject to other applicable substantive law.

See Legislative Note below, following Comments.

Comments

1. The scope of this Act is inherently limited by the fact that it only applies to transactions related to business, commercial (including consumer) and governmental matters. Consequently, transactions with no relation to business, commercial or governmental transactions would not be subject to this Act. Unilaterally generated electronic records and signatures which are not part of a transaction also are not covered by this Act. See Section 2, Comment 12.

2. This Act affects the medium in which information, records and signatures may be presented and retained under current legal requirements. While this Act covers all electronic records and signatures which are used in a business, commercial (including consumer) or governmental transaction, the operative provisions of the Act relate to requirements for writings and signatures under other laws. Accordingly, the exclusions in subsection (b) focus on those legal rules imposing certain writing and signature requirements which will **not** be affected by this Act.

3. The exclusions listed in subsection (b) provide clarity and certainty regarding the laws which are and are not affected by this Act. This section

provides that transactions subject to specific laws are unaffected by this Act and leaves the balance subject to this Act.

4. Paragraph (1) excludes wills, codicils and testamentary trusts. This exclusion is largely salutary given the unilateral context in which such records are generally created and the unlikely use of such records in a transaction as defined in this Act (i.e., actions taken by two or more persons in the context of business, commercial or governmental affairs). Paragraph (2) excludes all of the Uniform Commercial Code other than UCC Sections 1-107 and 1-206, and Articles 2 and 2A. This Act does not apply to the excluded UCC articles, whether in "current" or "revised" form. The Act does apply to UCC Articles 2 and 2A and to UCC Sections 1-107 and 1-206.

5. Articles 3, 4 and 4A of the UCC impact payment systems and have specifically been removed from the coverage of this Act. The check collection and electronic fund transfer systems governed by Articles 3, 4 and 4A involve systems and relationships involving numerous parties beyond the parties to the underlying contract. The impact of validating electronic media in such systems involves considerations beyond the scope of this Act. Articles 5, 8 and 9 have been excluded because the revision process relating to those Articles included significant consideration of electronic practices. Paragraph 4 provides for exclusion from this Act of the Uniform Computer Information Transactions Act (UCITA) because the drafting process of that Act also included significant consideration of electronic contracting provisions.

6. The very limited application of this Act to Transferable Records in Section 16 does not affect payment systems, and the section is designed to apply to a transaction only through express agreement of the parties. The exclusion of Articles 3 and 4 will not affect the Act's coverage of Transferable Records. Section 16 is designed to allow for the development of systems which will provide "control" as defined in Section 16. Such control is necessary as a substitute for the idea of possession which undergirds negotiable instrument law. The technology has yet to be developed which will allow for the possession of a unique electronic token embodying the rights associated with a negotiable promissory note. Section 16's concept of control is intended as a substitute for possession.

The provisions in Section 16 operate as free standing rules, establishing the rights of parties using Transferable Records *under this Act*. The references in Section 16 to UCC Sections 3-302, 7-501, and 9-308 (R9-330(d)) are designed to incorporate the substance of those provisions into this Act for the limited purposes noted in Section 16(c). Accordingly, an electronic record which is also a Transferable Record, would not be used for purposes of a transaction governed by Articles 3, 4, or 9, but would be an electronic record used for purposes of a transaction governed by Section 16. However, it is important to remember that those UCC Articles will still apply to the transferable record in their own right. Accordingly any other substantive requirements, e.g., method and manner of perfection under Article 9, must be complied with under those other laws. See Comments to Section 16.

7. This Act does apply, *in toto*, to transactions under unrevised Articles 2 and 2A. There is every reason to validate electronic contracting in these situations. Sale and lease transactions do not implicate broad systems beyond the parties to the underlying transaction, such as are present in check collection and

electronic funds transfers. Further sales and leases generally do not have as far reaching effect on the rights of third parties beyond the contracting parties, such as exists in the secured transactions system. Finally, it is in the area of sales, licenses and leases that electronic commerce is occurring to its greatest extent today. To exclude these transactions would largely gut the purpose of this Act.

In the event that Articles 2 and 2A are revised and adopted in the future, UETA will only apply to the extent provided in those Acts.

8. An electronic record/signature may be used for purposes of more than one legal requirement, or may be covered by more than one law. Consequently, it is important to make clear, despite any apparent redundancy, in subsection (c) that an electronic record used for purposes of a law which is *not* affected by this Act under subsection (b) may nonetheless be used and validated for purposes of other laws not excluded by subsection (b). For example, this Act does not apply to an electronic record of a check when used for purposes of a transaction governed by Article 4 of the Uniform Commercial Code, i.e., the Act does not validate so-called electronic checks. However, for purposes of check retention statutes, the same electronic record of the check is covered by this Act, so that retention of an electronic image/record of a check will satisfy such retention statutes, so long as the requirements of Section 12 are fulfilled.

In another context, subsection (c) would operate to allow this Act to apply to what would appear to be an excluded transaction under subsection (b). For example, Article 9 of the Uniform Commercial Code applies generally to any transaction that creates a security interest in personal property. However, Article 9 excludes landlord's liens. Accordingly, although this Act excludes from its application transactions subject to Article 9, this Act would apply to the creation of a landlord lien if the law otherwise applicable to landlord's liens did not provide otherwise, because the landlord's lien transaction is excluded from Article 9.

9. Additional exclusions under subparagraph (b)(4) should be limited to laws which govern electronic records and signatures which may be used in transactions as defined in Section 2(16). Records used unilaterally, or which do not relate to business, commercial (including consumer), or governmental affairs are not governed by this Act in any event, and exclusion of laws relating to such records may create unintended inferences about whether other records and signatures are covered by this Act.

It is also important that additional exclusions, if any, be incorporated under subsection (b)(4). As noted in Comment 8 above, an electronic record used in a transaction excluded under subsection (b), e.g., a check used to pay one's taxes, will nonetheless be validated for purposes of other, non-excluded laws under subsection (c), e.g., the check when used as proof of payment. It is critical that additional exclusions, if any, be incorporated into subsection (b) so that the salutary effect of subsection (c) apply to validate those records in other, non-excluded transactions. While a legislature may determine that a particular notice, such as a utility shutoff notice, be provided to a person in writing on paper, it is difficult to see why the utility should not be entitled to use electronic media for storage and evidentiary purposes.

Legislative Note Regarding Possible Additional
Exclusions Under Section 3(b)(4)

The following discussion is derived from the Report dated September 21, 1998 of The Task Force on State Law Exclusions (the "Task Force") presented to the Drafting Committee. After consideration of the Report, the Drafting Committee determined that exclusions other than those specified in the Act were not warranted. In addition, other inherent limitations on the applicability of the Act (the definition of transaction, the requirement that the parties acquiesce in the use of an electronic format) also militate against additional exclusions. Nonetheless, the Drafting Committee recognized that some legislatures may wish to exclude additional transactions from the Act, and determined that guidance in some major areas would be helpful to those legislatures considering additional areas for exclusion.

Because of the overwhelming number of references in state law to writings and signatures, the following list of possible transactions is not exhaustive. However, they do represent those areas most commonly raised during the course of the drafting process as areas that might be inappropriate for an electronic medium. It is important to keep in mind however, that the Drafting Committee determined that exclusion of these additional areas was not warranted.

1. Trusts (other than testamentary trusts). Trusts can be used for both business and personal purposes. By virtue of the definition of transaction, trusts used outside the area of business and commerce would not be governed by this Act. With respect to business or commercial trusts, the laws governing their formation contain few or no requirements for paper or signatures. Indeed, in most jurisdictions trusts of any kind may be created orally. Consequently, the Drafting Committee believed that the Act should apply to any transaction where the law leaves to the parties the decision of whether to use a writing. Thus, in the absence of legal requirements for writings, there is no sound reason to exclude laws governing trusts from the application of this Act.

2. Powers of Attorney. A power of attorney is simply a formalized type of agency agreement. In general, no formal requirements for paper or execution were found to be applicable to the validity of powers of attorney.

Special health powers of attorney have been established by statute in some States. These powers may have special requirements under state law regarding execution, acknowledgment and possibly notarization. In the normal case such powers will not arise in a transactional context and so would not be covered by this Act. However, even if such a record were to arise in a transactional context, this Act operates simply to remove the barrier to the use of an electronic medium, and preserves other requirements of applicable substantive law, avoiding any necessity to exclude such laws from the operation of this Act. Especially in light of the provisions of Sections 8 and 11, the substantive requirements under such laws will be preserved and may be satisfied in an electronic format.

3. Real Estate Transactions. It is important to distinguish between the efficacy of paper documents involving real estate between the parties, as opposed to their effect on third parties. As between the parties it is unnecessary to maintain existing barriers to electronic contracting. There are no unique characteristics to contracts relating to real property as opposed to other business and commercial (including consumer) contracts. Consequently, the decision whether to use an electronic medium for their agreements should be a matter for the parties to determine. Of course, to be effective against third parties state law generally requires filing with a governmental office. Pending adoption of electronic filing systems by States, the need for a piece of paper to file to perfect rights against third parties, will be a consideration for the parties. In the event notarization and acknowledgment are required under other laws, Section 11 provides a means for such actions to be accomplished electronically.

With respect to the requirements of government filing, those are left to the individual States in the decision of whether to adopt and implement electronic filing systems. (See optional Sections 1-719.) However, government recording systems currently require paper deeds including notarized, manual signatures. Although California and Illinois are experimenting with electronic filing systems, until such systems become widespread, the parties likely will choose to use, at the least, a paper deed for filing purposes. Nothing in this Act precludes the parties from selecting the medium best suited to the needs of the particular transaction. Parties may wish to consummate the transaction using electronic media in order to avoid expensive travel. Yet the actual deed may be in paper form to assure compliance with existing recording systems and requirements. The critical point is that nothing in this Act prevents the parties from selecting paper or electronic media for all or part of their transaction.

4. Consumer Protection Statutes. Consumer protection provisions in state law often require that information be disclosed or provided to a consumer in writing. Because this Act does apply to such transactions, the question of whether such laws should be specifically excluded was considered. Exclusion of consumer transactions would eliminate a huge group of commercial transactions which benefit consumers by enabling the efficiency of the electronic medium. Commerce over the internet is driven by consumer demands and concerns and must be included.

At the same time, it is important to recognize the protective effects of many consumer statutes. Consumer statutes often require that information be provided in writing, or may require that the consumer separately sign or initial a particular provision to evidence that the consumer's attention was brought to the provision. Subsection (1) requires electronic records to be retainable by a person whenever the law requires information to be delivered in writing. The section imposes a significant burden on the sender of information. The sender must assure that the information system of the recipient is compatible with, and capable of retaining the information sent by, the sender's system. Furthermore, nothing in this Act permits the avoidance of legal requirements of separate signatures or initialing. The Act simply permits the signature or initialing to be done electronically.

Other consumer protection statutes require (expressly or implicitly) that certain information be presented in a certain manner or format. Laws requiring information to be presented in particular fonts, formats or in similar fashion, as well as laws requiring conspicuous displays of information are preserved. Section 8(b)(3) specifically preserves the applicability of such requirements in an electronic environment. In the case of legal requirements that information be presented or appear conspicuous, the determination of what is conspicuous will be left to other law. Section 8 was included to specifically preserve the protective functions of such disclosure statutes, while at the same time allowing the use of electronic media if the substantive requirements of the other laws could be satisfied in the electronic medium.

Formatting and separate signing requirements serve a critical purpose in much consumer protection legislation, to assure that information is not slipped past the unsuspecting consumer. Not only does this Act not disturb those requirements, it preserves those requirements. In addition, other bodies of substantive law continue to operate to allow the courts to police any such bad conduct or overreaching, e.g., unconscionability, fraud, duress, mistake and the like. These bodies of law remain applicable regardless of the medium in which a record appears.

The requirement that both parties agree to conduct a transaction electronically also prevents the imposition of an electronic medium on unwilling parties See Section 5(b). In addition, where the law requires inclusion of specific terms or language, those requirements are preserved broadly by Section 5(e).

Requirements that information be sent to, or received by, someone have been preserved in Section 15. As in the paper world, obligations to send do not impose any duties on the sender to assure receipt, other than reasonable methods of dispatch. In those cases where receipt is required legally, Sections 5, 8, and 15 impose the burden on the sender to assure delivery to the recipient if satisfaction of the legal requirement is to be fulfilled.

The preservation of existing safeguards, together with the ability to opt out of the electronic medium entirely, demonstrate the lack of any need generally to exclude consumer protection laws from the operation of this Act. Legislatures may wish to focus any review on those statutes which provide for post-contract formation and post-breach notices to be in paper. However, any such consideration must also balance the needed protections against the potential burdens which may be imposed. Consumers and others will not be well served by restrictions which preclude the employment of electronic technologies sought and desired by consumers.

§4. Prospective Application

This [Act] applies to any electronic record or electronic signature created, generated, sent, communicated, received, or stored on or after the effective date of this [Act].

Comment

This section makes clear that the Act only applies to validate electronic records and signatures which arise subsequent to the effective date of the Act. Whether electronic records and electronic signatures arising before the effective date of this Act are valid is left to other law.

§5. Use of Electronic Records and Electronic Signatures; Variation by Agreement

(a) This [Act] does not require a record or signature to be created, generated, sent, communicated, received, stored, or otherwise processed or used by electronic means or in electronic form.

(b) This [Act] applies only to transactions between parties each of which has agreed to conduct transactions by electronic means. Whether the parties agree to conduct a transaction by electronic means is determined from the context and surrounding circumstances, including the parties' conduct.

(c) A party that agrees to conduct a transaction by electronic means may refuse to conduct other transactions by electronic means. The right granted by this subsection may not be waived by agreement.

(d) Except as otherwise provided in this [Act], the effect of any of its provisions may be varied by agreement. The presence in certain provisions of this [Act] of the words "unless otherwise agreed", or words of similar import, does not imply that the effect of other provisions may not be varied by agreement.

(e) Whether an electronic record or electronic signature has legal consequences is determined by this [Act] and other applicable law.

Comments

This section limits the applicability of this Act to transactions which parties have agreed to conduct electronically. Broad interpretation of the term agreement is necessary to assure that this Act has the widest possible application consistent with its purpose of removing barriers to electronic commerce.

1. This section makes clear that this Act is intended to facilitate the use of electronic means, but does not require the use of electronic records and signatures. This fundamental principle is set forth in subsection (a) and elaborated by subsections (b) and (c), which require an intention to conduct transactions electronically and preserve the right of a party to refuse to use electronics in any subsequent transaction.

2. The paradigm of this Act is two willing parties doing transactions electronically. It is therefore appropriate that the Act is voluntary and preserves the greatest possible party autonomy to refuse electronic transactions. The requirement that party agreement be found from all the surrounding circumstances is a limitation on the scope of this Act.

3. If this Act is to serve to facilitate electronic transactions, it must be applicable under circumstances not rising to a full fledged contract to use electronics. While absolute certainty can be accomplished by obtaining an explicit contract before relying on electronic transactions, such an explicit contract should not be necessary before one may feel safe in conducting transactions electronically. Indeed, such a requirement would itself be an unreasonable barrier to electronic commerce, at odds with the fundamental purpose of this Act. Accordingly, the requisite agreement, express or implied, must be determined from all available circumstances and evidence.

4. Subsection (b) provides that the Act applies to transactions in which the parties have agreed to conduct the transaction electronically. In this context it is essential that the parties' actions and words be broadly construed in determining whether the requisite agreement exists. Accordingly, the Act expressly provides that the party's agreement is to be found from all circumstances, including the parties' conduct. The critical element is the intent of a party to conduct a transaction electronically. Once that intent is established, this Act applies. See Restatement 2d Contracts, Sections 2, 3, and 19.

Examples of circumstances from which it may be found that parties have reached an agreement to conduct transactions electronically include the following:

A. Automaker and supplier enter into a Trading Partner Agreement setting forth the terms, conditions and methods for the conduct of business between them electronically.

B. Joe gives out his business card with his business e-mail address. It may be reasonable, under the circumstances, for a recipient of the card to infer that Joe has agreed to communicate electronically for business purposes. However, in the absence of additional facts, it would not necessarily be reasonable to infer Joe's agreement to communicate electronically for purposes outside the scope of the business indicated by use of the business card.

C. Sally may have several e-mail addresses home, main office, office of a non-profit organization on whose board Sally sits. In each case, it may be reasonable to infer that Sally is willing to communicate electronically with respect to business related to the business/purpose associated with the respective e-mail addresses. However, depending on the circumstances, it may not be reasonable to communicate with Sally for purposes other than those related to the purpose for which she maintained a particular e-mail account.

D. Among the circumstances to be considered in finding an agreement would be the time when the assent occurred relative to the timing of the use of electronic communications. If one orders books from an on-line vendor, such as Bookseller.com, the intention to conduct that transaction and to receive any correspondence related to the transaction electronically can be inferred from the conduct. Accordingly, as to information related to that transaction it is reasonable for Bookseller to deal with the individual electronically.

The examples noted above are intended to focus the inquiry on the party's agreement to conduct a transaction electronically. Similarly, if two people are at a meeting and one tells the other to send an e-mail to confirm a transaction the requisite agreement under subsection (b) would exist. In each case, the use of a business card, statement at a meeting, or other evidence of willingness to conduct a transaction electronically must be viewed in light of all the surrounding circumstances with a view toward broad validation of electronic transactions.

5. Just as circumstances may indicate the existence of agreement, express or implied from surrounding circumstances, circumstances may also demonstrate the absence of true agreement. For example:

A. If Automaker, Inc. were to issue a recall of automobiles via its Internet website, it would not be able to rely on this Act to validate that notice in the case of a person who never logged on to the website, or indeed, had no ability to do so, notwithstanding a clause in a paper purchase contract by which the buyer agreed to receive such notices in such a manner.

B. Buyer executes a standard form contract in which an agreement to receive all notices electronically in set forth on page 3 in the midst of other fine print. Buyer has never communicated with Seller electronically, and has not provided any other information in the contract to suggest a willingness to deal electronically. Not only is it unlikely that any but the most formalistic of agreements may be found, but nothing in this Act prevents courts from policing such form contracts under common law doctrines relating to contract formation, unconscionability and the like.

6. Subsection (c) has been added to make clear the ability of a party to refuse to conduct a transaction electronically, even if the person has conducted transactions electronically in the past. The effectiveness of a party's refusal to conduct a transaction electronically will be determined under other applicable law in light of all surrounding circumstances. Such circumstances must include an assessment of the transaction involved.

A party's right to decline to act electronically under a specific contract, on the ground that each action under that contract amounts to a separate "transaction," must be considered in light of the purpose of the contract and the action to be taken electronically. For example, under a contract for the purchase of goods, the giving and receipt of notices electronically, as provided in the contract, should not be viewed as discreet transactions. Rather such notices amount to separate actions which are part of the "transaction" of purchase evidenced by the contract. Allowing one party to require a change of medium in the middle of the transaction evidenced by that contract is not the purpose of this subsection. Rather this subsection is intended to preserve the party's right to conduct the next purchase in a non-electronic medium.

7. Subsection (e) is an essential provision in the overall scheme of this Act. While this Act validates and effectuates electronic records and electronic signatures, the legal effect of such records and signatures is left to existing substantive law outside this Act except in very narrow circumstances. See, e.g., Section 16. Even when this Act operates to validate records and signatures in an electronic medium, it expressly preserves the substantive rules of other law applicable to such records. See, e.g., Section 11.

For example, beyond validation of records, signatures and contracts based on the medium used, Section 7 (a) and (b) should not be interpreted as establishing the legal effectiveness of any given record, signature or contract. Where a rule of law requires that the record contain minimum substantive content, the legal effect of such a record will depend on whether the record meets the substantive requirements of other applicable law.

Section 8 expressly preserves a number of legal requirements in currently existing law relating to the presentation of information in writing. Although this Act now would allow such information to be presented in an electronic record, Section 8 provides that the other substantive requirements of law must be satisfied in the electronic medium as well.

§6. Construction and Application

This [Act] must be construed and applied:
    (1) to facilitate electronic transactions consistent with other applicable law;
    (2) to be consistent with reasonable practices concerning electronic transactions and with the continued expansion of those practices; and
    (3) to effectuate its general purpose to make uniform the law with respect to the subject of this [Act] among States enacting it.

Comments

1. The purposes and policies of this Act are
    (a) to facilitate and promote commerce and governmental transactions by validating and authorizing the use of electronic records and electronic signatures;
    (b) to eliminate barriers to electronic commerce and governmental transactions resulting from uncertainties relating to writing and signature requirements;
    (c) to simplify, clarify and modernize the law governing commerce and governmental transactions through the use of electronic means;
    (d) to permit the continued expansion of commercial and governmental electronic practices through custom, usage and agreement of the parties;
    (e) to promote uniformity of the law among the States (and worldwide) relating to the use of electronic and similar technological means of effecting and performing commercial and governmental transactions;
    (f) to promote public confidence in the validity, integrity and reliability of electronic commerce and governmental transactions; and
    (g) to promote the development of the legal and business infrastructure necessary to implement electronic commerce and governmental transactions.
2. This Act has been drafted to permit flexible application consistent with its purpose to validate electronic transactions. The provisions of this Act validating and effectuating the employ of electronic media allow the courts to apply them to new and unforeseen technologies and practices. As time progresses, it is anticipated that what is new and unforeseen today will be commonplace tomorrow. Accordingly, this legislation is intended to set a framework for the validation of media which may be developed in the future and which demonstrate the same qualities as the electronic media contemplated and validated under this Act.

§7. Legal Recognition of Electronic Records, Electronic Signatures, and Electronic Contracts

    (a) A record or signature may not be denied legal effect or enforceability solely because it is in electronic form.
    (b) A contract may not be denied legal effect or enforceability solely because an electronic record was used in its formation.

(c) If a law requires a record to be in writing, an electronic record satisfies the law.

(d) If a law requires a signature, an electronic signature satisfies the law.

Source: UNCITRAL Model Law on Electronic Commerce, Articles 5, 6, and 7.

Comments

1. This section sets forth the fundamental premise of this Act: namely, that the medium in which a record, signature, or contract is created, presented or retained does not affect its legal significance. Subsections (a) and (b) are designed to eliminate the single element of medium as a reason to deny effect or enforceability to a record, signature, or contract. The fact that the information is set forth in an electronic, as opposed to paper, record is irrelevant.

2. Under Restatement 2d Contracts Section 8, a contract may have legal effect and yet be unenforceable. Indeed, one circumstance where a record or contract may have effect but be unenforceable is in the context of the Statute of Frauds. Though a contract may be unenforceable, the records may have collateral effects, as in the case of a buyer that insures goods purchased under a contract unenforceable under the Statute of Frauds. The insurance company may not deny a claim on the ground that the buyer is not the owner, though the buyer may have no direct remedy against seller for failure to deliver. See Restatement 2d Contracts, Section 8, Illustration 4.

While this section would validate an electronic record for purposes of a statute of frauds, if an agreement to conduct the transaction electronically cannot reasonably be found (See Section 5(b)) then a necessary predicate to the applicability of this Act would be absent and this Act would not validate the electronic record. Whether the electronic record might be valid under other law is not addressed by this Act.

3. Subsections (c) and (d) provide the positive assertion that electronic records and signatures satisfy legal requirements for writings and signatures. The provisions are limited to requirements in laws that a record be in writing or be signed. This section does not address requirements imposed by other law in addition to requirements for writings and signatures See, e.g., Section 8.

Subsections (c) and (d) are particularized applications of subsection (a). The purpose is to validate and effectuate electronic records and signatures as the equivalent of writings, subject to all of the rules applicable to the efficacy of a writing, except as such other rules are modified by the more specific provisions of this Act.

Illustration 1: A sends the following e-mail to B: "I hereby offer to buy widgets from you, delivery next Tuesday. /s/ A." B responds with the following e-mail: "I accept your offer to buy widgets for delivery next Tuesday. /s/ B." The e-mails may not be denied effect solely because they are electronic. In addition, the e-mails do qualify as records under the Statute of Frauds. However, because there is no quantity stated in either record, the parties' agreement would be unenforceable under existing UCC Section 2-201(1).

Illustration 1: A sends the following e-mail to B: "I hereby offer to buy 100 widgets for $1000, delivery next Tuesday. /s/ A." B responds with the following e-mail: "I accept your offer to purchase 100 widgets for $1000, delivery next Tuesday. /s/ B." In this case the analysis is the same as in Illustration 1 except that here the records otherwise satisfy the requirements of UCC Section 2-201(1). The transaction may not be denied legal effect solely because there is not a pen and ink "writing" or "signature".

4. Section 8 addresses additional requirements imposed by other law which may affect the legal effect or enforceability of an electronic record in a particular case. For example, in Section 8(a) the legal requirement addressed is *the provision of information* in writing. The section then sets forth the standards to be applied in determining whether the provision of information by an electronic record is the equivalent of the provision of information in writing. The requirements in Section 8 are in addition to the bare validation that occurs under this section.

5. Under the substantive law applicable to a particular transaction within this Act, the legal effect of an electronic record may be separate from the issue of whether the record contains a signature. For example, where notice must be given as part of a contractual obligation, the effectiveness of the notice will turn on whether the party provided the notice regardless of whether the notice was signed (See Section 15). An electronic record attributed to a party under Section 9 and complying with the requirements of Section 15 would suffice in that case, notwithstanding that it may not contain an electronic signature.

§8. Provision of Information in Writing; Presentation of Records

(a) If parties have agreed to conduct a transaction by electronic means and a law requires a person to provide, send, or deliver information in writing to another person, the requirement is satisfied if the information is provided, sent, or delivered, as the case may be, in an electronic record capable of retention by the recipient at the time of receipt. An electronic record is not capable of retention by the recipient if the sender or its information processing system inhibits the ability of the recipient to print or store the electronic record.

(b) If a law other than this [Act] requires a record (i) to be posted or displayed in a certain manner, (ii) to be sent, communicated, or transmitted by a specified method, or (iii) to contain information that is formatted in a certain manner, the following rules apply:

(1) The record must be posted or displayed in the manner specified in the other law.

(2) Except as otherwise provided in subsection (d)(2), the record must be sent, communicated, or transmitted by the method specified in the other law.

(3) The record must contain the information formatted in the manner specified in the other law.

(c) If a sender inhibits the ability of a recipient to store or print an electronic record, the electronic record is not enforceable against the recipient.

(d) The requirements of this section may not be varied by agreement, but:

(1) to the extent a law other than this [Act] requires information to be provided, sent, or delivered in writing but permits that requirement to be varied by agreement, the requirement under subsection (a) that the information be in the form of an electronic record capable of retention may also be varied by agreement; and

(2) a requirement under a law other than this [Act] to send, communicate, or transmit a record by [first-class mail, postage prepaid] [regular United States mail], may be varied by agreement to the extent permitted by the other law.

Source: Canadian Uniform Electronic Commerce Act

Comments

1. This section is a savings provision, designed to assure, consistent with the fundamental purpose of this Act, that otherwise applicable substantive law will not be overridden by this Act. The section makes clear that while the pen and ink provisions of such other law may be satisfied electronically, nothing in this Act vitiates the other requirements of such laws. The section addresses a number of issues related to disclosures and notice provisions in other laws.

2. This section is independent of the prior section. Section 7 refers to legal requirements for a writing. This section refers to legal requirements for the provision of information in writing or relating to the method or manner of presentation or delivery of information. The section addresses more specific legal requirements of other laws, provides standards for satisfying the more particular legal requirements, and defers to other law for satisfaction of requirements under those laws.

. . .

§9. Attribution and Effect of Electronic Record and Electronic Signature

(a) An electronic record or electronic signature is attributable to a person if it was the act of the person. The act of the person may be shown in any manner, including a showing of the efficacy of any security procedure applied to determine the person to which the electronic record or electronic signature was attributable.

(b) The effect of an electronic record or electronic signature attributed to a person under subsection (a) is determined from the context and surrounding circumstances at the time of its creation, execution, or adoption, including the parties' agreement, if any, and otherwise as provided by law.

Comments

1. Under subsection (a), so long as the electronic record or electronic signature resulted from a person's action it will be attributed to that person the legal effect of that attribution is addressed in subsection (b). This section does not alter existing rules of law regarding attribution. The section assures that

such rules will be applied in the electronic environment. A person's actions include actions taken by human agents of the person, as well as actions taken by an electronic agent, i.e., the tool, of the person. Although the rule may appear to state the obvious, it assures that the record or signature is not ascribed to a machine, as opposed to the person operating or programing the machine.

In each of the following cases, both the electronic record and electronic signature would be attributable to a person under subsection (a):

A. The person types his/her name as part of an e-mail purchase order;

B. The person's employee, pursuant to authority, types the person's name as part of an e-mail purchase order;

C. The person's computer, programmed to order goods upon receipt of inventory information within particular parameters, issues a purchase order which includes the person's name, or other identifying information, as part of the order.

In each of the above cases, law other than this Act would ascribe both the signature and the action to the person if done in a paper medium. Subsection (a) expressly provides that the same result will occur when an electronic medium is used.

2. Nothing in this section affects the use of a signature as a device for attributing a record to a person. Indeed, a signature is often the primary method for attributing a record to a person. In the foregoing examples, once the electronic signature is attributed to the person, the electronic record would also be attributed to the person, unless the person established fraud, forgery, or other invalidating cause. However, a signature is not the only method for attribution.

3. The use of facsimile transmissions provides a number of examples of attribution using information other than a signature. A facsimile may be attributed to a person because of the information printed across the top of the page that indicates the machine from which it was sent. Similarly, the transmission may contain a letterhead which identifies the sender. Some cases have held that the letterhead actually constituted a signature because it was a symbol adopted by the sender with intent to authenticate the facsimile. However, the signature determination resulted from the necessary finding of intention in that case. Other cases have found facsimile letterheads NOT to be signatures because the requisite intention was not present. The critical point is that with or without a signature, information within the electronic record may well suffice to provide the facts resulting in attribution of an electronic record to a particular party.

In the context of attribution of records, normally the content of the record will provide the necessary information for a finding of attribution. It is also possible that an established course of dealing between parties may result in a finding of attribution Just as with a paper record, evidence of forgery or counterfeiting may be introduced to rebut the evidence of attribution.

4. Certain information may be present in an electronic environment that does not appear to attribute but which clearly links a person to a particular record. Numerical codes, personal identification numbers, public and private key combinations all serve to establish the party to whom an electronic record should be attributed. Of course security procedures will be another piece of evidence available to establish attribution.

The inclusion of a specific reference to security procedures as a means of proving attribution is salutary because of the unique importance of security procedures in the electronic environment. In certain processes, a technical and technological security procedure may be the best way to convince a trier of fact that a particular electronic record or signature was that of a particular person. In certain circumstances, the use of a security procedure to establish that the record and related signature came from the person's business might be necessary to overcome a claim that a hacker intervened. The reference to security procedures is not intended to suggest that other forms of proof of attribution should be accorded less persuasive effect. It is also important to recall that the particular strength of a given procedure does not affect the procedure's status as a security procedure, but only affects the weight to be accorded the evidence of the security procedure as tending to establish attribution.

5. This section does apply in determining the effect of a "click-through" transaction. A "click-through" transaction involves a process which, if executed with an intent to "sign," will be an electronic signature. See definition of Electronic Signature. In the context of an anonymous "click-through," issues of proof will be paramount. This section will be relevant to establish that the resulting electronic record is attributable to a particular person upon the requisite proof, including security procedures which may track the source of the click-through.

6. Once it is established that a record or signature is attributable to a particular party, the effect of a record or signature must be determined in light of the context and surrounding circumstances, including the parties' agreement, if any. Also informing the effect of any attribution will be other legal requirements considered in light of the context. Subsection (b) addresses the effect of the record or signature once attributed to a person.

§10. Effect of Change or Error

If a change or error in an electronic record occurs in a transmission between parties to a transaction, the following rules apply:

(1) If the parties have agreed to use a security procedure to detect changes or errors and one party has conformed to the procedure, but the other party has not, and the nonconforming party would have detected the change or error had that party also conformed, the conforming party may avoid the effect of the changed or erroneous electronic record.

(2) In an automated transaction involving an individual, the individual may avoid the effect of an electronic record that resulted from an error made by the individual in dealing with the electronic agent of another person if the electronic agent did not provide an opportunity for the prevention or correction of the error and, at the time the individual learns of the error, the individual:

(A) promptly notifies the other person of the error and that the individual did not intend to be bound by the electronic record received by the other person;

(B) takes reasonable steps, including steps that conform to the other person's reasonable instructions, to return to the other person or, if instructed by the other person, to destroy the consideration received, if any, as a result of the erroneous electronic record; and

(C) has not used or received any benefit or value from the consideration, if any, received from the other person.

(3) If neither paragraph (1) nor paragraph (2) applies, the change or error has the effect provided by other law, including the law of mistake, and the parties' contract, if any.

(4) Paragraphs (2) and (3) may not be varied by agreement.

Source: Restatement 2d Contracts, Sections 152-155.

§11. Notarization and Acknowledgment

If a law requires a signature or record to be notarized, acknowledged, verified, or made under oath, the requirement is satisfied if the electronic signature of the person authorized to perform those acts, together with all other information required to be included by other applicable law, is attached to or logically associated with the signature or record.

§12. Retention of Electronic Records; Originals

(a) If a law requires that a record be retained, the requirement is satisfied by retaining an electronic record of the information in the record which:

(1) accurately reflects the information set forth in the record after it was first generated in its final form as an electronic record or otherwise; and

(2) remains accessible for later reference.

(b) A requirement to retain a record in accordance with subsection (a) does not apply to any information the sole purpose of which is to enable the record to be sent, communicated, or received.

(c) A person may satisfy subsection (a) by using the services of another person if the requirements of that subsection are satisfied.

(d) If a law requires a record to be presented or retained in its original form, or provides consequences if the record is not presented or retained in its original form, that law is satisfied by an electronic record retained in accordance with subsection (a).

(e) If a law requires retention of a check, that requirement is satisfied by retention of an electronic record of the information on the front and back of the check in accordance with subsection (a).

(f) A record retained as an electronic record in accordance with subsection (a) satisfies a law requiring a person to retain a record for evidentiary, audit, or like purposes, unless a law enacted after the effective date of this [Act] specifically prohibits the use of an electronic record for the specified purpose.

(g) This section does not preclude a governmental agency of this State from specifying additional requirements for the retention of a record subject to the agency's jurisdiction.

Source: UNCITRAL Model Law on Electronic Commerce Articles 8 and 10.

§13. Admissibility in Evidence

In a proceeding, evidence of a record or signature may not be excluded solely because it is in electronic form.

Source: UNCITRAL Model Law on Electronic Commerce Article 9.

Comment

Like Section 7, this section prevents the nonrecognition of electronic records and signatures solely on the ground of the media in which information is presented.

Nothing in this section relieves a party from establishing the necessary foundation for the admission of an electronic record. See Uniform Rules of Evidence 1001(3), 1002,1003 and 1004.

§14. Automated Transaction

In an automated transaction, the following rules apply:

(1) A contract may be formed by the interaction of electronic agents of the parties, even if no individual was aware of or reviewed the electronic agents' actions or the resulting terms and agreements.

(2) A contract may be formed by the interaction of an electronic agent and an individual, acting on the individual's own behalf or for another person, including by an interaction in which the individual performs actions that the individual is free to refuse to perform and which the individual knows or has reason to know will cause the electronic agent to complete the transaction or performance.

(3) The terms of the contract are determined by the substantive law applicable to it.

Source: UNICTRAL Model Law on Electronic Commerce Article 11.

Comment

1. This section confirms that contracts can be formed by machines functioning as electronic agents for parties to a transaction. It negates any claim that lack of human intent, at the time of contract formation, prevents contract formation. When machines are involved, the requisite intention flows from the programming and use of the machine. As in other cases, these are salutary provisions consistent with the fundamental purpose of the Act to remove barriers to electronic transactions while leaving the substantive law, e.g., law of mistake, law of contract formation, unaffected to the greatest extent possible.

. . .

§15. Time and Place of Sending and Receipt

(a) Unless otherwise agreed between the sender and the recipient, an electronic record is sent when it:

(1) is addressed properly or otherwise directed properly to an information processing system that the recipient has designated or uses for the purpose of receiving electronic records or information of the type sent and from which the recipient is able to retrieve the electronic record;

(2) is in a form capable of being processed by that system; and

(3) enters an information processing system outside the control of the sender or of a person that sent the electronic record on behalf of the sender or enters a region of the information processing system designated or used by the recipient which is under the control of the recipient.

(b) Unless otherwise agreed between a sender and the recipient, an electronic record is received when:

(1) it enters an information processing system that the recipient has designated or uses for the purpose of receiving electronic records or information of the type sent and from which the recipient is able to retrieve the electronic record; and

(2) it is in a form capable of being processed by that system.

(c) Subsection (b) applies even if the place the information processing system is located is different from the place the electronic record is deemed to be received under subsection (d).

(d) Unless otherwise expressly provided in the electronic record or agreed between the sender and the recipient, an electronic record is deemed to be sent from the sender's place of business and to be received at the recipient's place of business. For purposes of this subsection, the following rules apply:

(1) If the sender or recipient has more than one place of business, the place of business of that person is the place having the closest relationship to the underlying transaction.

(2) If the sender or the recipient does not have a place of business, the place of business is the sender's or recipient's residence, as the case may be.

(e) An electronic record is received under subsection (b) even if no individual is aware of its receipt.

(f) Receipt of an electronic acknowledgment from an information processing system described in subsection (b) establishes that a record was received but, by itself, does not establish that the content sent corresponds to the content received.

(g) If a person is aware that an electronic record purportedly sent under subsection (a), or purportedly received under subsection (b), was not actually sent or received, the legal effect of the sending or receipt is determined by other applicable law. Except to the extent permitted by the other law, the requirements of this subsection may not be varied by agreement.

Source: UNCITRAL Model Law on Electronic Commerce Article 15.

Comment

1. This section provides default rules regarding when and from where an electronic record is sent and when and where an electronic record is received.

This section does not address the efficacy of the record that is sent or received. That is, whether a record is unintelligible or unusable by a recipient is a separate issue from whether that record was sent or received. The effectiveness of an illegible record, whether it binds any party, are questions left to other law.

. . .

§16.   Transferable Records

(a) In this section, "transferable record" means an electronic record that:

(1) would be a note under [Article 3 of the Uniform Commercial Code] or a document under [Article 7 of the Uniform Commercial Code] if the electronic record were in writing; and

(2) the issuer of the electronic record expressly has agreed is a transferable record.

(b) A person has control of a transferable record if a system employed for evidencing the transfer of interests in the transferable record reliably establishes that person as the person to which the transferable record was issued or transferred.

(c) A system satisfies subsection (b), and a person is deemed to have control of a transferable record, if the transferable record is created, stored, and assigned in such a manner that:

(1) a single authoritative copy of the transferable record exists which is unique, identifiable, and, except as otherwise provided in paragraphs (4), (5), and (6), unalterable;

(2) the authoritative copy identifies the person asserting control as:

(A) the person to which the transferable record was issued; or

(B) if the authoritative copy indicates that the transferable record has been transferred, the person to which the transferable record was most recently transferred;

(3) the authoritative copy is communicated to and maintained by the person asserting control or its designated custodian;

(4) copies or revisions that add or change an identified assignee of the authoritative copy can be made only with the consent of the person asserting control;

(5) each copy of the authoritative copy and any copy of a copy is readily identifiable as a copy that is not the authoritative copy; and

(6) any revision of the authoritative copy is readily identifiable as authorized or unauthorized.

(d) Except as otherwise agreed, a person having control of a transferable record is the holder, as defined in [Section 1-201(20) of the Uniform Commercial Code], of the transferable record and has the same rights and defenses as a holder of an equivalent record or writing under [the Uniform Commercial Code], including, if the applicable statutory requirements under [Section 3-302(a), 7-501, or 9-308 of the Uniform Commercial Code] are satisfied, the rights and defenses of a holder in due course, a holder to which a negotiable document of title has been duly negotiated, or a purchaser, respectively. Delivery, possession, and indorsement are not required to obtain or exercise any of the rights under this subsection.

(e) Except as otherwise agreed, an obligor under a transferable record has the same rights and defenses as an equivalent obligor under equivalent records or writings under [the Uniform Commercial Code].

(f) If requested by a person against which enforcement is sought, the person seeking to enforce the transferable record shall provide reasonable proof that the person is in control of the transferable record. Proof may include access to the authoritative copy of the transferable record and related business records sufficient to review the terms of the transferable record and to establish the identity of the person having control of the transferable record.

Source: Revised Article 9, Section 9-105.

§21. Effective Date

This [Act] takes effect. . . .

Comment: Commercial, Employment, and Consumer Arbitration

For years complaints have raged about the slowness and expense of the judicial process. Because of these concerns, critics of litigation have urged the use of alternative forms of dispute resolution, particularly arbitration. Although courts of an earlier day were extremely hostile to contracts providing for arbitration, regarding this as an attempt to oust them of their rightful jurisdiction, this attitude has given way to one that encourages arbitration as a means of relieving congested court dockets. See generally Ian R. MacNeil, American Arbitration Law: Reformation, Nationalization, Internationalization (1992); Linda R. Hirshman, The Second Arbitration Trilogy: The Federalization of Arbitration Law, 71 Va. L. Rev. 1305 (1985).

To change the restrictive common law rules dealing with arbitration, statutes providing for its use have been enacted at both the federal and state levels. In 1925 Congress enacted the United States Arbitration Act (the Federal Act), which establishes federal substantive law for arbitration of maritime matters or transactions involving interstate commerce. 9 U.S.C. §§1-16. In 1955 the National Conference of Commissioners on Uniform State Laws (NCCUSL)[1] promulgated the Uniform Arbitration Act to govern arbitration to the extent not superseded by the federal legislation. 7 U.L.A. 1 (1997). In 2000 NCCUSL produced a revised Arbitration Act. 7 U.L.A. (Supp. 2002). The initial Uniform Arbitration Act was adopted in 49 jurisdictions and, as of May 2012, the revised Arbitration Act had been adopted in 15 jurisdictions. The status of adoptions can be found at the NCCUSL website at www.uniformlaws.org.

Arbitration is now regularly used to resolve disputes arising from many employment contracts (including both unionized and individual employees), consumer transactions, securities transactions, construction agreements, and commercial contracts, both domestic and international. See Domke on Commercial Arbitration (3d ed., Larry E. Edmondson ed. 2011); Dennis R. Nolan, Labor and Employment Arbitration in a Nutshell (2d ed. 2006); Larry J. Pittman, Mandatory

---

1. NCCUSL is now also referred to as the Uniform Law Commission or ULC.

Arbitration: Due Process and Other Constitutional Concerns, 39 Cap. U. L. Rev. 853 (2011). Fundamental differences exist, however, with regard to arbitration of commercial disputes between sophisticated entities and arbitration of employment or consumer matters. This comment provides a brief overview of these various types of arbitration.

A dispute is subject to arbitration if the parties have entered into a valid contract calling for arbitration and the dispute is "arbitrable." While some types of disputes may not be subject to arbitration, the courts have greatly broadened the scope of matters subject to arbitration. See Vicki Zick, Comment, Reshaping the Constitution to Meet the Practical Needs of the Day: The Judicial Preference for Binding Arbitration, 82 Marq. L. Rev. 247 (1998).

Commercial Arbitration

The following is a typical, pre-dispute contractual provision calling for arbitration of a commercial matter:

> Any controversy or claim arising out of or relating to this contract, or the breach thereof, shall be settled by arbitration administered by the American Arbitration Association under its Commercial Arbitration Rules, and judgment on the award rendered by the arbitrator(s) may be entered in any court having jurisdiction thereof.

The American Arbitration Association (AAA), a private, nonprofit organization based in New York, has published rules on various types of arbitration proceedings. The AAA adopted revised Commercial Arbitration Rules and Mediation Procedures (hereinafter referred to as "CAR"), which became effective July 1, 2009. These rules, numbered R-1 to R-54, are available at the AAA's website (www.adr.org). You may recall that the arbitration agreements in the *Higgins* opinion in the authors' Problems in Contract Law casebook provided that arbitration would take place under AAA commercial arbitration rules.

If a dispute develops under a commercial contract containing an arbitration clause, a party who wishes to arbitrate the matter must file a written "demand" for arbitration with the AAA and pay its administrative fee, which is set by a schedule in accordance with the amount involved. The demand, which is usually much simpler than a complaint filed in court, should state the intent to arbitrate, contain a statement of the nature of the dispute, the names and addresses of all involved parties, the amount involved, the remedy sought, and the hearing locale requested. The demand is served on the opposing party, who has an opportunity to file an answer or counterclaim. CAR R-4.

Under the CAR, the fees for a case depend on the size of the claim. The AAA fee schedule, as amended in June 2010, provides that a claim involving less than $10,000 requires an initial filing fee of $775 and an additional final fee of $200 for all cases that proceed to an initial hearing; if the case involves $10,000 to $75,000, the initial filing fee is $975 and the final fee is $300; if the case involves $75,000 to $150,000, the initial filing fee is $1850 and the final fee is $750. As would be expected, the fees increase on a graduated scale for larger claims.

The Commercial Arbitration Rules contemplate that cases with claims that do not exceed $75,000 will also be governed by the "Expedited Procedures" (E-1 to E-10) and larger cases with claims of at least $500,000 will also be governed by the "Procedures for Large, Complex Commercial Disputes" (L-1 to L-4) published with the CAR. Moreover, the Expedited Procedures provide that a claim for $10,000 or less should be resolved by submission of documents. See CAR E-6.

If the party receiving a demand refuses to submit to arbitration, court proceedings to compel arbitration may be necessary. The party demanding arbitration could file a court action seeking an order compelling the other party to arbitrate the dispute. On the other hand, the party resisting arbitration could file an action to "stay" the arbitration proceeding, perhaps in response to a lawsuit initiated by the other side. Federal Act §3; Uniform Act §7. In each of these cases, the court must decide whether the parties entered into a valid agreement to arbitrate.

Assuming a matter has been effectively referred to arbitration, either because both parties have voluntarily submitted to arbitration or one party has obtained a court order, the next step in the process is the selection of an arbitrator. Sometimes the agreement will designate an arbitrator or provide a method for selection. CAR R-12. If the agreement is silent on the selection of an arbitrator, rules of the AAA provide a "list method" of selection. The AAA sends a list of ten proposed arbitrators, along with their biographical statements, to each of the parties who are asked to strike unacceptable names from the list and to rank acceptable candidates in order of preference. If possible, the AAA will appoint an arbitrator in accordance with the mutual preferences of the parties; if not, the AAA will choose one. CAR R-11. Commercial arbitrators are usually not lawyers; typically, they work in the relevant industry. Normally, one arbitrator is used, although the AAA in its discretion can direct the use of three arbitrators. CAR R-15.

Once the arbitrator is selected, a hearing date will be fixed. CAR R-22. In most jurisdictions, pretrial discovery is not allowed in arbitration proceedings, although the parties could agree to it informally. At the request of any party, the arbitrator has the power to order the production of documents and other information and the identification of witnesses to be called. At least five days before the hearing, parties are required to exchange exhibits they intend to submit at the hearing. CAR R-21. The arbitrator has the power to subpoena witnesses or documents for the hearing. Federal Act §7; Uniform Act §17. In addition, under the Uniform Act, the arbitrator may allow the taking of a deposition of a witness who cannot be subpoenaed or is unable to attend. Uniform Act §17. By agreement of the parties, it is also possible for a matter to be submitted to the arbitrator in writing for decision without a hearing. CAR R-30(c). If a hearing is held, it is less formal than the typical court proceeding. In particular, the arbitrator may consider any evidence that is relevant and material, even if it does not comply with the rules of evidence. CAR R-31.

After the close of the hearing, the arbitrator is required to reach a decision within 30 days. CAR R-41. Except in labor arbitration, the arbitrator's "award" typically states only the result without any reasons. CAR R-42. (This form of award is recommended in arbitration in order to insulate the award from judicial scrutiny.) Subject to the agreement of the parties, the award may provide for any legal or equitable remedy, including specific performance. See generally Michael F. Hoellering, Remedies in Arbitration, in Arbitration and the Law (1984) (Annual Report of General Counsel of AAA).

In many cases the award will be voluntarily honored by the losing party. While the losing party may seek judicial review, the grounds for "vacating" an award are extremely limited. An arbitration award cannot be overturned on the ground that it is contrary to the law or the evidence. The Federal Act lists the following bases for judicial review of an arbitration award:

(1) Where the award was procured by corruption, fraud, or undue means.
(2) Where there was evident partiality or corruption in the arbitrators, or either of them.
(3) Where the arbitrators were guilty of misconduct in refusing to postpone the hearing, upon sufficient cause shown, or in refusing to hear evidence pertinent and material to the controversy; or of any other misbehavior by which the rights of any party have been prejudiced.
(4) Where the arbitrators exceeded their powers, or so imperfectly executed them that a mutual, final, and definite award upon the subject matter submitted was not made.

Federal Act §10(a). Section 23 of the Uniform Act is similar.

After an award is issued, if the agreement to arbitrate so provides, the prevailing party may seek judicial "confirmation" of the award, the effect of which is to make the award a judgment of a court. Federal Act §9; Uniform Act§25.

Employment Arbitration

One of the areas in which arbitration first found acceptance was unionized employment. Dating back to the 1950s, the courts accepted that employers and unions could enter into binding agreements requiring arbitration of disputes between employers and unions, partly as a way of avoiding extended labor disputes, though in that early period the U.S. Supreme Court held that federal statutorily based antidiscrimination claims could be brought in court notwithstanding the union's arbitration agreement. See Frederick L. Sullivan, Accepting Evolution in Workplace Justice: The Need for Congress to Mandate Arbitration, 26 W. New Eng. L. Rev. 281, 290-293 (2004). Details of the collective-bargaining arbitration process are beyond the scope of this comment.

In subsequent years, the U.S. Supreme Court has interpreted the FAA in an expansive manner that resulted in the presumptive enforceability of mandatory arbitration agreements between employers and independent (or non-unionized) employees, even in claims concerning federal antidiscrimination laws. See Circuit City Stores, Inc. v. Adams, 532 U.S. 105, 109-10 (2001) (holding that the FAA applied to all employment except a narrow class of interstate transportation workers listed in the Act). As one article described, the application of the pro-arbitration policy of the FAA to a broad range of individual employees has resulted in "a tidal wave of employment contracts containing arbitration clauses." William H. Daughtrey, Jr. & Donnie L. Kidd, Jr., Modifications Necessary for Commercial Arbitration Law to Protect Statutory Rights Against Discrimination in Employment: A Discussion and Proposals for Change, 14 Ohio St. J. on Disp. Resol. 29, 31 (1998). The percentage of employers using arbitration to resolve disputes grew from less than 4 percent in 1993 to 19 percent in 1996, and the AAA caseload of employment arbitrations grew from three million in 1997 to six million in 2002. See Elizabeth Hill, Due Process at Low Cost: An Empirical Study of Employment Arbitration

Under the Auspices of the American Arbitration Association, 18 Ohio St. J. on Disp. Resol. 777, 779-780 (2003).

The expansion of the arbitration process to a broad range of employment (and consumer) disputes has engendered great controversy and criticism but it remains the applicable law. See, e.g., Jean R. Sternlight, Rethinking the Constitutionality of the Supreme Court's Preference for Binding Arbitration: A Fresh Assessment of Jury Trial, Separation of Powers, and Due Process Concerns, 72 Tul. L. Rev. 1 (1997); David L. Gregory; Edward McNamara, Mandatory Labor Arbitration of Statutory Claims, and the Future of Fair Employment: 14 Penn Plaza v. Pyett, 19 Cornell J.L. & Pub. Pol'y 429 (2010). Thus, the application of the FAA's pro-arbitration policy to individual employment contracts means that employees will find it difficult to avoid enforcement of an agreement to arbitrate. For an employee who does wish to avoid arbitration, the only avenue available is to find some general grounds for invalidating a contract, such as unconscionability, that can be applied specifically to the arbitration agreement. See Susan Randall, Judicial Attitudes Toward Arbitration and the Resurgence of Unconscionability, 52 Buffalo L. Rev. 185 (2004); Jeffrey W. Stempel, Arbitration, Unconscionability, and Equilibrium: The Return of Unconscionability Analysis as a Counterweight to Arbitration Formalism, 19 Ohio St. J. on Disp. Resol. 757 (2004). As indicated by the *Comment: Mandatory Arbitration and Unconscionability*, following the *Higgins* case in the authors' casebook, the once promising avenue of unconscionability as grounds for challenging pre-dispute arbitration agreements has been significantly narrowed by recent U.S. Supreme Court decisions. See also Thomas J. Stipanowich, The Third Arbitration Trilogy: Stolt-Nielsen, Rent-A-Center, Concepcion and the Future of American Arbitration, 22 Am. Rev. Int'l Arb. 323 (2011).

Assuming that the dispute between the individual employee and the employer is ultimately submitted to arbitration, the arbitral rules that are likely to be applied are derivative of the commercial arbitration model described above rather than the form of arbitration found in collective bargaining arrangements. See Michael H. LeRoy & Peter Feuille, Reinventing the Enterprise Wheel: Court Review of Punitive Awards in Labor and Employment Arbitrations, 11 Harv. Negotiation L. Rev. 199, 212-213 (2006). In 1996, the AAA issued National Rules for the Resolution of Employment Disputes to govern arbitration in employment settings. These rules are now known as the Employment Arbitration Rules and Mediation Procedures, most recently amended effective November 1, 2009. The rules are available at the AAA website (www.adr.org).

The 1996 National Rules for the Resolution of Employment Disputes reflected the "Due Process Protocol for Mediation and Arbitration of Statutory Disputes Arising Out of the Employment Relationship" promulgated in 1995 by a special task force composed of individuals representing management, labor, employment, civil rights organizations, private administrative agencies, government, and the AAA. The Due Process Protocol was designed to promote fairness and equity in resolving workplace disputes and has been endorsed by a broad range of organizations including the AAA, the Judicial Arbitration and Mediation Services, Inc. (JAMS), and the American Bar Association Section on Labor and Employment. See Margaret M. Harding, The Limits of the Due Process Protocols, 19 Ohio St. J. on Disp. Resol. 369, 403-405 (2004). By agreeing to arbitrate only agreements that meet the requirements of the Due Process Protocol, organizations such as AAA and JAMS are offering some procedural protection to the independent employee in arbitration.

A fundamental concern in employment arbitration is whether the employee can afford to pursue the claim. The AAA Employment Arbitration Rules create a division between two types of arbitration arrangements, one for disputes arising out of employer-promulgated plans that are imposed on employees as a condition of employment and the other for disputes arising out of individually-negotiated employment agreements. The AAA categorizes the claim when the arbitration is filed, but appeal can be made to the arbitrator. For arbitration under an employer-promulgated plan, the employee's nonrefundable filing fee is capped in the amount of $175, payable in full when a claim is filed unless the plan provides that the employee pay less. The employer pays an initial fee of $925 and other expenses of the hearing.

For individually-negotiated employment agreements, the employee must pay filing fees according to a schedule similar to that used in commercial arbitration. A claim involving less than $10,000 requires a filing fee of $775; if the case involves $10,000 to $75,000, the filing fee is $975; if the case involves $75,000 to $150,000, the filing fee is $1850. In addition, other arbitral expenses are generally borne equally by both sides. The AAA also adopted Supplementary Rules for Class Action Arbitration that adjust fees based on that factor. Procedures other than AAA may require that the employee pay a larger share of the costs, and the law in California may require that the employer pay a larger share.

Arbitration may begin either by joint submission of the parties or the submission of a demand by a single party. Employment Arbitration Rules-4. The appointment process contemplates that the parties may have agreed in advance to an arbitrator or a process for naming one, or may agree at the time the dispute arises. Alternatively, the AAA will provide a list of arbitrators and the parties will reach agreement through a process of objecting to some names and ranking the others. Employment Arbitration Rules-12.

The arbitrator has the ability to order such discovery as may appear necessary to the full exploration of the issues. Employment Arbitration Rules-9. Similarly, the parties are permitted to offer evidence deemed relevant and material to the dispute. Employment Arbitration Rules-30. The arbitrator is required to make an award in writing no later than 30 days from the date of closing of the hearing, in most cases, and the awards are made public and are deemed final and binding. The arbitrator is able to grant any remedy or relief that would have been available to the parties had the matter been heard in court including awards of attorney's fees and costs, in accordance with applicable law. Employment Arbitration Rules-39.

Consumer Arbitration

As suggested by the *Higgins* case and the notes following it, there has been a dramatic increase in the use of mandatory arbitration agreements in a wide variety of contracts involving consumers or otherwise noncommercial parties. The AAA describes consumer transactions as those involving goods or services primarily for personal, family, or household use, including:

> among other things, transactions involving: banking, credit cards, home loans and other financial services; health care services; brokerage services; home construction and improvements; insurance; communications; and the purchase and lease of motor vehicles and other personal property.

Comment on Arbitration

See Statement of Principles of the National Consumer Disputes Advisory Committee: Introduction, available under the "Consumer Due Process Protocol" at the AAA website: (www.adr.org). While there is a variety of fora in which a consumer arbitration procedure could be conducted, the AAA plays a leading role in this area as well. The Due Process Protocol for employment arbitration served as a model for a Consumer Due Process Protocol adopted in 1998 at the instigation of the AAA, and the latter document expands and refines many of the principles set forth in the employment protocol. The Consumer Protocol does not prohibit the use of mandatory pre-dispute arbitration clauses, but it does state that notice of mandatory arbitration should be "clear and adequate," and it preserves for consumers the right to go to the local small claims court instead of arbitration if the claim meets that court's jurisdictional requirements. The stated principles also establish as guidelines the norms that arbitration should be held in a location that is convenient for both parties and in a reasonably prompt fashion.

Similar to the employment protocol, the consumer rules indicate that the AAA will not participate in an arbitration governed by an agreement that does not meet its standards. Unlike the employment protocol, the Consumer Protocol explicitly requires that the any alternative dispute resolution program be independent of the parties. See Margaret M. Harding, The Limits of the Due Process Protocols, 19 Ohio St. J. on Disp. Resol. 369, 405-406 (2004). The AAA Consumer Protocol provides that it applies to standardized non-negotiable contracts between businesses and consumers.

For arbitrations that proceed before the AAA, the applicable rules are the Commercial Dispute Resolution Procedures described above, as altered by the AAA's Supplementary Procedures for Consumer-Related Disputes (numbered C-1 to C-8 and effective September 15, 2005). The stated goal of the AAA is to provide a low cost, streamlined process to resolve disputes between consumers and businesses. As with the commercial and employment procedures, the consumer process begins with a demand by the claimant. C-2. Unlike the other procedures, the arbitrators for consumer disputes are simply appointed by the AAA, subject to possible objection by the parties. C-4. For claims under $10,000, the expectation is that the arbitrator will decide the case based on submission of documents without a hearing, but the presumption is that a hearing will be conducted if the claim is for more than $10,000. C-5 and C-6. The arbitrator will normally make a written award within 14 days of the close of the hearing or receipt of the final documents, and the arbitrator may award any remedy that would be available under the applicable law. C-7.

A consumer is responsible for one-half the arbitrator's fees up to a maximum of $125 if the claim or counterclaim does not exceed $10,000. If the consumer's claim or counterclaim is greater than $10,000, but does not exceed $75,000, then the consumer is responsible for one-half the arbitrator's fees up to a maximum of $375. If the consumer's claim or counterclaim exceeds $75,000, or if the consumer's claim or counterclaim is non-monetary, then the consumer must pay an Administrative Fee in accordance with the Commercial Fee Schedule. The consumer can apply for a waiver of fees based on financial limitations. The arbitrator's fee is set at $250 for a desk arbitration that is decided on submission of papers or for a telephone hearing. The fees are set at $750 per day for an in-person hearing. The business must pay any administrative fees. C-8.

In theory, arbitration should offer consumers a quick and low cost process for resolving disputes. In reality, however, the agreements between consumers and businesses are rarely consensual, and businesses tend to stack the process in their favor by prohibiting consumer class actions, imposing prohibitive costs on individuals, limiting remedies, and setting up discovery rules that favor the business. See Richard M. Alderman, Pre-dispute Mandatory Arbitration in Consumer Contracts: A Call for Reform, 38 Hous. L. Rev. 1237 (2001); Mark E. Budnitz, Mandatory Arbitration: The High Cost of Mandatory Consumer Arbitration, 67 Law & Contemp. Prob. 133 (2004). On the other hand, there are studies which tend to prove that arbitration may work better for some consumers than the judicial process. See Sarah Rudolph Cole, On Babies and Bathwater: The Arbitration Fairness Act and the Supreme Court's Recent Arbitration Jurisprudence, 48 Hous. L. Rev. 457, 472-475 (2011) (citing studies which show that consumers pay lower fees, get faster results and greater remedies in arbitration). Given the nature of this debate, it is likely that consumers will continue to seek to avoid arbitration under the mandatory agreements typically found in consumer contracts but the courts will regularly continue to require that disputes be resolved through that process.

Contract Drafting: A Sample Problem

I. THE PROBLEM

Memorandum

To: File of Owens Chemical, Inc.
From: Attorney
Date: September 1, 2012

Tom Owens, owner of Owens Chemical, Inc., one of our clients, called me today. He wants me to draft a contract for his sales personnel.

The company sells cleaning chemicals to hotels, restaurants, and other businesses through commission salespeople. In the past the company has relied on oral agreements, but for several reasons Tom has now decided to have a written contract. He wants the contract to cover several points.

First, the company treats its sales force as independent contractors for tax purposes. This is important so that the company will not be responsible for withholding, Social Security, and other employment taxes. His accountant has said that it would be desirable to have this arrangement reflected in writing. Second, the company has had some problems with salespeople selling outside their territories. He says that the agreement should specify that salespeople are limited to certain territories.

I asked Tom about other provisions of the agreement. He said that sales personnel are paid a commission of 6 percent of gross sales each month and are responsible for paying all of their own automobile and other expenses. The company does not provide them with retirement or other employment benefits. I asked about duration of the contract, and he said that a one-year term would be fine.

Tom also said to keep it simple. He doesn't want a 20-page agreement and doesn't want a big bill.

II. THE LAWYER'S ROLE AND ETHICAL OBLIGATIONS IN CONTRACT DRAFTING

Contract drafting is a significant service that lawyers provide for their clients. Situations in which clients call on their lawyers to draft contracts typically fall in two categories. In the most common case, like the one involving Owens Chemical, the client asks the lawyer to draft a contract that the client will use in transactions with one or more other people. Examples of such contracts include leases of real property, contracts of purchase and sale of goods or real estate, and employment agreements.

In this first type of drafting situation, the lawyer does not have an attorney-client relationship with the other party, but only with the client for whom the lawyer drafted the contract. In fact, the lawyer may never even meet the other party to the contract. The other party may be represented by counsel, but it is often the case that this person will be unrepresented. If the lawyer does have any contact with an unrepresented party, the lawyer should be careful to make it clear that the lawyer does not represent that person. American Bar Association, Model Rules of Professional Conduct, Rule 4.3.

In the second type of drafting situation, a lawyer may be called on to serve as an intermediary between two or more persons, all of whom will be clients. For example, a lawyer might be asked to form a corporation and to prepare various agreements (such as employment and buy/sell contracts) between the shareholders. The lawyer could, of course, refuse to represent all the parties in this transaction and instead represent only one of the parties. In that case, the other participants would need to retain independent counsel or be unrepresented. To reduce legal fees and to facilitate the transaction, the parties to a business venture may prefer that one lawyer represent all their interests. Ethically, an attorney may do so, but the attorney must proceed with caution. The lawyer must fully advise all parties of the advantages and risks of multiple representation, must obtain their informed consent in writing, must treat all clients equally, and must withdraw from representation should an actual conflict of interest develop. See Model Rule 1.7 and comment 28.

The Owens Chemical situation involves the first type of transaction. Owens Chemical wants the lawyer to draft a standard form contract to be used to employ its sales personnel. Owens Chemical is the lawyer's client; the lawyer does not have an attorney-client relationship with the company's sales representatives. Since Owens is the client, the attorney has an ethical obligation to draft the contract to protect its interests. This does not mean, however, that the attorney has no ethical obligations to the sales personnel. Under the ABA Model Rules of Professional Conduct, a lawyer "shall not counsel a client to engage, or assist a client, in conduct that the lawyer knows is criminal or fraudulent." Model Rule 1.2(d). On occasion a client may ask a lawyer to draft a contract that would violate the criminal law, such as a price-fixing agreement.

Even if not criminal, some contractual provisions that a client might want to include would clearly be unenforceable. Some state statutes, for example, prohibit a seller of goods from disclaiming the implied warranty of merchantability in the sale of goods. See Cate v. Dover Corp., 790 S.W.2d 559, 566 (Tex. 1990) (citing statutes); Peter Millspaugh & Richard Coffinberger, Sellers' Disclaimers of Implied Warranties: The Legislatures Strike Back, 13 UCC L.J. 160 (1980). Drafting a clearly unenforceable disclaimer would be tantamount to fraud on the other person. If a client demands that a lawyer draft a contract that includes a clearly illegal or fraudulent provision, the lawyer should refuse to do so and should withdraw from representation if necessary. Model Rule 1.16(a) (1) (lawyer must withdraw if "representation will result in violation of the rules of professional conduct or other law"). In addition, as discussed below in the comments to the model agreement, the lawyer often must consider the fairness of provisions being drafted. See generally Lee A. Pizzimenti, Prohibiting Lawyers from Assisting in Unconscionable Transactions: Using an Overt Tool, 72 Marq. L. Rev. 151 (1989).

III. THE DRAFTING PROCESS

How does one begin the process of drafting a contract? The client will have given the lawyer some major points to include in the contract, as Mr. Owens has done for an agreement with his sales representatives. These include the following:

— independent contractor status
— definition of territory
— 6 percent commission
— responsibility for all expenses
— no retirement or other benefits
— one-year duration

Can the lawyer simply reduce to written form the points that the client wishes to include in the contract? Clearly not. Attorneys have a duty to represent their clients competently. Model Rule 1.1. Indeed, attorneys have been subject to professional discipline when they purported to do nothing more than act as a mere scrivener. See In re Solomon, 413 S.E.2d 808 (S.C. 1992) (rejecting "mere scrivener" defense to charge of representing conflicting interests). The lawyer's duty of competency in drafting a contract requires that the lawyer determine whether the client's expressed desires can be legally effectuated. Mr. Owens says that his company treats sales personnel as independent contractors for tax purposes, but is it proper for it to do so under federal and state tax law? The attorney or a specialist in tax law must research this point. See Horne v. Peckham, 158 Cal. Rptr. 714 (Ct. App. 1979) (in specialized area like tax law, lawyer must either refer matter to specialist or handle matter with degree of care and skill that would be exercised by specialist).

The duty of competency also means, however, that the lawyer cannot simply focus on the provisions that the client wishes to include in the agreement. The lawyer must determine whether other matters should be covered by the agreement or at least discussed with the client for possible addition to the contract.

Here the lawyer's duty of competency may encounter the economic realities of law practice. Owens says that he does not want a long contract; he wants to keep it simple and does not want a big bill. Yet, to adequately research and draft the contract may require considerable time. In some cases this may mean that the lawyer simply cannot bill the client for the actual time spent on the case. An attorney can view this unbilled time either as an investment in good client relations or as a cost that must be incurred along with the benefits of being a professional. What the attorney must *not* do, however, is consider the obligation to prepare the contract competently as somehow reduced because the client will not pay a full fee. It would be better to refuse the matter to begin with than to "cut corners."

How does a lawyer proceed to determine other provisions to consider including in the agreement? Experience and discussion with other lawyers can suggest some provisions that the agreement should contain. Usually, an attorney must turn to previously prepared agreements and checklists for guidance. Law offices typically maintain form files that an attorney can consult. In addition, commercial publishers offer form books of various types that normally include checklists, sample agreements, and commentary. Comprehensive sets of forms include the following:

American Jurisprudence, Legal Forms (2d ed.)
Nichols Cyclopedia of Legal Forms Annotated
Rabkin & Johnson, Current Legal Forms with Tax Analysis
West's Legal Forms (2d ed.)

After consulting these various sources, the lawyer should be able to prepare an outline of provisions to include in the agreement, along with suggested language for a number of these terms. The lawyer is now ready to prepare a draft of the contract.

IV. MODEL CONTRACT WITH COMMENTS

Independent Contractor Agreement[1]

Agreement entered into this _____ day of _____, 20____, between Owens Chemical, Inc. (the "Company"), of _____, and _____ ("Contractor") of _____.[2]

Recitals[3]

Company operates an industrial chemical business and wishes to hire Contractor as an independent contractor to sell chemicals on behalf of the Company.

Contractor is willing to perform sales services for the Company as an independent contractor.

In consideration[4] of the mutual covenants set forth below, the parties hereby agree as follows:

---

1. The Contract is titled "Independent Contractor Agreement" both for ease of identification and to bolster one of the client's major goals, to clarify the status of the sales personnel for tax purposes.

2. Contracts typically begin with an introduction that includes date, names of the parties, and the city in which they reside or do business. Shorthand references like "Company" and "Contractor" eliminate the need to fill in blanks. Avoid terms like "party of the first part," which are cumbersome and hard to follow.

3. Recitals are background facts and statements of the purposes of the agreement. Both may be useful should an issue of interpretation later develop. Older forms usually began the recitals with "Witnesseth." The trend in drafting is to use plain English whenever possible. Archaic language usually serves no useful purpose and should generally be eliminated. However, some "magic" phrases ("heirs and assigns," for example) have such an established meaning that it would be difficult and probably counterproductive to attempt to develop a modern equivalent.

4. The consideration clause is not strictly necessary since the contract contains mutual promises, but it is customary to include and serves as a transition to the body of the contract.

1. *Description of Work.*[5] Contractor shall devote his[6] full time and use his best efforts[7] to make sales of chemical products to the Company's customers.

2. *Territory.*[8] Contractor shall contact only customers whose principal place of business is located in the following territory: ———————————————
In case of doubt Contractor shall notify the Company and obtain permission to contact a customer. If Contractor learns of customers in other territories who are interested in purchasing the Company's products, Contractor shall promptly notify the Company of the names of these customers.

3. *Commission.* Company shall pay to Contractor a commission of six percent (6%) of gross sales.[9] Payment shall be made on the 15th of each month for sales made during the previous month.[10]

4. *Relationship of Parties.* The parties intend that an independent contractor-employer relationship will be created by this contract. The Company is interested only in the results to be achieved, and the conduct and control of the work will lie solely with the Contractor.[11]

5. *Expenses and Benefits.* Contractor shall be responsible for all expenses involved in performing duties under this agreement and shall not be entitled to any employee benefits, such as Social Security, workers' compensation, or insurance.

6. *Liability.* The work to be performed under this contract will be performed entirely at Contractor's risk. For the duration of this contract, Contractor will carry public liability insurance naming Company as an additional insured in the following amount: —————————. Contractor agrees to indemnify and hold the company harmless against any liability or loss arising from Contractor's negligence.[12]

---

5. The drafter should strive to have a logical order to the substantive provisions. In the Model Contract, Paragraphs 1 and 2 deal with the duties of the contractor. Paragraph 3 sets forth the compensation paid by the company. Paragraphs 4 through 6 focus on the various aspects of the independent contractor relationship. Paragraph 7 deals with termination of the relationship. Paragraph 8 is a merger clause. Contracts, particularly long ones, should include headings for easy reference.

6. In some contracts the use of gender-specific pronouns may be appropriate, but most standard form contracts apply to transactions with both men and women. Use of the plural rather than the singular can avoid the problem of choice of gender, but the plural does not always fit the context. (In the Owens Chemical contract, for example, it would be inappropriate to use the plural to refer to Contractors since the agreement is with an individual salesperson.) Some contracts use the male pronoun with a general statement that the male form is intended to include the female, but this form can give the impression of male dominance.

7. The obligation of sales personnel to devote full time and to use their best efforts on behalf of the Company was not mentioned by the client but was included by the drafter on the assumption that these provisions reflect the client's desires. Any provision that the drafter includes based on the drafter's view of what the client probably wants should be discussed with the client before the agreement is executed. See the letter to the client that follows the Model Contract.

8. Owens has said that the Company has a problem with sales representatives selling outside their territories. Drafting a clause to deal with this issue may appear to be a simple task, but it is not. Owens's customers may have more than one place of business; companies may also move or open additional places of business. How should the agreement deal with the fact that a customer may be physically located in more than one territory? Your tasks as a drafter are first to identify the problem and then to draft a solution that is compatible with the client's desires and business operation.

The agreement uses blanks for provisions that vary among the sales personnel. It is also common to group individual variations in an appendix to the standard form agreement.

9. Is the meaning of "gross sales" clear or is a definition needed? For example, are returns or credits deducted in determining the amount of gross sales to which the commission applies? This point should be raised with the client. The more general point is that operative terms in the agreement often need to be defined. When the agreement contains a number of definitions, the contract should contain a separate definitional paragraph.

10. Is the date for payment consistent with company practice?

11. Under federal income tax law, whether a person is treated as an employee or an independent contractor depends on a number of factors, especially whether the employer has the right to control the day-to-day activities of the Contractor. See Employment Status — Employee v. Independent Contractor (BNA) No. 391-2d (1993).

12. Paragraph 6 raises the issues of the lawyer's role in drafting and of the fairness of the agreement. The client has not mentioned the need for sales personnel to carry insurance or for indemnification against liability. The lawyer certainly has an ethical obligation to raise the issue of insurance with the client

7. *Duration and Termination.* This contract shall continue for one year from its execution. It shall be automatically renewed for additional one-year periods unless either party gives written notice of termination at least three (3) months before the anniversary of the execution of this agreement.[13] Provided, however, either party may terminate this agreement at any time for good cause.

8. *Entire Agreement.* This document constitutes the entire agreement between the parties. No agreements between the parties are binding on them unless incorporated in a writing signed by both parties. This agreement may be modified only in writing signed by both parties.[14]

In witness whereof,[15] the parties have executed[16] this agreement on the day and year first written above.

CONTRACTOR: OWENS CHEMICAL, INC.

_____   By: _____
                                                     Authorized Agent[17]

---

because the absence of such insurance could pose a substantial legal risk to the client and because it would not be unreasonable for sales personnel to be required to carry insurance.

The indemnification clause, however, is a different matter. Does the client really need the additional protection of an indemnification clause from sales personnel? If so, how broadly should the clause be drafted? Should it indemnify the Company against any loss resulting from the negligence of the salesperson, or should it protect the Company against any liability arising from the actions of the salesperson, whether negligent or not? As noted above, a lawyer may not draft a clause that is illegal or fraudulent, but this broad clause clearly does not violate those restrictions. Should the lawyer, therefore, include any provision that protects the client's interests, or should the lawyer strive to draft an agreement that reasonably protects the client's interests without being overreaching?

One possible answer to this question is that the lawyer should draft the agreement to protect the client to the maximum extent possible but also should discuss with the client the advantages and disadvantages of the provisions in question so that the client can make an informed decision. The difficulty with this approach is that the client will often turn to the lawyer for advice about what should be included. In addition, human inertia being what it is, the provision that the lawyer initially drafts will be more likely to remain in the agreement.

The drafter of this agreement has included an indemnification clause that the drafter believes reasonably protects the client's interest but without being overreaching. The clause, therefore, is limited to negligence by the salesperson. Do you agree with this approach? Or do you consider it inconsistent with the lawyer's fiduciary obligations to this client?

13. The automatic renewal clause avoids the necessity of additional paperwork to renew the contract each year, but the Company should be made aware of the requirement to give three months' written notice if it wishes to terminate a salesperson at the end of any year.

14. This merger clause is intended to invoke the application of the parol evidence rule and to prevent oral modifications.

15. This is a standard conclusion to a contract but could easily be eliminated.

16. Witnesses to a contract are not required for the validity of a contract but may be desirable if there is any possibility of a later dispute about execution or terms of the contract. Given the nature of this contract, witnesses seem unnecessary.

Certain contracts, particulary contracts involving real estate, may be recorded in public records if one of the parties wishes to give public notice of the existence of the contract. To be recorded, however, a contract must meet statutory requirements regarding number of witnessess, one of whom must be a "notary public" or other similar officer legally authorized to witness the execution of documents under oath. Since this contract will not be recorded, notarization is unnecessary.

Many older contracts stated that they were executed "under seal" or "L.S." (locus sigilli). The significance of the seal has largely disappeared in modern times. In some jurisdictions, execution under seal may have the benefit of lengthening the statute of limitations for suit for breach of the agreement, but this is a fairly minor point.

17. Whenever a corporation or other business entity is a party to an agreement, the authority of the agent who is signing the agreement on its behalf should be verified. This may be done by a certification from the secretary of the entity that the official has authority to act on behalf of the entity either under the bylaws or other governing document of the entity, or by virtue of a resolution adopted by the governing body of the entity (the board of directors of a corporation, for example). The president of a corporation normally has implied or inherent authority to execute contracts that are resonably necessary for the Company to take any formal action to authorize Owens to sign these contracts.

V. COUNSELING THE CLIENT

Once the attorney has prepared a draft of the contract, the attorney will then submit the draft to the client for review. Typically, the lawyer will do this with an accompanying cover letter pointing out the principal provisions in the agreement along with questions that the attorney would like the client to consider.

September 15, 2012

Mr. Tom Owens
Owens Chemical, Inc.
218 Local Street
Your Town, YS 91128

Dear Tom:

I enclose for your review a draft Independent Contractor Agreement for your sales personnel. Please consider the following points and questions as you review the agreement.

1. *Description of Work.* I included a provision stating that salespeople will devote their "full time" to Company sales. Is this satisfactory? Do you have or expect to have any part-timers? Do you have any sales representatives who also represent other chemical companies?

The provision also states that sales personnel will use their best efforts on behalf of the Company. Under paragraph 7 you can terminate any salesperson for good cause, which would include failure to use best efforts. You can also terminate a salesperson at the end of any year for any reason provided you give three months' written notice.

2. *Territory.* I drafted the territory clause to try to deal with the problem you mentioned about salespeople who contact customers outside their territories. A possible difficulty is that your customers may have places of business in several territories. This clause uses the principal place of business of a customer to define the territory in which the customer is located. Let's discuss this to determine if it meets your needs.

3. *Commission.* As you mentioned, this is based on 6 percent of gross sales. Do we need to define "gross sales"? Are there any deductions that should be made from gross sales, like returns or credits, for the purpose of determining commissions? Is payment of the commission on the 15th of the month for the previous month's sales consistent with your practice?

4. *Relationship of Parties.* This paragraph confirms that sales personnel are independent contractors. Under federal and state law, a salesperson will be treated as an independent contractor if the employer is concerned only about results and does not control the day-to-day activities of the sales personnel. This is a factual question. Despite what the agreement says, if you do try to control or direct the day-to-day activities of your personnel, they will no longer be independent contractors. Be aware of this fact as you conduct your business.

5. *Expenses and Benefits.* This confirms that the Company has no obligation to reimburse sales personnel for expenses or to provide any benefits.

6. *Liability.* We did not discuss the question of liability but I have drafted a clause requiring sales personnel to carry insurance and also providing that sales personnel must indemnify the Company for any liability arising from their negligence. Do you need or want this protection, or do you simply want to rely on your own insurance? In any event, you need to check with your insurance company to make sure your insurance covers the Company for any actions of its sales personnel.

7. *Duration and Termination.* The term of the agreement is one year, and the agreement automatically renews for additional one-year periods unless written notice of termination is given by either party three months before the end of any one-year period. The agreement may be terminated at any time for good cause. Are there any specific forms of misconduct that the agreement should specify as grounds for discharge?

8. *Entire Agreement.* This is a standard provision requiring that any modifications or additions to the agreement be in writing. The purpose of this clause is to reduce or eliminate disputes about the terms of the agreement. If you decide that change or modification of the agreement is necessary, you should reduce the provision to writing and have it signed by both the Company and the Contractor.

Other points to consider.

I did not include in the agreement a covenant not to compete. Do you want to consider including such a clause? For example, the agreement might prohibit a salesperson who leaves the Company from contacting any customer of the Company on behalf of a competitor of the Company for a designated period, such as one year. Courts sometimes refuse to enforce covenants not to compete, so if you wish to pursue this idea, we will need to discuss it further.

The agreement provides that if a salesperson learns of a potential customer outside the salesperson's territory, the salesperson will promptly notify the Company. Do you want to give sales personnel an incentive to make such contacts, such as giving them a referral fee if a sale results?

After you have had a chance to review the draft, give me a call so that we can discuss revisions and consider any suggestions you may have.

Best regards,

Helen T. Partner, Esq.

VI. BIBLIOGRAPHY

Given the importance of drafting, law schools are devoting increasing attention to the subject. In the past few years a number of fine books on drafting have been published. These include the following:

Scott Burnham, Drafting and Analyzing Contracts (3d ed. 2003)
Barbara Child, Drafting Legal Documents (2d ed. 1992)
Thomas R. Haggard, Contract Law from a Drafting Perspective (2002)
George W. Kuney, The Elements of Contract Drafting (3d ed. 2011)

Sample Examination Questions with Model Answers

EDITORS' NOTE

The sample examination questions and model answers that follow deal with issues covered in most contracts casebooks, although the order of their presentation may differ. The fifth problem is followed by a grading sheet that identifies the relevant issues and exemplifies how many professors award points in grading. Students using casebooks other than Knapp, Crystal & Prince, Problems in Contract Law (7th ed. 2012), should have little difficulty following the analysis. We have also included several questions without model answers, to be used by students for review or by instructors for class discussion.

CONTRACT FORMATION, DEFENSES, AND REMEDIES

You are an attorney practicing in a small midwestern town. One Monday morning you are consulted in your office by Karen Mackenzie, a local resident whom you know slightly but have not represented before. She tells you the following story:

"As you may know, my husband died several years ago. Our children were nearly grown then, and since I have a well-paying position at the hospital and he left a substantial estate, I haven't had severe financial worries. Now that our children are all through school and supporting themselves, I have moved into a smaller, less expensive apartment. As a result I find myself in quite comfortable circumstances, financially."

"Last week I got in the mail one of those promotional letters that said I had won a 'valuable prize' (you probably know the kind I mean), either a Jeep or a diamond ring or a set of luggage or $10,000 in cash. All I had to do to claim my prize, the letter said, was to come to Fairgate Hills, a new condominium development some 10 miles west of town, near the lake, and visit the 'prize redemption center.' Well, I knew there would be a sales pitch involved, but I was sort of curious to see the place, having heard about it from some friends of mine who live near there. And in fact I had thought a little about investing in some sort of vacation home where the kids could come and stay with me for a while. Now that they're all having families of their own, it's too crowded for them to visit my apartment in town."

"So last Saturday I took my 'Winner's Certificate' and drove out to Fairgate Hills. When I arrived I was met by a young woman named Abby something-or-other (I never did get her last name) who told me that before she could authorize my picking up the prize she would have to take me on a tour of Fairgate Hills and tell me about the terms on which condominium units were available there. I said I realized something like that would be involved, and that was okay with me — she should know I had no intention of buying anything, I said, but I did have some time to kill. So we walked around, and looked through some of the units, and I was pretty impressed, in spite of myself. There were tennis courts, too, and picnic areas, and the whole thing was very attractive. The more she talked the better it all seemed, and by the time we were finished, I had signed something and given her a check for $5000."

At this point, you ask Ms. Mackenzie if she has a copy of the paper she signed. She produces the following for your inspection:

Offer to Purchase

The undersigned, <u>Karen Mackenzie</u>, hereby offers to purchase condominium unit <u>54</u> in Fairgate Hills, a <u>three</u>-bedroom unit with two baths and <u>carport adjoining</u>. I agree that the seller, Fairgate Hills, Inc. (the "Seller"), may investigate my credit before accepting this offer, and I agree to provide such information and sign such consents as Seller may request for this purpose. I also agree that should this Offer be accepted, I will enter into the standard form of Sale and Mortgage Agreement used by the Seller for its sales of condominium units in Fairgate Hills (a copy of which has been made available for my inspection), with such changes therein as Seller and I may mutually agree to.

In earnest of my intention to perform all of my obligations hereunder, I have today paid to Seller the sum of <u>$5000.00,</u> which sum will be applied toward my total purchase price of <u>$165,000</u> should Seller accept this Offer. If my Offer is not accepted within sixty days of the date below, that sum will be refunded to me (subject to deduction of Seller's reasonable expenses incurred in connection with the processing of this Offer), and this Offer will thereupon terminate.

I understand and agree that this Offer is made for valuable consideration, and is irrevocable by me. I further understand and agree that the payment made by me today will not be refundable for any reason except the failure of the Seller to accept my Offer, and may in the event of my nonperformance of any obligation hereunder be retained by the Seller as damages for my nonperformance, without limitation of the Seller's right to any other remedy instead of, or in addition to, such sum.

<u>December 16, 2011</u>
Date

<u>(signed) Karen Mackenzie</u>
Purchaser

Karen Mackenzie's story continues: "After she had my check, Abby walked me over to the 'prize redemption center,' where they gave me my prize — a set of cheap plastic luggage, worth $50 at the most — and I left for home."

"All the way home, I kept having second thoughts. Even if I did want a vacation home, this one was too big for me, and too expensive. By the time I got home, I was sure I'd made a mistake. So right away I telephoned the office at Fairgate Hills, and asked to speak to Abby. As soon as she was on the phone, I identified myself and said I'd changed my mind, that I didn't want to buy a unit at Fairgate Hills after all. She said I must have misunderstood our conversation, that the paper I signed committed me to make the purchase, that it was an enforceable contract, and that if I tried to back out I'd not only lose my $5000, I'd be liable for damages, too. Is she right? Do I have to go through with this, or else lose a lot of money?"

You have some reason to think there may be provisions of federal or state statutory law that would be helpful to someone in Ms. Mackenzie's situation, and you resolve to do research in that area. First, however, you consider her position under traditional contract law. Is she legally bound to Fairgate Hills? Or can she freely terminate any potential obligation she may have incurred under the "Offer to Purchase" quoted above? If she is indeed bound by some sort of obligation, what kinds of liability might she face, should Fairgate Hills elect to enforce it? Finally, in light of your answers to these questions, what course of action would you advise her now to follow? If you need more facts in order to answer these questions, indicate what those facts might be and why they would be relevant to your conclusions.

OUTLINE OF ANSWER

1. Has Karen Mackenzie made an offer?
   a. Sufficiently definite and certain
   b. Finality of commitment
2. If offer was made, can it be revoked?
   a. Traditional rule of free revocability
   b. Presence of consideration
   c. Effectiveness of recital of consideration
   d. Application of statute
   e. Reliance by offeree
   f. Offer already revoked
   g. Offer already accepted (mailbox rule)
3. If offer accepted, enforceable contract?
   a. Sufficiently complete agreement
   b. Satisfaction of Statute of Frauds
   c. Possibility of avoidance for fraud or mistake
   d. Capacity to contract
   e. Unconscionability
4. Remedies of Seller
   a. Damages
   b. Specific performance
   c. Retention of down payment (vs. buyer's claim to restitution)

MODEL ANSWER

In order to counsel my client Karen Mackenzie (to whom I will refer for convenience as "Mackenzie"), I will first need to address several questions:

(1) Did Mackenzie make an offer to Fairgate Hills, Inc. ("Fairgate"), in the writing she signed during her Saturday visit to the condominium development?

(2) If Mackenzie did make an effective offer, is it one that she has the power to revoke?

(3) If Mackenzie has indeed made an offer, and does not effectively revoke that offer before Fairgate accepts it, has a contract enforceable against her been created?

(4) If Mackenzie is (or comes to be) bound to Fairgate by an enforceable contract, to what remedy would Fairgate be entitled if Mackenzie should refuse to perform?

These questions will be addressed below in the order stated above.

1. Has Mackenzie made an offer?

For a communication to reach the level of an "offer," creating in the one to whom it is addressed the power to bring a contract into being by making an acceptance, it must be such as to reasonably create in the mind of the (potential) "offeree" the belief that the person making it has stated a definite proposal for exchange, with sufficient commitment on the part of the "offeror" that no further expression of assent from her is necessary in order to complete the bargain. (See Restatement (Second) of Contracts §24 — offeree's "assent to that bargain is invited and will conclude it.")

In this case the writing signed by Mackenzie was clearly designed by Fairgate to be an offer, although one to be made by the potential purchasers of its condos, *not* by Fairgate itself. It uses the language of offer, and, with the incorporation by reference of Fairgate's standard form purchase agreement, probably has sufficient detail and certainty to satisfy that requirement as well. (The latter point is discussed further below.) As Mackenzie told her story to me, she did not seem to have been ignorant of the possibility that the writing she signed could in effect commit her to the purchase of a condo; rather, she apparently had assumed that she could back out if she chose before Fairgate had committed itself. (This goes more to the issue of irrevocability, discussed below.) Unless Mackenzie maintains that she was in fact deceived about the nature of the paper she was signing (she was told it was merely a receipt for her luggage "prize," for instance), it seems unlikely that she can successfully deny making an offer to purchase. (Her delivery to Abby of a $5000 check would undercut any "I thought I was only signing a receipt" argument — clearly one doesn't blithely hand over a check that large unless some substantial transaction is in process.) Before reaching a definite conclusion on this first point, however, I would quiz Mackenzie further as to just what Abby said to her about the writing she signed, and whether Mackenzie read it before signing (or at all).

2. If Mackenzie made an offer, can she revoke it?

This issue raises several questions: Was Mackenzie's offer (assuming for the moment it was indeed an offer) irrevocable when made? If not, has she revoked it already? If she has not, can she do so now? How?

Under the traditional common law of contract, an offeror may freely revoke her offer at any time before an effective acceptance is made, *even if* the offer expressly states that it is irrevocable. This rule sometimes appears to produce unjust results when used by a knowledgeable offeror against an unsophisticated offeree, who may have relied in various ways on the continuing availability of what was assumed to be in fact an irrevocable, or "firm," offer. In this case, however, the traditional rule could enable Mackenzie to escape from a bargain that she does not want and that, apparently, she believed she could avoid. A variety of exceptions to the general common law rule, however, might cause Mackenzie's offer to be irrevocable: She might be bound by a consideration-supported "option contract"; her offer might be irrevocable because of its form; the offeree might have reasonably relied on her apparent intention to make an irrevocable offer. It is even possible that her offer, even if it was in effect a revocable one from the start, has already been accepted by Fairgate and thus is no longer capable of being revoked. These possibilities will be explored in order below.

Even the most "classical" form of contract law allows for the possibility that an offer will be irrevocable for some period of time because the offeree has given "consideration" for its remaining open — has purchased an "option contract." Consideration was traditionally defined as a "benefit to the promisor" (who in the case of an option contract would be the offeror, promising to keep her offer open) or a "detriment to the promisee" (in this case, the offeree). The "benefit" or "detriment" involved may be of slight value, however, as shown by Hamer v. Sidway. Under the more modern definition of consideration, virtually anything may serve as consideration if it was bargained for and given in exchange for the promise. (Restatement (Second) of Contracts §71).

In Mackenzie's case, it is difficult to find anything in the facts as related which could serve the function of consideration to keep her offer open. Mackenzie did in fact suffer a variety of "detriments," some quite substantial (the $5000) and some less so (driving out to Fairgate Hills, taking the tour and enduring Abby's sales pitch). These are also "benefits" to Fairgate, in varying degrees. But they move the wrong way — Mackenzie in this case would be the "promisor" (promising to keep her offer open), so the benefit must move *to* her, not *from* her; similarly, the detriment must be suffered by Fairgate, not by Mackenzie.

On the facts as related, the only thing that might serve as consideration for the making of an irrevocable offer by Mackenzie is the set of luggage she received at the end of her Saturday visit. The modest value of the luggage is no obstacle — clearly $50 or the equivalent in goods could be sufficient consideration for an option contract, *if bargained for.* This latter point appears crucial, however. If the luggage was indeed given to Mackenzie by Fairgate as the "exchange" or the "price" for anything at all (rather than being just a "gift," which is what "prize" connotes, probably), it was the price for Mackenzie's willingness to travel several miles to Fairgate Hills, or perhaps for that plus her willingness to sit through a sales pitch. Although the presentation of the luggage was not characterized by Fairgate as an exchange, the luggage may have served in effect to purchase the presence of a potential buyer. Thus, if Fairgate had not come through with the luggage at the end of her tour, Mackenzie might in theory have had a cause of action against Fairgate for the luggage or its value. (Note that this scenario is different from Williston's "tramp" hypothetical, because Mackenzie's presence at the condo development, unlike the tramp's trip to obtain the overcoat, could have been — and in fact was — of benefit to Fairgate.) But to call the luggage consideration for the making of an irrevocable offer by Mackenzie seems to stretch the facts too far. It was never so characterized, and Mackenzie never understood that the luggage was given in exchange for anything other than, perhaps, her presence at the condo long enough for the sales pitch to be made.

If no consideration was in fact given for Mackenzie's offer, can Fairgate claim the benefit of the suggested rule of Restatement (Second) of Contracts §87(1)(a)? This rule applies to an offer that meets certain specific requirements: It is in writing and signed (which Mackenzie's is), recites a "purported consideration" for the making of the offer, and "proposes an exchange on fair terms within a reasonable time." Applying this rule to Mackenzie's situation could create problems. The "offer" Mackenzie signed recites that it is made for consideration, but doesn't otherwise identify that consideration. Must it do so to satisfy §87(1)(a)? That's not clear from the statement of the rule. Does her offer propose an exchange "on fair terms"? Until I conduct some investigation of the facts, I have no idea whether the $165,000 price is a reasonable one. Is the proposed exchange one that will take place "within a reasonable time"? Again, I can't know this from reading the offer itself; the form it refers to may have a provision governing the time by which the sale is to be closed. (It seems unlikely, however, that the seller would draft a form unreasonably *delaying* the closing.)

The proposed rule of §87(1)(a) has not been embraced by the courts; not all courts have addressed it, and not all that have done so have adopted it. I would have to examine the case law of my jurisdiction to know whether a mere recital of consideration would be given this effect. If our courts have not yet adopted the rule of §87(I)(a), we can in good faith take the position that it is not good law (and unlikely to become so). Moreover, there is also room to argue that this is not an appropriate case for the application of that rule. If I understood her correctly, Mackenzie did not in fact believe that she was making an offer that she could not revoke, and did not know that the "recital of consideration" could have that effect. This by itself may not be persuasive, however, since a court might not believe her or might conclude that she *should* have understood the writing to have that effect.

A clearer rebuttal can be given to another possible argument in favor of irrevocability. The Uniform Commercial Code in §2-205 provides that written, signed "firm" offers may be binding without consideration. That section applies only to sales of goods, however, and only to offers made by "merchants." Fairgate might be considered a "merchant," as Article 2 uses that rather broad term, but *Mackenzie* probably is not. Moreover, the condo is not "goods" as defined in the Code. UCC §2-205 thus does not directly apply, and in view of Mackenzie's nonmerchant status should not be applied even "by analogy." (Note also that §2-205 calls for separate signing, or at least initialing, when a "firm offer" is made on a form supplied by the *offeree,* another reason why that section should have no relevance here.) A few states, such as New York, have broader statutes making "firm" offers irrevocable, a point that also needs research. (For the moment, I will assume that my jurisdiction does not have such a statute.)

Since the decision in Drennan v. Star Paving Co., courts have been willing to consider the possibility that reliance on an offer by the offeree may be sufficient to deprive the offeror at least temporarily of the power to revoke. Despite its incorporation in Restatement (Second) of Contracts §87(2), however, this application of "promissory estoppel" seems unlikely to help Fairgate, even if the courts of my jurisdiction would be willing to apply the *Drennan* principle in nonconstruction-bidding cases, as the Restatement suggests. According to Mackenzie's story, she called Abby as soon as she returned home from her trip to Fairgate Hills; the facts we know suggest that the time lag cannot have been more than a few hours, at most. It is difficult to imagine any actions Fairgate might have taken during that brief interval other than to initiate a credit check on Mackenzie, an action that by itself seems unlikely to be viewed by the court as the sort of "substantial" action that under §87(2) might result in injustice if the offer were freely revocable. Once Mackenzie notified

Fairgate that she did not wish to proceed with the transaction, it seems that any further reliance on her willingness to honor an apparent promise of irrevocability would be unreasonable and thus should have no effect on her power to revoke. Moreover, when Abby told Mackenzie the offer could not be withdrawn, she did not mention any change of position on Fairgate's part to justify that conclusion; she seemed to be arguing simply on the strength of the language of the offer. This by itself is not conclusive, of course, but it strengthens our argument that any reliance on Fairgate's part was insubstantial at that point.

This leads logically to another, related question. Assuming that Mackenzie's offer is not, in legal effect, an irrevocable one, has she already revoked it? Her telephone call, as she recounted it, seems to have been sufficient to give Abby notice that Mackenzie no longer wanted to make the purchase, and it may have had the effect suggested above on Fairgate's power to reasonably rely. Whether it also served effectively as a revocation is less clear. Abby took the strong position that Mackenzie simply had no power to withdraw from the transaction, and it may be that Mackenzie's response to that assertion was sufficiently equivocal to leave her offer on the table. In any event, recollections of a conversation (and the credibility of those recollections) may differ. Since it is at least possible that Mackenzie has the power to revoke, she should do so immediately in a written letter to Fairgate. (This point is explored further at the end of the discussion.)

It should be noted here that, although perhaps unlikely, one other factor could make it impossible for Mackenzie now to revoke her offer. That is the possibility that Fairgate has already accepted it. Mackenzie wrote her offer and left it with Abby for Fairgate to consider; clearly the offer did not call only for an immediate acceptance. Under these circumstances, the offer is probably susceptible of acceptance by mail, under the traditional "deposited acceptance," or "mailbox," rule. Conceivably Mackenzie's call to Abby triggered an immediate mailing of such an acceptance (if only for the purpose of giving Fairgate an even stronger claim to retention of Mackenzie's $5000 payment). At this point we don't know whether that happened. In case it did, we should take the position (which on the facts we can, in good faith) that Mackenzie's telephone call was itself a revocation sufficient to terminate any power of acceptance. Any letter of revocation sent now by Mackenzie should therefore take the position that revocation has already been effected orally and that the letter is simply to confirm that fact.

3. If Fairgate does accept before Mackenzie effectively revokes her offer, will an enforceable contract result?

This general question raises a number of distinct issues: Would a mere acceptance by Fairgate without further assent by Mackenzie conclude an effective contract? Would Mackenzie have the ability to avoid that contract, or have a defense against its enforcement, under some applicable rule of law?

In discussing the "offer" status of Mackenzie's signed writing, it was suggested that the incorporation by reference of Fairgate's standard form could satisfy the requisite certainty of terms that common law courts (with varying degrees of scrutiny) look for in a contract. Not actually having seen the form, I cannot be sure of that, but for the moment I can assume it, given the nature of Fairgate and the likelihood that the form was drafted by a competent attorney. (If a dispute with Fairgate develops, at some point we will demand and get a copy of that form, of course.) The offer refers to the possibility of amending the terms of that standard form, to the extent that the parties may both agree. The possibility of such modifications probably would not undercut the agreement so greatly as to make it ineffective for vagueness or "agreement to agree" character, however, whether or not we hypothesize some degree of obligation on Fairgate's part to bargain in good faith over possible amendments to the form.

A second rule of law that can make an agreement unenforceable is the Statute of Frauds. A condominium is an interest in land (as contrasted with a "cooperative," which technically is a shareholder's interest in a land-owning corporation), and clearly the Statute of Frauds could — at least at this point — be a defense to any enforcement by Mackenzie *against* Fairgate. But Mackenzie has signed an offer, and the offer coupled with the incorporated-by-reference terms of the standard agreement probably satisfies the writing requirement of the Statute of Frauds, as against her. (Some research again is called for, to see whether our courts have imposed an unusually high threshold for completeness or land-description.) Traditionally the Statute of Frauds only requires a writing signed by the "party to be charged," and in this case that is Mackenzie.

If Mackenzie's offer once accepted is sufficient in form and content to satisfy the ordinary rules of contract law, are there any grounds on which she might seek to avoid its enforcement? One set of rules focuses on possible misconduct by the other party. Did Fairgate misrepresent any material fact, intentionally or otherwise? Here again, a more searching conversation with Mackenzie is needed to determine precisely what Mackenzie was and was not told during her visit to Fairgate Hills. Nothing Mackenzie has said so far suggests any misrepresentation by Abby, other than her assertion that Mackenzie cannot now withdraw her offer. That assertion was made after the offer was signed, however, and therefore played no role in inducing Mackenzie's entry into this transaction. Moreover, it was at worst a misrepresentation by one party of the other party's legal position, which is the sort of assertion that is not likely to be actionable fraud, if only because — like "puffing" — it is not an assertion on which the other party should reasonably rely. It should also be noted that although Mackenzie quickly concluded that this purchase was for her a "mistake," this is not the sort of mistake that provides a legal power of avoidance. That requires a later-discovered material fact that at the time of contracting was unknown either to both parties or at least to the one seeking to avoid. Absent more facts, we have nothing like that here.

Although we know that Mackenzie is old enough to have grown children with families of their own, she sounds too vigorous (physically as well as mentally) to be able to make a viable claim of legal incompetence to contract (even if she wanted to, which seems doubtful). Could she have been the victim of undue influence? Presumably Abby is a well-trained, high-pressure salesperson, and an effective one, too; by itself, however, this is not enough. Mackenzie seems to have understood from the start that she was letting herself in for a sales talk. The sales pitch seems to have had real substance, and the condos to have been attractive, but nothing (other than the lure of her "prize") appears to have kept Mackenzie at any point from just picking up her marbles and walking away.

Can this agreement be "unconscionable," and for that reason unenforceable? To answer this, I need to see the standard Sale and Mortgage Agreement referred to in the offer. Even if the price itself is a fair one, other terms in that form may appear shocking to the conscience of a court, such as stronger-than-ordinary rights for the seller upon buyer's default. I also need to ask Mackenzie whether she even saw that form, whether she was given an opportunity to study it, and (if so) whether she did. If the price is shockingly high or the terms unusually onerous, the transaction is one — sophisticated seller, unsophisticated and uncounseled buyer, hasty decision — that could qualify for unconscionability treatment. (This is not confined to sales of goods, of course, even though the modern law of unconscionability can be traced in large part to UCC §2-302.) For a number of reasons, however, the unconscionability defense is best as a backstop. First, courts are often reluctant to apply it; second, Mackenzie may not be an ideal candidate. (She is hardly a poor or illiterate person — did she have an "absence of meaningful choice"?) Even if successful, it might result only in staving off further liability, not in a refund of Mackenzie's $5000.

4. If Mackenzie is bound by an enforceable contract, what remedies might be available to Fairgate if she refuses to perform?

The potential remedies for Fairgate fall into three categories: money damages, specific performance, and liquidated damages (retention of the down payment).

The vendor's money damages for breach of a contract to purchase real estate are traditionally computed as the excess of the purchase price over the value of the property, plus incidental and consequential damages occasioned by the breach. The first question here is one we have already raised above: What is the market value of the condo at issue? If it is worth about what Mackenzie agreed to pay for it, then Fairgate's money damages for her breach could consist only of the "incidental" damages involved in finding another buyer. The chance of consequential damages to Fairgate appears nil — nothing Mackenzie has told me suggests she had any reason at the time of her meeting with Abby to foresee any unusual damages to Fairgate from a buyer's refusal to perform, so the traditional Hadley v. Baxendale rule would protect her. (As an analogy, consider that the UCC doesn't even expressly contemplate the recovery of consequential damages by a *seller*.) Suppose, however, that the condos Fairgate is selling are in fact worth much less on the market than the price stated to Mackenzie. (If so, this could also be a first step — but *only* a first step — toward an argument that material misrepresentations were made to her.) In this case, Fairgate's money damages for a breach by Mackenzie could range from little or nothing to quite a lot of money. (Note that even if the clause providing for Fairgate's retention of the down payment is valid and effective as in effect a liquidated remedy, the clause itself is specific on the point that retention of the deposit is not necessarily the *only* remedy to which Fairgate might be entitled.)

Could Fairgate succeed in an action for specific performance? Traditionally this remedy has been available in land cases, to sellers as well as to buyers. We might well argue, however, that money damages here would certainly be adequate; some courts would accept that argument by a defendant-buyer where the property is readily resaleable and the plaintiff-seller's damages can be fixed with sufficient accuracy. Specific performance is also sometimes withheld because the exchange appears to be an unfair one; thus, the greater the disparity between contract and market prices, the less likely it is that specific performance will be granted. (Paradoxically, this disparity would also *increase* the likelihood of substantial money damages unless the court found the contract to be unenforceable for some other reason, such as fraud or mistake.)

Assuming the money damages available to Fairgate would in fact be small, can we successfully claim the right to a refund of Mackenzie's $5000? If the contract is not otherwise vulnerable to our defense or avoidance, Mackenzie's right (as a party in breach) to restitution will depend on our jurisdiction's attitude toward the retention-of-deposit clause in the offer form. Traditionally such provisions have been regarded as valid and enforceable, the breaching party being considered ineligible for restitution. More recently, however, many courts have been disposed to recognize in principle the possibility that even a breaching party might be entitled to restitution of benefits conferred. Once that position is taken, the validity of clauses like this will be judged under the broader rules governing liquidated damages in general. Under that approach, the breaching party may be granted restitution of all or part of her down payment where the other party has not been damaged at all by the breach, or where the injury from breach is demonstrably less than the amount being retained as damages. Research into the case law of our jurisdiction is again called for here. In the end, Mackenzie might (with my counsel) decide to surrender her claim to all or part of the $5000 in order to obtain a release from further liability to Fairgate.

5. What counsel should I give to Mackenzie?

Besides communicating to Mackenzie my conclusions about her legal position, as set forth above, I should in light of those conclusions counsel her to do two things without further delay.

First, she should send a letter to Fairgate, confirming her previous declaration that she does not wish to purchase the condo and asserting that any offer she may have made to that effect was withdrawn by her and is no longer open for acceptance. That letter should also state that Mackenzie demands prompt return of her $5000 payment to Fairgate and that she intends to pursue legal action if Fairgate does not comply. It should also assert that Mackenzie's attorney is ready to discuss the matter if Fairgate does not simply accede to Mackenzie's position. This letter should be sent in such a manner as to arrive reliably and speedily at Fairgate's offices. (Q.: Does Fairgate have a fax number?)

Second, I would urge Mackenzie to stop payment immediately on the check she gave to Abby. Of course, it may be too late to prevent Mackenzie's bank from honoring the check, and in any event merely stopping the check will not improve Mackenzie's substantive position vis-à-vis liability to Fairgate. It can, however, tremendously improve her *tactical* position: The burden of suing to change the status quo would then be on Fairgate, rather than on Mackenzie (as it otherwise would be, with respect to restitution of the $5000 payment). It is important to caution here that some state statutes make it a crime to obtain property or services by giving a check that is later dishonored. It is unlikely, however, that such a statute would apply to Mackenzie's situation since she didn't receive anything from Fairgate for her check. Still, before advising her to stop payment, I would research statutory law dealing with dishonored checks to determine whether this step would pose any risk to Mackenzie.

As suggested earlier, statutory rules may regulate either the substance or the form of contracts like this one (rules mandating written disclosure of interest rates, for instance, or giving the purchaser a "cooling-off period" within which free withdrawal is permitted). In the absence of such more specialized rules, however, the above analysis would apply.

JUSTIFICATIONS FOR NONPERFORMANCE
AND REMEDIES

John Sanders owns Sanders's Steak and Ale, a local restaurant. Several months ago Sanders decided to sell his restaurant and retire to Florida. In response to one of Sanders's advertisements in the newspaper, Leyman Boyle approached Sanders about purchasing the business. Boyle told Sanders that he had recently retired from the military and was looking for a business that he could operate. After inspecting Sanders's operation, Boyle expressed interest in engaging in serious negotiations.

One of the first questions that Boyle asked was about Sanders's license to sell alcoholic beverages. Sanders told him that the sale of his restaurant included his rights to the liquor license. He told Boyle that Boyle would be required to obtain approval from the Alcoholic Beverages Commission to have the license transferred to him.

Boyle hired an accountant who reviewed the books and records of the restaurant and gave him advice about the value of the business. Based on this advice Boyle made an offer to Sanders to purchase the restaurant, including the land and building, for $300,000. During the negotiations, Boyle informed Sanders that he had not actually retired from the military but had been dishonorably discharged because he had been convicted of distributing drugs. Sanders knew that this would cause Boyle a problem in obtaining transfer of the liquor license, but he did not say anything to Boyle about this.

After some lengthy negotiations Sanders and Boyle agreed on a price of $310,000 for the sale of the business. The parties executed a written contract calling for a closing of the sale within 60 days. Boyle gave Sanders a check for $60,000 as a deposit for purchase of the business. Paragraphs 16 and 17 of the contract provided as follows:

16. *Transfer of License to Sell Alcoholic Beverages.* Sanders agrees to transfer to Boyle all right, title, and interest in his license to sell alcoholic beverages at the restaurant. Sanders agrees to cooperate fully with Boyle to obtain the approval of the Alcoholic Beverages Commission to transfer the liquor license to Boyle.

17. *No Warranties.* This document constitutes the entire agreement between the parties. The seller makes no representations or warranties other than those specifically contained in this document. The restaurant is being sold "AS IS."

After execution of the contract Boyle contacted the Alcoholic Beverages Commission to apply for a transfer of the license. He received several forms to complete. One question asked whether the applicant had ever been convicted of a crime or subject to court martial. Boyle disclosed his conviction on his application. When members of the Commission staff reviewed the application, they informed Boyle that his application for transfer of the license would be denied because state law prohibited ownership of a liquor license by anyone convicted of a serious crime. Boyle asked whether he could form a corporation to own the license, but he was told that the law applied not only to individuals but to any entity, whether a corporation or a partnership, in which one of the principals had been convicted of a crime.

Boyle immediately contacted Sanders, told him of his problem with the Commission, and indicated that he would be unable to go forward with the purchase of the restaurant. Sanders said that he was sorry that Boyle had this problem, but that he expected Boyle to go ahead with the purchase. Boyle responded that the restaurant was worthless without the license. Sanders pointed out that the restaurant would still be profitable, even without a liquor license. The parties ended their meeting without any resolution of the matter.

A few days before the scheduled closing, Sanders's attorney wrote Boyle to remind him of the upcoming closing and to insist on performance of the contract. Boyle hired his own lawyer, who wrote a letter to Sanders stating that his client took the position that his obligations under the contract were discharged because of his inability to obtain transfer of the liquor license. He demanded return of the $60,000 deposit.

When Boyle did not appear at the closing, Sanders's lawyer wrote another letter informing Boyle that Sanders was giving him 30 days to complete purchase of the business. Sanders's lawyer informed Boyle that his failure to complete the purchase would cause Sanders to be unable to acquire an interest in a real estate limited partnership at a very favorable price. (The price of the interest was $250,000 and its value was $350,000.) Boyle's attorney wrote back protesting that his client had been discharged from any obligations under the contract and again demanding return of the $60,000 deposit. Because Boyle failed to complete the purchase, Sanders was unable to acquire the limited partnership interest.

Sanders's lawyer responded that Sanders was holding Boyle to his obligations under the contract. Sanders then proceeded to hire a manager to operate the business while he moved to Florida. He agreed to pay the manager a salary of $2,500 per month. Sanders also employed a broker to try to sell the business, but he was unable to find a purchaser.

Sanders has continued operating the restaurant through a manager (he has paid the manager $20,000 to date) and has now brought suit against Boyle seeking to enforce the contract or to obtain damages for breach. An expert is prepared to testify that the fair market value of the restaurant was $300,000 at the date set for performance, but the value has now declined to $225,000. Discuss fully (a) the defenses that Boyle could raise in an action by Sanders for breach of contract and (b) Sanders's remedies if Boyle is found to have breached the contract. Assume that a court would apply general common law principles rather than the UCC.[1]

OUTLINE OF ANSWER

I. Boyle's defenses
  A. Failure of condition
    1. Was obtaining license a condition? Question of interpretation.
    2. Consider language, preliminary negotiations, antiforfeiture maxim. Restatement (Second) §227.
  B. Nondisclosure
    1. Was there a duty? Restatement (Second) §161.
    2. Effect of disclaimer.
  C. Mistake
    1. Unilateral rather than mutual. Restatement (Second) §153.
    2. Does Boyle bear risk? Restatement (Second) §154. Effect of "AS IS" clause.

---

1. Article 2 of the UCC might apply in whole or in part to this transaction, depending on how the sale was structured and the assets involved in the sale. Tangible assets, such as equipment and inventory, constitute "goods" subject to Article 2 of the Code. Intangible assets, such as common stock or real property, are not subject to the Code.

    D. Impossibility/impracticability/frustration of purpose
       1. Performance not impossible. Could still buy restaurant.
       2. Impracticability and frustration require Boyle to act without fault. Restaurant may still be profitable. Also, "as is" clause may bar relief.
    E. Restitution
       1. If not in breach, can obtain restitution. Restatement (Second) §§376, 377. Would get deposit back.
       2. If in breach, could still seek restitution but subject to damages. Restatement (Second) §374.
II. Sanders's remedies
    A. Specific performance
       1. Must show damage remedy inadequate. May be difficult to do because can compute damages. Restatement (Second) §360.
       2. Question of whether this is unfair under Restatement (Second) §364. Involves mistake and perhaps nondisclosure.
    B. Expectation damages
       1. General measure is difference between contract price and market price.
       2. Normally measure at time of breach, but would not fully compensate. Could measure by market value now.
    C. Incidental and consequential damages
       1. Cost of manager. Recoverable as part of mitigation. Restatement (Second) §350(2).
       2. Consequential damages. Lost profit on investment. Subject to *Hadley* rule. Generally must determine at time of contract, not later.
    D. Attorney fees, punitive damages, and damages for emotional distress
       1. Generally no recovery of attorney fees unless contract provision or statute.
       2. No recovery of punitive damages unless breach also a tort.
       3. No recovery of damages for emotional distress unless bodily harm or emotional distress particularly likely to result.

MODEL ANSWER

I. Boyle's Defenses

The first issue to address is whether Boyle breached the contract by failing to complete the purchase of the restaurant. Boyle's failure to perform amounts to a breach unless Boyle has a justification for nonperformance. See Restatement (Second) of Contracts §235, Comment *b*. Boyle can argue that his nonperformance was justified because of failure of condition, nondisclosure by Sanders, mistake, and impossibility/impracticability/frustration of purpose.

A. Failure of Condition

Boyle can argue that transfer of the liquor license to him was an express condition and that the failure of this condition to occur discharged his obligation to purchase the restaurant. Whether an event is a condition of a party's duty to perform is a question of interpretation. A court will examine a variety of factors in making this determination, including the language of the agreement, preliminary notifications, and maxims of interpretation.

The language of the agreement points against Boyle's position. The agreement provides in Paragraph 16 that Sanders agrees to transfer his interest in the liquor license to Boyle and "to cooperate fully with Boyle to obtain the approval of the Alcoholic Beverages Commission to transfer the liquor license to Boyle." The agreement does not, however, specifically state that transfer of the license is a condition to Boyle's duty to perform.

The preliminary negotiations between the parties also are against Boyle's position. Boyle raised the issue of transfer of the license when he first discussed purchasing the business with Sanders, but Sanders immediately told him that he would be required to obtain Commission approval. While Sanders later learned that Boyle had been dishonorably discharged, he said nothing that could have misled Boyle. (The issue of nondisclosure is discussed below.)

Restatement (Second) of Contracts §227 sets forth certain maxims of interpretation regarding conditions. A crucial factor in the application of these maxims is whether the event in question is one within the control of the obligee (Sanders). Since obtaining a liquor license was not within Sanders's control, the maxims do not appear to favor Boyle.

Based on the language of the agreement, preliminary negotiations, and maxims of interpretation, it appears likely that a court would find that obtaining a liquor license is not a condition to Boyle's duty to perform the contract.

B. Nondisclosure

A contract may be rescinded by a party because of a material misrepresentation made by the other party. Restatement (Second) of Contracts §164(1). Here Sanders does not appear to have made any actual misrepresentations. Nondisclosure by one party is the equivalent of a misrepresentation *if* that party has a "duty" to disclose. A party has a duty to disclose when (a) disclosure is necessary to prevent a previous representation from being a misrepresentation; (b) disclosure would correct a mistake about a basic assumption about the contract and the failure to disclose amounts to a "failure to act in good faith and in accordance with reasonable standards of fair dealing"; (c) disclosure is necessary to correct a mistake about the contents or effect of a writing evidencing an agreement between the parties; or (d) a fiduciary relationship exists between the parties, Restatement (Second) of Contracts §161.

Only (b) is potentially applicable here. (Note that no fiduciary relationship exists between the parties since this is an arm's-length business transaction.) Because Boyle appears to have labored under a mistake about a basic assumption regarding the contract — his ability to obtain a transfer of the liquor license — the analysis must focus on whether Sanders failed to act in good faith and in accordance with reasonable standards of fair dealing. Sanders originally told Boyle of his need to check with the Commission about transfer of the license, but when he learned of Boyle's dishonorable discharge, he said nothing even though he knew this was a problem. Good faith means, at a minimum, "honesty in fact." It seems that Sanders was not acting honestly when he allowed Boyle to proceed with the transaction even though he knew that Boyle placed great importance on obtaining the license and even though he knew that Boyle would have difficulty obtaining a transfer of the license because of his military record. The issue is probably a question of fact for the jury to decide.

One problem that Boyle will face, however, in trying to avoid the contract on the ground of nondisclosure is the presence in the contract of a disclaimer of all warranties and representations and a statement that the restaurant is being sold "as is." A party may not rescind a contract because of nondisclosure unless the party would be "justified in relying" on the other party's failure to disclose. Restatement (Second) of Contracts §§161, 164. On the one hand, the presence of the disclaimer arguably makes any reliance by Boyle unjustified. On the other hand, some courts have held that "fraud vitiates any transaction," and a court might treat an intentional nondisclosure as fraudulent.

C. Mistake

Boyle can argue that his nonperformance is excused because he labored under a mistake of fact regarding his ability to obtain a transfer of the restaurant's liquor license. Since Sanders knew that Boyle had been dishonorably discharged and that this would cause Boyle problems in obtaining a transfer of the license, the mistake is unilateral rather than mutual. Under Restatement (Second) of Contracts §153, a unilateral mistake is a basis for avoiding enforcement of a contract if the following requirements are met:

— a mistake by one party deals with a basic assumption on which that party made the contract;
— the mistake has a material effect on the agreed exchange;
— enforcement of the contract would be unconscionable, or the other party knew of the mistake;
— the party attempting to avoid the contract does not bear the risk of the mistake.

Boyle should be able to meet each of the first three elements, but the fourth requirement, that he not bear the risk of the mistake, will cause him problems.

Under Restatement (Second) of Contracts §154, a party bears the risk of a mistake when:

— the mistake is allocated to the party by the agreement;
— the party acts on the basis of limited knowledge; or
— the court allocates the risk to the party because under the circumstances it is reasonable to do so.

All three of these, but especially the first, could apply. The agreement itself provides that Sanders made no representations or warranties other than those specifically contained in the document and that the restaurant was being sold "as is." Sanders told Boyle that he would need to obtain permission from the Beverage Commission to transfer the license, but Boyle apparently did not check with the Commission until after he signed the contract. Finally, the court might well conclude that it is reasonable to allocate the risk to Boyle because he was informed about the need to obtain Commission approval.

Boyle could counter that under the Restatement a party's fault does not bar avoidance unless the party failed to act in good faith and in accordance with reasonable standards of fair dealing. Restatement (Second) of Contracts §157. Although Boyle may have been negligent in not obtaining information from the Commission before signing the contract, there is no evidence that he acted in bad faith. In addition, the common understanding of "as is" clauses is that they relate to the condition of the property. Boyle might argue that the "as is" clause does not reasonably apply to a situation that involves the legality of operating the business rather than the condition of the premises.

D. Impossibility/Impracticability/Frustration of Purpose

Performance by Boyle is not literally impossible—he could still buy the restaurant—so the classical doctrine of impossibility is inapplicable. Boyle could argue, however, that his nonperformance should be justified under the doctrine of impracticability because the restaurant without a liquor license is substantially less valuable than a restaurant with a license. Restatement (Second) of Contracts §261. He could also rely on the doctrine of frustration of purpose, contending that his principal purpose in entering into the contract has been substantially frustrated. Restatement (Second) of Contracts §265. Boyle faces difficulties in convincing a court to apply these doctrines. First, both impracticability and frustration require the party seeking relief to act "without fault." Boyle knew that he had a problem in his background, and Sanders had told him that he must seek Commission approval to transfer the license. Second, Sanders has claimed that the restaurant would still be profitable even without a liquor license. (It might be quite difficult to prove whether the restaurant would be profitable or unprofitable without a liquor license. How could a court determine whether customers would continue to come to the restaurant if it could no longer serve alcoholic beverages?) The burden of proof on the issue probably rests with Boyle, however, since he is trying to avoid enforcement of the contract. Unless Boyle could show that the restaurant would be unprofitable without a liquor license, he is unlikely to succeed in his claim that his performance is impracticable or that his principal purpose has been substantially frustrated. Finally, under the Restatement formulation of both doctrines a court can refuse relief if "language or the circumstances indicate the contrary." As with nondisclosure and mistake, the disclaimer and "as is" clauses could prevent Boyle from obtaining relief.

E. Restitution

If the court accepts Boyle's claim that his nonperformance was justified, Boyle will be able to obtain restitution from Sanders. See Restatement (Second) of Contracts §§376, 377. The amount of his claim for restitution would be the $60,000 deposit that he paid to Sanders. If the court finds that Boyle has breached the contract, Boyle would still be entitled to restitution of his deposit as a breaching party, less any damages that Sanders can establish. Restatement (Second) of Contracts §374(1).

II. Sanders's Remedies

A. Specific Performance

To obtain specific performance of the contract, Sanders must establish that a damage remedy is "inadequate," Restatement (Second) of Contracts §359(1), and that neither equitable nor practical factors, Restatement (Second) of Contracts §§364, 366, should prevent such relief. Sanders will have some difficulty meeting these requirements. Boyle can argue that specific performance should be denied because expectation damages can be established with reasonable certainty. The expectation measure of damages for breach of a contract of sale by the buyer is the difference between the contract price and the market price. An expert is prepared to testify regarding the value of the business both at the date set for performance and now, so there should be no difficulty in proving expectation damages with reasonable certainty. Sanders can argue, however, that a damage remedy may be inadequate even if damages can be proven with reasonable certainty. See Restatement (Second) of Contracts §360. Sanders has moved to Florida; to award him expectation damages means that he will need to make arrangements either for the continued operation of the business or for its resale. Further, the business has declined in value since Boyle has refused to perform, and Sanders has been unable to find a purchaser. Under these circumstances, a court might conclude that an expectation measure of damages would be inadequate because it would not fully compensate Sanders.

While it would be practical to enter an award of specific performance because this contract does not involve supervision, a court might find that such a holding would be unfair. Evidence shows that Sanders was acting in bad faith by not disclosing to Boyle that his dishonorable discharge would cause him problems in obtaining transfer of the liquor license. Although this factor might not be sufficient to amount to a defense on Boyle's behalf (see the discussion of nondisclosure above), a court could consider this conduct in deciding whether to order specific performance. In addition, a court might find that specifically enforcing the contract would cause hardship to Boyle because he cannot obtain a liquor license, while Sanders already has one. At the same time, denial of specific performance will impose a hardship on Sanders because of his move to Florida and the decline in value of the business.

B. Expectation Damages

As discussed previously, the formula normally used to measure expectation damages for breach of a contract of sale by the buyer is the difference between the contract price and the market price plus incidental and consequential damages. The contract price was $310,000. Sanders's expert is prepared to testify that the value of the business at the date set for performance was $300,000 but that the business has now declined in value to $225,000. Normally, expectation damages are measured at the date set for performance on the theory that the nonbreaching party can then take steps to mitigate damages. If this traditional approach is used, Sanders's expectation damages would be $10,000 (increased by an incidental and consequential damages, discussed below) but reduced by Boyle's claim for restitution (see above). Sanders might be able to convince a court to use the $225,000 figure, however, since he took reasonable (albeit unsuccessful) steps to mitigate damages. To award him any less would be inconsistent with the compensation principle on which expectation damages are based.

C. Incidental and Consequential Damages

In addition to "loss in value" of the contract, the nonbreaching party is also entitled to recover "other loss," including incidental and consequential damages. See Restatement (Second) of Contracts §347. Incidental damages consist of expenses reasonably incurred to deal with the consequences of breach, including reasonable expenses in mitigation of damages. The $20,000 expense incurred by Sanders to hire a manager to run the restaurant after Boyle's breach seems to be a reasonable expense in mitigation.

Consequential damages refer to losses incurred in other contracts as a result of the breach of the principal contract. Sanders lost the benefit of a favorable real estate contract ($100,000) because of Boyle's breach. The problem that Sanders will face in recovering this amount is that consequential damages must pass the foreseeability test of Hadley v. Baxendale. The *Hadley* test provides that consequential damages are recoverable only if they either arise in the ordinary course of events or result from special circumstances of which the breaching party had reason to know. Loss of a favorable real estate contract would not arise in the ordinary course of events from breach of a contract to sell a business, and there is no evidence that Boyle had "reason to know of this contract" when he entered into the contract with Sanders. While Boyle was informed of the real estate contract prior to his breach, the *Hadley* test is applied at the date of the formation of the contract, not at the date of breach. (The breaching party could have protected itself against liability for the consequential damages if that party had reason to know of those damages at the time the contract was formed.)

D. Attorney Fees, Punitive Damages, and Damages for Emotional Distress

According to the "American Rule," a litigant may not recover legal fees unless a contract, statute, or court rule provides for recovery of fees. There is no indication that the contract provided for recovery of attorney fees. The dispute appears to be an ordinary breach of contract action that is not governed by any statute. There is also no evidence of bad faith or other improper conduct that would justify an award of attorney fees under court rule.

Punitive damages are normally not awarded in an action for breach of contract but may be allowed when the conduct that constitutes the breach also amounts to a tort. Restatement (Second) of Contracts §355. Even if a court finds that Boyle breached the contract, it is doubtful that his breach also amounts to a tort.

Damages for emotional distress are also generally unavailable in an action for breach of contract unless the breach also caused bodily injury or emotional disturbance was a "particularly likely result." Restatement (Second) of Contracts §353. Sanders has not suffered any bodily injury. Since this is a commercial contract, emotional disturbance is not likely.

CONDITIONS AND JUSTIFICATIONS FOR NONPERFORMANCE

Part A

Jessica Dandy is a 69-year-old resident of your community. Four years ago, Dandy retired from her job as an English teacher in the local junior high school. She receives a modest monthly pension from the public employees' retirement fund, as well as Social Security payments from the federal government. By the time of her retirement, she also had built up savings of some $250,000 (her own savings from her earnings, plus the remainder of her deceased husband's estate), which she invested primarily in long-term savings certificates and bonds. (She owns no real estate, having sold five years earlier the small home she had for several years occupied with her late husband.) Her two children are grown and self-supporting; one daughter is a veterinary surgeon in the midwest and the other (herself a mother of two teenage children) is, with her husband, co-owner of a small pharmacy in Florida, which they manage themselves. Influenced by the bad experiences some of her friends had undergone when they reached retirement years and faced living alone, Dandy recently began to investigate the possibility of moving into a retirement living facility, which would provide her with apartment-style living accommodations, prepared meals, if she wishes, and health and even nursing care, should that become necessary. Eventually she decided on the Vintage Valley Senior Center, a retirement complex on the outskirts of your town. She was impressed by the facility during her visits there, she knew several people living at the Center who had praise for their accommodations and service received, and she was led to believe by its manager that there were apt to be at any given time a substantial number of persons seeking admission to the limited number of accommodations at the Center.

Last November, Dandy entered into a written "Residence Agreement" with Vintage Valley, Inc., operator of the Center. In this agreement, she agreed to pay Valley the sum of $150 as a nonrefundable application fee, in consideration of its receiving and processing her application for admission to the Center. She further agreed that if her application were accepted she would pay Valley the sum of $125,000, in exchange for which Valley agreed to provide her with a two-bedroom apartment, meals upon request, and nursing care as and when required for the remainder of her life. Additional medical care as needed by Dandy was also to be provided by Valley, conditioned on Dandy's participating in Valley's group health insurance plan. In addition to the $125,000 "accommodation fee," Dandy agreed to pay a $175 monthly maintenance fee (subject to periodic increases at no more than cost-of-living-index-increases rates). The Residence Agreement (which was signed by Dandy and Valley) contained among others the following provisions:

> 4. *Effective Date.* Upon Applicant's completion of the Center's application form and payment of the non-refundable $150 processing fee, Valley shall forthwith consider Applicant's application, and shall notify him/her in writing promptly upon its approval. It shall be a condition to Applicant's entry into the Center that Applicant shall be examined by a physician of Valley's choosing and shall be determined to be in satisfactory health. When Valley has notified Applicant of its approval, Applicant shall within thirty days move into the

designated apartment in the Center, and shall pay the $125,000 Accommodation Fee provided hereunder. The date on which Applicant moves into the Center shall be the Commencement Date of this Residence Agreement. . . .

6. *Probationary Period.* There shall be a Probationary Period of 90 days from the Commencement Date, during which this Agreement may be canceled by either party. In the event of such termination, refund of the Accommodation Fee shall be made promptly, subject to the retention by Valley of reasonable per diem charges for any accommodations and other benefits received by Applicant hereunder. From and after the end of the Probationary Period, the Accommodation Fee shall be non-refundable, and in the event of the death of Applicant, no portion thereof shall be refundable to anyone, including without limitation Applicant's estate or any person claiming thereunder. The Accommodation Fee shall in such event be retained by Valley as payment in full for all services rendered to Applicant under this Residence Agreement.

Within two weeks after her signing of the Residence Agreement, Dandy had been examined by Valley's physician and had selected the apartment she intended to occupy at the Center. On December 28 she was informed by Valley that her application had been approved. On January 9 she paid Valley the $125,000 Accommodation Fee and moved her personal belongings from her old apartment into the Center. She lived there comfortably and without incident until April 5, when on a trip to a nearby shopping mall she became unconscious and collapsed. She was taken by ambulance to a local hospital, where she remained unconscious until April 11. At that time her condition began to improve, and by April 14 she was told by the attending physician that she could return to her home. At the same time, however, Dandy was advised that she was suffering from a serious coronary illness, in an advanced stage, which could at any time cause a recurrence of the attack she had just suffered. She was also told that for a younger person with her condition, surgery would be indicated, but that at her age the necessary surgery would pose a very grave risk; on the other hand, she was told, without it she could not expect to live more than 6 to 12 months. At Dandy's request, her attending physician at the hospital agreed to forward her medical records to the doctor's office at the Center.

On April 15 Dandy returned to her apartment at the Center, where she began to reflect on the events of the past ten days, and eventually determined that she had made a mistake in entering into the Residence Agreement. She wrote the following note, which on April 16 she delivered to the office of Norman Bates, manager of the Center and Vice-President of Valley:

Dear Mr. Bates:

During my recent hospitalization, I learned of my serious physical condition, which makes it likely that my life will be cut short much sooner than I had ever anticipated. As a result, I have been thinking about myself and my family, and about the proper disposition of my property among them when my time does come. I have concluded that it does not make sense for me to pay the Vintage Valley Center such a large sum for what is clearly going to be a short lifetime. I therefore must elect to terminate my residence here and to request a refund of my Accommodation fee, subject of course to a reasonable deduction for the accommodations and services I have enjoyed since January 9, when I moved in. I am sorry to do this, for I have enjoyed my brief time here, but I am sure you will agree that my resources would be better employed elsewhere at this point.

Please let me know when we can meet to finalize this matter.

Sincerely,
Jessica Dandy

The next day, Dandy received the following response from Bates:

Dear Ms. Dandy:

Thank you for your note. I am glad to know you have found your accommodations here at the Vintage Valley Center enjoyable. In response to your request to terminate your residence at the Center, you are of course free to come and go as you wish. I must, however, call your attention to the fact that the Accommodation Fee you paid upon commencement of your residence here is nonrefundable for any reason, and to remind you that your obligation to pay maintenance fees for your accommodations here at the Center is also a binding obligation, not subject to termination. We should be very disappointed should you elect to breach the obligations you undertook to us, but of course we would have no alternative in that event but to assert our right to damages under your Residence Agreement with us. Our continuing responsibility to all our residents requires us to act prudently in conserving and applying our resources, so as to insure all our residents the very best of care and comfort.

With all best regards,
Norman Bates

Immediately after receiving the above letter from Bates, Dandy telephones you at your law office and requests an appointment. When she arrives at your office, she tells you the above story. She declares to you her desire to terminate her relationship with Valley and to obtain a refund of all (or as much as she can) of the Accommodation Fee already paid by her. She asks you if she can accomplish this, and how she should proceed.

What do you tell her, and why?

Part B

Upon receiving the above letter from Bates, Dandy does not consult you immediately. Instead, she requests and receives an appointment with Bates in his office. On April 19 she meets with him and reiterates her desire to terminate her relationship with the Center and to receive a refund of the $125,000 fee she has paid. He tells her that in Valley's opinion the Residence Agreement is binding and cannot be terminated by her. He also asserts Valley's willingness to take her to court if she should cease making the maintenance fee payments called for by the Residence Agreement and tells her that the damages she would have to pay in that event could substantially eat into the remainder of her savings. He suggests that she simply accept the existence and binding effect of her agreement with Valley and rely on the Center to care for her as her needs dictate. When she again declares her unwillingness to accept this state of affairs, Bates suggests that Valley would be willing to refund 20 percent of her Accommodation Fee in return for her agreement to move out at once and for her signature of a general release of all claims. Dandy reluctantly agrees, and in exchange for Valley's check for $25,000 signs and delivers to Bates the following statement:

> In consideration of $25,000, receipt of which is hereby acknowledged, I, Jessica Dandy, hereby do release and relinquish any and all claims I may now or hereafter have against Vintage Valley, Inc., its officers, agents, and/or employees, arising out of or in any way related to my execution of the Vintage Valley Resident's Agreement and/or my residence in the Vintage Valley Senior Center. This release shall be binding henceforth and in perpetuity upon me, my estate, and anyone claiming thereunder.

> Signed:
> *Jessica Dandy*

On April 20, Dandy for the first time visits you at your law office and informs you of the above events. She tells you she fears she got a bad deal from Bates and asks if there is any way she can avoid the above release so as to assert any claims that (before its execution) she might have had against Valley.

What do you tell her, and why?

OUTLINE OF ANSWER FOR PART A

I. Does Dandy have a right to terminate the Residence Agreement and obtain restitution under terms of agreement?
   A. Should 90-day probationary period be strictly enforced or should strict compliance be excused?
      1. interpretation;
      2. impossibility;
      3. immateriality;
      4. to avoid forfeiture.
   B. Can agreement be terminated because she was not in "satisfactory" health?
      1. interpretation of "satisfactory" health
      2. for whose benefit was condition of satisfactory health?
II. Does Dandy have right to avoid the Residence Agreement?
   A. Mistake
      1. Fundamental issue of who bears risk of mistake. Risk may be allocated to Dandy by agreement, but may be reasonable to allocate to Valley because it required medical examination.
      2. If Valley claims that mistake was unilateral rather than mutual, Dandy may still be able to rescind for unilateral mistake, either because agreement was unconscionable or because Valley knew of her mistake.
   B. Impossibility, Impracticability, and Frustration of Purpose
      1. Agreement not literally impossible.
      2. Frustration of purpose may be difficult to establish because Dandy still receives substantial benefits under contract.

C. Capacity, Duress, and Undue Influence
1. Incapacity inapplicable because Dandy does not lack either cognitive or volitional capacity.
2. Duress not applicable because no wrongful threat.
3. Undue influence also does not apply because no excessive pressure and because agreement provided for probationary period.
D. Unconscionability claim seems remote because Dandy did not lack meaningful choice and because agreement was not unreasonably favorable at time of making.
E. Fraud and Nondisclosure
1. Strongest argument may be for nondisclosure. While Valley did not engage in actual fraud, good faith and fair dealing may require disclosure of her health condition.
2. Also relationship with doctor may give rise to duty to disclose because of fiduciary relationship. Although nondisclosure arose after agreement was signed, it nonetheless relates to exercise of rights during probationary period.

OUTLINE OF ANSWER FOR PART B

A. Unlikely that release can be rescinded for impossibility, impracticability, or frustration because she knew state of her health when she signed release.
B. Mistake also a weak basis to rescind release because release does not appear to be unconscionable.
C. Release may be avoided on ground of economic duress. Valley's threats and actions may well be wrongful, and a lawsuit during the last few months of one's life is not a reasonable alternative.
D. Release may also be subject to rescission for undue influence. Valley applied excessive pressure, and given Dandy's age and physical condition, she was susceptible to such pressure.
E. Valley may have engaged in fraud or nondisclosure with regard to Dandy's legal position.
F. Unconscionability seems relatively weak. Although Dandy may have lacked meaningful choice, the terms of the release may not be viewed as unreasonably favorable.

MODEL ANSWER — PART A

Based on the story related to me by Ms. Dandy, there are two possible approaches to the question of whether her relationship with Vintage Valley can be terminated so as to entitle her to a refund of all or some of her Accommodation Fee. First, she may assert a right to terminate and recover the fee paid under the terms of the Residence Agreement itself. Or, she may assert the power to avoid that agreement, which would entitle her to restitution of all or at least most of the Accommodation Fee. I will consider these two alternatives below.

I. Termination Under Provisions of Residence Agreement

The Residence Agreement contains two provisions that might allow for termination, one explicit and the other (arguably) implicit. Both involve the notion of *conditions* to contractual liability. The Agreement provides that once the Applicant (in this case, Dandy) has moved into the Center, there is to be a 90-day Probationary Period during which either party may terminate without liability and Valley is to refund the Accommodation Fee, except that it may in that event retain from the Accommodation Fee a reasonable amount to cover per diem charges for the Applicant's stay at the Center. Dandy will presumably be happy to concede that Valley is entitled to retain some portion of her Accommodation Fee on account of her approximately 90-day stay there; she does, however, want to assert her right to terminate and recover the balance of that $125,000. The Agreement provides that at the end of the Probationary Period, the Agreement is *not* freely cancellable, and all sums paid by the Applicant are to be retained. (This is of course apart from the question of liability for monthly maintenance fees or health insurance premiums.) Dandy's first line of argument should be that under this provision of the Agreement, she was entitled to and in fact did exercise a power of termination by her letter of April 16. (There is, incidentally, no indication that a notice of termination must be given in any particular form, such as certified mail; Bates's response appears to acknowledge his receipt of her April 16 letter, so that letter should be sufficient to exercise her power of termination, if timely sent.)

A. Excuse of Strict Compliance with Probationary Period

The principal issue here is how long Dandy retained her power of termination. The Probationary Period began on January 9, so it should have terminated no earlier than the end of April 9 (or April 8, if this is a leap year). She was incapacitated—indeed, unconscious—from April 5 to April 11 (and also not resident at the Center during that six-day period); she remained hospitalized, and away from the Center, for another three days. From the Applicant's point of view, the purpose of the Probationary Period seems obviously to allow an informed decision about making a permanent investment in a Center apartment on the basis of a 90-day test of Center living. (From Valley's point of view, it is probably so they can without liability extricate themselves from a long-term relationship with an Applicant who appears problematic for some reason—an incredibly difficult personality, for instance.) If so, it can well be argued that Dandy's Probationary Period should be extended beyond 90 calendar days if, because of events not within her control, she would otherwise have less than the full 90 days' trial run on which to make her judgment. For Dandy to have the benefit of the last four days of the Probationary Period (from April 5 through April 9), she would need an extension of an additional four days. Dandy did regain consciousness on April 11, but her condition did not improve enough to return to the Center until April 14. An extension of four additional days after April 14 would give her until April 18 to make her election to terminate. In fact she made it on April 16.

This argument can be made in several slightly different forms. It can be argued that by the terms of the Agreement itself, properly understood (90 days in residence to make a decision) her letter of termination was simply not late at all, and should for that reason be effective. Or, it can be argued that because it was literally impossible for her to give that notice until April 11, and at least impracticable until April 14, she should be entitled to make her election within a reasonable time after that impracticability had ended. (See Restatement of Contracts (Second) §271.) Or, it can be argued that her lateness in giving notice was so slight as to be non-material (a week at the very most, compared with a lifetime relationship), and that the condition of timely notice should be excused to avoid a forfeiture. (See Restatement (Second) §229.) The forfeiture of her Accommodation Fee would be "disproportionate" because of her newly discovered short life expectancy. It should be emphasized that this latter argument does not involve a contention that the *giving* of notice of termination is a "non-material" condition, only that *timely* notice is not material, at least not when the lateness is no more than a few days.

A hypothetical case may help to clarify this argument. Suppose that after Dandy had been living in the Center for 60 days, there was a serious fire in the building where she was staying, so that she and some of the other tenants had to be moved out to temporary lodging in a near-by motel for six weeks. Could Valley rightfully claim that after 30 days in the motel her 90-day Probationary Period expired, even though she had lived in the Center itself for only 60 days? Seemingly not, because she was deprived of the full 90 days' trial of Center residency through no fault of her own. The same argument should be available here, where her illness was the intervening event that interrupted her probationary stay at the Center.

All of these arguments — especially the one based on forfeiture — are strengthened by the fact that Dandy was told originally by the Valley that there was usually a waiting list of Applicants for space in the Center. Even apart from the possibility of mitigation of damages by Valley, the equities of Valley's position are weak in comparison with Dandy's. They can readily replace her with someone else, it appears, and would be losing only the windfall of a large profit from a surprisingly short lifetime stay. She, on the other hand, will forfeit half of her life's savings if not permitted to terminate now and recover her Accommodation Fee.

B. Meaning of Condition of "Satisfactory Health"

The second argument based on the principle of conditions to liability is less obvious from the terms of the Agreement. It is derived from the provision which makes Dandy's "satisfactory health" (as determined after examination by a physician of Valley's choosing) a "condition" to her entry into the Center. We have reason to believe that at the time she was examined for entry, her health was indeed in *poor* condition, since she has been told she is suffering from a chronic, potentially fatal heart condition "in an advanced stage." The problem here is largely one of interpreting the effect of the contract's language. First, what is "satisfactory" health? To Dandy, obviously a terminal illness is *not* satisfactory health. But the provision was put in the contract by Valley, and so the question may be, what is "satisfactory" from Valley's point of view? The intent may have been to screen out not fatal illnesses, but conditions that will entail expensive care for long periods of time — Alzheimer's, for instance, or "Lou Gehrig's disease." From that perspective, an illness that might kill quickly is not necessarily "unsatisfactory" to Valley. Indeed, it might be eminently *satisfactory* to Valley, if it meant the windfall of a large Accommodation Fee for a very short lifetime of residence and care.

The second question of interpretation under this line of analysis is this: Even if we assume that Dandy's health was not "satisfactory" when she was examined and when she entered the Center, can she invoke that condition now to avoid liability on the Agreement? Valley will argue that the condition was included for the benefit of *Valley*, not the Applicant, and that Valley can, if it chooses, *waive* the condition — as, in effect, it has in this case. Valley can also point to the language of the provision, which does not say that all the parties' contractual obligations are conditioned, merely that "Applicant's entry into the Center" is conditioned. Here, Valley would argue, it had the privilege at the outset of denying her entry into the Center and, in effect, abrogating any further contractual relation with her. Once Valley elected to admit her, however, that provision had no further effect on the parties' contractual relationship. That seems persuasive, although as we shall see below Valley's knowledge of her condition might generate other arguments in her favor.

II. *Avoidance of Residence Agreement*

The preceding arguments on Dandy's behalf do not challenge the validity of the Residence Agreement, but seek to establish Dandy's rights under that Agreement to terminate and recover her Accommodation Fee. There are numerous other arguments she can make, however, for the proposition that the Agreement can be *avoided*, entitling her to restitution of the Accommodation Fee. (Under this approach, Valley would still probably be entitled to retain some of the Accommodation Fee as a reasonable charge for her stay at the Center, not by virtue of the terms of the Agreement but under general principles of restitution, or "quasi-contract.") Some of these arguments are premised not on any misconduct by Valley, but on neutral principles applicable to cases of mistake or changed circumstances. Others involve the possibility of conduct on Valley's part that might be viewed as fraudulent or otherwise "wrongful."

A. Mistake

Dandy appears to have thought she was in good health at the time of her entry into the Residence Agreement and her move into the Center. Obviously, she was mistaken. If Valley also had no reason to think she was in other than good health at the time, then the mistake was probably a "mutual" one. Under Restatement (Second) §§152 and 154, such a mutual mistake ("mistake of both parties") may make a contract voidable by the one adversely affected, if it goes to a basic assumption on which the contract was made and had a material effect on the agreed exchange of performances, unless that person bore the risk of the mistake. Here the mistake does go to a basic assumption: Dandy assumed herself to be in good health, and would not knowingly have agreed to transfer half her wealth to Valley for a few months of residence and care. Also, the disproportion between what she expected to receive and what she will in fact receive is surely material. The problem here is to determine whether Dandy bore the risk of this mistake. Valley presumably enters into an agreement like this one with each of its residents. (The contract appears to be a form, with blanks filled in.) From Valley's point of view, the agreement is a fair one, even though some residents may live only a short time thereafter, because other, more fortunate, residents do in fact live on for years and years, and receive value in excess of what they pay. Thus the risk of early death was allocated to the Applicant under the agreement, Valley would argue, just as the risk of an Applicant's extreme longevity was allocated to Valley. (See Restatement (Second) §154(a).)

Valley would also argue that if Dandy was worried about the state of her health at the time she entered into the Residence Agreement, she had available to her an easy answer: See a physician and get a physical exam. If she chose to make a contract like this one without being sure of her own health, then under Restatement (Second) §154(b) (Valley would argue), she elected to "treat her limited knowledge as sufficient."

In the ordinary case, Valley's arguments under §154(a) and (b) would probably prevail. If an elderly person makes a contract like this, she can win big or lose big—but either way it is a gamble she consciously takes, like buying an annuity. Here, however, an important part of the Agreement was the physical exam which Valley insisted on (as a "condition" to its accepting her as a resident). Even though the examining physician was not "her" physician, in the ordinary sense, Dandy could reasonably have assumed that she would be told if the exam revealed any dangerous health condition. (I'm no expert on medical ethics, but surely that would be appropriate, no matter who was paying the doctor's fee.) If so, then Dandy did not consciously take the risk of limited knowledge—she thought her knowledge would *not* be limited, but would be informed by competent medical advice. Therefore, under Restatement (Second) §154(c), the risk of this mistake should be allocated to *Valley*—because in these circumstances it is "reasonable to do so."

If the argument based on mistake is directed to the time of the contract's making, then the mistake was probably a "mutual" one. On the other hand, by the time Dandy entered into the Center, Valley either knew or at least "had reason to know" of her heart condition. If Valley argues that this makes applicable the somewhat more stringent "unilateral mistake" rule of Restatement (Second) §153 ("mistake of one party"), two responses are possible: First, the Agreement in these circumstances is indeed "unconscionable" in its gross disproportion, so the rule of §153 can also be satisfied by Dandy. Second, this additional fact leads to arguments based on fraud or wrongful disclosure (to which I will return below).

B. Impossibility, Impracticability, and Frustration of Purpose

Before going on to those points, I should briefly discuss the possible effect of a trio of related doctrines: impossibility, impracticability, and frustration of purpose. We have already considered the effect of "impossibility" or "impracticability" in the context of the contract's condition of notice; now these issues reappear in a broader context. Although Dandy's illness apparently existed before the Agreement was made, it is newly discovered. In that sense, this is a "change of circumstances" occurring since the making of the Residence Agreement. Is it one which gives rise to a power of avoidance on the part of the one adversely affected (i.e., Dandy)? Probably not. The Agreement is not in fact impossible, or even impracticable, of performance on either side. Valley can still provide Dandy with lifetime residency at the Center and medical and nursing care as needed until she dies, and has expressed willingness to do so. For her part, Dandy can also still perform—indeed, she already *has* performed a major part of her obligation, and there is no reason to think she is unable to make the other payments called for. Her complaint really is one of "frustration of purpose"—like the empty room with no view of the Coronation, in Krell v. Henry—the deal she has made with Valley has lost its utility for her because it now appears she will get very little in return for what she has given up, compared with what she could reasonably expect to receive.

Like the arguments above based on mistake, the argument of frustration is substantial, but may not succeed. True, Dandy anticipated a better-balanced exchange than the one she is apparently getting. But the courts have been resistant to the doctrine of frustration, often insisting that the contract has lost virtually all value for the one complaining. This contract will still provide Dandy with adequate housing, board, and medical and nursing care for life (assuming the capability of Valley to perform its obligations, which so far we have no reason to doubt). This is hardly de minimis — for many people, it would be an unattainable dream. And in cases like this, the courts are likely to say that someone in Dandy's position assumes the risk that the bargain will turn out to be unfavorable — just as Valley does.

C. Capacity, Duress, and Undue Influence

On the facts we know, it seems unlikely that Dandy, despite her somewhat advanced age and ill health, lacked capacity to contract as of December and January. Clearly she has cognitive capacity, and her belief in her own good health was far from being an "irrational delusion" — she was just badly mistaken about the facts. Nor do we have apparent grounds for asserting that duress or undue influence on the part of Valley induced her to sign the Residence Agreement. She appears to have "shopped around" in an intelligent way, and to have made a rational decision on reasonable grounds without "high-pressure" selling techniques or improper threats or force on Valley's part. Perhaps some further conversation with her would disclose something more along this line, but it seems unlikely. And the substance of the Residence Agreement itself undercuts the notion of duress or undue influence, because it gives the Applicant a 90-day Probationary Period, during which she can apparently cancel with impunity for any reason at all, or indeed for no reason. (Cf. the "sale on approval," in UCC §2-326, which allows for non-cause termination.)

D. Unconscionability

For similar reasons, the Residence Agreement *at the time of its making* does not appear to be vulnerable to claims of unconscionability. The contract does appear to be a standard form (as one would expect in these circumstances), and possibly a "contract of adhesion" in the sense that it was offered on a "take it or leave it" basis. On the other hand, there is no indication that Dandy was prevented from reading the form, or that she would have been incapable of understanding it if she did read it, or that she was pressured into signing it without seeking counsel. Certainly she had the financial means of employing an attorney or other adviser if she had wished to do so. (Thus there seems to have been no "procedural" unconscionability.) And the Agreement is probably not unduly unbalanced in substance, unless the price charged in the circumstances was a grossly high one for the size and quality of the apartment provided to Dandy, in light of her (presumed) life expectancy. (This is a question of fact, of course, but Dandy does not seem to be complaining that the price was too high in that sense.) In short, there appears to have been no "absence of meaningful choice" on Dandy's part, nor terms that were *at the outset* unduly favorable to the other party. The thing that makes this transaction unconscionable — if anything does — is not improper selling tactics, or a basically unfair deal; it is the conduct of Valley in withholding from Dandy the knowledge it had presumably acquired of her potentially fatal heart condition.

E. Fraud and Nondisclosure

Dandy's strongest argument for avoiding this contract appears to be that it was procured by fraud or at least by wrongful nondisclosure, the equivalent of fraud for the purpose of asserting the power to avoid. There may have been no actual *misrepresentation* in this case; Dandy appears to have inspected the Center for herself before signing and to have found her period of residence there satisfactory. It should be remembered, however, that a misrepresentation in order to justify rescission need not be fraudulent; it may be innocent and still suffice, if material. (See Restatement (Second) §164(1).) Although further conversation with Dandy about this is called for, it is not clear from what she has told me so far that Valley or any of its agents (including Bates) made any misrepresentations of fact to induce her to sign the Residence Agreement and pay the Accommodation Fee. I would need to see any brochures or selling material Valley may have provided to Dandy, to see if any possible misrepresentations were made there. These could present a parol evidence problem, of course. Although ordinarily even a strong merger clause in a written contract will not bar a showing of extrinsic fraudulent representations made to induce a contract, some jurisdictions will give effect to strong contract language negating representations of various sorts. I would have to study the Residence Agreement's language in this regard, and perhaps also do some research in the law of my jurisdiction on the point. Dandy's argument along this line would probably be somewhat strengthened by the fact that she would be seeking rescission and restitution of the Agreement, rather than damages for fraud.

The more likely successful argument here, however, is one of *wrongful nondisclosure*. If one uses the standard suggested by Restatement (Second) §161, there are two possible grounds for asserting that Valley has been guilty of a nondisclosure which in the circumstances is the equivalent of a wrongful misrepresentation. Under the general "good faith and reasonable standards of fair dealing" test (161(b)), Valley's failure to disclose to Dandy the existence of her potentially fatal health condition surely should be regarded as wrongful. Not only has it induced her to make a decision she now regrets, it also has kept her from taking earlier steps to ameliorate her heart condition, or at least to deal with it. (What if her attack had occurred while she was driving a car?) It also could be contended that in the circumstances, Valley had a clear duty of disclosure under §161(d), because of a "relation of trust and confidence" between them. This is a little tricky, because ordinarily Valley and Dandy would be regarded (at least at the time of making of their contract) as dealing at arms' length, with no fiduciary role on Valley's part. That might well change once Dandy becomes a resident of the Center, with Valley contractually obligated to provide her with not only room and board, but medical and nursing care to the extent required. Even at the outset, however, at least as regards the physical exam of Dandy by Valley's physician, it seems that once the physician (as Valley's agent for this purpose) acquires knowledge of Dandy's condition, s/he — and thus Valley — has a fiduciary duty to disclose it to Dandy. This assumes, of course, that the physician performed the exam competently, and did discover Dandy's heart condition at the time. If not, then the argument based on nondisclosure has to be one of "negligent" nondisclosure; this is not completely off-the-wall, but it is a lot harder to make stick.

The principal problem with an argument of wrongful nondisclosure by Valley is the timing: the fact that Valley's knowledge of Dandy's illness would not have been acquired until after Dandy had entered into the Residence Agreement. Ordinarily, for fraud to be a basis for avoidance of a contract, it must be an inducing cause of the complaining party's entry into the Agreement. Here Valley can correctly claim that Dandy's initial decision was made without any wrongful nondisclosure on Valley's part; that came later. This argument is superficially persuasive, but should not succeed. The terms of the Residence Agreement permit either party freely to withdraw until the end of the Probationary Period; each party thus retains the power to choose whether to continue or not until that period has ended. If Dandy had stayed on at the Center without incident until two weeks *after* April 9, and then suffered her heart attack, she could properly claim that her decision to allow the Period to expire without terminating was induced by her ignorance of her extreme ill health. The only difference between that hypothetical and Dandy's actual case is that her attack occurred earlier, depriving her of what would have been the last few days of her Probationary Period. Valley's nondisclosure is probably fraudulent and certainly material, and in the circumstances was an inducing cause of Dandy's not exercising her power to withdraw from the Residence Agreement.

Conclusion

In all the circumstances, I would counsel Dandy that she has the right to a refund of her $125,000 Accommodation Fee, subject only to a reasonable deduction for her stay at the Center from January through early April, either on the ground that the Agreement itself (properly interpreted and applied) gives her that right, or on the ground that she is entitled for at least one and probably several reasons to avoid the Agreement and have restitution of benefits conferred on Valley by her under it.

MODEL ANSWER — PART B

If Dandy can successfully claim that she is not bound by the release she signed on April 19, then she can assert the defenses and claims discussed in the answer to Part A. Her situation is complicated, however, by the fact that she acted on her own before consulting an attorney, and signed a document purporting to release Valley from any and all claims she may have against it, in exchange for Valley's payment of $25,000 to her. (I am assuming at this point that she still has the $25,000 check and has not cashed or deposited it.) If that release is binding upon her, Dandy will have no right to a refund of any of the $100,000 unrefunded remainder of her Accommodation Fee. Her ability to assert the underlying claim for refund of the Accommodation Fee depends on her being able to avoid that release on some legally sufficient ground.

A. Impossibility, Impracticability, and Frustration of Purpose

In attempting to avoid the Residence Agreement, Dandy may as we have seen assert that circumstances have changed (or at least her perception of them has changed) since that Agreement was made, so that impossibility, impracticability or at least frustration of purpose might apply. With respect to avoiding the release, however, such claims appear weak. By the time she signed the release, Dandy knew the true state of her health, and knew that the Residence Agreement looked like a bad deal for her. The only thing that has changed since yesterday is her decision to seek legal counsel, resulting in her having a better understanding of her legal relationship with Valley. This alone will not be enough, since virtually every contract made without counsel and later regretted would otherwise be voidable at will by the disappointed party.

B. Mistake

Similarly, Dandy's claim of mistake seems unlikely to succeed. If she asserts that her rights against Valley were in fact stronger than she thought when she signed the release, this would presumably have been at most a unilateral mistake, and by itself will probably be an insufficient ground for avoidance. Even if we were successful in asserting that Valley had reason to know of her mistake (which is likely, on the facts), Dandy must also show that the resulting contract is "unconscionable," in order to qualify for relief under the rule of Restatement (Second) §153. Although I have earlier contended that Dandy should be entitled to rescind the Residence Agreement and recover her $125,000 (with some offset), her right to do so was not on April 19 so clear and beyond reasonable dispute that it could not legitimately be the subject of a compromise settlement agreement. The payment she received in exchange for the release only gives her 20 cents on the dollar, but whether this is so grossly disproportionate as to be "unconscionable" within the meaning of §153(a) is another question. Another factor that might bolster a claim of unconscionability (for the purpose of applying §153) is the fact that the release nowhere provides for a release by Valley of the rights that Bates has threatened to enforce against Dandy; indeed, it doesn't even mention any obligation of Dandy under the Residence Agreement. If the document signed by Dandy on April 12 were really construed as releasing her claims against Valley but not *vice versa*, that might indeed be viewed as unconscionable, within the old English definition: such an agreement as no *sane* person would make and no *fair* one would accept.

C. Duress

Even if Dandy's lack of understanding of her legal position is not sufficient for avoidance grounded on mistake, it may also be relevant to another, stronger claim Dandy can make for avoidance of the release: a claim of either duress or undue influence. It does not appear that Dandy was subjected to any physical duress, or even the kind of "browbeating" that might cause a person in poor health to sign an agreement she did really want to make. But courts have also found "economic duress" to be a sufficient basis for rescission. Here, Dandy had already paid over to Valley roughly half of her life savings. She was told by Bates, Valley's agent, that if she tried to withdraw from the Center not only would Valley refuse to refund the Accommodation Fee, it would sue her for the monthly maintenance payments she was obligated to make under the Residence Agreement. If Valley's wrongful nondisclosure was responsible for her entry into residence at the Center in the first place (as discussed in the answer to Part A), then Valley was taking advantage of a situation wrongfully created by it to pressure Dandy into a further agreement prejudicial to her interests.

Valley may claim that duress is inapplicable here because it made no threat against Dandy, other than a threat to enforce its rights against her by legal action if necessary. That does not necessarily negate the argument that a threat is wrongful, however. Under Restatement (Second) §176, even a threat to take legal action may be wrongful if it is a breach of the duty of good faith and fair dealing (1(d)), or if "the effectiveness of the threat is significantly increased by prior unfair dealing by the party making the threat" (2(b)). Both of those should apply here, particularly the latter: by permitting Dandy to enter into residence at the Center while concealing from her the true state of her health, until the 90-day Probationary Period had expired (if indeed it did expire, an arguable point), Valley allowed Dandy to put herself in a position where Valley's grossly unfair settlement proposal appeared to her to be a reasonable alternative to the status quo.

Valley will presumably argue that Dandy had a reasonable alternative other than acceding to Bates's offer of a compromise weighted in Valley's favor, because her remaining resources were ample to hire an attorney and bring suit to recover her Accommodation Fee. To counter that, Dandy can argue that not only was she wrongfully deprived of half of her resources, she believed herself to be a person with possibly only a few months to live. To face spending her last few months on earth fighting a lawsuit (and perhaps leaving it for her heirs to deal with) may not have appeared to her to be a reasonable alternative, at least at that time. If so, that seems in the circumstances not an unreasonable reaction on her part.

D.   Undue Influence

Similar to duress, and perhaps even stronger, is Dandy's claim of undue influence. Clearly, Dandy was a vulnerable person: advanced in years, in extremely poor health, and facing the prospect of a time-consuming and emotionally draining legal dispute. Bates's threat that Valley would sue to recover her maintenance fees, followed by his offer of a settlement if she would move out "at once," may be seen as a kind of undue pressure, particularly if—as seems likely—Valley's claim to recover those fees would in fact have been substantially diminished or undercut entirely by its ability to mitigate damages through a replacement tenant. (Remember the waiting list of applicants for the Center?) The claim of undue influence would also be substantially strengthened if Valley as of April 19 were seen as standing in a fiduciary relation to Dandy. Pretty clearly it could be in that position with respect to the elements of her care that Valley has undertaken to provide, such as medical and nursing care. Whether that fiduciary relation would also extend more generally to the negotiation of a release is another question. Since by April 19 Dandy was aware that she was embroiled in a dispute with Valley, and that their interests were adverse to hers in that regard, it seems more likely that Valley and Dandy will be seen as having engaged in an "arm's-length" negotiation.

Even without the aid of a fiduciary relation, however, the case for undue influence seems strong, particularly when one focuses on the mental and physical state of Dandy on April 19. Although advanced in years, Dandy was not yet at the point of being an "aged" person; up until her heart attack earlier in April she apparently had every reason to believe she would live to a ripe old age, to enjoy the life at Valley and occasional visits with her family. Now, suddenly, all is changed for her: She faces what may be an imminent demise, and her personal affairs are in what appears to her to be disarray. For Bates to insist upon her signing a release and moving out immediately as the price of a financial settlement (and an inadequate one at that), rather than giving her time to consider her position and to consult an attorney or other advisor (not to mention members of her family), in these circumstances seems "undue" indeed. All in all, Bates and Dandy fit the pattern of "dominant" and "subservient" bargainers, and the release she signed should be void for undue influence.

E. Fraud and Nondisclosure

Elements of duress and undue influence in this case are also mingled with indicia of fraud or wrongful nondisclosure. Bates as manger of Valley (apparently with authority to enter into settlement agreements such as this on its behalf) can be assumed to have an accurate idea of what Dandy's legal obligations to Valley were, and his statements to her about those obligations can be seen as fraudulent and material to her entry into the release agreement. Here as in the earlier problem, the hardest issue is reasonable reliance by Dandy. Ordinarily, one party to a dispute is presumed to know that the other party is not a reliable source of legal counsel about that dispute, and misrepresentations of law or legal rights for that reason have typically been held not actionable as fraud. Whether Dandy could overcome that tendency is questionable. Even if not sufficient in themselves to support rescission, however, statements by Bates that exaggerated the strength of Valley's legal position could bolster the arguments of undue influence or duress.

F. Unconscionability

I have already suggested that the release agreement might be regarded as "unconscionable," as that term is used in Restatement (Second) §151. Whether it could also be unconscionable in the broader sense (see UCC §2-302, Restatement (Second) §208) is less clear. The release that Dandy signed is not a fine-print form that she would have had difficulty reading or understanding, so it might be argued by Valley that she had no "absence of meaningful choice." But to some degree Dandy was the victim of bargaining tactics that seem to shock the sense of justice; and the resulting agreement is one that may seem grossly unfair. Perhaps an unconscionability analysis could succeed as an omnibus approach if the various more specific grounds discussed above seemed weak for some reason. Or, it could be a backstop, an additional reason for voiding the release agreement.

Conclusion

I would advise Dandy that she has a number of substantial grounds for asserting that the release she signed is invalid, in order to pursue her claim for refund of the Accommodation Fee, as described in response Part A. I would advise her that her claim for rescission should be promptly asserted by me on her behalf, and that consistent with that claim she should not cash the check given to her by Bates. I would offer to hold the check for her pending resolution of her dispute with Valley.

CONTRACT DEFENSES: MISTAKE AND MISREPRESENTATION

Ben Benson is a middle-aged doctor, whose hobby is collecting jazz and early rock recordings and musical memorabilia of various kinds. He is a single man with an excellent income, and so he has the extra money to spend on rare and expensive items; his collection is well-known to other collectors in the area. Recently Ben was driving home from his office, and saw a garage sale with several tables full of what looked like 78 and 33-1/3 rpm records. He stopped to browse through the merchandise and found several recordings that he did not already have in his collection, including a large batch of 45 rpm records by the Spyders, a legendarily successful English rock group from the '60s. When he went to pay for the items he wanted to buy, Ben struck up a conversation with the seller, Sam Samson, a young man probably in his early 20s. Sam commented on the Spyders recordings that Ben was buying, saying, "Do you really like that stuff? I can't stand them myself." Ben assured Sam that indeed he did like the Spyders (as did most of the civilized world, he might have added), and that he was pleased to find some of their recordings that he did not already own. "Well, if you really like music from that era," Sam responded, "you might be interested in this stuff over here." He showed Ben a suitcase full of scrapbooks, records, notebooks, and several of what appeared to be reel-to-reel tape recordings. "This was my grandpa's stuff," Sam continued. "He was a drummer for a bunch of different groups back in the '60s; maybe even did a tour with the Spyders, or so he said. It's probably pretty much all junk, but you can have it for a song—if you'll pardon the pun. You can have the lot for $5,000."

While Sam went off to attend to other customers, Ben began to look through the items in the suitcase. At first he was only acting out of idle curiosity, but soon Ben's interest was aroused, and his pulse quickened. The items all appeared to be related to the Spyders, including scrapbooks full of clippings and photos, and the tapes were labeled "Recording Sessions—July 1964." If they were genuine, and particularly if the tapes were of unreleased recordings, they could be worth many thousands of dollars—perhaps even hundreds of thousands. Ben closed the suitcase, took it over to Sam, and said, "Well, most people would think this was junk, I guess, but I just go for this kind of thing. I'll give you $2500 for it." Sam agreed, and Ben wrote him a check for $2500 (which Sam deposited in his bank the same day).

Additional Facts and Questions

1. **Assume** that when Ben gets the suitcase home and starts to go through it, he discovers that it is an even more significant find than he had thought possible. The tape recordings, of which there are several, do appear to be genuine, and to contain recording sessions not previously released. The scrapbooks and photos are genuine, and rare. After consultation with experts in the field, he concludes that the suitcase and its contents are probably worth at least half a million dollars, maybe more. Word of the find is published in the local newspapers, where Sam Samson reads about it.

   Question: Assuming Ben still has all the material that he purchased from Sam, does Sam have any possible legal claim against Ben? What would be the nature of that claim, if any, and what relief could Ben seek?

2. **Instead** of the additional facts in item 1 above, **assume** that when Ben gets the suitcase home and looks more carefully at the contents, he discovers they are essentially worthless. The scrapbooks and photos are just photocopies of readily available material, and the recordings are just home-made copies of commercial recordings of which Ben and most other Spyders fans already have numerous copies.

    Question: Does Ben have any possible legal claim against Sam? What would be the nature of that claim, if any, and what relief could Ben seek?

3. **In addition to** the facts given in item 2 above, **assume** one more fact: Neither of Sam's grandfathers ever played a musical instrument of any kind, much less playing with a group of rock musicians, and Sam is well aware of that.

    Question: Does this affect any of your answers to item 2 above? If so, how; if not, why not?

OUTLINE OF ANSWER

1. Question 1
    a. Mutual Mistake
    b. Unilateral Mistake
    c. Nondisclosure
2. Question 2
    a. Mistake — Unilateral or Mutual
    b. Implied Warranties
3. Question 3
    a. Misrepresentation
    b. Tort Claim for Fraud

MODEL ANSWER

Preliminary observation: The things that Ben buys from Sam in this question (the suitcase and all of its contents) are all classified as "goods" — tangible, physical, moveable things — and to that extent are governed by Article 2 of the Uniform Commercial Code. See UCC §2-105. While Article 2 does govern sales of goods generally, the various defenses considered in this question are not codified by the UCC, and remain subject to the general principles of the common law of contract. See UCC §1-103(b). On the other hand, Ben has hopes that the goods will be valuable to him not just as rare physical objects, but also because he hopes to exploit the intellectual property that they incorporate: the photographs, clippings, etc., and especially the musical recordings. These kinds of property rights are intangible personal property. To some extent, more specialized rules of law, such as federal or state copyright law, etc., will apply to them. This answer will assume, however, that nothing in those bodies of law overrides the general contract principles discussed below.

Question 1

Question 1 involves the discovery that the facts at the time the contract was made are not as one of the parties thought them to be. The buyer, Ben, was aware that the lot of goods he was buying might be considerably more valuable than the price he was paying, although it now appears that perhaps the goods are worth even more than he thought was possible. It follows that they are also even more valuable than the seller, Sam, thought them to be. Does this fact give Sam any basis for overturning the transaction?

One way to analyze this transaction would be to view it as an example of "mutual mistake." See Restatement (Second) of Contracts §§152 and 154. If both parties believed the goods were worth no more than Ben paid for them, and it turned out that they were indeed worth much, much more, Sam might claim that this was a "mutual mistake of fact," an erroneous assumption shared by both parties, which makes the contract much more disadvantageous to Sam than he had supposed. Such a mistake could make the contract voidable by Sam. To reach that conclusion, however, the court would have to conclude not only that the mistake was indeed shared by both parties, and of sufficient materiality to justify rescission, but that Sam did not bear the risk of the mistake, under Restatement (Second) §154.

Some of these conclusions are doubtful, however. To begin with, Ben seems to have had an idea that the goods were worth much more than Sam was asking, so the two parties may not have had a shared mistake, even if Ben did underestimate their true worth. (That fact might be relevant to another argument, considered below.) It is probably correct that Sam's mistake was material to him, because if he had known the true value of this material he would probably not have sold it for that price to Ben — and perhaps he would not have sold it to Ben or anyone else at all, or at least not in that fashion, all in one bundle. It will be difficult, however, for Sam to establish that he does not bear the risk of his mistake under Restatement (Second) §154.

One might well take the position that in sales like this ("yard sales" or "garage sales"), it is customary for the buyer to take the goods "as is" and for both parties to take the risk that their value may not be the same as the price charged. ("Flea markets" are another example of this genre.) In that sense, one might say that the risk of a mistake in value is tacitly allocated by the agreement to *both* parties — each one takes the risk that he will have made a bad deal. See §154(a). Even if that is not the case, it is hard not to conclude that on these facts (at this point we are still assuming that Sam told the truth about his grandfather) Sam knew or should have known that the goods might be genuine and indeed might have some substantial value. If so, under §154(b) he probably bears the risk, because he proceeded with what he knew was limited knowledge about the value of the goods, rather than seeking expert evaluation. Finally, under §154(c) (which would be determinative only if (a) or (b) were not), the court is likely to feel that it is reasonable for Sam to bear the risk of this mistake, although this is less clear.

Of course, the above discussion is premised on a "mutual mistake" of fact. But what if we treat the mistake as essentially a "unilateral" one, because Ben actually knew or at least suspected that the goods were indeed worth much more? Then we would be operating under the rule of Restatement (Second) §153. Sam would have to meet the additional requirements that the contract can be seen as "unconscionable" (which in this context simply means grossly unbalanced and unfair) and that Ben had some reason to know of Sam's mistake. The extreme disparity between price and value might be thought to make the contract an "unconscionable" one, but the other reservations about the operation of §154 would remain.

The "unilateral" character of Sam's mistake might enable him to make a different kind of argument, however. If Ben is seen as having some idea of the goods' real value (even if a conservative one) while Sam was essentially ignorant of that fact, then

Sam might argue that Ben had intentionally and wrongfully failed to disclose to him a material fact, one that would clearly be material to Sam's entry into the sale contract. See Restatement (Second) §161, which provides that nondisclosure of a material fact may sometimes be wrongful, and the legal equivalent of active fraud. Although Ben does have to some extent the knowledge of an expert in this area (he is a well-known collector), and thus does have a bargaining advantage over Sam, there is no confidential relationship between them (Restatement (Second) §161(d)). Does nondisclosure by Ben amount to a failure to act "in accordance with reasonable standards of good faith and fair dealing"? American courts are generally resistant to the notion that a buyer who because of expertise or industry has better knowledge than the seller is obliged to share that knowledge with the seller. (See the old *Laidlaw* case.) It is possible that a court might be influenced to find for Sam if it feels that Ben was armed with superior knowledge and took a conscious advantage of a vulnerable, ignorant, and needy person. Whether Sam meets that description seems doubtful, however. He seems just to have been somewhat careless, and perhaps lazy.

It might be noted that the facts here bear a structural resemblance to the old "pregnant cow" case, Sherwood v. Walker, discussed in the *Lenawee County* opinion, where the seller was permitted to rescind a sale contract when the cow he sold turned to be not only not barren, but actually pregnant with a calf, and thus much more valuable. It should also be noted, however, that in deciding the *Lenawee County* case, the court expressed considerable doubt about the decision in *Sherwood*, preferring to apply the analysis expresssed in the Restatement (Second) sections cited and discussed above.

If any of the above claims were successful, the result for Sam would be avoidance of the contract, which would mean rescission and restitution would be the appropriate remedies. Sam would have to return the amount of the purchase price, and in return would be entitled to recover the goods from Sam. ("Specific restitution.")

Question 2

In this question, the tables are turned, and it is the buyer who is disappointed by the outcome of the transaction. Here we are not yet assuming any misrepresentation by Sam (that doesn't come until Question 3), and Sam has not made any statements about the goods that could amount to express warranties under UCC §2-313, so this question is simply the flip side of the mistake analysis. The same sections of Restatement (Second) are relevant, and the analysis probably comes out the same way.

The mistake here is made by Ben (and maybe by Sam as well, if he thinks the goods have at least *some* value—he did ask a substantial amount for them, after all). Even if Ben did believe the goods were worth at least what he paid for them (and maybe more), he certainly was aware that he had limited knowledge as to their value. See §154(b). And a court is not likely to find that it is reasonable to allocate the risk to Sam, given Ben's apparently greater expertise. The relief sought by Ben would again be rescission and restitution—he would return the goods to Sam in exchange for the money he paid—but there is probably little chance of Ben achieving that outcome.

The fact that this transaction is an Article 2 sale of goods does not mean that the seller is bound by implied warranties with respect to the goods. Sam is not a professional merchant of goods, so the implied warranty of merchantability under §2-314 does not arise, and there seem to be no grounds for a warranty of fitness for a particular purpose under §2-315; although that section does not require that the seller be a merchant, it does require that the buyer be relying on the seller's expertise to furnish goods fit for a particular use, not apparent on these facts. Sam probably does make an implied warranty of title under §2-312, but there is no indication that anyone else has a claim to these goods — the question is merely as to their worth — so that warranty has presumably not been broken. (As noted earlier, someone else might have a claim to the intellectual property embodied in these goods, but this is beyond the scope of Article 2, and of our Question here.)

Question 3

At this point we add to the mix a conscious misrepresentation of fact by Sam. It could hardly have been an oversight or an accident on his part. Sam knew what he said was false, and he had to know that it could be material in inducing Ben to make the purchase — as indeed it was, although not at the price that Sam asked originally, but still at a price much greater than the value of the goods. This is more than a "unilateral mistake," or even a possibly wrongful nondisclosure — it is a conscious misrepresentation. See Restatement (Second) §162. A misrepresentation that is either fraudulent OR material entitles the other party to avoid the contract; here we have a misrepresentation that is undoubtedly *both*. See Restatement (Second) §164. This is not just a statement of the seller's "opinion," or "puffing," like the statements in *Syester*, which are often tolerated by the law (although they were not in the *Syester* case). See Restatement (Second) §§167, 168. This is a statement of fact by Sam about his grandfather. Ben would have no way of corroborating the statement, or knowing its falsity. And it would be material because if Sam's grandfather really did play with the Spyders, the genuineness of the articles, if not their ultimate worth, would at least be more likely.

Ben might also have a tort action against Sam for fraud, in which case his damages might be somewhat higher than what he would gain from rescission and restitution, particularly if punitive damages were assessed. But under contract law, Ben should at least be entitled to avoid the contract, return the goods to Sam, and have a refund of his money.

BREACH AND REMEDIES

Dawn Upshaw graduated from college as the premier basketball player in the country. She was picked number one in the draft of the AWBA, the newly formed American Women's Basketball Association, by the Dallas Dynamos. In anticipation of her probable signing, the Dynamos employed a marketing firm and paid it $750,000 to develop a national marketing strategy built around Upshaw.

A few weeks later, Upshaw signed a three-year $30 million contract with the Dynamos. The Dynamos also paid her a signing bonus of $1 million. Following her signing the Dynamos launched an extensive advertising campaign referring to the team as "Dawn's Dynamos." The Dynamos predicted that ticket sales (both season tickets and individual game tickets) would more than double because of her presence on the team.

"Dynamos Dumped!!!" was the shocking headline three months later when Upshaw announced that she had changed her mind about playing professional basketball and had instead decided to attend the Jameston Law School to study under world-renowned contracts professor Nathan Glassfield. In announcing her decision, Upshaw said, "I'd rather develop my intellectual ability and jump through Glassfield's hoops than shoot hoops any day." It might have been wise, however, for Upshaw to have taken Glassfield's course before making her decision, because she failed to take into account her possible contractual liability to the Dallas Dynamos.

Shortly after Upshaw announced her decision to go to law school, she received the following letter from Scott Hayes, counsel for the Dynamos. Hayes is a nationally-known attorney who is feared for his slashing courtroom style.

Dear Ms. Upshaw:

I write as counsel for the Dallas Dynamos to demand that you honor your contractual commitment to the team, and to inform you of the steps that the team will take if you refuse to do so. Under your contract you have a three-year obligation to the team. Should you fail to report to camp by October 1, as required by your contract, the team will seek to enforce the contract by way of specific performance, injunction, or damages. I must inform you that the Dynamos have already received requests for refunds for many of the tickets that have been sold. We will hold you responsible for any refunds that your breach of contract makes necessary as well as loss of anticipated ticket sales and associated concession revenue. If litigation is necessary to enforce the team's contractual rights, the team will also seek recovery of any expenses of litigation, including attorney fees. Please be advised that the team considers your willful breach of contract to be egregious. Indeed, the Dynamos question whether you truly intended to play pro ball when you signed your contract. Accordingly, we will seek punitive as well as actual damages.

I trust that this letter conveys the seriousness by which the team treats this matter. At the same time, however, the Dynamos would welcome your return and I am authorized to tell you that management is willing to forget this unfortunate incident if you decide to rejoin the team. I hope that you will reconsider your decision and avoid what will surely be painful litigation.

Sincerely,
/s/ Scott Hayes

P.S. On a more personal note, I think you are making a horrible mistake going to law school, especially to take Glassfield's Contracts class. His best days are behind him and you won't learn much contract law. The best you could hope for would be a few stale jokes.

Discuss fully the issues of contract law raised by this situation.

GRADING SHEET FOR ESSAY QUESTION ON BREACH AND REMEDIES

1. <u>Breach.</u> Has Upshaw committed an <u>anticipatory repudiation?</u> Test: refusal to perform or conduct that renders obligor unable to perform. Restatement (2d) §250. Repudiation can be retracted before change of position by obligee or notice that they will treat as total breach. Restatement (2d) §256. Neither limitation on retraction is present here. Dynamos state they would welcome her back to team and have given her until October 1.

Weight   6   Points   _____

2. <u>Equitable relief by way of specific performance or injunction.</u> (a) No specific performance of personal service contracts is available. Restatement (2d) §367(1)(b). Even though services are unique, court is unlikely to grant an injunction because Upshaw is not working for a competitor. Restatement (2d) §367; pages 1028-1029 of casebook.

Weight   8   Points   _____

3. <u>Expectation damages.</u> Loss in value is value of performance or $30 million plus $1 million bonus. Other loss consists of consequential damages. Lost ticket sales and lost concessions are clearly foreseeable but questions may exist about proof with reasonable certainty. Sales that have already been made can be proven with reasonable certainty, but future sales and concessions may be speculative. Cost avoided is the $30 million in salary they will not have to pay. Dynamos must use reasonable efforts to mitigate damages. Do they have to refund sales that have been made? Can they trade for a star that might make up for the lost sales?

Weight   10   Points   _____

4. <u>Reliance or restitutionary damages.</u> If the Dynamos cannot recover expectation because damages are too uncertain, Dynamos may recover reliance damages. Restatement (2d) §349. Reliance damages would include bonus paid and other expenses incurred in preparation or part performance. Recovery of $750,000 advertising expenditures may be difficult because the expense was incurred before the contract was signed. On the other hand, the expenses were incurred in reliance on contract and Dynamos expected to recover. Restitutionary damages as alternative remedy for breach seem undesirable because the Dynamos would not be able to recover any expenses except for bonus. This is not a losing contract where restitutionary damages may be desirable. See *Algernon Blair*, in Chapter 12, Section B of the authors' casebook, and Restatement (2d) §373.

Weight   8   Points   _____

5. <u>Attorney fees.</u> Under American rule, no recovery of attorney fees. However, if contract contains attorney fee provision, they may be recovered. See Chapter 11, Section D of the authors' casebook.

Weight   4   Points   _____

6. <u>Punitive damages.</u> Punitive damages not available for breach of contract unless breach was a tort for which punitive damages are recoverable. Restatement (2d) §355. Here may be able to establish fraud if she did not intend to perform but was only trying to get bonus. Query whether she did anything to show her intent, such as paying school deposit before signing contract?

Weight   4   Points   _____

Total   40   Points   _____

Sample Examination Questions without Model Answers

MUTUAL ASSENT AND THE STATUTE OF FRAUDS

Lance Anderson owns 25 acres of lakefront property. Through Army Reserve meetings, Lance has come to know Ronald Bending, a young, aggressive businessman. Several years ago Anderson mentioned to Bending that he owned lakefront property and Bending expressed an interest in purchasing the property both for himself personally and for development. Anderson said he might be willing to sell at the right price, but Bending did not pursue the matter. From time to time, Bending has raised the possibility of purchasing the property. Anderson always responded by saying to Bending, "Make me an offer." But Bending never made an offer.

About six months ago, Bending again asked Anderson whether he would be willing to sell the property. Anderson responded: "Ron, how many times have we gone through this song and dance? I tell you what, I'll make you an offer you can't refuse. I'll sell you the property for $100,000. I know I'll hear from you soon, probably about the time the Falcons win the Super Bowl. Ha! Ha! Ha!"

Anderson was surprised when a week later he received a letter from Bending. The letter read as follows:

Dear Lance:

This letter is my formal acceptance of your offer to sell me your property on Lake Jones. The price is $100,000. I have arranged for financing with the First National Bank. To approve the loan the bank requires a formal contract of purchase and sale. I am enclosing the contract for your signature. I have already signed the contract. I understand that it contains the standard provisions for the sale of real estate.

I look forward to living on the property, watching the sun go down over Lake Jones, while my big screen TV shows the Falcons winning the Super Bowl.

Your friend,
Ron

Anderson immediately wrote back to Bending as follows:

Dear Ron:

All right. You proved your point and called my bluff. You win. But let's not let this get out of hand. No way am I selling the property for that price. The property is worth twice that amount. Maybe more. The whole thing was a big joke, so let's forget it.

Lance

But Bending wasn't willing to forget the sale or to treat the transaction as a joke. He told Anderson that he had signed a contract with a general contractor to construct a home on the property. Bending said that he had paid the contractor a nonrefundable deposit of $5000.

Anderson was shocked that matters had gone this far. He told Bending that he had acted totally unreasonably. This only added fuel to Bending's fire. Bending has now brought suit against Anderson. Discuss fully Bending's rights against Anderson under contract law.

BATTLE OF THE FORMS: UCC §2-207

On May 1, the Roberts County School Board submitted a purchase order to the Sealy Desk Company for 1000 school desks for a new elementary school that was to open in the fall. The order was based on the price stated in Sealy's published catalogue. The purchase order provided that delivery was to be made by July 15 and that the School Board reserved the right to cancel the order and to return the desks within 15 days of delivery if "the desks were not satisfactory to the Board in any respect."

On May 10, Sealy responded to the Board's order by sending a document entitled "Sales Contract." The document confirmed that Sealy would deliver 1000 school desks at its catalogue price by July 15. The contract also contained the following clause:

> Sealy warrants that its products will be free from defects in materials or workmanship for a period of one year from the date of delivery. Except as provided in this document, there are no warranties, representations, or agreements whatsoever with respect to the products. Sealy hereby DISCLAIMS THE IMPLIED WARRANTIES OF MERCHANTABILITY AND FITNESS FOR A PARTICULAR PURPOSE.
>
> If a defect in any product occurs during the one-year period after the date of delivery, Sealy will replace the product free of charge. Replacement of any defective product shall be the buyer's sole remedy under this contract. SEALY SHALL NOT BE LIABLE FOR INCIDENTAL OR CONSEQUENTIAL DAMAGES OF ANY TYPE WHATSOEVER.

Sealy delivered the desks on July 7. On July 15, the Board notified Sealy that it was returning the desks because they were unsatisfactory. When Sealy asked the Board to specify the problem with the desks, it learned that the Board had found another desk supplier who was willing to sell desks at a cheaper price. Attempts to resolve the matter without litigation were unsuccessful, and Sealy has not brought suit against the Board for damages for breach of contract. Discuss Sealy's right to recover from the Board for breach of contract. You may assume that the School Board would be subject to the same rules of contract law (common law or statutory) that would apply to a private party.

INTERPRETATION

Samantha Eaden owns one of the country's largest collections of Japanese art. For some time a number of museums had been trying to convince Eaden to sell her collection. In the past Eaden had rejected all offers because she wished to have her collection maintained as a whole. About a year ago, the relatively new, up-and-coming Southwestern Museum indicated a willingness to purchase Eaden's collection and to house it in a new wing that the museum had added.

On September 1, Eaden received the following letter from Ronald Hildebrand, the Director of the Southwestern Museum.

Dear Ms. Eaden:

This letter is a formal offer from the Southwestern Museum to purchase your collection of Japanese art. As I indicated in my discussions with you, the collection will be housed in a large gallery in the recently added Jawinski Wing of the museum. The gallery will be named "The Herbert Eaden Collection of Japanese Art" in honor of your late father.

The purchase price for the collection will be negotiated between you and the museum once the collection is inventoried and appraised. After we complete the inventory and agree on price, we will have our lawyers prepare a written contract of sale. You reserve the right to cancel the contract if our plans for your collection are unsatisfactory.

The opportunity to purchase your collection is an exciting prospect for the museum. I believe that the arrangements we can make to house your collection are second to none in the world. I hope that you will decide to place your collection with the Southwestern.

Sincerely,
Ronald Hildebrand
Director

One week later, after consulting with her family and advisers, Eaden telephoned Hildebrand to inform him that she had decided to accept the Southwestern's offer. That same day, September 8, Hildebrand wrote Eaden the following letter:

Dear Ms. Eaden:

On behalf of the Southwestern Museum I wish to express my appreciation to you for accepting our offer to purchase your collection of Japanese art. We look forward to presenting your collection to the world.

Most sincerely,
Ronald Hildebrand
Director

A short time later, Hildebrand's staff members began to inventory the collection. Hildebrand also hired two noted experts in Japanese art to appraise the works in the collection. With Eaden's approval, he also held a press conference to announce the acquisition of the Eaden collection.

Unfortunately, during inventory, a dispute developed over five paintings by artist Winston Ambrose. Ambrose was born and educated in the United States but spent a number of years living and working in Japan. (Indeed, while retaining his American citizenship, Ambrose exhibited his art under the name of Winston Oh.) Ambrose's art focuses on the impact of industrialization on Japanese culture. Eaden considers Ambrose's art an important part of her collection and wants it prominently displayed. The Southwestern's curator of Japanese art does not classify Ambrose's work as Japanese art, but rather as art about Japan by an American. In addition, the curator's opinion is that Ambrose's work is far inferior to the other works in Eaden's collection. This opinion is shared by other noted experts on Japanese art.

The dispute now threatens the entire purchase. Eaden says that she will not go through with the transaction unless the Southwestern purchases Ambrose's art and displays it prominently as part of the collection. The Southwestern contends that it has an enforceable contract for the collection excluding the Ambrose paintings.

Discuss fully the issues of contract law raised by this fact situation.

BREACH AND REMEDIES

On April 11, 2010, the Collins Construction Company (Contractor) entered into a contract with the Oswald Development Company for the construction of an office building. The contract included the pertinent provisions summarized below:

1. *Contract Price.* $30 million. (Collins estimated the cost of construction at $28 million, producing an anticipated profit of $2 million.)

2. *Construction Schedule.* Construction was to begin by June 1, 2010, with final completion scheduled for December 1, 2011. The contract also included a detailed progress schedule for the work.

3. *Contract Documents.* The "contract documents" consisted of the agreement between Collins and Oswald, along with designs and specifications prepared by Aaron & Aaron, architects employed by Oswald, who would act as Oswald's agent in supervising the construction.

4. *Progress Payments.* Collins could apply for progress payments for work done on the building. Payment was to be made by Oswald to the extent the architect certified that the work complied with the contract documents. Oswald was allowed to withhold up to 10 percent of all progress payments as retainage until completion of the project.

5. *Substantial Completion.* When Collins had substantially completed the work, it was to notify the architect, who would inspect the work done and prepare a "punch list" of defects that Collins was required to correct.

6. *Final Payment.* When Collins had corrected all defects, the architect would issue a certificate of completion, at which time Oswald was required to make final payment to Collins.

7. *Use of Retainage.* Oswald was required to deposit the retainage in a separate interest-bearing account. Oswald could use the retainage to correct any defects in the work that Collins was unable or unwilling to correct after notification from the architect. When the architect issued the certificate of completion, Oswald was required to pay the balance in the retainage account to Collins.

8. *Termination.* Oswald could terminate the contract for a variety of causes, including violation by Collins of the contract documents in "any substantial way."

9. *Delays.* The contract provided that time was of the essence. It also stated that time for performance would be extended if delay resulted from "causes beyond the control of the contractor."

10. *Subcontractors.* Collins had responsibility for selection and performance of all subcontractors.

11. *Liquidated Damages.* If the project was not completed by December 1, 2011, Collins would be required to pay liquidated damages of $10,000 per day, the amount estimated to be the profit lost for each day of delay in occupancy of the building.

12. *Litigation.* The contract provided that "in the event either party recovers damages from the other for breach of this contract, the prevailing party shall be entitled to recover its reasonable attorney fees, not to exceed 1/3 of the amount recovered."

Work began on time, and for the first few months progressed in accordance with the schedule. By January 2011, however, Collins had fallen 15 days behind schedule. On January 12, 2011, Aaron wrote Collins to complain about its failure to adhere to the construction schedule; the letter demanded strict compliance with the schedule. Collins responded that the delay had been caused by subcontractors, but that it expected to be able to make up the time as the work progressed. By March, Collins was 20 days behind schedule. On March 15, 2011, Aaron wrote a letter to Collins stating that Oswald insisted on compliance with the construction schedule. The letter warned Collins that "unless your performance of the contract improves, you run the risk that the owner will elect to terminate the contract." In a letter written in response, Collins objected to the threat. The contractor claimed that Oswald did not have the right to terminate the contract because the delay was caused by subcontractors and was, in any event, too short to justify termination of the contract.

On April 15, 2011, writing on behalf of Oswald, Aaron notified Collins that Oswald had elected to terminate the contract because of Collins's failure to honor the construction schedule. At that time, Collins was 30 days behind schedule.

When Oswald terminated the contract, Collins had submitted requests for progress payments totaling $15 million. The architect had approved these requests and Oswald had made full payment, less $1.5 million held in retainage. Collins had also completed an additional $500,000 of work for which a request for payment had not yet been submitted. Oswald quickly employed a new contractor who was able to complete the project by January 1, 2012, one month late, for a contract price of $16 million.

Collins has brought suit against Oswald for breach of contract, and Oswald has counterclaimed for damages. Discuss the rights of the parties.